The Laws of Imitation

Tarde, Gabriel de, Parsons, Elsie Worthington Clews

BIBLIOLIFE

THE
LAWS OF IMITATION

BY

GABRIEL TARDE
Professor in the College de France, Member of the Institute

TRANSLATED FROM THE SECOND
FRENCH EDITION BY

ELSIE CLEWS PARSONS
Lecturer on Sociology in Barnard College

WITH AN INTRODUCTION BY

FRANKLIN H. GIDDINGS
Professor of Sociology in Columbia University

NEW YORK
HENRY HOLT AND COMPANY
1903

INTRODUCTION

GABRIEL TARDE, whose most interesting and important book is here given to American readers, is Professor of Modern Philosophy in the *Collège de France,* and a member of the *Institut.* A true philosopher, but also a man of affairs, with wide intellectual sympathies, M. Tarde is a writer of great charm, and his influence among his own countrymen and abroad has steadily increased since he began, in 1880, to contribute to the *Revue philosophique.* American scholars, long familiar with M. Tarde's suggestive works, have felt that his thought should be made more accessible to English-speaking readers. Hitherto only a little book, *Les Lois sociales,* presenting a mere outline of his philosophy, has been translated.

M. Tarde was born in 1843, at Sarlat, Dordogne. After school days were over, instead of entering upon university life at Bordeaux, or Montpellier, or Paris, he took up legal studies, and presently became *juge d'instruction* in his native town. This office he held for nearly eighteen years, years of keen observation, but also of much solitude, of patient reflection, of the gradual unfolding of original ideas of man, of society, and of the world, which were presently to combine in a complete philosophical scheme.

A born student of human nature, M. Tarde was from the first interested in that oldest of philosophical problems, the explanation of motive. He early perceived not only that motive may be resolved into terms of belief and desire, but also that it may be measured. This discovery had, of course, been made before by Bentham, Cournot, Menger, Walras, and Jevons, but Tarde's presentation of the subject in his first contribution to the *Revue philosophique,* on *La Croyance et le désir, possibilité de leur mesure,* was independent and original.

But motives, and those impersonal forces that are not motives, work out results in an orderly fashion, by definite modes, which are the chief subject-matter of scientific study, and to the explanation of modes of activity M. Tarde was to make noteworthy contributions. Among the phenomena that early arrested his attention was imitation. From his office of magistrate he observed the large part that imitation plays in criminal conduct. Does it play a smaller part in normal conduct? Very rapidly M. Tarde's ardent mind ranged over the field of history, followed the spread of Western civilisation, and reviewed the development of language, the evolution of art, of law, and of institutions. The evidence was overwhelming that in all the affairs of men, whether of good or of evil report, imitation is an ever-present factor; and to a philosophical mind the implication was obvious, that there must be psychological or sociological laws of imitation, worthy of most thorough study.

At this time sociology was represented in France by disciples of Comte and by a few interested readers of Herbert Spencer. The thoughts of the Comtists did not range far beyond the "hierarchy of the sciences," and the "three stages" of history. To demonstrate the place of sociology in the "hierarchy," or to show that a social fact belonged to one or another "stage," was very nearly the limit of Comtist sociological ambition. The Spencerians, on the other hand, seizing upon Spencer's proposition that society is an organism,—but neglecting most of the psychological and historical elements of his system,—were busy elaborating biological analogies.

With such notions M. Tarde had, and could have, no sympathy. He felt that if the study of society was to be erected into a science, a beginning must be made, not by demonstrating the logical and rightful place of sociology in the sisterhood of sciences, and not by exploiting the analogy of institutions to organic life, but rather by thoroughly examining the nature and combinations of some distinctively *social* phenomenon. The fact—the relationship or activity—if such there be, in virtue of which society is *itself*, a differentiated thing, and not merely a part of something else, that fact the sociologist should understand through and through, and in all its bearings, and should make it the corner-stone of his system. That elemental social fact M. Tarde believed he had discovered in the phenomenon of imitation.

Too profoundly philosophical, however, to view any fact in even partial isolation, M Tarde perceived that imitation, as a social form, is only one mode of a universal activity, of that endless repetition, throughout nature, which in the physical realm we know as the undulations of ether, the vibrations of material bodies, the swing of the planets in their orbits, the alternations of light and darkness, and of seasons, the succession of life and death. Here, then, was not only a fundamental truth of social science, but also a first principle of cosmic philosophy.

His first tentative studies of the laws of universal repetition in physical nature and in history, and of imitation as the distinctive social fact, M. Tarde published between 1882 and 1884 in the *Revue philosophique*. Among articles which, in substance, afterwards reappeared as chapters of *Les Lois de l'imitation,* were those entitled *Les Traits communs de la nature et de l'histoire, L'Archéologie et la statistique,* and *Qu'est-ce qu'une société?* Other articles, setting forth the same underlying principles, but having a more practical aim, and presenting views born of the author's professional experience as a magistrate, were afterwards incorporated in the volumes, *La Criminalité comparée* and *La Philosophie pénale* (1891). Of these and other writings by our author on criminology, Havelock Ellis says: " He touches on all the various problems of crime with ever-ready intelligence and acuteness, and a rare charm of literary style, illuminating with suggestive criticism everything that he touches." [1]

The first edition of *Les Lois de l'imitation* appeared in 1890; a second in 1895. M. Tarde had now conceived a complete philosophy of phenomenal existence, and he

[1] *The Criminal,* p 42.

rapidly converted it into literary embodiment. Unlike philosophers in general, M. Tarde is compact and brief in his systematic work; discursive in his varied writings illustrative of principles or practical by application. His whole philosophical system is set forth in three volumes of moderate dimensions. *Les Lois de l'imitation* is an exposition of the facts and laws of universal repetition. In *La Logique sociale,* which appeared in 1895, we have our author's explanation of the way in which elemental phenomena, undergoing endless repetition, are combined in concrete groups, bodies, systems, especially mental and social systems. This process is a *logic,* a synthesis, of repetitions. It includes adaptation, invention, and organisation. The chapters on the laws of invention are brilliant examples of M. Tarde's originality and many-sided knowledge. The third volume of the system, *L'Opposition universelle,* was published in 1897. Here was developed the theory of a third universal form and aspect of natural phenomena—namely, conflict.

The chronological order of these publications did not correspond exactly to their logical order, as parts of a system. The latter was presented in a series of lectures in 1897 at the *Collège Libre des Sciences Sociales.* The order there given was "The Repetition of Phenomena," "The Opposition of Phenomena," "The Adaptation of Phenomena." These lectures were published in 1898, under the title already mentioned, *Les Lois sociales.*

M. Tarde's abilities, and in particular his knowledge of criminal statistics and penology, had ere this drawn attention to him as a man whom the state could not overlook, and in 1894 he was called to Paris to assume charge of the Bureau of Statistics of the Ministry of Justice. This position he held until his election as Professor of Modern Philosophy in the *Collège de France* in 1900. In this latter year he was elected also a member of the Institute of France.

M. Tarde's later writings present his philosophical and sociological views under many aspects. They include: *Les Transformations du droit, Les Transformations du pouvoir, L'Opinion et la foule, Études pénales et sociales, Essais et Mélanges sociologiques, Études de psychologie pénale,* and *Psychologie économique.*

It is not the purpose of these brief lines of introduction to attempt any estimate of M. Tarde's place in philosophy, or to offer any criticism of his sociological views. The object is rather to indicate the place which " The Laws of Imitation" holds among the many writings of a gifted and widely influential author, in the belief that those who read this volume will wish to look into at least some of the others.

Of the quality of Mrs. Parsons' translation the reader himself will judge. It is enough here to say that Mrs. Parsons has sought with painstaking fidelity to convey to English readers the exact meaning of the original text.

FRANKLIN H. GIDDINGS

Columbia University

PREFACE TO THE FIRST EDITION

IN this work I have endeavoured to point out as clearly as possible the *purely social* side of human phenomena, as distinct from their vital and physical characteristics. It just happens, however, that the point of view which is helpful in noting this distinction is the very one which presents the greatest number of the closest and most natural analogies between the facts of society and the facts of nature. Many years ago I formulated and partly developed in the *Revue philosophique* my fundamental thought, — "the key to almost every lock," as one of our greatest philosophers of history graciously wrote to me;—and as the plan of the present work was already in my mind at that time, many of those articles have been readily incorporated as chapters of this book.[1] I am but setting them in the place for which they were originally intended. Sociologists who have already honoured these fragmentary expositions with their notice, now have the opportunity, if they desire it, to criticise my point of view in its entirety. Any harsh treatment of myself I will forgive, providing my thought be received with leniency. This is not at all impossible. In fact, my conception might have a grievance against me just as seed might complain of its soil. But then I hope that through this publication it will reach someone better fitted to develop it than I am.

I have tried, then, to outline a *pure sociology*. This is

[1] They have been modified, or amplified, as Chapters I, III, IV, V. Chapter I was published in September, 1882; Chapter III, in 1884; Chapter IV, in October and November, 1883; Chapter V, in 1888. Several other sociological articles were published in the same collection and were also intended for future revision, but it has seemed unnecessary to embody them in this volume

In another work, *La Philosophie pénale,* I have developed the application of my point of view to social crime and punishment. My *Criminalité comparée* is an earlier attempt in the same direction.

tantamount to saying a general sociology. The laws of such a science, as I understand it, apply to every society, past, present, or future, just as the laws of general physiology apply to every species, living, extinct, or conceivable. The simplicity of such principles equals their generality, and I grant that it is much easier to lay them down and even to prove them, than to follow them through the labyrinth of their particular applications. Their formulation is nevertheless necessary.

Formerly, a *philosophy of history* or *nature* meant a narrow system of historical or scientific interpretation. It sought to explain the whole group or series of historic facts or natural phenomena, as presented in some inevitable order or sequence. Such attempts were bound to fail. The actual can be explained only as a part of the vast contingent, that is, of that which, given certain conditions, is necessary. In this it swims, like a star in infinite space. The very idea of law rests upon the conception of such a firmament of facts.

Given certain unknown primordial conditions, existence was, of course, bound to be as it is. But why were these conditions given and no others? There is something irrational here at the bottom of the inevitable. Moreover, in the worlds of life and matter, as well as in that of society, the actual seems to be a mere fragment of the potential. Witness the character of the heavens, dotted arbitrarily with suns and nebulæ. Witness the strange nature of certain faunas and floras. Witness the distorted and disjointed aspects of those societies that lie heaped up side by side under social ruins and abortions. In this respect, as in many others which I shall indicate in passing, the three great divisions of existence are very much alike.

Chapter V, on the Logical Laws of Imitation, is merely the toothing-stone of a future work which is intended to complete this one. A proper development of the subject would have led me beyond the limits of this volume.

The ideas which I have presented may supply new solutions for the political or other questions upon which we now stand divided. But it seemed to me that it was unnecessary to undertake to deduce them. It would, moreover, have taken me away from my immediate subject. Nor will the class of readers for whom I am writing reproach me for resisting the charm of such concrete subjects. Besides, I could not have succumbed to it without going beyond the limits of this work.

One word more in justification of my dedication. I am not the pupil, or even the disciple, of Cournot. I have never met him. But I take it as one of the happy chances of my life that I read a great deal of this writer after I left college. I have often thought that he needed only to have been born in England or Germany and to have had his work translated into a French teeming with solecisms to be famous among us all. Above all, I shall never forget that at a dreary period of my youth, when I was suffering from my eyes, and limited of necessity to one book, it was Cournot who saved me from mental starvation. But I shall certainly be ridiculed unless I add another much less disinterested sentiment to this old-fashioned one of intellectual gratitude. If my book fail of a welcome,—a contingency for which a philosopher must always be prepared in France, even if he have hitherto had but to congratulate himself upon the good will of the public,—this dedication will prove a consolation to me. Cournot was the Sainte-Beuve of philosophic criticism; possessed of originality and discrimination, he was a thinker of universal erudition as well as insight; he was a profound geometrician, an unparalleled logician, and as an economist he was the unrecognised precursor of modern economists; to sum it all up, Cournot was an Auguste Comte, purified, condensed, and refined. In realising, then, that such a man continued to be obscure during his lifetime, and that even since his death he has not been very well known, in realising this how could I ever dare to complain of not having had greater success?

PREFACE TO THE SECOND EDITION

SINCE the first edition of this book I have published its sequel and complement under the title of *La Logique sociale*.

In saying this I think that I have implicitly answered certain objections which the reader of *The Laws of Imitation* might have raised. However, it will not be useless to give a few brief points of explanation on this subject.

I have been criticised here and there " for having often called by the name of *imitation* certain facts which this name did not at all fit." This criticism, coming from a philosophic pen, astonishes me. In fact, when a philosopher needs a word to express a new generalisation, he must choose between two things; he must choose a neologism, if he is put to it, or he must decide, and this is unquestionably better, to stretch the meaning of some old term. The whole question is one of finding out whether I have overstretched —I do not say from the point of view of the dictionary definition, but from that of a deeper conception of things—the meaning of the word imitation.

Now I am well aware that I am not conforming to ordinary usage when I say that when a man unconsciously and involuntarily reflects the opinion of others, or allows an action of others to be suggested to him, he imitates this idea or act. And yet, if he knowingly and deliberately borrows some trick of thought or action from his neighbour, people agree that in this case the use of the word in question is legitimate. Nothing, however, is less scientific that the establishment of this absolute separation, of this abrupt break, between the voluntary and the involuntary, between the conscious and the unconscious. Do we not pass by insensible degrees from deliberate volition to almost mechanical habit? And does the same act absolutely change its nature during this transition? I do not mean to say that I deny the importance of the psychological change that is produced in this way. But on its social side the phenomenon has remained the same. No one has a right to criticise the extension of the meaning of the word in question as unjustifiable unless in extending it I have deformed or obscured its sense. But I have always given it a very precise and characteristic meaning, that of the action at a distance of one mind upon another, and of action which consists of a quasi-photographic reproduction of a cerebral image upon the sensitive plate of another brain.[1] If the photographic plate became conscious at a given moment of what was happening to it, would the nature of the phenomenon be essentially changed? By imitation I mean every impression of an inter-psychical photography, so to speak, willed or not willed, passive or active. If we observe that wherever there is a social relation between two living beings, there we have imitation in this sense of the word (either of one by the other or of others by both, when, for example, a man converses with another in a common language, making new verbal *proofs* from very old negatives), we shall have to admit that a sociologist was justified in taking this notion as a look-out post.

I might have been much more justly criticised for having overstretched the meaning of the word *invention*. I have certainly applied this name to all individual *initiatives*, not only without considering the extent in which they are self-conscious—for the individual often innovates unconsciously, and, as a matter of fact, the most imitative man is an innovator on some side or other—but without paying the slightest attention in the world to the degree of difficulty or merit of the innovation in question. This is not because I have failed to recognise the importance of this last consideration. Some *inventions* are so easy to conceive of that we may admit the fact that they have arisen of themselves, without

[1] Or of the same brain, if it is a question of imitation of self; for memory or habit, its two branches, must be connected, in order to be well understood, with imitation of others, the only kind of imitation which we are concerned with here. The psychological is explained by the social just because the social, sprang from the psychological.

borrowing, in almost all primitive societies, and that their first accidental appearance here or there has little significance. Other discoveries, on the contrary, are so difficult that the happy advent of the genius who made them may be considered a pre-eminently singular and important chance of fortune. Well, in spite of all this, I think that even here I have been justified in doing some slight violence to common speech in characterising as inventions or discoveries the most simple innovations, all the more so because the easiest are not always the least fruitful nor the most difficult the least useless. What is really unjustifiable, on the other hand, is the elastic meaning that is given by many naturalistic sociologists to the word *heredity*. They use this word indifferently to express the transmission of vital characteristics through reproduction and the transmission of ideas and customs, of social things, by ancestral tradition, by domestic education, and by custom-imitation.

Let me add that a neologism from the Greek would have been the easiest thing in the world to conceive of. Instead of saying *invention* or *imitation* I might have readily forged two new words. Now let me dismiss this petty and uninteresting quibble. I have been sometimes charged with exaggeration, and this is a more serious thing, in the use of the two notions in question. It is rather a commonplace criticism, to be sure, and one which every innovator must expect even when he has erred on the side of too much reserve in the expression of his thoughts. We may be sure that if a Greek philosopher had undertaken to say that the sun might possibly be as big as the Peloponnesus, his best friends would have been unanimous in recognising the fact that there was something true at the bottom of his ingenious paradox, but that he was evidently exaggerating. In general, my critics did not consider the end which I had in view. I desired to unfold the purely sociological side of human facts, intentionally ignoring their biological side, although I am well aware that the latter is inseparable from the former. My plan allowed me to indicate, without developing to any extent, the relations of the *three principal forms of universal repetition,* especially the relation of heredity to imitation. But I have said enough, I think, to leave no doubt as to my views on the importance of race and physical environment.

Besides, if I say that the distinctive character of every social relation, of every social fact, is to be imitated, is this saying, as certain superficial readers have seemed to believe, that in my eyes there is no social relation, no social fact, no social cause, but imitation? One might as well say that every function of life could be reduced to reproduction and every vital phenomenon to heredity because in every living being everything is a matter of generation and inheritance. Social relations are as manifold, as numerous, and as diverse, as the objects of the desires and ideas of man, and as the helps or hindrances that each of these desires and ideas lends or presents to the similar or dissimilar tendencies and opinions of others. In the midst of this infinite complexity we may note that these varied social relations (talking and listening, beseeching and being beseeched, commanding and obeying, producing and consuming, etc.) belong to two groups; the one tends to transmit from one man to another, persuasively or authoritatively, willingly or unwillingly, a belief; the other, a desire. In other words, the first group consists of various kinds or degrees of instruction; the second, of various kinds or degrees of command. And it is precisely because the human acts which are imitated have this dogmatic or commanding character that imitation is a social tie, for it is either dogma[1] or power which binds men together. (People have seen only the half of this truth, and seen that badly, when they have said that social facts were distinguished by their constrained and coercive character. In saying this, they have failed to recognise the spontaneity of the greater part of popular credulity and docility.)

Therefore I think that I have not erred through exag-

---

[1] Dogma, that is to say, any idea, religious or otherwise, political, for example, which takes root in the mind of any social unit through the pressure of his environment.

geration in this book; and so I have reprinted it without eliminating anything. I have sinned rather through omission. I have said nothing at all about a form of imitation which plays a big rôle in societies, particularly in contemporary societies, and I shall make haste here to make good this omission. There are two ways of imitating, as a matter of fact, namely, to act exactly like one's model, or to do exactly the contrary. Hence the necessity of those divergences which Spencer points out, without explaining, in his law of progressive differentiation. Nothing can be affirmed without suggesting, no matter how simple the social environment, not only the idea that is affirmed, but the negation of this idea as well. This is the reason why the supernatural, in asserting itself through theologies, suggests naturalism, its negation. (See Espinas on this subject.) This is the reason why the affirmation of idealism gives birth to the idea of materialism; why the establishment of monarchy engenders the idea of republicanism, etc.

Let us say, then, from this wider point of view, that a society is a group of people who display many resemblances produced either by imitation or by *counter-imitation*. For men often counter-imitate one another, particularly when they have neither the modesty to imitate directly nor the power to invent. In counter-imitating one another, that is to say, in doing or saying the exact opposite of what they observe being done or said, they are becoming more and more assimilated, just as much assimilated as if they did or said precisely what was being done or said around them. Next to conforming to custom in the matter of funerals, marriages, visits, and manners, there is nothing more imitative than fighting against one's natural inclination to follow the current of these things, or than pretending to go against it. In the Middle Ages the *black mass* arose from a counter-imitation of the Catholic mass. In his book on the expression of the emotions, Darwin very properly gives a large place to the need of *counter-expression*.

When a dogma is proclaimed, when a political programme is announced, men fall into two unequal classes ;

there are those who are enthusiastic about it and those who are not enthusiastic.   There is no manifestation which does not recruit supporters and which does not provoke the formation of a group of non-supporters.   Every positive affirmation, at the same time that it attracts to itself mediocre and sheep-like minds, arouses somewhere or other in a brain that is naturally rebellious,—this does not mean naturally inventive,—a negation that is diametrically opposite and of about equal strength.   This reminds one of *inductive currents* in physics.   But both kinds of brains have the same content of ideas and purposes.   They are associated, although they are adversaries, or, rather, because they are adversaries.   Let us clearly distinguish between the imitative propagation of questions and that of solutions.   Because a certain solution spreads in one place and another elsewhere, this does not prevent the problem from having spread in both places.   Is it not evident that in every period, among people in constant communication, particularly in our own day because international relations have never before been so manifold, is it not evident that the calendar of social and political debates is always the same?   And is not this resemblance due to a current of imitation that may itself be explained by a diffusion of wants and ideas through prior contagions of imitation?   Is not this the reason why labour questions are being agitated at the present moment throughout Europe?   No opinion is discussed by the press, about which, I repeat, the public is not daily divided into two camps, those who agree with the opinion and those who disagree.   But the latter as well as the former admit that it is impossible to be concerned for the time being with anything other than the question which is thus forced upon them.   Only some wild and undisciplined spirit will ruminate, now and then, in the whirl of the social sea in which he is plunged, over strange and absolutely hypothetical problems.   Such men are the inventors of the future.

We must be very careful not to confuse counter-imitation with invention, its dangerous counterfeit.   I do not mean that the former is worthless. Although it fosters the spirit of partisanship, the spirit of either peaceful or warlike division between men, it introduces them to the wholly social pleasure of discussion. It is a witness to the sympathetic origin of contradiction itself; the back currents themselves are caused by the current. Nor must we confuse counter-imitation with systematic non-imitation, a subject about which I should also have spoken in this book. Non-imitation is not always a simple negative fact. The fact of not imitating when there is no contact—no social contact through the practical impossibility of communication—is merely a non-social relation, but the fact of not imitating the neighbour who is in touch with us, puts us upon a footing of really anti-social relations with him. The refusal of a people, a class, a town or a village, of a savage tribe isolated on a civilised continent, to copy the dress, customs, language, industry, and arts which make up the civilisation of their neighbourhood is a continual declaration of antipathy to the form of society in question. It is thereby declared absolutely and forever alien. Similarly, when a people deliberately undertakes not to reproduce the examples of its forefathers in the matter of rights, usages, and ideas, we have a veritable *disassociation* of fathers and sons, a rupture of the umbilical cord between the old and the new society. Voluntary and persistent non-imitation in this sense has a purgative rôle which is quite analogous to that filled by what I have called the *logical duel*. Just as the latter tends to purge the social mass of mixed ideas and volitions, to eliminate inequalities and discords, and to facilitate in this way the synthetic action of the *logical union;* so non-imitation of extraneous and heterogeneous models makes it possible for the harmonious group of home models to extend and prolong themselves, to entrench themselves in the custom-imitation of which they are the object; and for the same reason non-imitation of anterior models, when the moment has come for civilising revolution, cuts a path for fashion-imitation. It no longer finds any hindrance in the way of its conquering activity.

Is the unique or principal cause of this invincible obstinacy—momentarily invincible—of non-imitation, as the naturalistic school was led to think some years ago, racial difference? Not the least in the world. In the first place, in the case of non-imitation of ancestral examples, in revolutionary periods, it is clear that this cause could not be brought forward, since the new generation belongs to the same race as the prior generations whose traditions it casts aside. Then, in the case of non-imitation of the foreigner, historical observation shows that resistance to outside influences is very far from being in proportion to the dissimilarities of the physical traits which differentiate populations. Of all the nations conquered by Rome none was more allied to her through blood than the populations of Greek origin; and yet these were precisely the communities where her language failed to spread and where her culture and genius failed to be assimilated. Why was this? Because they alone, in spite of their defeat, were able to retain their fierce pride, their indelible feeling of superiority. On the side of the idea that it is impossible for separate races to borrow from one another one of the strongest arguments that could have been cited thirty years ago was the hermetical shutting out by the peoples of the Far East, Japan and China, of all European culture. But from the still recent day when the Japanese, foreign as they were to us in colour, lineaments, and physical constitution, felt for the first time that we were their superiors, they left off trying to shut out the imitative radiation of our civilisation by the opaque screen they had used before. They gave it, on the contrary, the warmest of welcomes. The same thing will happen to China if she ever makes up her mind to recognise that in certain respects—not in all, I hope, for her sake—we have the better of her. It is idle to argue that the transformation of Japan in the direction of Europe is more apparent than real, more superficial than deep, that it is due to the initiative of certain intelligent men who are followed by a part of the upper classes, but that the great mass of the nation remains hostile to this foreign inundation. To argue after this fashion is to ignore the fact that every intellectual and moral revolution that is destined to utterly recast a people always begins in this way. A chosen few have always imported the foreign examples that come little by little to spread by fashion, to be consolidated into custom, and to be developed and systematised by social logic. When Christianity first reached the Germans, the Slavs, the Finns, it started in the same way. Nothing is more consistent with the "laws of imitation."

Does this mean that the action of race upon the course of civilisation is overlooked from my point of view? Not at all. I have said that in passing from one ethnical environment to another the radiation of imitation is refracted; and I add that this refraction may be enormous without its leading to any consequence that is in the least contradictory to the ideas developed in this book. Only race as I see it is a national product where, in the crucible of a special civilisation, different prehistoric races have been melted together, intermingled, and assimilated. For every given civilisation that is formed of ideas of genius, hailing a little from everywhere and brought into logical agreement somewhere or other, creates in the long run the race, or races, in which it is for a time embodied; and the inverse of this is not true, namely, that every race makes its own civilisation. This means, at bottom, that different human races, which are quite different in this respect from different living species, are collaborators as well as competitors; that they are called upon not only to fight and destroy each other for the good of a small number of survivors, but to aid each other in the age-long achievement of a common social work, of a great final society whose unity will be the fruit of their very diversity.

The *laws of heredity* that have been so well studied by naturalists do not contradict in any respect the "laws of imitation." On the other hand, they complete them, and there is no concrete sociology that could separate these two orders of consideration. If I separate them here, it is, I repeat, because the proper subject of this work is sociology pure and abstract. Besides, I do not fail to point out what their place is in the biological considerations which I am purposely ignoring because I am leaving them to more competent hands. And this place is three-fold. To begin with, in expressly developing the nation from the family—for the primitive horde is made up of emigrants or exiles from the family—I have clearly affirmed that if the social fact is a relation of imitation, the social *tie,* the social *group,* is both imitative and hereditary. In the second place, invention, from which I derive everything that is social, is not, in my opinion, a purely social fact in its origin. It arises from the intersection of an individual genius, an intermittent and characteristic racial product, the ripe fruit of a series of happy marriages, with the currents and radiations of imitation which one day happened to cross each other in a more or less exceptional brain. You may agree, if you wish, with M. de Gobineau, that only the white races are inventive, or with a contemporary anthropologist, that this privilege belongs exclusively to the dolichocephalic races—all this matters little from my point of view. And I might even pretend that the radical and vital separation that is thus established between the inventiveness of certain privileged races and the imitativeness of all races is fitted to emphasise, a little unjustifiably, as a matter of fact, the truth of my point of view. Finally, I have not only recognised the influence of the *vital environment* upon imitation, an environment in which it spreads while it is refracted, as I said above, but in stating the law of the normal return of fashion to custom, the rooting of innovations in customs and traditions, have I not again made heredity the necessary prop of imitation? But we may accord to the biological side of social facts the highest importance without going as far as to maintain that there is a water-tight bulkhead between different races, presumably primitive and *presocial,* which makes any *endosmosis* or *exosmosis* of imitation impossible. And this is the only thing which I deny. Taken in this false and unjustifiable sense, the idea of race leads the sociologist who has taken it for a guide to conceive of the end of social progress as a disintegration of peoples who are walled about and shut off from one another and everlastingly at war with one another. This kind of naturalism is generally associated with a defence of militarism. On the other hand, if we take the ideas of invention, imitation, and social logic as a guiding thread, we are led to the more reassuring perspective of a great future confluence—alas, that it is not immediate—of multiple divisions of mankind into a single peaceful human family. The idea of *indefinite progress,* which is such a vague and obstinate idea, has neither a clear nor precise meaning except from this point of view. The *necessity* of a progressive march *towards* a great but distant goal is an outcome of the laws of imitation. This goal, which becomes more and more accessible in spite of apparent, although only transitory, set-backs, is the birth, the development, and the universal spread,—whether under an imperial or federated form is insignificant,—of a unique society. And, as a matter of fact, among all the predictions of Condorcet relating to social progress, the only ones that have been realised—that, for example, relating to the extension and gradual levelling down of European civilisation—are consequences of the laws in question. But if he had considered these laws he would have expressed his thought more exactly and precisely. When he predicts that the *inequality* of different nations will continue to diminish, he should have said *social dissimilarity,* and not inequality. For between the smallest and largest states the disproportion of power, of territory, and even of wealth, goes on increasing, and yet this condition does not stand in the way of a constant progress of international *assimilation.* And is it certain that inequality between individuals must continually diminish in all respects as our illustrious philosopher also predicted? Inequality of genius or talent? Not at all. Of comfort and wealth? I doubt it. It is true that their inequality before the law has disappeared or will before long disappear altogether. But why is this so? Because the growing resemblance of individuals between whom all the customary barriers of reciprocal imitation have been broken down, and who imitate one another more and more freely, to be sure, and yet more and more necessarily, makes them feel with a growing and, eventually, irresistible power the injustice of privilege.

Let us be sure, however, that we understand one another about this progressive resemblance of individuals. Far from smothering their true originality, it fosters and favours it. What is contrary to personal pre-eminence is the imitation of a single man whom people copy in everything. But when, instead of patterning one's self after one person or after a few, we borrow from a hundred, a thousand, or ten thousand persons, each of whom is considered under a particular aspect, the elements of thought or action which we subsequently combine, the very nature and choice of these elementary copies, as well as their combination, expresses and accentuates our original personality. And this is, perhaps, the chief benefit that results from the prolonged action of imitation. We might demand to what extent this collective dream, this collective nightmare of society, was worth its cost in blood and tears, if this grievous discipline, this deceptive and despotic prestige, did not serve to free the individual in calling forth, little by little, from the depths of his heart, his freest impulses, his boldest introspection, his keenest insight into nature, and in developing everywhere, not the savage individualities, not the clashing and brutal soul-stuffs of bygone days, but those deep and harmonious traits of the soul that are characteristic of personality as well as of civilisation, the harvest of both the purest and most potent individualism and of consummate sociability.

G. T.

May, 1895

CONTENTS

CHAPTER I.—UNIVERSAL REPETITION

CHAPTER II—SOCIAL RESEMBLANCES AND IMITATION

CHAPTER III—WHAT IS A SOCIETY?

CHAPTER IV.—WHAT IS HISTORY? ARCHÆOLOGY AND STATISTICS

CHAPTER V—THE LOGICAL LAWS OF IMITATION

CHAPTER VI.—EXTRA-LOGICAL INFLUENCES

CHAPTER VII.—EXTRA-LOGICAL INFLUENCES (CONTINUED)— CUSTOM AND FASHION

Contents xxix

CHAPTER VIII.—REMARKS AND COROLLARIES

LAWS OF IMITATION

CHAPTER I

UNIVERSAL REPETITION

I

CAN we have a science or only a history, or, at most, a philosophy of social phenomena? This question is always open. And yet, if social facts are closely observed from a certain point of view, they can be reduced, like other facts, to series of minute and homogeneous phenomena and to the formulas, or laws, which sum up these series. Why, then, is the science of society still unborn, or born but recently, among all its adult and vigorous sister sciences? The chief reason is, I think, that we have thrown away the substance for its shadow and substituted words for things. We have thought it impossible to give a scientific look to *sociology* except by giving it a biological or, better still, a mechanical air. This is an attempt to light up the known by the unknown. It is transforming a solar system into a non-resolvable nebula in order to understand it better. In social subjects we are exceptionally privileged in having veritable causes, positive and specific acts, at first hand; this condition is wholly lacking in every other subject of investigation. It is unnecessary, therefore, to rely for an explanation of social facts upon those so-called general causes which physicists and naturalists are obliged to create under the name of force, energy, conditions of existence, and other verbal palliatives of their ignorance of the real groundwork of things.

But are we to consider that human acts are the sole factors of history? Surely this is too simple! And so we bind ourselves to contrive other causes on the type of those useful fictions which are elsewhere imposed upon us, and we

congratulate ourselves upon being able at times to give an
entirely impersonal colour to human phenomena by reason
of our lofty, but, truly speaking, obscure, point of view. Let
us ward off this vague idealism. Let us likewise ward off
the vapid individualism which consists in explaining social
changes as the caprices of certain great men. On the other
hand, let us explain these changes through the more or less
fortuitous appearance, as to time and place, of certain
great ideas, or rather, of a considerable number of both
major and minor ideas, of ideas which are generally anonymous and usually of obscure birth; which are simple or
abstruse; which are seldom illustrious, but which are always
novel. Because of this latter attribute, I shall take the
liberty of baptising them collectively *inventions* or *discoveries*. By these two terms I mean any kind of an innovation
or improvement, however slight, which is made in any previous innovation throughout the range of social phenomena
—language, religion, politics, law, industry, or art. At the
moment when this novel thing, big or little as it may be, is
conceived of, or determined by, an individual, nothing appears to change in the social body,—just as nothing changes
in the physical appearance of an organism which a harmful
or beneficent microbe has just invaded,—and the gradual
changes caused by the introduction of the new element seem
to follow, without visible break, upon the anterior social
changes into whose current they have glided. Hence arises
the illusion which leads philosophers of history into affirming
that there is a real and fundamental continuity in historic
metamorphoses. The true causes can be reduced to a chain of
ideas which are, to be sure, very numerous, but which are
in themselves distinct and discontinuous, although they are
connected by the much more numerous acts of imitation
which are modelled upon them.

Our starting-point lies here in the re-inspiring initiatives
which bring new wants, together with new satisfactions,
into the world, and which then, through spontaneous and
unconscious or artificial and deliberate imitation, propagate
or tend to propagate, themselves, at a more or less rapid,

but regular, rate, like a wave of light, or like a family of termites. The regularity to which I refer is not in the least apparent in social things until they are resolved into their several elements, when it is found to lie in the simplest of them, in combinations of distinct inventions, in flashes of genius which have been accumulated and changed into commonplace lights. I confess that this is an extremely difficult analysis. Socially, everything is either invention or imitation. And invention bears the same relation to imitation as a mountain to a river. There is certainly noth-' ing less subtle than this point of view; but in holding to it boldly and unreservedly, in exploiting it from the most trivial detail to the most complete synthesis of facts, we may, perhaps, notice how well fitted it is to bring into relief all the picturesqueness and, at the same time, all the simplicity of history, and to reveal historic perspectives which may be characterised by the freakishness of a rock-bound landscape, or by the conventionality of a park walk. This is idealism also, if you choose to call it so; but it is the idealism which consists in explaining history through the ideas of its actors, not through those of the historian.

If we consider the science of society from this point of view, we shall at once see that human sociology is related to animal sociologies, as a species to its genus, so to speak. That it is an extraordinary and infinitely superior species, I admit, but it is allied to the others, nevertheless. M. Espinas expressly states in his admirable work on *Sociétés animales,* a work which was written long before the first edition of this book, that the labours of ants may be very well explained on the principle " *of individual initiative followed by imitation.*" This initiative is always an innovation or invention that is equal to one of our own in boldness of spirit. To conceive the idea of constructing an arch, or a tunnel, at an appropriate point, an ant must be endowed with an innovating instinct equal to, or surpassing, that of our canal-digging or mountain-tunnelling engineers. Parenthetically it follows that imitation by masses of ants of such novel initiatives strikingly belies the spirit of mutual

hatred which is alleged to exist among animals.[1]   M.
Espinas is very frequently impressed in his observation of
the societies of our lower brethren by the important rôle
which is played in them by individual initiatives.   Every
herd of wild cattle has its leaders, its influential heads.   Developments in the instincts of birds are explained by the
same author as " individual inventions which are afterwards
transmitted from generation to generation through direct
instruction." [2]   In view of the fact that modification of instinct is probably related to the same principle as the
genesis and modification of species, we may be tempted
to enquire whether the principle of the imitation of invention, or of something physiologically analogous, would not
be the clearest possible explanation of the ever-open problem
of the origin of species.   But let us leave this question and
confine ourselves to the statement that both animal and
human societies may be explained from this point of view.

In the second place, and this is the special thesis of this
chapter, the subject of social science is seen, from this
standpoint, to present a remarkable analogy to the other
domains of general science, and, in this way, to become
re-embodied, so to speak, in the rest of the universe, where
it had before this the air of an outsider.

In every field of study, affirmations pure and simple enor-
mously outnumber explanations.   And, in all cases, the
first data are simply affirmed; they are the extraordinary
and accidental facts, the premises and sources from which
proceeds all that which is subsequently explained.   The
astronomer states that certain nebulæ, certain celestial

---

[1] Among the higher species of ants, according to M. Espinas, " *the
individual develops an astonishing initiative* " [*Des Sociétés animales*,
p. 223; Alfred Espinas, Paris, 1877.   The italics are M Tarde's —*Tr.*].
How do the labours and migrations of ant-swarms begin?   Is it
through a common, instinctive, and spontaneous impulse which starts
from all the associates at the same time and under the pressure of
outward circumstances which are experienced simultaneously by all?
On the contrary, a single ant begins by leaving the others and undertaking the work; then it strikes its neighbours with its antennæ to
summon their aid, and the contagion of imitation does the rest.

[2] [*Ibid*, p 272.—*Tr.*]

bodies of a given mass and volume and at a given distance, exist, or have existed. The chemist makes the same statement about certain chemical substances, the physicist, about certain kinds of ethereal vibrations, which he calls light, electricity, and magnetism; the naturalist states that there are certain principal organic types, to begin with, plants and animals; the physiographer states that there are certain mountain chains, which he calls the Alps, the Andes, *et cetera*. In teaching us about these capital facts from which the rest are deduced, are these investigators doing the work, strictly speaking, of scientists? They are not; they are merely *affirming* certain facts, and they in no way differ from the historian who chronicles the expedition of Alexander or the discovery of printing. If there be any difference, it is, as we shall see, wholly to the advantage of the historian. What, then, do we know in the *scientific* sense of the word? Of course, we answer that we know causes and effects. And when we have learned that, in the case of two different events, the one is the outcome of the other, or that both collaborate towards the same end, we say that they have been explained. But let us imagine a world where there is neither resemblance nor repetition, a strange, but, if need be, an intelligible hypothesis; a world where everything is novel and unforeseen, where the creative imagination, unchecked by memory, has full play, where the motions of the stars are sporadic, where the agitations of the ether are unrhythmical, and where successive generations are without the common traits of an hereditary type. And yet every apparition in such a phantasmagoria might be produced and determined by another, and might even, in its turn, become the cause of others. In such a world causes and effects might still exist; but would any kind of a science be possible? It would not be, because, to reiterate, neither resemblances nor repetitions would be found there.

This is the essential point. Knowledge of causes is sometimes sufficient for foresight; but knowledge of resemblances always allows of enumeration and measurement. and science depends primarily upon number and measure.

More than this is, of course, necessary.   As soon as a new science has staked out its field of characteristic resemblances and repetitions, it must compare them and note the bond of solidarity which unites their concomitant variations.   But, as a matter of fact, the mind does not fully understand nor clearly recognise the relation of cause and effect, except in as much as the effect resembles or repeats the cause, as, for example, when a sound wave produces another sound wave, or a cell, another cell.   There is nothing more mysterious, one may say, than such reproductions. I admit this, but when we have once accepted this mystery, there is nothing clearer than the resulting series.   Whereas, every time that *production* does not mean *reproduction of self,* we are entirely in the dark.[1]

When like things form parts of the same or of supposedly the same whole, like the molecules of a volume of hydrogen, or the woody cells of a tree, or the soldiers of a regiment, the resemblance is referred to as a quantity instead of a group.   In other words, when the things *which repeat themselves* remain united as they increase, like vibrations of heat or electricity, accumulating within some heated or electrified object, or like cells multiplying in the body of a growing child, or like proselytes to a common religion, in such cases the repetition is called a growth instead of a series.   In all of this I fail to see anything which would differentiate the subject of social science.

Besides, whether resemblances and repetitions are intrinsic or extrinsic, quantities or groups, growths or series, they are the necessary themes of the differences and variations which exist in all phenomena.   They are the canvas of their embroidery, the measure of their music.   The wonder world which I was picturing would be, at bottom, the least

1 " Scientific knowledge need not necessarily take its starting-point from the most minute hypothetical and unknown things. It begins wherever matter forms units of a like order which can be compared with and measured by one another, and wherever such units combine as units of a higher order and thus serve in themselves as a standard of comparison for the latter " (Von Naegeli. Address at the congress of German naturalists in 1877).

richly differentiated of all possible worlds. How much greater a renovator than revolution is our modern industrial system, accumulation as it is of mutually imitative actions! What is more monotonous than the free life of the savage in comparison with the hemmed-in life of civilised man? Would any organic progress be possible without heredity? Would the exuberant variety of geological ages and of living nature have sprung into existence independently of the periodicity of the heavenly motions or of the wave-like rhythm of the earth's forces?

Repetition exists, then, for the sake of variation. Otherwise, the necessity of death (a problem which M. Delbœuf considers in his book upon animate and inanimate matter, almost impossible of solution), would be incomprehensible; for why should not the top of life spin on, after it was wound up, forever? But under the hypothesis that repetitions exist only to embody all the phases of a certain unique originality which seeks expression, death must inevitably supervene after all these variations have been fully effected. I may note in this connection, in passing, that the relation of universal to particular, a relation which fed the entire philosophic controversy of the Middle Ages upon nominalism and realism, is precisely that of repetition to variation. *Nominalism* is the doctrine in accordance with which individual characteristics or idiosyncracies are the only significant realities. *Realism,* on the other hand. considers only those traits worthy of attention and of the name of reality through which a given individual resembles other individuals and tends to reproduce himself in them. The interest of this kind of speculation is apparent when we consider that in politics individualism is a special kind of nominalism, and socialism, a special kind of realism.

All repetition, social, vital, or physical, *i. e., imitative, hereditary,* or *vibratory* repetition (to consider only the most salient and typical forms of universal repetition), springs from some innovation, just as every light radiates from some central point, and thus throughout science the normal appears to originate from the accidental. For the propagation of an attractive force or luminous vibration from a heavenly body, or of a race of animals from an ancestral pair, or of a national idea or desire or religious rite from a scholar or inventor or missionary, seem to us like natural and regular phenomena; whereas we are constantly surprised by the strange and partly non-formulable sequence or juxtaposition of their respective centres, *i. e.,* the different crafts, religions, and social institutions, the different organic types, the different chemical substances or celestial masses from which all these radiations have issued. All these admirable uniformities or series,—hydrogen, whose multitudinous, star-scattered atoms are universally homogeneous, protoplasm, identical from one end to the other of the scale of life, the roots of the Indo-European languages, identical almost throughout civilisation, the expansion of the light of a star in the immensity of space, the unbroken sequence from geological times of incalculable generations of marine species, the wonderfully faithful transmission of words from the Coptic of the ancient Egyptians to us moderns, etc.,—all these innumerable masses of things of like nature and of like affiliations, whose harmonious co-existence or equally harmonious succession we admire, are related to physical, biological, and social accidents by a tie which baffles us.

Here, also, the analogy between social and natural phenomena is carried out. But we should not be surprised if the former seem chaotic when we view them through the medium of the historian, or even through that of the sociologist, whereas the latter impress us, as they are presented by physicist, chemist, or physiologist, as very well ordered worlds. These latter scientists show us the subject of their science only on the side of its characteristic resemblances and repetitions; they prudently conceal its corresponding heterogeneities and transformations (or transsubstantiations). The historian and sociologist, on the contrary, veil the regular and monotonous face of social facts,—that part in which they are alike and repeat themselves,—and show us only their accidental and interesting, their infinitely novel and diversified, aspect. If our subject were, for example, the Gallo-Romans, the historian, even the philosophic historian, would not think of leading us step by step through conquered Gaul in order to show us how every word, rite, edict, profession, custom, craft, law, or military manœuvre, how, in short, every special idea or need which had been introduced from Rome had begun to spread from the Pyrenees to the Rhine, and to win its way, after more or less vigorous fighting against old Celtic customs and ideas, to the mouths and arms and hearts and minds of all the enthusiastic Gallic imitators of Rome and Cæsar. At any rate, if our historian had once led us upon this long journey, he would not make us repeat it for every Latin word or grammatical form, for every ritualistic form in the Roman religion, for every military manœuvre that was taught to the legionaries by their officer-instructors, for every variety of Roman architecture, for temple, basilica, theatre, hippodrome, aqueduct, and atriumed villa, for every school-taught verse of Virgil or Horace, for every Roman law, or for every artistic or industrial process in Roman civilisation that had been faithfully and continuously transmitted from pedagogues and craftsmen to pupils and apprentices. And yet it is only at this price that we can get at an exact estimate of the great amount of regularity which obtains in even the most fluctuating societies.

Then, after the introduction of Christianity, our historian would certainly refrain from making us renew this tedious peregrination in connection with every Christian rite which propagated itself, in spite of resistance, through heathen Gaul, like a wave of sound through air that is already in vibration. Instead of this, he would inform us at what date Julius Cæsar conquered Gaul, or, again, at what date certain saints came to that country to preach Christianity. He might also enumerate the diverse elements out of which the Roman civilisation and the Christian faith and morality that were introduced into the Gallic world, were composed. In this case, his problem is to understand and rationally, logically, and scientifically, describe the extraordinary superposition of Christianity upon Romanism, or rather, the gradual process of Christian upon the gradual process of Roman assimilation. In the separate treatment of both Romanism and Christianity, he will meet with an equally difficult problem in giving a rational explanation of the strange juxtaposition of the very heterogeneous Etruscan, Greek, Oriental, and other fragments which constituted the former, and of the incoherent Jewish, Egyptian, and Byzantine ideas, ideas which were incoherent even in each distinct group, which constituted the latter. This, however, is the arduous task which the philosopher of history sets before himself and which he thinks that he cannot slur over if he is to do the work of a scholar. He will, therefore, wear himself out in trying to bring order out of disorder by discovering some law or reason for these historic chances and coincidences. He would do better to investigate how and why harmonies sometimes proceed from these coincidences and in what these harmonies consist. I will undertake to do this further on.

In short, a historian of this kind is like the botanist who would feel bound to ignore everything about the generation of plants of the same species or variety, as well as everything about their growth or nutrition, a kind of cellular generation or regeneration of tissues; or like the physicist who disdained to study the propagation of light or heat or sound waves as they passed through different mediums which were themselves in vibration. Can we conceive of the former believing that the proper and exclusive object of his science was an interlinking of unlike species, beginning with the first alga and ending with the last orchid, plus a profound justification of such a concatenation? Can we conceive of the latter convinced that the sole end of his studies was investigation into the reason why there were precisely seven known kinds of luminous undulation, and why, including electricity and magnetism, there were no other kinds of ethereal vibration? These are certainly interesting questions, but although they are open to philosophic, they are not open to scientific, discussion, since their solution does not seem capable of admitting of that high kind of probability which science exacts. It is clear that the first condition of becoming an anatomist or physiologist is the study of tissues, the aggregates of homogeneous cells and fibres and blood vessels, or the study of functions, the accumulations of minute homogeneous contractions, innervations, oxidations, or deoxidations, and then, and above all, belief in the great architect of life, in heredity. It is equally clear that it is of primary importance to the chemist and physicist to examine many kinds of gaseous, liquid, and solid masses, masses composed of corpuscles which are absolutely alike, or of so-called physical forces which are prodigious accumulations of minute, homogeneous vibrations. In fact, in the physical world, everything refers, or is in course of being referred, to vibration. Here everything is taking on more and more an essentially vibratory character, just as in the animate world the reproductive faculty, or the property of transmitting the smallest peculiarities (which are usually of unknown origin) through inheritance, is coming more and more to be thought inherent in the smallest cell

And now my readers will realise, perhaps, that the social being, in the degree that he is social, is essentially imitative, and that imitation plays a rôle in societies analogous to that of heredity in organic life or to that of vibration among inorganic bodies. If this is so, it ought to be admitted, in consequence, that a human invention, by which a new kind of imitation is started or a new series opened,—the invention of gunpowder, for example,[1] or windmills, or the Morse telegraph,—stands in the same relation to social science as the birth of a new vegetal or mineral species (or, on the hypothesis of a gradual evolution, of each of the slow modifications to which the new species is due), to biology, or as the appearance of a new mode of motion comparable with

[1] When I speak of the invention of gunpowder, of the telegraph, of railroads, etc., I mean, of course, the group of accumulated and yet distinguishable and numerable inventions which have been necessary for the production of gunpowder, or telegraphy, or railroads.

light or electricity, or the formation of a new substance, to physics or chemistry. Therefore, if we are to make a just comparison, we must not compare the philosophic historian who strives to discover a law for the odd groups and sequences of scientific, industrial, æsthetic, and political inventions, to the physiologist or physicist, as we know him, to Tyndall or Claude Bernard, but to a philosopher of nature like Schelling or like Haeckel in his hours of riotous imagination.

We should then perceive that the crude incoherence of historic facts, all of which facts are traceable to the different currents of imitation of which they are the point of intersection, a point which is itself destined to be more or less exactly copied, is no proof at all against the fundamental regularity of social life or the possibility of a social science. Indeed, parts of this science exist in the petty experience of each of us, and we have only to piece the fragments together. Besides, a group of historic events would certainly be far from appearing more incoherent than a collection of living types or chemical substances. Why then should we exact from the philosopher of history the fine symmetrical and rational order that we do not dream of demanding from the philosopher of science? And yet there is a distinction here which is entirely to the credit of the historian. It is but recently that the naturalist has had any glimpses that were at all clear of biological evolution, whereas the historian was long ago aware of the continuity of history. As for chemists and physicists, we may pass them by. They dare not even yet forecast the time when they will be able to trace out, in their turn, the genealogy of simple substances, or when a work on the origin of atoms, as successful as Darwin's *Origin of Species,* will be published. It is true that M. Lecoq de Boisbaudran and M. Mendelejeff thought that they had distinguished a natural series of simple substances, and it is true that Boisbaudran's discovery of *gallium* was made in connection with his eminently philosophic speculations along this line But upon close consideration, perhaps neither the remarkable attempts of these scientists nor the various systems of our evolutionists on the genealogical ramification of living types present any greater degree of precision or certainty than sparkles in the ideas of Herbert Spencer, or even in those of Vico, upon the so-called periodic and predestined evolutions of society. The origin of atoms is much more mysterious than the origin of species, and the origin of species is, in turn, more mysterious than the origin of civilisations. We can compare extant living species with those which have preceded them, the remains of which we find in the earth's strata; but we have not the slightest trace of the chemical substances which must have preceded in prehistoric astronomy, so to speak, in the unfathomable and unimaginable depths of the past, the actual chemical substances of the earth and stars. Consequently, chemistry, which cannot even propound a problem of origins, is less advanced, in this essential particular, than biology; and, for like reason, biology is, in reality, less advanced than sociology.

From the foregoing, it is evident that social science and social philosophy are distinct; that social science must deal exclusively, like every other science, with a multitude of homogeneous facts, with those facts which are carefully concealed by the historians; that new and heterogeneous facts, or historical facts, strictly speaking, are the special domain of social philosophy; that from this point of view social science might be as advanced as the other sciences, and that social philosophy is actually much more so than any other philosophy.

In the present volume, we are concerned only with the science of society; moreover, we shall confine our discussion to imitation and its laws. Later on, we shall have to study the laws, or pseudo-laws, of invention.[1] The two questions are quite different, although they cannot be wholly separated.

[1] Since this was written I have outlined a theory of invention in my *Logique sociale* (F Alcan, 1895).

II

After these long preliminaries, I must develop an important thesis which has so far been obscure and involved. Science, as I have said, deals only with quantities and growths, or, in more general terms, with the resemblances and repetitions of phenomena.

This distinction, however, is really superfluous and superficial. Every advance in knowledge tends to strengthen the conviction that *all resemblance is due to repetition.* I think that this may be brought out in the three following propositions:

1. All resemblances which are to be observed in the chemical, or physical, or astronomical worlds (the atoms of a single body, the waves of a single ray of light, the concentric strata of attraction of which every heavenly body is a centre), can be caused and explained solely by periodic, and, for the most part, vibratory motions.

2. All resemblances of vital origin in the world of life result from hereditary transmission, from either intra- or extra-organic reproduction. It is through the relationship between cells and the relationship between species that all the different kinds of analogies and homologies which comparative anatomy points out between species, and histology, between corporeal elements, are at present explained.

3. All resemblances of *social origin* in society are the direct or indirect fruit of the various forms of imitation,—custom-imitation or fashion-imitation, sympathy-imitation or obedience-imitation, precept-imitation or education-imitation, naive imitation, deliberate imitation, etc. In this lies the excellence of the contemporaneous method of explaining doctrines and institutions through their history. It is a method that is certain to come into more general use. It is said that great geniuses, great inventors, are apt to cross each other's paths. But, in the first place, such coincidences are very rare, and when they do occur, they are always due to the fact that

both authors of the same invention have drawn independently from some common fund of instruction. This fund consists of a mass of ancient traditions and of experiences that are unorganised or that have been more or less organised and imitatively transmitted through language, the great vehicle of all imitations.

In this connection we may observe that modern philologists have relied so implicitly upon the foregoing proposition, that they have concluded, through analogy, that Sanskrit, Latin, Greek, German, Russian, and other kindred tongues, belong in reality to one family, and that it had a common progenitor in a language which was transmitted, with the exception of certain modifications, through tradition. Each modification was, in truth, an anonymous linguistic invention which was, in turn, perpetuated by imitation. In the next chapter I will return to the development and re-statement of our third proposition.

There is only one great class of universal resemblances which seem at first as if they could not have been produced by any form of repetition. This is the resemblance of the parts of infinite space whose juxtaposition and immobility are the very conditions of all motion whatsoever, whether vibratory, or reproductive, or propagative and subduing. But we must not pause over this apparent exception. It is enough to have mentioned it. Its discussion would lead us too far afield.

Turning aside from this anomaly, which may be illusory, let us maintain the truth of our general proposition, and note one of its direct consequences. If quantity signifies resemblance, if every resemblance proceeds from repetition, and if every repetition is a vibration (or any other periodic movement), a phenomenon of reproduction or an act of imitation, it follows that, on the hypothesis that no motion is, or ever has been, vibratory, no function hereditary, no act or idea learned and copied, *there would be no such thing as quantity in the universe,* and the science of mathematics would be without any possible use or conceivable application. It also follows upon the inverse hypothesis, that if our physical, vital, and social spheres were to enlarge the range of their vibratory, reproductive, and propagative activities, our field of calculation would be even more extensive and profound. This fact is apparent in our European societies where the extraordinary progress of fashion in all its forms, in dress, food and housing, in wants and ideas, in institutions and arts, is making a single type of European based upon several hundreds of millions of examples. Is it not evident that it is this prodigious levelling which has from its very beginning made possible the birth and growth of statistical science and of what has been so well called *social physics,* political economy? Without fashion and custom, social quantities would not exist, there would be no values, no money, and, consequently, no science of wealth or finance (How was it possible, then, for economists to dream of formulating theories of value in which the idea of imitation had no part?) But the application of number and measure to societies, which people are trying to make nowadays, cannot help being partial and tentative. In this matter the future has many surprises in store for us!

III

At this point we might develop the striking analogies, the equally instructive differences, and the mutual relations of the three main forms of universal repetition. We might also seek for the explanation of their majestically interwoven rhythms and symmetries; we might question whether the content of these forms resembled them or not, whether the active and underlying substance of these well-ordered phenomena shared in their sage uniformity, or whether it did not perhaps contrast with them in being essentially heterogeneous, like a people which gave no evidence in its military or administrative exterior of the tumultuous idiosyncracies which constituted it and which set its machinery in motion.

This twofold subject would be too vast   In the first part of it, however, there are certain obvious analogies which we should note. In the first place, repetitions are also multiplications or self-spreading contagions. If a stone falls into the water, the first wave which it produces will repeat itself in circling out to the confines of its basin. If I light a match, the first undulation which I start in the ether will instantly spread throughout a vast space. If one couple of termites or of phylloxeras are transported to a continent, they will ravish it within a few years. The pernicious *erigeron* of Canada, which has but quite recently been imported from Europe, flourishes already in every uncultivated field. The well-known laws of Malthus and Darwin on the tendency of the individuals of a species to increase in geometrical progression, are true laws of human radiation through reproduction. In the same way, a local dialect that is spoken only by certain families, gradually becomes, through imitation, a national idiom. In the beginning of societies, the art of chipping flint, of domesticating dogs, of making bows, and, later, of leavening bread, of working bronze, of extracting iron, etc., must have spread like a contagion; since every arrow, every flake, every morsel of bread, every thread of bronze, served both as model and copy. Nowadays the diffusion of all kinds of useful processes is brought about in the same way, except that our increasing density of population and our advance in civilisation prodigiously accelerate their diffusion, just as velocity of sound is proportionate to density of medium. Every *social thing*, that is to say, every invention or discovery, tends to expands in its social environment, an environment which itself, I might add, tends to self-expansion, since it is essentially composed of like things, all of which have infinite ambitions.

This tendency, however, here as in external nature, often proves abortive through the competition of rival tendencies. But this fact is of little importance to theory; besides, it is metaphorical. Desire can no more be attributed to ideas than to vibrations or species, and the fact in question must be understood to mean that the scattered individual forces which are inherent in the innumerable beings composing the environment where these forms propagate themselves, have taken a common direction. In this sense, this tendency towards expansion presupposes that the environment in question is homogeneous, a condition which seems to be well fulfilled by the ethereal or aërial medium of vibrations, much less so by the geographical and chemical medium of species, and infinitely less so by the social medium of ideas. But it is a mistake, I think, to express this difference by saying that the social medium is more complex than the others. On the contrary, it is perhaps because it is numerically much more simple, that it is farther from presenting the required homogeneity; since a homogeneity that is real on the surface merely, suffices. Besides, as the agglomerations of human beings increase, the spread of ideas in a regular geometrical progression is more marked. Let us exaggerate this numerical increase to an extreme degree, let us suppose that the social sphere in which an idea can expand be composed not only of a group sufficiently numerous to give birth to the principal moral varieties of the human species, but also of thousands of uniform repetitions of these groups, so that the uniformity of these repetitions makes an apparent homogeneity, in spite of the internal complexity of each group. Have we not some reason for thinking that this is the kind of homogeneity which characterises all the simple and apparently uniform realities which external nature presents to us? On this hypothesis, it is evident that the success of an idea, the more or less rapid rate at which it circulated on the day of its appearance, would supply the mathematical reason, in a way, of its further progression. Given this condition, producers of articles which satisfied prime needs and which were therefore destined for universal consumption, would be able to foretell from the demand in a given year, at a certain price, what would be the demand in the following year, at the same price, providing no check, prohibitive or otherwise, intervened, or no superior article of the same class were discovered.

It has been said that the faculty of foresight is the criterion of science. Let us amend this to read, the faculty of *conditional* foresight. The botanist, for example, can foretell the form and colour of the fruit which a flower will produce, provided it be not killed by drought, or provided a new and unexpected individual variety (a kind of secondary biological invention) do not develop. The physicist can state, at the moment a rifle-shot is discharged, that it will be heard in a given number of seconds, at a given distance, provided nothing intercept the sound in its passage, or provided a louder sound, a discharge of cannon, for example, be not heard during the given period. Now it is precisely on the same ground that the sociologist is, strictly speaking, a scientist. Given the centres, the approximate velocities, and the tendency to separate or concurrent motion of existing imitations, the sociologist is in a position to foretell the social conditions of ten or twenty years hence, provided no reform or political revolution occur to hinder this expansion and provided no rival centres arise meanwhile.

In this case, to be sure, the conditioning of events is highly probable, more probable, perhaps, than in the others. But it is only a difference of degree. Besides, let us observe (as a matter that belongs to the philosophy and not to the science of history), that the successful discoveries and initiatives of the present vaguely determine the direction of those of the future. Moreover, the social forces of any real importance at any period are not composed of the necessarily feeble imitations that have radiated from recent inventions, but of the imitations of ancient inventions, radiations which are alike more intense and more widespread because they have had the necessary time in which to spread out and become established as habits, customs, or so-called physiological " race instincts."[1] Our ignorance, therefore, of the unforeseen discoveries which will be made ten,

[1] I must not be accused of the absurd idea of denying in all of this the influence of race upon social facts. But I think that on account of the number of its acquired characteristics, race is the outcome, and not the source, of these facts, and only in this hitherto ignored sense does it appear to me to come within the special province of the sociologist.

twenty, or fifty years hence, of the art-inspiring masterpieces which are to appear, of the battles and revolutions
and deeds of violence which will be noised abroad, does not
hinder us from almost accurately predicting, on the foregoing hypothesis, the depth and direction of the current of
ideas and aspirations which our statesmen and our great
generals, poets, and musicians will have to follow and render navigable, or stem and combat.

As examples in support of the geometrical progress of
imitations, I might cite statistics of locomotive construction, or of the consumption of coffee, tobacco, etc.,
from the time they were first imported, to the time they
began to overstock the market.[1] I will mention a discovery which appears to be less favourable to my argument,
the discovery of America. This discovery was *imitated*
in the sense that the first voyage from Europe to America,
which was conceived of and executed by Columbus, came
to be repeated more and more frequently by subsequent
navigators. Every variation in these after-voyages constituted a little discovery, which was grafted upon that of
the great Genoese, and which, in turn, found imitators.

I will take advantage of this example to open a parenthesis. America might have been discovered two centuries earlier, or two centuries later, by an imaginative navi-
gator. If two centuries earlier, if in 1292, the opening
out of a new world had been offered to Philip the Fair,
during his bouts with Rome and his bold attempt at seculari-
sation and administrative centralisation, his ambition would

---

[1] The objection may be raised that increasing or diminishing series
as shown in the continuous statistics of a given number of years, are
never regular, and are often upset by checks and reactions. Without
dwelling upon this point, I may say that, in my opinion, these checks
and reactions are always indicative of the interference of some new
invention, which, in its turn, is spread abroad. I explain diminishing
series in the same way, and in considering them we must be careful
not to infer that at the end of a certain time, after it has been imitated
more and more, a social thing tends to become *disimitated*. On the
contrary, its tendency to invade the world continues unchanged, and
if there be, not any disimitation, but any continuous falling off of imitation, its rivals are alone to blame.

have surely been excited, and the arrival of the Modern Age precipitated. Two centuries later, in 1692, America would unquestionably have been of greater value to the France of Henry IV. than to Spain, and the latter country, not having had this rich prey to batten upon for two hundred years, would have been, at that time, less rich and prosperous. Who knows whether, under the first hypothesis, the Hundred Years' War might not have been precluded and, under the second, the empire of Charles V.? At any rate, *the need of having colonies, a need which was both created and satisfied* by the discovery of Christopher Columbus and one which has played such a leading rôle in the political life of Europe since the fifteenth century, would not have arisen until the seventeenth century, and, at the present time, South America would belong to France, and North America would not as yet amount to anything politically. What a difference to us! And to think that Christopher Columbus succeeded by a mere hair's breadth in his enterprise! But a truce to these speculations upon the *contingencies of the past,* although, in my opinion, they are as well-founded and as significant as those of the future.

Here is another example, the most striking of all. The Roman Empire has perished; but, as has been well said, the conquest of Rome lives on forever. Through Christianity, Charlemagne extended it to the Germans; William the Conqueror extended it to the Anglo-Saxons; and Columbus, to America. The Russians and the English are extending it to Asia and to Australia, and, prospectively, to the whole of Oceanica. Already Japan wishes for her turn to be invaded; it seems as if China alone would offer any serious resistance. But if we assume that China also will become assimilated, we can say that Athens and Rome, including Jerusalem, that is to say, the type of civilisation formed by the group of their combined and co-ordinated initiatives and master-thoughts, have conquered the entire world. All races and nationalities will have contributed to this unbounded contagious imitation of Greco-Roman civilisation. The outcome would certainly have been different if Darius or Xerxes had conquered Greece and reduced it to a Persian province; or if Islam had triumphed over Charles Martel and invaded Europe; or if peaceful and industrious China had been belligerent during the past three thousand years, and had turned its spirit of invention towards the art of war as well as towards the arts of peace; or if, when America was discovered, gunpowder and printing had not yet been invented and Europeans had proved to be poorer fighters than the Aztecs or Incas. But chance determined that the type to which we belong should prevail over all other types of civilisation, over all the clusters of radiant inventions which have flashed out spontaneously in different parts of the globe. Even if our own type had not prevailed, another type would certainly have triumphed in the long run, for one type was bound to become universal, *since all laid claim to universality*, that is to say, since all tended to propagate themselves through imitation in a geometrical progression, like waves of light or sound, or like animal or vegetal species.

IV

Let me point out a new order of analogies. Imitations are modified in passing from one race or nation to another, like vibrations or living types in passing from one environment to another. We see this, for example, in the transition of certain words, or religious myths, or military secrets, or literary forms, from the Hindoos to the Germans, or from the Latins to the Gauls. In certain cases, the record of these modifications has been sufficiently full to suggest what their general and uniform trend has been. This is especially true of language; Grimm's, or, better still, Raynouard's, laws might well be called the laws of linguistic refraction.

According to Raynouard, when Latin words come under Spanish or Gallic influences, they are consistently and characteristically transformed. According to Grimm's laws, a given consonant in German or English is equivalent to another given consonant in Sanskrit or Greek. This fact means, at bottom, that in passing from the primitive Aryan to the Teutonic or Hellenic or Hindoo environments, the parent-language has changed its consonants in a given order, substituting, in one case, an aspirate for a hard check, in another a hard check for an aspirate, etc.

If there were as many religions as there are languages (and there are hardly enough of these to give an adequate basis of comparison to certain general observations that might be formulated into linguistic laws), and, above all, if religious ideas were as numerous in every religion as words in a language, we might have laws of mythological refraction analagous to those of language. As it is, we can only follow a given myth like that of Ceres or Apollo, for example, through the modifications which have been stamped upon it by the genius of the different peoples who have adopted it. But there are so few myths to compare in this way, that it is difficult to see any appreciable common traits in the turns which they have been given by the same people at different times, or anything more than a general family resemblance. And yet have we not much to observe in a study of the forms which the same religious ideas have taken on as they passed from the Vedas to the doctrines of Brahma or Zoroaster, from Moses to Christ or Mahomet, or as they circulated through the dissentient Christian sects of the Greek, Roman, Anglican, and Gallic churches? Perhaps I should say that all that could be has already been observed along this line and that we have only to draw upon this material.

Art critics have likewise had a confused premonition of the laws of artistic refraction, so to speak. These laws are peculiar to every people, in all epochs, and belong to every definite centre of painting, music, architecture, and poetry, to Holland, Italy, France, etc. I will not press my point. But is it purely metaphorical and puerile to say that Theocritus is refracted in Virgil; Menander, in Terence; Plato, in Cicero; Euripides, in Racine?

Another analogy. Interferences occur between imitations, between social things, as well as between vibrations and between living types. When two waves, two physical *things* which are pretty much alike, and which have spread separately from two distinct centres, meet together in the same physical *being,* in the same particle of matter, the impetus of each is increased or neutralised, as its direction coincides with, or is diametrically opposed to, the direction of the other. In the first case, a new and complex wave sets in which is stronger than the others and which tends to propagate itself in turn; in the second, struggle and partial destruction follow, until one of the two rivals has the better of the other. In the same way we know what happens when two specific and sufficiently near types, two vital things, which have been reproduced independently of each other, generation after generation, come into mutual contact, not merely in one place (as in the case of animals which fight or devour one another, which would be a strictly physical encounter), but, more than that, in the same living being, in a germ cell fertilised by hybrid copulation, the only kind of encounter and interference which is really vital. In this case, either the offspring has greater vitality than its parents and, being at the same time more fruitful and prolific, transmits its distinctive characteristics to a more numerous progeny, a veritable discovery of life, or it is more puny, and gives birth to a few stunted descendants, in whom the divorce of the incompatible characters of their unnaturally united progenitors is hastened by the distinct triumph of one in expelling the other. In the same way, when two beliefs or two desires, or a belief and a desire, in short, when two social things (in the last analysis all social facts are beliefs or desires under the different names of dogmas, sentiment, laws, wants, customs, morals, etc.), have for a certain time travelled their separate roads in the world by means of education or example, *i. e.,* of imitation, they often end by coming into mutual contact. In order that their encounter and interference may be really psychological and social, co-existence in the same brain and participation in the same state of mind and heart is not only necessary, but, in addition, one must present itself either in support of, or in opposition to the other, either as a principle, of which the other is a corollary, or as an affirmative, of which the other is the negative. As for the beliefs and desires which seem neither to aid nor injure, neither to confirm nor contradict, each other, they cannot interfere with each other any more than two heterogeneous waves or two living types which are too distant from each other to unite. If they do appear to help or confirm each other, they combine by the very fact of this appearance or perception into a new practical or theoretic discovery, which is, in turn, bound to spread abroad, like its components, in contagious imitation. In this case, there has been a gain in the force of desire or belief, as in the corresponding cases of propitious physical or biological interference there was a gain in motor power or vitality. If, on the other hand, the interfering social things, theses or aims, dogmas or interests, convictions or passions, are mutually hurtful and antagonistic in the soul of an individual, or in that of a whole people, both the individual and the community will morally stagnate in doubt and indecision, until their soul is rent in two by some sudden or prolonged effort, and the less cherished belief or passion is sacrificed. Thus life chooses between two miscoupled types. A particularly important case and one which differs slightly from the preceding is that in which the two beliefs or desires, as well as the belief and the desire, which interfere happily or unhappily in the mind of an individual, are not experienced exclusively by him, but in part by him, and in part by one of his fellows. Here the interference consists in the fact that the individual is aware of the confirmation or disproof of his own idea by the idea of others, and of the advantage or injury accruing to his own will from the will of others. From this, sympathy and agreement, or antipathy and war, result.[1]

[1] The likeness which I have pointed out between heredity and imitation is verified even in the relation of each of these two forms of universal Repetition to its special form of Creation or Invention. As long as a society is young, vigorous, and progressive, inventions, new proj-

But all of this, I feel, needs to be elucidated. Let us distinguish between three hypotheses. the propitious interference of two beliefs, of two desires, and of a belief and a desire; and let us subdivide each one of these divisions as the subjects of interference are, or are not, found in the same individual. Later on, I shall have a word to say about unpropitious interferences.

1. If a conjecture which I have considered *fairly probable* comes into my mind while I am reading or remembering a fact which I think is *almost certain,* and if I suddenly perceive that the fact confirms the conjecture of which it is a consequence (*i. e.,* the particular proposition which expresses the fact is included in the general proposition which expresses the conjecture), the conjecture immediately becomes much more probable in my eyes, and, at the same time, the fact appears to me to be an absolute certainty. So that there is a *gain in belief* all along the line. And the perception of this logical inclusion is a discovery. Newton discovered nothing more than this when, having brought his conjectured law of gravitation face to face with the calculation of the distance from the moon to the

ects, and successful initiatives follow one another in rapid succession, and hasten social changes; then, when the inventive sap is exhausted, imitation still continues upon its course India, China, and the late Roman Empire are examples in point Now this is also true of the world of life. For example, M Gaudry says in referring to the *crinoïdea* (echinoderms) [*Enchaînment du monde animal* (secondary period)]: " They have lost that marvellous diversity of form which was one of the luxuries of the primary period; *no longer having the power of much self-mutation, they still retain that of producing individuals like themselves* " But this is not always so. In the geological epochs, certain families or types of animals disappeared after their most brilliant period. This was the case with the *ammonite,* that wonderful fossil which flourished in such exuberant variety, during the secondary period, and which was, subsequently, annihilated forever This was also the case with those brief and brilliant civilisations which, like ephemeral stars, glittered for a day in the sky of history, and were then suddenly extinguished I refer to the Persia of Cyrus, to some of the Greek republics, to the south of France at the time of the war of the Albigenses, to the Italian republics, etc When the creative power of these civilisations was worn out, not even the power to reproduce themselves remained In fact, in most cases, they would have been precluded from doing so by their own violent destruction.

earth, he perceived that this fact confirmed his hypothesis. Let us suppose that, for a century long, an entire people is led by one of its teachers, by St. Thomas Aquinas, for example, or by Arnaud or Bossuet, to prove, or to think that it is proving, that a like agreement exists between its religious dogmas and the contemporaneous state of its sciences. Then we shall see such an overflowing river of faith as that which fructified the logical and inventive and warlike thirteenth and the Janseist and Gallican seventeenth centuries. A harmony like this is nothing less than a discovery. The Summa, the catechism of Port-Royal and the French clergy, and all the philosophic systems of the period, from Descartes himself to Leibnitz, are, in different degrees, its various expressions. Now let us somewhat modify our general proposition. Let us suppose that I am inclined to endorse a principle which the friend with whom I am talking absolutely refuses to accept. On the other hand, he tells me certain facts which he thinks are true, but which I take to be unverified. Subsequently, it seems to me, or rather, if flashes upon me, that if these facts were proved, they would fully confirm my principle. From now on, I, also, am inclined to credit them; but the only gain in belief has been one in regard to them, not in regard to my principle. Besides, this kind of discovery is incomplete; it will have no social effect until my friend either succeeds in imparting to me, through proofs, his belief, which is greater than mine, in the reality of the facts, or I myself can prove to him the truth of my principle. Here is precisely the advantage of a wide and free intellectual commerce.

2. The first mediæval merchant who was both vain and avaricious and who, in his unwillingness to forego either commercial wealth or social position, came to perceive the possibility of making avarice serve the ends of vanity, through the purchase of a title of nobility for himself and his family, thought he had made a fine discovery. And, as a matter of fact, he had numerous imitators. Is it not true that after this unhoped-for prospect, both his passions redoubled in strength? Did not his avarice increase because

gold had gained a new value in his eyes, and his vanity, because the object of his ambitious and hitherto-despaired-of dream had come within reach? To give, perhaps, a more modern illustration, the first lawyer who reversed the usual order of things by going into politics in order to make his fortune, introduced neither a bad idea nor an ineffective initiative. Let us take other instances. Suppose that I am in love and that I also have a passion for rhyming. I turn my love to inspiring my metromania. My love quickens and my rhyming mania is intensified. How many poetical works have originated in this kind of an interference! Suppose, again, that I am a philanthropist and that I like notoriety. In this case, I will strive to distinguish myself in order to do more good to my fellows, and I will strive to be useful to them, in order to make a name for myself, etc., etc. In history the same phenomenon occurs. After a long period of mutual opposition, Christian zeal combined with the contemporary passion for warlike expeditions and produced the outbreak of the Crusades. The invasion of Islam, the Jacqueries of '89 and of the years following, and all revolutions in which so many base passions are yoked to noble ones, are notable examples. But, happily, a still more contagious example was set in the beginnings of social life by the first man who said: " I am hungry and my neighbour is cold; I will offer him this garment, which is useless to me, in exchange for some of the food which he has in excess, and so *my* need of food will help satisfy *his* need of clothing, and *vice versa*. In this excellent and very simple, but, for that time, highly original, idea, industry, commerce, money, law, and all the arts originated. (I do not date the birth of society from this idea, for society undoubtedly existed before exchange. It began on the day when one man first copied another).

Let us note that all new forms of professional work, that all new crafts, have arisen from analogous discoveries. These discoveries have generally been anonymous, but they are none the less positive and significant.

3. In historical importance, however, no mental inter-

ference equals that of a desire and a belief. But the numerous cases in which a conviction or opinion fastens itself upon an inclination, and effects it merely through inspiring another desire, must not be included in this category. After these cases have been eliminated, there still remains a considerable number in which the supervening idea acts directly upon the desire it has fallen in with and stimulated. Suppose, for example, that I would like to be an orator in the Chamber of Deputies, and I am straightway persuaded by the compliment of a friend that I have recently displayed true oratorical talent. This conviction enhances my ambition, and my ambition itself contributed to my conviction. For the same reason, there is no historical error, no atrocious or extravagant calumny or madness, which is not readily entertained by the very political passion which it helps to inflame. A belief will also stimulate a desire, now by making its object seem more attainable, now by stamping it with its approval. It also happens, to complete our analysis, that a man may realise that his own scheme will be helped by the belief of others, although he may have no share in their belief, nor they in his scheme. Such a realisation is a *find* that many an impostor has exploited and still exploits.

This special kind of interferences and the important unnamed discoveries which result from them, are to be counted among the chief forces which rule the world. What was the patriotism of Greek or Roman but a passion nourished by an illusion and *vice versa;* what was it but ambition, avarice, and love of fame nourished by an exaggerated belief in their own superiority, by the *anthropocentric* prejudice, the mistake of imagining that this little point in space, the earth, was the universe, and that on this little point Rome or Athens was alone worthy of the gods' consideration? What are, in large part, the fanaticism of the Arab, the proselytism of the Christian, and the propagandism of Jacobin and revolutionary doctrines but prodigious outgrowths of illusion-fed passions and passion-fed illusions? And these forces always arise from one person, from a single *centre,* long

in advance, to be sure, of the moment when they break forth
and take on historical importance. An enthusiast, eaten up
with an impotent desire for conquest, or immortality,
or human regeneration, chances upon some idea which
opens an unhoped-for door to his aspirations. The idea
may be that of the Resurrection or the Millennium,
the dogma of popular sovereignty or some other formula
of the *Social Contract.* He embraces the idea, it exalts
him, and behold, a new apostle! In this way a political
or religious contagion is spread abroad. In this way a
whole people may be converted to Christianity, to Islam,
and, to-morrow, perhaps, to socialism.

In the preceding paragraphs we have discussed only
interference-combinations, interferences which result in
discovery and gain and add to the two psychological quantities of desire and belief. But that long sequence of opera-
tions in moral arithmetic, which we call history, ushers in
at least as many *interference-conflicts.* When these subjective antagonisms arise between the desires and beliefs of
a single individual, and only in this case, there is an absolute
diminution in the sum of those quantities. When they occur obscurely, here and there, in isolated individuals, they
pass by unnoticed except by psychologists. Then we have
(1) on the one side, the deceptions and gradual doubts of
bold theorists and political prophets as they come to see facts
giving the lie to their speculations and ridiculing their predictions, and the intellectual weakening of sincere and well-
informed believers who perceive the contradiction between
their science and their religion or philosophic systems; and,
on the other side, the private and juristic and parliamentary discussions in which belief is rekindled instead of
smothered Again, we have (2) on the one side, the enforced and bitter inaction, the slow suicide of a man strug-
gling between two incompatible aptitudes or inclinations,
between scientific ardour and literary aspirations, between
love and ambition, between pride and indolence, and, on the
other side, those various rivalries and competitions which
put every spring into action—what we call in these days

the struggle for existence. Finally, we have (3) on the one side, the malady of despair, a state of intense longing and intense self-doubt, the abyss of lovers and of those weary with waiting, or the anguish of scruple and remorse, the feeling of a soul which thinks ill of the object of its desire, or well of the object of its aversion; and, on the other side, the irritating resistance which is made to the undertakings and eager passions of children and innovators by parents who are convinced of their danger and impracticability and by people of prudence and experience.

When these same phenomena (at bottom they are always the same) are enacted upon a large scale and multiplied by a large and powerful social current of imitation, they attain historical importance. Under other names, they become, (1) on the one hand, the enervating scepticism of a people caught between two hostile churches or religions or between the contradictions of its priests and its scientists; on the other, the religious wars which are waged by one people against another merely because of differences in religious belief; (2) on the one hand, the failure and inertia of a people or class which has created for itself artificial passions contrary to its natural instincts (*i. e.*, at bottom, to passions which also began by being artificial, by being adopted from foreign sources, but which are much older than the former passions), or desires inconsistent with its permanent interests, the desire for peace and comfort, for example, when a redoubling of military spirit was indispensable; on the other hand, the majority of external political wars; (3) on the one hand, civil warfare and oppositions strictly speaking, struggles between conservatives and revolutionists; on the other, the despair of a people or class which is gradually sinking back into the historical oblivion whence it had been drawn by some outburst of faith and enthusiasm, or the irritation and oppression of a society distressed by a conflict between its ancient maxims and traditions and its new aspirations, between Christianity and chivalry, for example, and industrialism and utilitarianism.

Now in the case of both individuals and societies, the

doleful states of scepticism, inertia, and despair, and, still more, the violent and more painful states of dispute, combat, and opposition are quick to push man on to their own undoing. Nevertheless, although man often succeeds in delivering himself for long periods from the former, which imply the immediate weakening of his two master forces, he never overcomes the latter, or if he does free himself from them it is merely to fall into them again, since, up to a certain point, they bring with them momentary gains of belief and desire. Whence the interminable dissensions, rivalries, and contradictions which befall mankind and which each one can settle for himself only by adopting some logical system of thought and conduct. Whence the impossibility, or the seeming impossibility, of extirpating the wars and litigations from which everybody suffers, although the subjective strife of desires and opinions which afflicts some people generally ends for them in definite treaties of peace. Whence the endless rebirth of the eternal hydra-headed social question, a question which is not peculiar to our own time, but which belongs to all time, for it does not investigate into the outcome of the debilitating, but into that of the violent, states of desire and belief In other words, it does not ask whether science or religion will, or should, ultimately prevail in the great majority of minds; whether desire for social order or rebellious outbursts of social envy, pride, and hatred will, or should, ultimately prove the stronger in human hearts; whether a positive and courageous resignation of old pretensions or, on the contrary, a new outburst of hope and self-confidence will help our sometime ruling classes to rid themselves to their honour of their present torpor; whether the old morality will have the right and the power to influence society again, or whether the society of the future will legitimately establish a code of honour and morality in its own likeness. The solution of these problems will not be long delayed, and it is not difficult, even at present, to foresee its nature. Whereas the problems which really constitute the social question are arduous and difficult. The problems are these:

Is it a good or a bad thing for a complete intellectual unanimity to be established through the expulsion or the more or less tyrannical conversion of a dissenting minority, and will this ever come about? Is it a good or a bad thing for commercial or professional or personal competition between individuals, as well as political and military competition between societies, to come to be suppressed, the one through the much-dreamed-of organisation of labour, or, at least, through state socialism, and the other through a vast, universal confederation, or, at least, through a new European equilibrium, the first step towards the United States of Europe? Does the future hold this in store for us? Is it a good or a bad thing for a strong and free social authority, an absolutely sovereign authority, capable of grandiose things, as philanthropic and intelligent as possible, to arise, untrammelled by outside control or resistance, as a supreme imperial or constitutional power in the hands of a single party or a single people? Have we any such prospect in view?

This is the question, and stated thus it is a truly redoubtable one. Mankind, as well as the individual man, always moves in the direction of the greatest truth and power, of the greatest sum of conviction and confidence, in a word, of the greatest attainable belief; and we may question whether this *maximum* can be reached though the development of discussion, competition, and criticism, or, inversely, through their suppression and through the boundless opening out through imitation of a single expanding and at the same time compact thought or volition.

V

But the preceding digression has made us anticipate questions which can be discussed more advantageously elsewhere. Let us return to the subject of this chapter, and, after reviewing the principal analogies between the three forms of Repetition, let us note for a moment their equally instructive points of difference. In the first place, the soli-

darity of these forms is not reciprocal, it is one-sided.
Generation depends upon undulation, but undulation does
not depend upon generation.   Imitation depends upon them
both, but they do not depend upon imitation   After two
thousand years, the manuscript of Cicero's *Republic* was
recovered and published.   It became a source of inspiration.   This posthumous imitation would not have occurred
if the molecules of the parchment had not surely continued
to vibrate (if only from the effect of the surrounding temperature); and if, in addition, human reproduction had
not gone on from Cicero to us without interruption.   It is remarkable that here, as elsewhere, the most
complex and unconditioned term is always supported by
those which are least so.   The inequality of the three
terms in this respect is, indeed, obvious.   Vibrations are
linked together, being both isochronous and contiguous,
whereas living things are detached and separate from
each other, and their duration varies considerably.   Moreover, the higher up in the scale they are, the more independent they become   Generation is a free kind of undulation,
whose waves are worlds in themselves.   Imitation does
still better; its influence is exerted not only over a great
distance, but over great intervals of time.   It establishes
a pregnant relation between the inventor and his copier,
separated as they may be by thousands of years, between
Lycurgus and a member of the French Convention, between
the Roman painter of a Pompeiian fresco and the modern
decorator whom it has inspired.   Imitation is generation
at a distance.[1]   It seems as if these three forms of repetition were three undertakings of its single endeavour to extend the field of its activity, to successfully cut off every

---

[1] If, as Ribot thinks, memory is only the cerebral form of nutrition,
if, on the other hand, nutrition is only an internal generation, finally,
if Imitation is nothing but social memory (see my *Logique sociale* on
this subject), it follows that there is not only an analogy, as I have
shown, between Generation and Imitation, but a fundamental identity.
Imitation, the elementary and persistent social phenomenon, would be
the social sequel and equivalent of Generation taken in its most comprehensive sense to include Nutrition.

chance of revolt in elements which are always quick to overthrow the yoke of law, and by more and more ingenious and potent methods to constrain their tumultuous crowd to proceed in orderly masses of constantly increasing strength and organisation. This advance may be illustrated by comparing it to that of a cyclone or epidemic or insurrection. A cyclone whirls from neighbourhood to neighbourhood; none of its blast ever tears from it to leap over intervening space and carry its virus to a distance. An epidemic, on the other hand, rages in a zig-zag line; it may spare one house or village among many, and it strikes down almost simultaneously those which are far apart. An insurrection will spread still more freely from workshop to workshop, or from capital to capital. It may start from a telegraphic announcement, or, at times, the contagion may even come from the past, out of a dead and buried epoch.

There is still another important difference. In imitation, the product is generally in a state of complete development; it is spared the fumblings of the first workman. This artistic kind of process is consequently much more rapid than the vital process; embryonic phases and phases of infancy and adolescence are suppressed. And yet life itself does not ignore the art of abbreviation. For if, as is thought, embryonic phases repeat (with certain restrictions) the zoölogical and paleontological series of preceding and allied species, it is clear that this individual recapitulation of a prolonged race elaboration must have become marvellously succinct at last. But during the course of the generations which pass under our own observation, periods of gestation and growth are not noticeably curtailed. The only fact that can be determined in this direction is the reproduction of hereditary traits or diseases at an earlier age in the offspring than in the parent. Let us compare this slight advance with the progress of our manufactures. Our watches, pins, textiles, all our goods, are manufactured in one-tenth or one-hundredth part of the time which they originally required. As for vibration, in what an infinitesimal degree it shares in this faculty of acceleration! Successive waves would be strictly isochronous, that is, would take the same amount of time to be born, mature, and die in, if their temperature remained constant. But their oscillation necessarily results in the heating of their medium (this fact is known, at least, in the case of sound waves, according to the correction made in Newton's formula by La Place), and in the consequent acceleration of their rate. This brings with it but little saving of time, however. There is infinitely more time gained from the mechanisms for repetition which characterise life and, especially, society; for the products of imitation, as I have said before, are entirely free from the obligation to traverse, even in abridgment, the steps of prior advances. Changes in the world of life are also much less rapid than those in society. The most earnest upholder of the doctrine of rapid evolution will readily admit that the wing of the bird did not replace the limb of the reptile as rapidly as our modern locomotives were substituted for stage-coaches. One of the consequences of this observation is to relegate historic naturalism to its true place. According to this view, social institutions, laws, ideas, literature, and arts must always, of necessity, spring from the very bottom of a people to slowly germinate and blossom forth like bulbs. Nothing can ever be created, complete in all its parts, in a nation's soil. This proposition holds true as long as a community has not passed beyond the natural phase of its existence, that in which, under the dominating rule of *custom-imitation,* to which I will refer later on, its changes are as much conditioned by heredity as by imitation pure and simple. But as soon as imitation becomes freer, as soon as a spirit of radicalism arises which threatens to carry out its revolutionary programme overnight, we must beware of any undue reassurance, against the possibility of such a danger, that we might base upon the alleged laws of historic growth. It is a mistake in politics not to believe in the improbable and never to foresee what has not already been seen.

CHAPTER II

SOCIAL RESEMBLANCES AND IMITATION

IN the preceding chapter I merely stated, without developing, the thesis that imitation is the cause of all social likeness. But this formula must not be lightly accepted; to grasp its truth and that of the two analogous formulas relating to biological and physical resemblances, it must be thoroughly understood. Upon our first glance at societies, exceptions and objections seem to abound.

1. In the first place, many points of anatomical or physiological likeness between two living species belonging to different types cannot be explained, apparently, by hereditary repetition, because in many cases the common progenitor to whom they may both be traced, is, or theoretically should be, without the characteristics in question. The whale, for example, assuredly does not inherit its fishlike shape from the common hypothetical forefather from which both fish and mammals must have developed. If a bee reminds us in its flight of a bird, we have still less reason for thinking that bird and bee have inherited their wings and elytra from their very remote ancestor, who was probably a creeping and non-flying creature. The same observation may be made about the similar instincts that are displayed, according to Darwin and Romanes, by many animals of very distant species. Take, for example, the instinct to sham death as a means of escape from danger. This instinct is common to the fox, to certain insects, spiders, serpents, and birds. In this case, similarity of instinct can be accounted for only through homogeneity of physical environment. All these heterogeneous creatures have depended upon the same environment for the satisfaction of those fundamental wants which are essential to all life and which are identical in each one of them. Now,

homogeneity of physical environment is nothing else but the uniform propagation of homogeneous waves of light or heat 'or sound through air or water that is itself composed of atoms in constant and uniform vibration. As for the homogeneity of the fundamental functions and properties of every cell, of all protoplasm (of nutrition, for example, or of irritability), must it not be explained through the molecular constitution of the ever homogeneous chemical elements of life, that is, according to hypothesis, through the inner rhythms of their indefinitely repeated movements, rather than through the transmission of characteristics, by fission or some other kind of reproduction, from the first protoplasmic germ, admitting that in the beginning only a single germ was spontaneously formed? Therefore, although the above class of analogies is not due to the vital or hereditary form of repetition, it has originated in its physical or vibratory form.

In like manner there are always between two separate peoples who have reached an original civilisation by independent routes, certain general resemblances in language, mythology, politics, industry, art, and literature, where mutual imitation plays no part. Quatrefages relates that " when Cook visited the New Zealanders, they were strangely like the Highlanders of Rob Roy and MacIvoy " (*Espèce humaine,* p. 336). Now, resemblance between the social organisation of the Maoris and the ancient Scotch clans is certainly not due to any common ground of traditions, and no philologist would amuse himself by deriving their respective tongues from a common parent language. When Cortez reached Mexico, he found that the Aztecs, like many Old-World nations, were possessed of a king and orders of nobility and of agricultural and industrial classes. Their agriculture, with its floating islands and perfected system of irrigation, was suggestive of China; their architecture, their painting, and their hieroglyphic writing, of Eygpt. Their calendar testified, in spite of its peculiar character, to astronomical knowledge which corresponded to that of contemporary Europeans. Although their religion was sanguinary, it resembled Christianity in some of its rites, particularly in those of baptism and confession. In certain instances the coincidences of detail are so astonishing that they have led some people to believe that Old-World arts and institutions were brought over directly by shipwrecked Europeans.[1] But in these comparisons and in an infinite number of others of the same kind, is it not nearer the truth to recognise the fundamental unity of human nature on the one hand and the uniformity of external nature on the other? In human nature, those organic wants whose satisfaction is the end of all social evolution are everywhere the same; all human beings have the same senses and the same brain structure. In external nature, about the same resources are offered for the satisfaction of about the same wants, and approximately the same spectacles to approximately the same eyes, consequently the world's industries, arts, perceptions, myths, and theories must be all pretty much alike. These resemblances, like those referred to above, would be instances of the general principle that all likeness is born of repetition. But, although they are themselves social, they are caused by repetitions of a biological or physical order, by the hereditary transmission of the human functions and organs which constitute the human races, and by the vibratory transmission of the temperatures, colours, sounds, electrical currents, and chemical affinities which constitute the climes and soils inhabited and cultivated by man.

Here we have the objection or the exception in its full

[1] In fact, there are many striking points of comparison. Civilisation in America, as in Europe, has passed successively " from the age of stone to the age of bronze by the same methods and under the same forms. The *teocalli* of Mexico correspond to the pyramids of Egypt; the *mounds* of North America may be compared to the *tumuli* of Brittany and Scythia; the *pylônes* of Peru reproduce those of Etruria and Egypt " (Clémence Royer, *Revue scientifique*, July 31, 1886). It is a still more surprising fact that the only affinities of the Basque tongue seem to be with certain of the American languages   The bearing of these resemblances is weakened by the fact that the points of comparison are not drawn from two given civilisations, but, more artificially, from a large number of different civilisations in both the Old World and the New.

force. In spite of its apparent gravity, it merely offers an opportunity of copying in sociology a distinction that is usual in comparative anatomy between *analogies* and *homologies*. Now, resemblances such as that between the insect's elytra and the bird's wings seem superficial and meaningless to the naturalist. They may be very striking, but he pays no attention to them.[1] He almost denies their existence. Whereas he attaches the highest value to resemblances between the wing of the bird, the limb of the reptile, and the fin of the fish. From his point of view these are close and deep-seated resemblances, quite different from the former kind. If this form of discrimination is legitimate for the naturalist, I do not see why the sociologist should be refused the right of treating the *functional analogies* of different languages, religions, governments, and civilisations with equal contempt, and their *anatomical homologies* with equal respect. Philologists and mythologists are already filled with this spirit. To the philologist there is no significance in the fact that the word for deity in Aztec is *teotl,* and in Greek, *théos.* In this he sees nothing but a coincidence; consequently he does not assert that *teotl* and *théos* are the same word. On the other hand, he does undertake to prove that *bischop* is the same word as *episcopus.*[2] The reason of this is that no linguistic element should ever be detached at any instant in its evolution from all its anterior transformations nor considered apart from the other elements which it reflects and which reflect it. Accordingly, any likeness that may be proved to exist between the isolated phases of two vocables which have been taken from their own language families and so separated

[1] The phenomenon of *mimicry* receives more attention. Hitherto this enigma has been undecipherable, but if the key to it were really given by natural selection, it might be explained by the ordinary laws of heredity, by the hereditary fixation and accumulation of the individual variations most favourable to the welfare of the species which, in this way, comes to take on the lineaments of another as a disguise.

[2] The coincidence is the more singular, too, because the *tl* in *teotl* may be ignored, since this combination of consonants is the regular termination of Mexican words. Téo and théô (in the dative) have absolutely the same sense and the same sound.

from all that which goes to make up their real life is only a factitious connection between two abstractions and not a true link between two real things This consideration may be generalised.[1]

But this answer, which is nothing more than the denial of troublesome resemblances, is inadequate. On the contrary, I hold that there certainly are many real and important resemblances which have been spontaneously produced between civilisations without any known or probable means of intercommunication. Moreover, I admit that, in general, when the current of human genius has once set towards inventions and discoveries, it finds itself confined by a sum of subjective and objective conditions, like a river by its banks, between narrow limits of development. Accord-

[1] Although customs of mutilation, circumcision, for example, tattooing, or cutting the hair, in sign of religious or political subordination, are found in the most distant parts of the globe, in America and in Polynesia, as well as in the Old World; although the totems of the South American savages remind us, if only a little, of the coats of arms of our mediæval knights, etc ; these *coincidences* and resemblances merely prove that actions are governed by beliefs, and that beliefs are largely suggested to man through the phenomena of external nature and through the innate tendencies of his own nature. The depths of human nature are the same everywhere, and in the phenomena of external nature there is, in spite of climatic variation, more similarity than dissimilarity I admit that such analogies may not be caused by imitation. But they are at any rate only gross and indefinite. They are without sociological significance, just as the fact that insects are possessed of limbs, like vertebrates, and of eyes and wings, like birds, is insignificant from a biological point of view. On the other hand, although the bird's wing looks very different from the wing of the bat, they are really part of the same evolution and are possessed of the same past and of the possibility of experiencing the same future. In their successive transformations, these organs correspond in an endless number of particulars They are *homologous*. Whereas, the bird's wing never has anything in common with the wing of the insect, except during one phase of their very unlike developments.

Did the same ceremonies and the same religious meaning attach to circumcision among the Aztecs as among the Hebrews? On the contrary, there was as much difference between them as between the Aztec rite of confession and ours And yet this matter of ceremonies is the important thing from the social point of view; for it is the special part of the social environment which is directed by individual activity. Besides, this part is constantly on the increase.

ingly, even in distant regions there may be a certain approximate similarity between its channels. It may even chance to show, less often, however, than we might suppose, a parallelism of certain pregnant ideas,[1] of ideas which may be very simple or, at times, quite complicated, which have appeared independently and which are equivalent to, if not identical with, one another.[2] But, in the first place, in as much as men have been forced by the uniformity of their organic wants to follow the same trend of ideas, we have a fact that belongs to the biological, and not to the social, order of resemblances. Consequently the biological and not the social principle of repetition is applicable. Parallelly when conditions of light and sound, identical to all intents and purposes, force animals belonging to different families to develop organs of sight and hearing which are not without some points of resemblance, the likeness, in this respect, is physical, not biological; it depends upon vibration, and therefore comes under the principle of physical repetition.

Finally, how and why did human genius come to run its course at all, unless by virtue of certain initial causes which, in arousing it from its original torpor, also stirred up, one by one, the deep potential wants of the human soul? And were not these causes certain primordial and capital inventions and discoveries which began to spread through imitation and which inspired their imitators with a taste for invention and discovery? The first crude conceptions of the rudiments of language and religion on

[1] They are all the more apt to be simple ideas, ideas exacting but a slight effort of the imagination. This is true of some of the strangest freaks of custom For example, in reading the work of M. Jametel upon China, I was surprised to see an account of the custom of *eructation* practised as *an act of courtesy* at the close of a meal Now, according to M Garnier and M Hugonnet (*La Grèce nouvelle*, 1889), the same ceremony is observed by modern Greeks. In both countries, evidently, the desire to give ample proof of repletion had suggested this ridiculous, although natural, custom

[2] The same needs, for example, both in the Old World and in the New, prompted the ideas of domesticating the ox and taming the chamois in the former, and in the latter, of taming the bison, the buffalo, and the llama. (See Bourdeau, *Conquête du monde animal*, p 212)

the part of some ape-man (I will speculate later on upon how this was done) carried man over the threshold from the animal to the social world   This difficult step must have been an unique event; without it, our richly developed world would have been chained to the limbo of unrealised possibilities.   Without this spark, the flame of progress would never have been kindled in the primæval forests of savagery.   This original act of imagination and its spread through imitation was the true cause, the *sine qua non* of progress.   The immediate acts of imitation which it prompted were not its sole results.   It suggested other acts of imagination which in turn suggested new acts and so on without end.

Thus everything is related to it.   Every social resemblance precedes from that initial act of imitation of which it was the subject.   I think I may compare it to that no less extraordinary event which occurred on the globe, many thousands of centuries in advance, when, for the first time, a tiny mass of protoplasm originated in some unknown way and began to multiply by fission.   Every resemblance between existing forms of life is the outcome of this first repetition in heredity.   For it would be futile to conjecture, purely gratuitously, that protoplasm, or language, or mythology originated at more than one centre of creation.   As a matter of fact, granted the hypothesis of polygenism, we could not deny that, after a more or less prolonged struggle and competition, the best and most prolific of the different spontaneous specimens must have triumphed alone in the extermination or assimilation of its rivals.

There are two facts which we should not overlook: first, that the desire to invent and discover grows, like any other desire, with its satisfaction; second, that every invention resolves itself into the timely intersection in one mind of a current of imitation with another current which re-enforces it, or with an intense perception of some objective fact which throws new light on some old idea, or with the lively experience of a need that finds unhoped-for resources in some familiar practice.   But if we analyse the feelings

and perceptions in question, we shall find that they themselves may be resolved almost entirely, and more and more
completely as civilisation advances, into psychological elements formed under the influence of example.   Every
natural phenomenon is seen through the prisms and coloured
glasses of a mother tongue, or national religion, or ruling
prejudice, or scientific theory, from which the most unbiassed
and unimpassioned observation cannot emancipate itself
without self-destruction.   Moreover, every organic want is
experienced in the characteristic form which has been sanc-
tioned by surrounding example.   The social environment,
in defining and actualising this form, has, in truth, appro-
priated it.   Even desires for nutrition and reproduction
have been transformed, so to speak, into national products.
Sexual desire is changed into a desire to be married according to the different religious rites of different localities.
Desire for food is expressed in one place as a desire for a
certain kind of bread or meat, in another, for a certain kind
of grain or vegetable.   This is all the more true of the natural desire for amusement.   It expresses itself as desire for
circus sports, for bull-fights, for classical tragedies, for naturalistic novels, for chess, for piquet, for whist.   From this
point of view several lines of imitation intersected one
another in the brilliant eighteenth-century idea of applying the steam-engine, which had already been em-
ployed in factories, to the satisfaction of the desire for ocean
travel—a desire which had originated through the spread
of many antecedent naval inventions.   The subsequent adaptation of the screw to the steamboat, both of which had
been known of separately for a long time, was a similar
idea.   When Harvey had optical proof of the valves of the
veins, and when this combined in his mind with his existing anatomical knowledge, he discovered the circulation of
the blood.   This discovery was hardly anything more, on
the whole, than the encounter of traditional truths with
others (namely, with the methods and practices which
Harvey had long followed docilely as a disciple, and which
alone enabled him to finally advance his master proposi-

tion). The development of a new theorem in the mind of a geometrician through the combination of two old theorems is pretty nearly analogous.

Since, then, all inventions and discoveries are composed of prior imitations; excepting certain extraneous accretions, of themselves unfruitful, and since these composites are themselves imitated and are destined to become, in turn, elements of still more complex combinations, it follows that there is a genealogical tree of such successful initiatives and that they appear in an *irreversible,* although otherwise indeterminate, sequence, suggestive of the pangenetic theory of the old philosophers. Every successful invention actualises one of the thousand possible, or rather, given certain conditions, necessary, inventions, which are carried in the womb of its parent invention, and by its appearance it annihilates the majority of those possibilities and makes possible a host of heretofore impossible inventions. These latter inventions will or will not come into existence according to the extent and direction of the radiation of its imitation through communities which are already illuminated by other lights. To be sure, only the most useful, if you please, of the future inventions—and by most useful I mean those which best answer the problems of the time—will survive, for every invention, like every discovery, is an answer to a problem. But aside from the fact that these problems,[1] inasmuch as they are themselves the vague expressions of certain indefinite wants, are capable of manifold solutions; the point of interest is to know how, why, and by whom they have been raised; why one date was chosen rather than another, and, finally, why one solution was chosen in one place, and another in another place.[2]

[1] In politics they are called *questions:* the Eastern question, the social question, etc

[2] Sometimes the same solution is adopted almost everywhere, although the problem may have lent itself to other solutions. That is, you may say, because the choice in question is the most natural one. True, but is not this the very reason, perhaps, why, although it was disclosed only in one place, and not everywhere at the same time, it ended by spreading in all directions? For example, almost all primitive peoples think of the future abode of the wicked as subterranean and of that of the good

All this depends upon individual initiatives, upon the nature
of the scholars and inventors of the past.   From the earliest
of these, the greatest, perhaps, our avalanche of progress
has rolled down out of the zenith of history.

It is difficult for us to imagine how necessary genius and
exceptional circumstances were for the development of the
simplest ideas.   To tame and make use of harmless indigenous animals, instead of merely hunting them, would
seem at first to be the most natural, as well as the
most fruitful, of initiatives, an inevitable initiative, in
fact.   Yet we know that, although the horse originally belonged to the American fauna, it had disappeared from
America when that continent was discovered, and, according
to Bourdeau, its disappearance is generally explained (*Conquête du monde animal*) on the ground that "in many
places (in the Old World as well) it had been annihilated by
the hunter for food, before the herdsman had conceived the
idea of domesticating it."   And so we see that this idea was
far from being an inevitable one.   The domestication of the
horse depended upon some individual accident.   It had to
occur in some one place whence it could spread through imitation.   But what is true of this quadruped is undoubtedly
true of all domestic animals and of all cultivated plants.
Now, can we imagine humanity without these prime inventions!

In general, if we do not wish to explain resemblances between communities which are separated by more or less insurmountable obstacles (although these may not have
existed in the past), through the common possession of
some entirely forgotten primitive model, only one other explanation, as a rule, remains.   Each community must have
exhausted all the inventions which were possible in a given
line save the one adopted, and eliminated all its other

as celestial. The similarity of such conceptions is often minute According to Tylor, the Salish Indians of Oregon believe that the bad
dwell after death in a place of eternal snow, where they "are tantalised
by the sight of game which they cannot kill, and water which they
cannot drink" [*Primitive Culture,* II, 84, Edward B. Tylor, London,
1871.—*Tr*]

useless or less useful ideas. But the comparative barrenness of imagination which characterises primitive people is opposed to this hypothesis. We should then accept the former hypothesis and refuse to renounce it without good reason. Is it certain, for example, that the idea of building lake dwellings came to the ancient inhabitants of both Switzerland and New Guinea without any suggestion of imitation? The same question arises in relation to the cutting and polishing of flints, to the use of tendons and fishbones for sewing, or to the rubbing together of two pieces of wood for fire. Before we deny the possibility of a diffusion of these ideas through a world-wide process of gradual and prolonged imitation, the immense duration of prehistoric times must be brought to mind, and we must not overlook the evidence of the existence of relations between very distant peoples not only in the age of bronze, when tin was sometimes brought from a great distance, but also in the smooth stone and perhaps even in the rough stone age. The great invasions which have raged at all periods of history must have aided and often universalised the spread of civilising ideas. Even in prehistoric times this was true. Indeed it must have been especially true in those times, for the ease with which great conquests are effected depends upon the primitive and disintegrated nature of the people to be conquered. The irruption of the Mongols in the thirteenth century is a good instance of these periodic deluges, and we know that it broke down, in the full tide of mediævalism, the closest of race barriers and put China and Hindustan into communication with each other and with Europe.[1]

[1] In a very interesting article in the *Revue des Deux Mondes* of May 1, 1890, M. Goblet d'Alviella aptly comments upon the rapidity and facility of the circulation of religious symbols by means of travellers, of slavery, and of *currency*, the latter of which is a veritable system of moving bas-reliefs This is true also of political symbols. The *two-headed eagle*, for example, on the arms of both the Emperor of Austria and the Czar of Russia has come down to them from the ancient Germanic empire. It was brought there through the Eastern expedition of Frederick the Second in the thirteenth century, when he borrowed it from the Turks. Furthermore, M. Goblet d'Alviella says

Even in default of such violent events, a world-wide interchange of examples could not have failed to take place eventually. At this point, let me make the following general remark: The majority of historians are not inclined to admit the influence of one civilisation upon another unless they can prove the existence of some intercommercial or military relations. They think, implicitly, that the action of one nation upon another at a distance, of Egypt upon Mesopotamia, for example, or of China upon the Roman Empire, presupposes the transportation of troops or the sending of ships or caravans from one to the other. They would not admit, for example, that currents of Babylonian and Egyptian civilisation may have intermingled before the conquest of Mesopotamia by Egypt in the sixteenth century before our era. Oppositely, in virtue of the same point of view, as soon as a similarity of works of art, of monuments, of tombs, of mortuary relics, proves to them the action of one civilisation upon another, they at once conclude that wars or regular transactions of some kind must have occurred between them.

In view of the relations which I have established between the three forms of universal repetition, the above preconception suggests the error of the old-time physicists, who saw in every physical action between two distant bodies, like the imparting of heat or light, the proof of a transmission of matter Did not Newton himself think that the diffusion of solar light was produced by the emission of particles projected by the sun through boundless space? There is as much difference between my point of view and the ordinary one as there is in optics between the vibratory theory and the theory of emission. Of course I do not deny that

that there are reasons for thinking that the astonishing likeness between this two-headed eagle and the eagle which is also two-headed and which figures upon the most ancient bas-reliefs of Mesopotamia, is due to a series of imitations Note in this same article the reference to the widespread imitation of the *Gamma* cross as a luck piece It is probable, on the other hand, that the idea of using the cross to symbolise the god of the air or the compass-card arose spontaneously and not through imitation in Mesopotamia and in the Aztec empire.

social action is effected, or rather aroused, by the movements of armies or merchant vessels; but I challenge the view that such movements are the sole or even the principal mode through which the contagion of civilisation takes place. Men of different civilisations come into mutual contact on their respective frontiers, where, independently of war or trade, they are naturally inclined to imitate one another. And so, without its being necessary for them to displace one another in the sense of checking the spread of one another's examples, they continually and over unlimited distances react upon one another, just as the molecules of the sea drive forward its waves without displacing one another in their direction. Consequently, long before the arrival of Pharaoh's army in Babylon, sundry external observances and industrial secrets had passed from hand to hand, in some way or other, from Egypt to Babylon.

Here we have the first principle of history. Let us note closely the continuity, the power and the irresistibility of its action. Given the necessary time, it will inevitably reach out to the ends of the earth. Now, in view of the fact that man's past is to be reckoned in hundreds of thousands of years, there is ample reason to think that it must have spread through the entire universe before the nearby historic ages which we call antiquity, began.

Moreover, it is not necessary that the thing which is propagated should be beautiful or useful or rational. In the Middle Ages, for example, a grotesque custom existed in many different places of parading, seated backwards upon an ass, husbands who had been beaten by their wives. Obviously such an absurd idea could not have arisen spontaneously at the same time in different brains. Was it not due to imitation? And yet M. Baudrillart is led by current prejudice to believe that popular festivals originated of themselves without any conscious or deliberate individual initiative. "The festivals of *Tarasque* at Tarascon, of *Graouilli* at Metz, of *Loup vert* at Jumièges, of *Gargouille* at Rouen, and many others, he says, were never established, in all probability, by a formal decree [I admit this] or by premeditated desire [the error is here]; they were made periodic by unanimous and *spontaneous* agreement. . . ." Imagine thousands of people simultaneously conceiving and *spontaneously* carrying out such extraordinary things!

To sum up, everything which is social and non-vital or non-physical in the phenomena of societies is caused by imitation. This is true of both social similarities and dissimilarities. And so, the epithet *natural* is generally and not improperly bestowed upon the spontaneous and non-suggested resemblances which arise between different societies in every order of social facts. If we like to look at societies on the side of their spontaneous resemblances, we have the right to call this aspect of their laws, cults, governments, customs and crimes, natural law, natural religion, natural governments, natural industry, natural art (I do not mean naturalistic art), natural crime. Now, such spontaneous resemblances have, of course, some significance. But, unfortunately, we waste our time in trying to get at their exact meaning, and because of their irremediable vagueness and arbitrariness of character, they must end by repelling the positive and scientifically trained mind.

I may be reminded of the fact that although imitation is a social thing, the tendency to imitate in order to avoid the trouble of inventing, a tendency which is born of instinctive indolence, is an absolutely natural thing. But although this tendency may, of necessity, precede the first social act, the act whereby it is satisfied, yet its own strength and direction varies very much according to the nature of existing habits of imitation. It may still be argued that this tendency is only one form of a desire which I myself hold to be innate and deep-seated and from which I deduce, later on, all the laws of social reason, namely, desire for a maximum of strong and stable belief. If these laws exist, the resemblances which they produce in people's ideas and institutions have, in as much as there can be nothing social in their origin, a natural and non-social cause. For example, the savages of America, Africa, and Asia all explain sickness on the ground of diabolical possession, the entrance of evil spirits into the body of the diseased—this, in itself, is quite a singular coincidence; then when they have once adopted this explanation they all conceive of the idea of curing through exorcism as a logical outcome. In reply, I say that although it cannot be denied that there is a certain logical orientation on the part of the presocial man, the desire for logical co-ordination has been enhanced and directed by the influences of the social environment, where it is subject to the widest and strangest fluctuations, and where, like every other desire, it waxes strong and definite according to the measure of satisfaction which it receives. We shall see the proof of this at another time

2. This leads me to examine another leading objection which may be raised against me. As a matter of fact, I have gained little in proving that all civilisations, even the most divergent, are rays from a single primordial centre, if there are reasons for thinking that, after a certain point, the distance between them begins to diminish rather than increase, and that, whatever may have been the point of departure, the evolution of languages, myths, crafts, laws, sciences, and arts has been drawing nearer and nearer to a beaten track, so that their goal must always have been the same, predetermined and inevitable.

It is for us to ascertain if this hypothesis be true. It is not true. Let me first point out the extravagant consequence that it involves. It implies that, given sufficient time, the scientific spirit must lead, no matter what its path of speculation may be, to the infinitesimal calculus in mathematics, to the law of gravitation in astronomy, to the union of forces in physics, to atomism in chemistry, and in biology to natural selection or to some other ulterior form of evolution. Moreover, since the industrial and the military and the artistic imagination must have depended upon this would-be unique and inevitable science in their search for the means of satisfying virtually innate wants, it follows that the invention of the locomotive and the electric telegraph, for example, of torpedoes and Krupp guns, of Wagnerian opera and naturalistic novels, was a necessary thing, more necessary, perhaps, than the simplest expression of the art of pottery. Now, unless I am much mistaken, one might as well say that from its very beginnings and throughout all its metamorphoses, life tended to give birth to certain predetermined forms of existence and that the duck-bill, for example, or the lizard or ophrys or cactus or man himself was a necessary occurrence. Would it not be more plausible to admit that the ever fresh problem of life was of itself undertermined and susceptible of multiple solutions?

The illusion which I am opposing owes its verisimilitude to a kind of *quid pro quo*. The progress of civilisation is unquestionably manifest in the gradual equalisation that is being established throughout an ever vaster territory. This process is so thorough that some day, perhaps, a single stable and definite social type will cover the entire surface of a globe[1] that was formerly divided up among a thousand different unrelated or rival types. But does the work of universal equalisation in which we are taking part reveal the slightest common movement on the part of different societies towards the same pole? Not in the least, since the equalisation is plainly due to the submersion of the greater number of our original civilisations by the overflow of one whose waters are advancing in continually enlarging circles of imitation. To see how far independent civilisations are from tending to merge together spontaneously, let us compare in their stages of final development the Byzantine Empire of the Middle Ages, for example, with the Chinese Empire of the same epoch. Both civilisations had long since put forth all their fruit and reached their extreme limits of growth. The question at issue is whether in this final state of consummation they resembled each other more than they did at any previous

[1] In the long run, however, as we shall see later on, the exclusive imitation of *custom* will have to prevail over the proselyting imitation of *fashion* As a result of this law, the disintegration of mankind into distinct states and civilisations may very possibly be the final stage of society Only, these civilisations will be less in number and greater in scale than those of past or present times.

time.   It seems to me that the very opposite is much more true.   Compare Saint Sophia with its mosaics to a pagoda with its porcelains, the mystic miniatures of Byzantine manuscripts to the flat paintings of Chinese vases, the life of a mandarin occupied with literary frivolities and setting but an intermittent example of labour to that of a Byzantine bishop, devoted to the mingled ruses and subtleties of diplomacy and theology, etc.   The contrast is complete between the ideal of exquisite landscape gardening, of swarming families, and of lowered morality that is dear to one of these peoples, and the ideal of Christian salvation, of monastic celibacy and of ascetic perfection which fascinates the other.   It is difficult to class under the same term of religion the ancestor-worship which is the basis of the one, and the worship of divine personages or of saints which is the soul of the other.   But if I go back to the most ancient ages of those Greeks and Romans whose twofold culture was amalgamated and completed in the Lower Empire, I shall find a family organisation which would seem to be patterned after that of China   In fact, in the ancient Aryan, and, I may add, Semitic, family, we find, as in the Chinese family, not only the worship of ancestors and of household gods, we also find the same contrivances for honouring the dead, namely, food offerings and the singing of hymns accompanied by genuflexion. We find, too, the same fictions, particularly the fiction of adoption whose purpose is to accomplish, in spite of the occasional barrenness of wives, the chief end in view, the perpetuation with the family of the family-cult.

We shall have the counterproof of this truth, if, instead of comparing two original peoples at two successive phases of their history, we compare two classes or two social levels in each of them.   The traveller, to be sure, will observe that there is greater dissimilarity in many European countries, even in the most backward, between the common people who have remained faithful to their ancient customs than between persons belonging to the upper classes   But it is because the latter have been the first to be touched by the rays of invading fashion; here the resemblance is obviously the child of imitation. On the other hand, when two nations have remained hermetically shut off from each other, there are certainly greater differences between the ideas, the tastes, and the habits of their nobles or clergy than between those of their farmers or mechanics.

The reason of this is that the more civilised a nation or class becomes, the more it escapes from the narrow banks in whose thraldom the same universal corporeal wants have hemmed its development. It flows out into the freedom of the æsthetic life, where its ship of art is wafted at the pleasure of the breezes with which its own past fills its sails. If civilisation were only the full expansion of organic life by means of the social environment, this would not be so; but it seems as if life, in expanding in this way, sought above all to free itself from itself, to break through its own circle; as if it bloomed only to wither away, as if nothing were more essential to it (this is the case with all reality, perhaps), than to rid itself of its very essence. Accordingly, the superfluity, the luxury, the thing of beauty, I mean the special thing of beauty which every nation and every age makes its own, is, in every society, the pre-eminently social thing; it is the *raison d'être* of all the rest, of all that which is useful and necessary. Now we shall see that the exclusively imitative origin of resemblances becomes more and more indisputable as one passes from things of use to things of beauty. Artistic habits of eye, born of ancient individual caprice in art, become super-organic wants which the artist is obliged to satisfy, and which singularly limit the field of his fancy. But this imitation, which has nothing vital in it, varies as much as possible with time and place. Thus the eye of the Greek, beginning with a certain epoch, needed to see his columns in keeping with the Ionic or Corinthian order, whereas the eye of the Egyptian, under the Old Empire, exacted a square pier, and, under the Middle Empire, a column with lotos-bulb capital. Here, in this sphere of pure art, or rather of almost pure art, for architecture will always be an industrial art, my formula relating to imitation as the unique cause of true social resemblances, applies to the very letter.

It would apply still more exactly in sculpture, painting, music, and poetry. In fact, the æsthetic ideas and judgments to which art corresponds, do not exist before it. They have nothing in them that is fixed and uniform. They differ from the bodily wants and sense-perceptions which in a certain measure predetermine works of industry and force them to repeat themselves vaguely among different peoples. When a product belongs both to industry and to art, we must expect it to be like other products from foreign and independent sources in its industrial characteristics and to differ from them on its æsthetic side. In general, this differential element seems of slight importance to the practical man. Are not the monuments, the vases, the furniture, and the hymns and epics of different civilisations differentiated from each merely in detail? But detail, the characteristic shade, the turn of the sentence, the peculiar colouring, all this is style and manner; to the artist it is more important than anything else. The pointed arch of one place, the semi-circular of another, the pediment of still another, is both the most visible and most significant character of its respective society. It is the master-form which controls, instead of being controlled by, utilities, and, in this respect, it may well be likened to those morphological characteristics which rule over functions and by which living types are recognised. This is the reason why we can deny from the æsthetic, that is, from the most purely social, point of view, that any real likeness exists between works which differ from each other only in detail. We can assert, for example, that the graceful little Egyptian temple at Elephante is, in spite of its appearance, unlike a peripteral Greek temple. Consequently, we can set aside the question of ascertaining if this resemblance is not a proof that, as Champollion thought, Greece copied Egypt. After all, this amounts to saying that the formula applies the more exactly, the more it is a question of like products satisfying wants which are more artificial than natural, that is, which belong to a social

rather than vital order of things.   From this we may infer
that if certain products ever intersected each other, products
that were inspired by exclusively social motives, and that
were absolutely disconnected from any vital functions, this
principle would be verified with the utmost exactness.

There has been much talk among artists of an alleged law
of development which would subject the fine arts to turn
forever in the same circle and repeat themselves indefinitely.
Unfortunately no one has ever been able to formulate it with
any precision without running foul of the facts.   This observation may be likewise applied, although in a lesser degree, as we should expect from what has preceded, to the
development of religions, languages, governments, laws,
morals, and sciences.   Although M. Perrot shares in the
aforesaid current prejudice, yet in his *Histoire de l'art*
he is forced to admit that the evolution of architectural
orders did not pass through analagous phases in Egypt and
Greece.   When the most ancient stone columns of both
places came to take the place of wooden piers, they undoubtedly began by more or less faithfully imitating them
and they retained for a long-time this counterfeit character;
and in both countries the native plants, the acanthus in
Greece, the lotos or palm in Egypt, were reproduced in the
ornamentation of the capitals.   Again, without doubt, the
Greek or Egyptian column, massive and undivided as it
was in the beginning, came to be subdivided into three
parts, the capital, the shaft, and the base.   Finally, the
decoration of the capital in Greece and of the entire column
in Egypt undoubtedly went on, becoming more and more
complicated and surcharged with fresh ornamentation.

But of these three analogies, the first is only another
witness to our first principle, the instinctive imitativeness of
social man, and the third sets off for us a necessary corollary of this principle, the gradual accumulation of non-contradictory inventions, thanks to the conservation and diffusion of each of them through the imitation of which each
is the centre of radiation   As for the second, it is one of
those functional analogies of which I spoke above.   In fact,
as soon as the need of shelter came to require dwellings of

a certain elevation for its satisfaction, this tripartite division of the column was pretty much necessitated by the nature of the materials used and by the law of gravity. If we wish to get at the truth of the pseudo-law of religious or political or other kinds of development which I have just been criticising in passing, we shall see that it may be resolved into resemblances which fall within the three preceding categories. If any fails to fall within them, it is because imitation has intervened. For example, the point of similarity between Christianity and Buddhism, but especially between Christianity and the worship of Krishna, are so multiple, that they have seemed sufficient to some of the most learned authorities, notably to Weber, to justify the affirmation that an historical relationship exists between the aforesaid religions. The conjecture is the less astonishing because it is about proselyting religions.

Besides,—and here the significant divergences will stand out,—among the Greeks the proportion of the supports were always modified in the same direction, " a higher and higher fraction expressed the ratio between the height of the shaft and its diameter. The Doric of the Parthenon is more slender than that of the old temple of Corinth; it is less so than the Roman Doric. This was not the case in Egypt, its forms did not tend to grow more tapering with the lapse of the centuries. The proportions of the polygonal or of the fascicular column of Beni-Hassan are not more thickset than those of the columns of much earlier monuments." [1] We even find the contrary of this, the exact inverse of Hellenic evolution. " There are thus," concludes the author I cite from, " capricious oscillations in the course of Egyptian art. It is less regular than that of classic art; it does not seem to be governed by an equally severe internal logic." [2]

I prefer to say that it follows from this that art is unwilling to be shut up in a formula, since, at times, this formula, if formula there be, seems to apply, whereas at

[1] [*Histoire de l'art*, I, 574, Georges Perrot and Charles Chipiez, Paris, 1882.—*Tr.*]

[2] [*Ibid*, II, 575 —*Tr.*]

other times it is plain that it does not apply at all, and precisely in that which to the eyes of those who know concerns the most important, the most expressive, and the most
profound characteristics When it is a question of looking at the column from the utilitarian point of view, external conditions narrowly circumscribe the field of architectural invention and impose certain fundamental ideas
upon it like themes for variation. But when once the
strait was crossed along which all schools had to follow in
almost parallel courses, the schools turned in different directions and drifted apart; and yet they were not more free,
only each obeyed merely the inspirations of its own peculiar
genius. From now on, there is an end to coincidences, and
dissimilarities are deepened [1] The individual influence of
great masters, either living or dead, becomes sovereign and
preponderant in the transformations of their arts   In this
way the "capricious oscillations" of Egyptian architecture may be explained; and, if the development of Greek
architecture appears to be more rectilinear, is this not an illusion? If we do not limit ourselves to the consideration of
two or three remarkable centuries of Greek development, if
we include the entire unfolding of Greek art from its scarcely
known beginnings to its final Byzantine transformations,
shall we not see that that increasing need of more slender
proportions which M. Perrot points out, begins, at a certain
epoch, to diminish? The birth and growth of this optical
need was due to a series of elegant and graceful artists, just
as generations of solid builders made the need of massive
solidity a general and permanent thing on the banks of the
Nile. And yet contributions of a different style were not
lacking when an architect of originality, one less inclined to
conform to the national genius than to reform it, made his
appearance on the scene. But how much these considerations would gain by being illustrated by examples taken
from the higher arts, from painting and poetry and music!

[1] Do we find anything analogous to the obelisk outside of Egypt?
It is because obelisks do not answer to a need that is for the most part
natural, like doors or windows or like columns in so far as they are
supports, but to a need that is almost entirely social.

CHAPTER III

THE meaning which I attach to *society* can be clearly enough inferred from what has preceded, but it is proper to express this fundamental notion still more precisely.

I

What is a society? The general answer is as follows: It is a group of distinct individuals who render one another mutual services. But this definition is as false as it is clear. It has been the source of all those confusions which have so often been made between so-called animal societies, or the majority of them, and the only true societies, which do include, in a certain connection, a small number of animals.[1]

For this wholly economic notion, a notion which bases the social group upon mutual helpfulness, it might be an advantage to substitute a purely juristic conception of society. In this case, an individual would not be associated with those to whom he was useful or who were useful to him, but with those, and only with those, who had established over him recognised rights of law, custom, and conventionality, or over whom he had analogous rights, with or without reciprocity. But we shall see that although this is a preferable point of view, yet it unduly restricts the social group, just as the economic point of view unduly enlarges it. Finally, we might think of the social tie as entirely political or religious in character. Belief in the same religion or collaboration for the same patriotic purpose, a purpose common to all the associates and one absolutely distinct from their different individual wants, for whose

---

[1] I should be sorry to have the reader find any implicit criticism in these lines of the work of M. Espinas upon " Animal Societies " That work is redeemed by too many true and profound insights to be arraigned for the confusion referred to in the text.

satisfaction it matters little whether they aid each other or not, would constitute a true social relationship. Such moral and mental unanimity is undoubtedly characteristic of mature societies; but it is also true that social ties may begin without it. They exist, for example, among Europeans of different nationalities. Consequently, this definition is too narrow. Moreover, the conformity of aims and beliefs of which we are speaking, this mental likeness, which may characterise tens and hundreds of millions of men at the same time, is not born all of a sudden. It is produced little by little, and extends from one man to another by means of imitation. This, then, is always the point to which we must return.

If the relation of one social unit to another consisted essentially of an exchange of services, we should not only have to recognise the right of animal groups to be called societies, we should have to admit that they were the societies *par excellence*. The mutual services of shepherd and husbandman, of hunter and fisherman, of baker and butcher, are far less than those which the different sexes of white ants render one another. Among animals themselves, the most typical societies would not be formed by the highest, by bees, ants, horses, and beavers, but by the lowest, by the siphonophoræ, for example, where division of labour is so complete that eating and digesting are carried on separately by different individuals. There can be no more signal interchange of services than this. Applying this view to mankind it might be said, without irony, that the strength of the social tie between men was in proportion to the degree of their reciprocal usefulness. The master who shelters and nourishes his slave and the noble who defends and protects his serf, in return for their subordinate services, are examples of mutual service. The reciprocity is gained, to be sure, by force; but that fact is insignificant if the economic point of view is the primary one and if we think that it is bound to encroach more and more upon the juristic point of view. . . Consequently, the social tie between the Spartan and the helot, or between a noble and his serf, or between a Hindoo warrior and a Hindoo merchant, is stronger than that between free Spartan citizens, or that between the feudal nobles of a single country, or that between the helots or serfs who live in the same village, in spite of the fact that the members of all these classes may possess the same customs and language and religion!

We have erred in thinking that societies in becoming civilised have favoured economic at the expense of juristic relations. In doing this, we forget that all labour and service and exchange is based upon a true system of contract, a system which is guaranteed by more and more formal and complex legislation; and we forget that to this accumulation of legal rules are added commercial and other kinds of usages which have the force of law, besides a host of all kinds of *procedures*, from the simple but general formalities of polite manners to electoral and parliamentary practices.[1] Society is far more a system of mutually determined engagements and agreements, of rights and duties, than a system of mutual services. This is the reason why it is established between beings who are alike or who differ little from each other. Economic production exacts a specialisation of aptitudes. If this specialisation were fully developed in accordance with the logically inevitable although unexpressed wish of economists, we should have as many distinct human species as there are miners, farmers, weavers, lawyers, physicians, etc. But, fortunately, the assured and undeniable preponderance of juridical relations prevents any excessive differentiation of workers. In fact, it is continually diminishing such distinctions. Here Law, it is true, is only one form or outcome of man's inclination towards imitation. Is it from the standpoint of utilitarianism that the peasant is given an education and instructed in his rights when as the result of this kind of education the rural population may desert its plough and spade and the double mammal of husbandry and herding may dry up? The

---

[1] It is a mistake to think that the rule of *ceremony,* of *ceremonial government,* to use Spencer's term, is on the decline. At the side of outgrown conventions or dying-out ceremonial, vigorous ceremonies arise and multiply under the name of conventions.

cult of equality has outweighed any fear of this latter contingency. We have wished to promote in the social scale certain classes which formerly, in spite of a constant exchange of services, did not come in for so much consideration and, consequently, we have appreciated that it was necessary *to assimilate them through the contagion of imitation* with the members of a higher grade of society. To put it better, it was necessary to bring into their mental and *social* life ideas, desires, and needs, in a word, individual elements like those which constituted the mind and character of the members of that society.

Beings which differ greatly in kind, the shark, for example, and the little fish which he uses as a mouth scavenger, or man and the domestic animals, can be of much service to each other, and at times, like the huntsman and his dog or like men and women very different as they often are from each other, work together in a common undertaking But the recognition and assumption by two beings of mutual rights and obligations involves one indispensable condition, the possession of a common foundation of ideas and traditions, of a common language or interpreter. These close points of likeness are formed by education, which is one of the forms by which imitation spreads. For this reason the recognition of mutual responsibilities never arose between the Spanish or English conquerors of America and the conquered natives. In this case, racial dissimilarity either played a much smaller rôle than difference of language, custom, or religion; or it served merely as an added cause of incompatibility.[1]   This is the reason, on the other hand, that a close chain of reciprocal rights and obligations united all members of the feudal tree from its topmost branch to its nethermost root in an eminently juridical institution. Here, in fact, Christian propagandism had

[1] In the sixteenth and seventeenth centuries, when military and civil populations were radically unlike, the standards of the time justified the perpetration of every kind of outrage, of rape, pillage, massacre, etc., by campaigning troops upon either friendly or hostile civilians. But *among themselves* soldiers were more sparing of one another.

produced in the twelfth century the most profound mental assimilation from the emperor to the serf that has ever been seen.   And it was essentially because of this network of rights, that feudal Europe formed from one end of it to the other a true society, the society of *Christendom,* which was as widespread as *Romanism (Romanitas)* in the best days of the Roman Empire.   If we require any counter-proof of this, we may find it in the fact that a real social tie is never established between the Chinese and Hindoo emi-grants to the Antilles and their white masters by their reciprocity of services, or even by their bilateral contracts, for they never become assimilated to one another.   Here two or three distinct civilisations, two or three distinct groups of inventions which have spread out through imita-tion in their own particular spheres, come into mutual con-tact and mutual service, but there is no society in the true sense of the word.

The Hindoo caste system was based mainly on an eco-nomic conception of society.   Castes were distinct races which were of vast assistance to one another.   We see, then, that the tendency to subordinate moral considerations of rights to utilitarian considerations of service and occupa-tion does not denote an advanced state of civilisation. This tendency diminishes, in fact, as mankind improves and as industry itself progresses[1]   In reality, the civilised man of to-day is inclined to do without the assistance of his fellow.   He appeals less and less to the professional

---

[1] In his remarkable work on Cinematics, Reuleaux, the German director of the Industrial Academy of Berlin, observes that industrial progress demonstrates more clearly every day that economists err in attaching undue importance to the division of labour.   It is the co-ordination which results from it that deserves the chief praise   This is true also of " the division of organic labour ", without an admirable organic harmony, it would not be in the slightest degree a step in vital progress.   " The principle of machine work," M. Reuleaux remarks in particular, " contradicts, in part, at any rate, the principle of division of labour .   . In the most improved modern factories, the men who tend the different machines are shifted from one place to another in order to break the monotony of their work"   An increasing special-isation in the work of the machine produces the opposite result in the work of the mechanic.   Otherwise, as Reuleaux observes, the workman would become more mechanical as the machine became a better workman.

specialist who is fundamentally unlike himself and more
and more to the forces of subjugated nature. Is not the
social ideal of the future the enlarged reproduction of the
city of antiquity, where slaves would be replaced by machines,—an idea that has been tediously reiterated,—and
where a small homogeneous group of citizens in constant
imitation and assimilation of one another, but independent and self-sufficient in other respects, in times of
peace at least, would constitute the sum total of civilised
men? Economic solidarity establishes a vital rather than
a social tie between workers and no organisation of labour
will ever be comparable, in this respect, to the most imperfect organism. Juridical solidarity has, on the other
hand, a purely social character, because it presupposes the
kind of similarity that is due to imitation. Given this similarity, and we have, notwithstanding a lack of recognised
rights, a beginning of society. Louis XIV did not recognise the fact that his subjects had any claims whatsoever
upon him, and his subjects shared his delusion; nevertheless,
he was socially related to them, because both he and they
were products of the same classical and Christian education, because everyone from the Court at Paris to the heart
of Brittany and Provence looked up to him as a model,
and because he himself was unconsciously reacted upon by
the influence of his courtiers, a kind of *diffused* imitation
experienced by him in return for that *radiating* from him.

Social relations, I repeat, are much closer between individuals who resemble each other in occupation and education, even if they are competitors, than between those
who stand most in need of each other. Lawyers, journalists, magistrates, all professional men, are cases in point.
So society has been properly defined by common speech
as a group of people who, although they may disagree in
ideas and sentiments, yet, having had the same kind of
bringing up, have a common meeting ground and see and
influence one another for pleasure. As for the employees
of the same shop or factory who meet together for mutual
assistance or collaboration, they constitute a commercial or

industrial society, not a society pure and simple, not a society in the unqualified sense of the word.[1]

A *nation*, which is a kind of super-organic organism made up of co-operative castes and classes and professions, is quite different from a *society*. This distinction is obvious in the *denationalisation* and *socialisation* which is taking place to-day among hundreds of millions of men. It does not seem to me that the multiple uniformities to which we are hastening in language, education, instruction, etc., have as yet proved to be the fittest ways to assure the accomplishment of the innumerable tasks which nations and associations of individuals have heretofore divided up among themselves. It may well be that the scholar-peasant is not a better farmer for his learning, nor the soldier a better disciplined or, who knows, a braver fighter. But when we bring the steadfast partisans of progress face to face with these threatening possibilities, it is because we do not have the point of view which they, perhaps unconsciously, hold. They wish for the most intense kind of socialisation, not for the highest and strongest kind of social organisation, quite a different thing. They would be satisfied, if need be, by an exuberance of social life in a weakened social organisation. We have still to learn how desirable this end may be. Let us hold this question in reserve.

The fret and instability of modern societies must seem inexplicable to economists and, in general, to those sociologists who base society upon reciprocal utility. As a matter of fact, reciprocity of services between different classes and different nations does plainly exist, and it increases day by day, thanks to the co-operation of law and custom, with the utmost rapidity. But we forget that the in-

[1] Both lawyers and physicians vie with fellow professionals for public patronage, but, in the legal profession, community of work tempers the heat and bitterness of competition and selfish resentment and necessarily develops certain fraternal relations. Among physicians, on the contrary, nothing takes the edge off their struggle and rivalry; for as a rule they do not work together. Consequently, paroxysms of professional hatred and animosity characterise the medical fraternity, and, I may add, all bodies of men, such as notaries, pharmacists, or merchants, who work independently of one another.

dividuals who compose these classes and nations are becoming even more rapidly and thoroughly assimilated, although this process of imitation is still hindered by irritating obstacles, by customs, and even by laws which are, perhaps, the more irritating the less discouraging they appear to be.

Contemporary civilisation in England, America, France, in all modern countries, tends to diminish the intellectual difference, which was becoming more and more deep and far-reaching, between men and women by opening up most of men's occupations to women and by letting the latter share in almost all the advantages of training and education of the former. In this respect, civilisation treats the weaker sex just as it treated the peasant or free agricultural labourer when it took him out of the distinct caste into which it had gradually come to put him and replaced him in the big social group. Now, is social utility the end in view in either case? Were these transformations brought about to enable either class to be more successful in performing its special function, in cultivating the soil, or in nourishing and caring for children? On the contrary, many pessimists like myself foresee the time when, in consequence of these changes, we shall be without agricultural labourers, without nurses, and even without mothers who can or will nourish the continually decreasing number of their children. *But because the enlargement of the social circle was the end in view and because the assimilation of women with men, of peasants with townsmen, was an indispensable condition of this socialisation,* assimilation had to occur.

As early as the eighteenth century, in a more restricted social circle, in the brilliant social life of the common meeting ground of the *salon,* both sexes were brought closer together in tastes and ideas than they were in the Middle Ages; and we know that this social advantage was bought at the price of family fruitfulness and even at that of family honour. And yet people were happy under these circumstances, because a higher necessity impels the social circle, be it what it may, to continually widen its circumference.

Am I socially related to other men who may belong to the same physical type and possess the same organs and the same senses that I do? Am I socially related to an educated deaf mute who may closely resemble me in face and figure? No, I am not. Inversely, the animals of La Fontaine's fables, the fox, the cricket, the cat, and the dog, live together in society, in spite of the difference in species which separates them, because they all speak the same language.[1] We eat, drink, digest, walk, or cry without being taught. These acts are purely vital. But talking requires the hearing of conversation, as we know from the case of deaf mutes who are dumb because they are deaf. Consequently, I begin to feel a social kinship with everyone who talks, even if it be in a

---

[1] Romanes devotes one very interesting chapter in his *Mental Evolution in Animals* to the influence of imitation upon the origin and development of instincts. This influence is much greater and more far-spread than we suppose. It is not only the related and even the un-related individuals of the same species who copy one another,—many song birds learn to sing only through the teaching of their mothers or companions.—individuals of different species as well borrow both the useful and the unmeaning peculiarities of one another. Here we see the deep-seated desire to imitate for the sake of imitation, the desire which is the original source of all our arts A mocking-bird can imitate a cock's crow so accurately that the very hens are deceived Darwin thought that some hive-bees that he had observed had borrowed from the humble-bees their ingenious method of sucking the nectar of certain flowers by boring their under sides. Certain birds and insects and animals are creatures of genius, and genius even in the animal world can count upon some measure of success. Only, these social attempts prove abortive for lack of language Not man only, but every animal, reaches out according to his degree of mentality to a social life as the *sine qua non* of mental development Why is this? Because the cerebral function, the mind, is distinguished from other functions in not being a simple adaptation of definite means to definite ends, but in being an adaptation to many indeterminate ends which depend more or less upon chance to be made definite through the same far-reaching means by which they are in the first instance pursued, namely, through imitation of outside things. This infinite outside, this outer world which is pictured, represented. *imitated,* by sensation and intelligence, is primarily universal nature in its continual and irresistible action by suggestion upon the animal's brain and muscular system; later on, however, it is pre-eminently the social environment.

strange tongue, providing our two idioms appear to me to have some common source. This social tie may be weak and inadequate, but it gains in strength as other common traits, all originating in imitation, are added to it.

Society may therefore be defined as a group of beings who are apt to imitate one another, or who, without actual imitation, are alike in their possession of common traits which are ancient copies of the same model.

II

We must not confuse the social type of a given place or period, as it is more or less incompletely reproduced in every member of the social group, with the social group itself. What constitutes this type? A certain number of wants and ideas which have been created by thousands of time-accumulated inventions and discoveries. These wants harmonise to a certain extent, that is, they contribute to the supremacy of some dominant desire which is the soul of a given epoch or people. The ideas or beliefs also harmonise more or less; that is, they are logically related to one another or, at least, they do not in general mutually contradict one another. This twofold, always incomplete, and, in certain notes, discordant accord, which is gradually established between things which have been fortuitously produced and brought together, may be perfectly well compared to what is called in a living body organic adaptation. But it has the advantage of being free from the mystery which is inherent in this latter kind of harmony; it points out in extremely clear terms the relations of means to an end or of consequences to a principle, two relations which amount, after all, to one, the latter one of the two. What is the meaning of the incompatibility or discord that may exist between two organs, or conformations, or characteristics taken from two different species? We do not know, but we do know that when two ideas are incompatible it means that one of them implies a negative to the affirmative of the other and that for the same reason the consistency of two ideas means the lack, or the apparent lack, of all such implications. Finally, we know that when two ideas more or less agree, it is because the one implies in a more or less considerable number of its aspects the affirmation of a more or less considerable number of the points which the other affirms. There is nothing less obscure, nothing more enlightening, than these psychical acts of affirmation and negation. In them the whole life of the mind is wrapped up. Nor is there anything more intelligible than their opposition. In it is expressed the opposition between desire and repulsion, between *velle* and *nolle*. Thus we see that a social type or what is called a particular civilisation is a veritable system, a more or less coherent theory, whose inner contradictions eventually strengthen themselves or eventually break out and force its disruption. Under such conditions it is easy to understand why there are certain pure and strong types of civilisation and certain mixed and feeble types, and why the purest types change and decay upon the addition of new inventions which stimulate new desires and beliefs and disturb the balance of old desires and faiths; why, in other words, all inventions cannot be added to others, and why many can merely be substituted for others, those, namely, that stimulate desires and beliefs which are implicitly or explicitly contradictory in all the logical exactness of the word. Therefore, in the oscillations of history there is nothing but endless additions and subtractions of quantities of faith or desire which are brought forward by discoveries and which reinforce or neutralise one another, like intersecting vibrations.

This is the national type which, as I have said, is repeated in every member of the nation. It is like a great seal, which makes an imperfect mark upon the bits of wax which it stamps, but which could not be completely recast without comparing all its impressions.

III

What I defined above was really not so much *society*, in the common sense of the word, as *sociality* A society is always in different degrees an association, and association is to sociality, to *imitativeness,* so to speak, what organisation is to vitality, or what molecular structure is to the elasticity of the ether.   Here are some new analogies in addition to those which seemed to me to be presented in such abundance by the three great forms of Universal Repetition.   But, perhaps, in order to fully understand sociality in its relative form, the only one in which in various degrees it actually occurs, it may be well to conceive of it, hypothetically, as perfect and absolute.   In its hypothetical form it would consist of such an intense concentration of urban life that as soon as a good idea arose in one mind it would be instantaneously transmitted to all minds throughout the city.   This hypothesis is analogous to that of physicists who state that if the elasticity of the ether were perfect, luminious excitations, etc., would be transmitted without lapse of time.   Would it not be useful for biologists to conceive, on their part, of an absolute irritability incarnated in a kind of ideal protoplasm, a conception which would help them to understand the varying vitality of real protoplasm?

With this for our starting point, if we wish to carry our analogy straight through, life would be merely the organisation of protoplasmic irritability, matter, the organisation of ethereal elasticity, and society, the organisation of imitativeness.   Now, it is almost superfluous to remark that the hypothesis which was conceived of by Thompson and adopted by Wurtz on the origin of atoms and molecules, the vortex theory, extremely plausible and probable as it is, to say the least, as well as the universally accepted protoplasmic theory of life, fully answers one of the demands of our point of view.   Given a mass of children who have been brought up together and given the same education in the same environment and who have not yet separated into classes and professions, and we have the groundmatter of society. It kneads this mass, and then, through an artificial and inevitable differentiation of functions, develops it into a nation.   Given a mass of protoplasm, *i. e.,* of homogeneous molecules, which can be, but have not been, organised, and which have all been assimilated by virtue of the obscure mode of reproduction from which they originated, and we have the ground-matter of life. From it, cells, tissues, individuals, and species are formed. Finally, given a mass of homogeneous ether whose elements are thrilled by the same rapidly exchanging vibrations, according to our theoretical chemists, and we have the ground-matter of matter. From this the corpuscles of all bodies, however heterogeneous they may be, are made. For a body is merely an accord of differentiated and subordinated vibrations which have been separately produced in distinct and interwoven series, just as an organism is only an accord of different elementary and harmonious inward reproductions, of distinct and interwoven kinds of histological elements, or just as a nation is only an accord of traditions, customs, teachings, tendencies, and ideas which have spread in different ways through imitation, but which are subordinate to one another in a fraternal and mutually helpful hierarchy.

The law of differentiation, then, comes into play here. But it is not superfluous to note that the homogeneity upon which it acts under three superimposed forms is a superficial, although real, homogeneity, and that, if we continue the analogy, our sociological point of view would lead us to admit that in protoplasm there are some elements which have highly individualistic features under their mask of apparent uniformity, and that in ether itself the atoms are individually as characteristic as the children of the best disciplined school may be. Heterogeneity, not homogeneity, is at the heart of things. Could anything be more improbable or more absurd than the co-existence of an endless number of elements created to be co-eternally alike? Things are not born alike, they become alike. And, besides, is not the inborn diversity of the elements the sole possible justification of their *variability?*

I might be willing to go still further and say that without this initial and fundamental heterogeneity, the homogeneity which screens and disguises it never would or could have occurred. In fact, all homogeneity is a likeness of parts and all likeness is the outcome of an assimilation which has been produced by the voluntary or non-voluntary repetition of what was in the beginning an individual innovation. But there is something more to be said. When the homogeneity in question, when ether or protoplasm, when a mass of people who have been levelled down and put upon a footing of equality, becomes differentiated in order to become organised, do we not find, judging from what passes in our own societies at least, that the change in its character is another effect of the very same cause? After proselytism has assimilated a people, despotism steps in to rule over them and impose a hierarchy upon them; but despot and apostle are alike refractory individuals upon whom the democratic or aristocratic yoke of others has been a burden. For every individual conflict or outbreak which succeeds in this way there are, of course, hundreds of millions which are suppressed, but which are, nevertheless, the nursery of the great innovations of the future. This wealth of variations, this exuberance of picturesque fancies and erratic designs which Nature unrolls so magnificently under her austere garb of time-honoured laws, repetitions, and rhythms can have but one source; the tumultuous originality of elements that have been but partly brought under these yokes of nature, the radical and innate diversity that bursts out through all these uniformities of law to be transfigured upon the fair surface of things.

I will not follow up these last considerations, for they would lead us away from our subject. I only wished to point out that our search for law, *i. e.*, for like facts either in nature or history, must not make us forget their hidden agents, agents which are both original and individual. Passing on, then, we may draw a useful lesson from what preceded, namely, that the assimilation together with the equalisation of the members of a society is not, as we are led to think, the final term of a prior social progression; it is, on the contrary, the point of departure for a new social advance. Every new form of civilisation be-

gins in this way.   In the homogeneous and democratic
communities of the early Christians, the bishop was merely
one of the faithful and the pope was not to be distinguished
from the bishop.   In the Frankish army, booty was dis-
tributed in equal portions between the king and his compan-
ions-in-arms.   The first caliphs to succeed Mahomet argued
in court like simple Mahometans; the equality of all the sons
of the Prophet before the Koran had not yet become the
mere fiction which the equality of Frenchmen or Europeans
before the law is eventually bound to become.   Then, by
degrees, a radical inequality, the condition of solid organisation, came to be hollowed out in the Arab world, somewhat as the ecclesiastical hierarchy of Catholicism or the
feudal pryamid of the Middle Ages was formed.   The past
speaks for the future.   Equality is only a transition between
two hierarchies, just as liberty is only a passage between
two disciplines.   But this does not mean that the confidence
and power, the knowledge and security, of every citizen do
not go on increasing from age to age.

Now let us take up another aspect of our foregoing
thought.   Homogeneous and democratic communities precede churches and states, for the same reason, I say, that
tissues precede organs.   Moreover, once tissues and communities have been formed, they become organic and hierarchical for the same reason which caused their formation
in the first place.   The growth of still undifferentiated and
unutilised tissue is evidence of the peculiar ambition and
eagerness of the germ which propagates itself in this way,
just as the creation of a club or circle or fraternity of
kindred spirits is evidence of the ambition of the enterprising man who originated it in order to spread some plan
or idea of his own.   Now, the community becomes consolidated into a hierarchical corporation, and tissue becomes organic, for the sake of self-propagation and self-
defence against existing or anticipated enemies   For the
living or for the social being, to act and function is a
necessary condition for the conservation and extension of its
essential nature, for the early development of which it was

at first enough for it to multiply uniform copies of itself.
But self-propagation and not self-organisation is the prime
demand of the social as well as of the vital thing. Organisation is but the means of which propagation, of which
generative or *imitative* repetition, is the end.

To sum up, to the question which I began by asking:
What is society? I have answered: Society is imitation.
We have still to ask: What is imitation? Here the soci-
ologist should yield to the psychologist.

IV

1. Taine sums up the thought of the most eminent
physiologists when he happily remarks that the brain is a
repeating organ for the senses and is itself made up of
elements which repeat one another. In fact, the sight of
such a congery of like cells and fibres makes any other idea
impossible. Moreover, direct proof is at hand in the numerous observations and experiments which show that the
cutting away of one hemisphere of the brain, and even the
removal of much of the substance of the other, affects only
the intensity, without at all changing the integrity, of the
intellectual functions. The part that was removed, therefore, did not collaborate with the part that remained; both
parts could only copy and reinforce each other. Their
relation was not economic and utilitarian, but imitative and
social in the sense that I use that term. Whatever may be
the cellular function which calls forth thought (a highly
complex vibration, perhaps?), there is no doubt that it is
reproduced and multiplied in the interior of the brain every
moment of our mental life and that to every distinct perception a distinct cellular function corresponds. The indefinite and inexhaustible continuation of these intricate and
richly intersecting radiations constitutes memory and habit.
When the multiplying repetition in question is confined to
the nervous system, we have memory; when it spreads
out into the muscular system, we have habit. Memory,

so to speak, is a purely nervous habit; habit is both a nervous and a muscular memory.

Thus every act of perception, in as much as it involves an act of memory, which it always does, implies a kind of habit, an unconscious imitation of self by self. There is, evidently, nothing social in this. When the nervous system is sufficiently excited to set in motion a certain set of muscles, habit, properly speaking, appears. It is another case of non-social, or, as I might better say, of *presocial* or *subsocial* self-imitation. This does not mean that, as alleged, an idea is an abortive act. Action is only the following up of an idea, the acquisition of a steadfast faith. Muscle works only for the enrichment of nerves and brain.

But if the remembered idea or image was originally lodged in the mind through conversation or reading, if the habitual act originated in the view or knowledge of a similar act on the part of others, these acts of memory and habit are social as well as psychological facts, and they show us the kind of imitation of which I have already spoken at such length.[1] Here we have memory and habit which are not individual, but collective. Just as a man does not see, listen, walk, stand, write, play the flute, or, what is more, invent or imagine, except by means of many co-ordinated muscular memories, so a society could not exist or change or advance a single step unless it possessed an untold store of blind routine and slavish imitation which was constantly being added to by successive generations.

2. What is the essential nature of the suggestion which passes from one cerebral cell to another and which consti-

[1] While correcting the proofs of my second edition, I read in the *Revue de métaphysique* a brief review of an article of Mr. Baldwin's which appeared in 1894 in *Mind* under the title of *Imitation. A Chapter in the Natural History of Consciousness.* " Mr Baldwin," writes his reviewer, " wishes to define and generalise the theories of Tarde. Biological imitation, or imitation which is primarily subcortical, is a circular reaction of the nerves, that is, it reproduces its own stimulus. Psychological or cortical imitation is *habit* (expressed in the principle of identity) and *accommodation* (expressed in the principle of sufficient reason). It is, in short, sociological, plastic, and only secondarily subcortical."

tutes mental life?   We do not know.¹   Do we know anything more about the essence of the suggestion which passes
from one person to another and which constitutes social
life?   We do not; for if we take this phenomenon in itself,
in its higher state of purity and intensity, we find it related to one of the most mysterious of facts, a fact which
is being studied with intense curiosity by the baffled philosophic alienists of the day, *i. e.*, somnambulism.²   If you
re-read contemporaneous works on this subject, especially
those of Richet, Binet and Féré, Beaunis, Bernheim, Delbœuf, I shall not seem fanciful in thinking of the social man
as a veritable somnambulist   I think, on the contrary, that
I am conforming to the most rigorous scientific method in
endeavouring to explain the complex by the simple, the compound by the element, and to throw light upon the mixed
and complicated social tie, as we know it, by means of a
social tie which is very pure, which is reduced to its
simplest expression, and which is so happily realised for the
edification of the sociologist in a state of somnambulism.
Let us take the hypothetical case of a man who has been removed from every extra-social influence, from the direct
view of natural objects, and from the instinctive obses-
sions of his different senses, and who has communication
only with those like himself or, more especially, to simplify
the question, with one person like himself.   Is not such an
ideal subject the proper one through which to study by ex-
periment and observation the really essential characteristics
of social relations, set free in this way from all com-
plicating influences of a natural or physical order?   But

¹ At the time when the foregoing and the following considerations
first appeared in print, in November, 1884, in the *Revue philosophique,*
hypnotic suggestion was but barely spoken of and the idea of universal social suggestion, an idea which has since been so strongly em-
phasised by Bernheim and others, was cast up against me as an un-
tenable paradox   Nothing could be commoner than this view at
present.

² This old-fashioned term shows that at the time of the first publication of this passage the word *hypnotism* had not as yet been altogether
substituted for somnambulism.

are not hypnotism and somnambulism the exact realisation of this hypothesis? Then I shall not excite surprise if I briefly review the principal phenomena of these singular states and if I find both magnified and diminutised, both overt and covert, forms of them in social phenomena. Through such a comparison, we may perhaps come to a better understanding of the fact that is called abnormal by showing to what extent it is general, and of the fact that is general by perceiving its distinctive traits in high relief in the apparent anomaly.

The social like the hypnotic state is only a form of dream, a dream of command and a dream of action. Both the somnambulist and the social man are possessed by the illusion that their ideas, all of which have been suggested to them, are spontaneous. To appreciate the truth of this sociological point of view, we must not take ourselves into consideration, for should we admit this truth about ourselves, we would then be escaping from the blindness which it affirms; and in this way a counter argument might be made out. Let us call to mind some ancient people whose civilisation differs widely from our own, the Egyptians, or Spartans, or Hebrews. Did not that people think, like us, that they were autonomous, although, in reality, they were but the unconscious puppets whose strings were pulled by their ancestors or political leaders or prophets, when they were not being pulled by their own contemporaries? What distinguishes us modern Europeans from these alien and primitive societies is the fact that the magnetisation has become mutual, so to speak, at least to a certain extent; and because we, in our democratic pride, a little exaggerate this reciprocity, because, moreover, forgetting that in becoming mutual, this magnetisation, the source of all faith and obedience, has become general, we err in flattering ourselves that we have become less credulous and docile, less imitative, in short, than our ancestors. This is a fallacy, and we shall have to rid ourselves of it. But even if the aforesaid notion were true, it would nevertheless be clear that before the relations of model and copyist, of mas-

ter and subject, of apostle and neophyte, had become reciprocal or alternative, as we ordinarily see them in our
democratic society, they must of necessity have begun by
being one-sided and irreversible. Hence castes. Even in the
most democratic societies, the one-sidedness and irreversibility in question always exist at the basis of social imitations, *i. e.*, in the family. For the father is and always will
be his son's first master, priest, and model. Every society,
even at present, begins in this way.

Therefore, in the beginning of every old society, there
must have been, *a fortiori,* a great display of authority exercised by certain supremely imperious and positive individuals. Did they rule through terror and imposture, as
alleged? This explanation is obviously inadequate. They
ruled through their *prestige.* The example of the magnetiser alone can make us realise the profound meaning of this
word. The magnetiser does not need to lie or terrorise to
secure the blind belief and the passive obedience of his magnetised subject. He has prestige—that tells the story.
That means, I think, that there is in the magnetised subject
a certain potential force of belief and desire which is anchored in all kinds of sleeping but unforgotten memories, and
that this force seeks expression just as the water of a lake
seeks an outlet. The magnetiser alone is able through a
chain of singular circumstances to open the necessary outlet
to this force. All forms of prestige are alike; they differ
only in degree. We have prestige in the eyes of anyone
in so far as we answer his need of affirming or of willing some given thing. Nor is it necessary for the magnetiser to speak in order to be believed and obeyed. He
need only act; an almost imperceptible gesture is sufficient.

This movement, together with the thought and feeling
which it expresses, is immediately reproduced. Maudsley
says that he is not sure that the somnambulist is not enabled
to read unconsciously what is in the mind through " an
unconscious imitation of the attitude and expression of the
person whose *exact* muscular contradictions are *instinctively*

copied."[1]   Let us observe that the magnetised subjects imitates the magnetiser, but that the latter does not imitate the former. *Mutual imitation,* mutual prestige or *sympathy,* in the meaning of Adam Smith, is produced only in our so-called waking life and among people who seem to exercise no magnetic influence over one another.   If, then, I have put prestige, and not sympathy, at the foundation and origin of society, it is because, as I have said before, the unilateral must have preceded the reciprocal.[2]   Without an age of authority, however surprising this fact may be, an age of comparative fraternity would never have existed.   But, to return, why should we really marvel at the one-sided, passive imitation of the somnambulist?   Any act of any one of our fellows inspires us who are lookers-on with the more or less irrational idea of imitation.   If we at times resist this tendency, it is because it is neutralised by some antagonistic suggestions of memory or perception.   Since the somnambulist is for the time being deprived of this power of resistance, he can illustrate for us the imitative quiescence of the social being in so far as he is social, *i. e.,* in so far as he has relations exclusively with his fellows and, especially, with one of his fellows.

If the social man were not at the same time a natural being, open and sensitive to the impressions of external nature and of alien societies, he would never be capable of change.   Like associates would remain forever incapable of changing spontaneously the type of traditional ideas and desires which had been impressed upon them by the conventional teaching of their parents, priests, or leaders.   Certain peoples have been known to approach singularly close to this condition.   Nascent communities, like young children, are, in general, indifferent and insensible to all which

[1] *The Pathology of Mind* [p. 69. Henry Maudsley, M. D., New York, 1890   The italics are the author's.—*Tr.*].

[2] On this point I need correction.   Sympathy is certainly the primary source of sociability and the hidden or overt soul of every kind of imitation, even of imitation which is envious and calculating, even of imitation of an enemy   Only, it is certain that sympathy itself begins by being one-sided instead of mutual.

does not concern man or the kind of man whom they resemble, the man of their own race or tribe.[1] "The somnambulist sees and hears," says A. Maury, "only what enters into the preoccupations of his dream." In other words, all his power of belief and desire is concentrated on a single point. Is not this the exact effect of obedience and imitation *through fascination?* Is not fascination a genuine neurosis, a kind of unconscious *polarisation* of love and faith?

Now many great men from Rameses to Alexander, from Alexander to Mahomet, from Mahomet to Napoleon, have thus polarised the soul of their people! How often has a prolonged gaze upon the brilliant point of one man's glory or genius thrown a whole people into a state of catalepsy! The torpor that appears in somnambulism is, as we know, only superficial; it masks an intense excitement. This is the reason why the somnambulist does not hesitate to perform great feats of strength and skill. A similar phenomenon occurred at the beginning of the nineteenth century when military France fell into a passive and, at the same time, feverish state of mingled torpor and excitement and performed prodigies in obedience to the gesture of its imperial fascinator. There is nothing better fitted than this atavistic phenomenon to plunge us into the remote past, to make us realise the influence which must have been exerted upon their contemporaries by those great semi-mythical persons to whom all civilisations trace their origin and to whom their legends attribute the revelation of all their knowledge, laws, and industries. Oannes in Babylon, Quetz-alcoatl in Mexico, the *divine* pre-Menes dynasties in Egypt, etc., are cases in point.[2] Under close observation, all these *king-*

---

[1] Science, then, is the source of every social revolution. It is this extra-social research which opens for us the windows of the social phalanstery in which we live and lets in the light of the universe. How many phantoms are scattered by this light! But then, too, how many perfectly preserved mummies it crumbles into dust!

[2] In his profound Asiatic studies of the religious and social customs of the Far East, Sir Alfred Lyall (who seems to have studied on the spot the actual formation of tribes and clans in certain parts of India)

gods who figure in mythologies and dynasties are seen to be inventors or importers of foreign inventions. They are, in a word, initiators. Thanks to the deep and intense stupor caused by their first miracles, each of their assertions and commands opened out an immense vent to the vast, vague, and impotent aspirations, to the blind and futile desires for faith and activity, which they had called into being.

At present, when we speak of obedience, we mean a conscious and voluntary act. But primitive obedience was far different. When the subject weeps at the bidding of the hypnotist, it is not the ego only, but the whole organism, that obeys. The obedience of crowds and armies to their demagogues and captains is, at times, almost equally strange. And so is their credulity. "It is a curious sight," says M Charles Richet, "to see a somnambulist make gestures of distaste and nausea and experience real suffocation when an empty bottle is put under his nose and he is told that it contains ammonia, or, on the other hand, to see him inhale ammonia without showing the least discomfort when he is told that it is pure water" We have a strange analogy in the artificial, absurd, and extravagant, but none the less deep, active, and obstinate, beliefs of ancient peoples, of those, indeed, who were the freest and the most cultivated of all the ancients; and this, too, long after

---

attributes a preponderating influence in primitive societies to the individual action of men of note "To borrow Carlyle's words," he says, "the perplexed jungle of primitive society springs out of many roots, but the hero is the tap-root from which in a great degree all the rest were nourished and grown. In Europe, where the landmarks of nationalities are fixed, and the fabric of civilisation firmly entrenched, people are often inclined to treat as legendary the enormous part in the foundation of their race or institutions attributed by primitive races to their heroic ancestor. Yet it may be difficult to overrate the impression which must have been produced by daring and successful exploits upon the primitive world, where the free impulsive play of a great man's forces is little controlled by artificial barriers. . . In such times, whether a group which is formed upon the open surface of society shall spread out into a clan or tribe, or break up prematurely, seems to depend very much upon the strength and energy of its founder" [*Asiatic Studies, Religious and Social*, p 168, Sir Alfred C. Lyall, K. C B., C. I. E., second edition, London, 1884—*Tr*].

their first phase of autocratic theocracy had passed away.
Were not the most abominable monstrosities, Greek love, for
example, deemed worthy of the songs of Anacreon and
Theocritus and of the philosophy of Plato? Were not serpents, cats, bulls, and cows worshipped by prostrate populations? Were not mysteries, metempsychoses, dogmas in absolute contradiction to the direct evidence of the senses, not
to speak of such absurdities as the arts of augury, astrology,
and sorcery, unanimously believed in? On the other hand,
were not the most natural sentiments repressed with horror,
paternal love, for example, in communities where the uncle
took precedence over the father, or sexual jealousy among
tribes whose wives were owned in common? Has not the
most impressive beauty of nature or art been overlooked or
condemned, and this even in modern times, because it vio-
lated the taste of the period? The attitude of the Romans towards the picturesqueness of the Alps or Pyrenees, or that
of our own seventeenth and eighteenth centuries towards
the masterpieces of Shakespeare or the art of Holland, is an
example.   In short, are not the clearest experiences and
observations controverted and the most palpable truths arraigned, whenever they come into opposition with the traditional ideas that are the antique offspring of prestige and
faith?

Civilised peoples flatter themselves with thinking that
they have escaped from this *dogmatic slumber*. Their
error can be explained. The oftener a person has been
magnetised, the easier and quicker is it for him to be re-
magnetised. This fact shows us how it is that societies
come to imitate one another with increasing ease and rapidity. As they become civilised and, consequently, more
and more imitative, they also become less and less aware
that they are imitating. In this particular, mankind is like
the individual man. A child is, unquestionably, a true somnambulist; the older it grows, the more complex its dream
becomes, until it thinks that, because of this very complexity, it has been awakened. But the child errs. When a
ten- or twelve-year-old boy leaves his family for school, he

seems to himself to have become demagnetised, to have been aroused from his dream of parental respect and admiration. Whereas, in reality, he becomes still more prone to admiration and imitation in his submission to the ascendency of one of his masters or, better still, of some prestigeful classmate. The alleged awakening is only a change or piling up of slumbers. In the substitution of *fashion-magnetisation* for *custom-magnetisation,* the usual symptom of incipient social revolution, we have an analogous, although magnified, phenomenon.

We should also observe, however, that as the suggestions of example become more numerous and diversified around an individual, each of them loses in intensity, and the individual becomes freer to determine his choice according to the preference of his own character, on the one hand, and on the other, according to certain logical laws which I will discuss elsewhere. Thus it is certain that the progress of civilisation renders subjection to imitation at once more *personal* and more *rational.* We are just as much enslaved as our ancestors by the examples of our environment, but we make a better use of them through our more logical and more individual choice, one adapted to our own ends and to our particular nature. And yet, as we shall see, this does not keep extra-logical and prestigeful influences from always playing a very considerable part.

This part is remarkably potent and interesting in the case of an individual who suddenly passes from an impoverished environment to one rich in all kinds of suggestions. Then there is no need of such a brilliant and striking object as personal glory or genius to bewitch him and to put him to sleep. The college freshman, the Japanese traveller in Europe, the countryman in Paris, are as stupefied as if they were in a state of catalepsy. Their attention is so bent upon everything they see and hear, especially upon the actions of the human beings around them, that it is absolutely withdrawn from everything they have previously seen and heard, or even thought of or done. It is not that their memory is destroyed, *for it has never been as alert* or as quick to re-

spond to the slightest word which recalls to them, with a
wealth of hallucinating detail, their distant country, their
home, or their previous existence. But memory becomes
absolutely paralysed; all its own spontaneity is lost In
this singular condition of intensely concentrated attention,
of passive and vivid imagination, these stupefied and fevered
beings inevitably yield themselves to the magical *charm* of
their new environment. They believe everything that they
see, and they continue in this state for a long time. It is
always more fatiguing to think for one's self than to think
through the minds of others. Besides, whenever a man
lives in an animated environment, in a highly strung and
diversified society which is continually supplying him with
fresh sights, with new books and music and with constantly
renewed conversation, he gradually refrains from all intellectual effort; his mind, growing more and more stulti-
fied and, at the same time, more and more excited, becomes, as I have said, somnambulistic. Such a state of
mind is characteristic of many city dwellers. The noise
and movement of the streets, the display of shop-windows,
and the wild and unbridled rush of existence affect them
like magnetic passes. Now, is not city life a concentrated
and exaggerated type of social life?

If these persons end by becoming *examples* themselves,
this also is due to imitation. Suppose a somnambulist
should imitate his medium to the point of becoming a medium himself and magnetising a third person, who, in turn,
would imitate him, and so on, indefinitely. Is not social
life this very thing? Terraces of consecutive and connected magnetisations are the rule; the mutual magnetisation of which I spoke above is exceptional. In general, a
naturally prestigeful man will stimulate thousands of people
to copy him in every particular, even in that of his prestige,
thereby enabling them to influence, in turn, millions of inferior men. It is only at rare moments, after the movement
down the scale is spent, that an inverse movement takes
place and that, in a period of democracy, millions of men
collectively fascinate and tyrannise over their quondam

mediums. If every society stands forth as a hierarchy, it is because every society reveals the terracing of which I have just spoken and to which, *in order to be stable,* its hierarchy must correspond.

Besides, social somnambulism, as I have said already, is not brought about through fear or the power of conquest, but through admiration and a sense of brilliant and irksome superiority. And so it sometimes happens that the conqueror is magnetised by the conquered. Just as a savage chief or a social upstart is all eyes and ears, is *charmed* or *intimidated* in spite of his pride, in the midst of a great city, or in a fashionable drawing room. But he sees and hears only what astonishes him and holds him captive; for a singular mixture of anæsthesia and hyperæsthesia of the senses is the dominant characteristic of somnambulists. Consequently, they copy all the usages, the language, the accent, etc., of their new environment. The Germans did this in the Roman world. They forgot German and spoke Latin. They composed hexameters. They bathed in marble baths. They dubbed themselves patricians. The Romans themselves did this in the Athens which they had conquered. The Hyksos conquerors of Egypt were subjugated by its civilisation.

But is there any need to ransack history for examples? Let us look nearer home. The kind of momentary paralysis of mind, tongue, and arm, the profound agitation of the whole being and the lack of self-possession which is called *intimidation,* deserves special study. The intimidated man loses, under the gaze of another person, his self-possession and is wont to become manageable and malleable by others. He feels this and struggles against it, but his only success lies in bringing himself to an awkward standstill; he is still strong enough to neutralise any external impetus, but not strong enough to regain the mastery of his own power of motion. It will be admitted, perhaps, that this singular state, a state that we have all more or less passed through at a certain age, has a great many points in common with somnambulism. But when timidity is routed, when one is put

at his ease, as they say, has demagnetisation set in? Far
from that, to be put at one's ease in a given society is to
adopt its manners and fashions, to speak its dialect, to copy
its gestures, in short, to finally abandon one's self unresist-
ingly to the many surrounding currents of subtle influences
against which one first struggled in vain, and to abandon
one's self so completely that all consciousness of this
self-abandonment is lost. Timidity is a conscious and, consequently, an incomplete magnetisation. It may be compared to that drowsy state which precedes the profound
slumber in which the somnambulist moves and speaks. It
is a *nascent* social *state* which accompanies every transition from one society to another, or from the limits of the
family to a wider social life.

It is for this reason, perhaps, that so-called rough dia-
monds, people who strongly rebel against assimilation and
who are really unsociable, remain timid during their whole
life. They are but partially subject to somnambulism. On
the other hand, are not people who never feel awkward
and embarrassed, who never experience any real timidity
upon entering a drawing room or a lecture hall, or any corresponding stupor in taking up a science or art for the first
time (for the trouble produced by entrance into a new calling whose difficulties frighten one and whose prescribed
methods do violence to one's old habits, may be perfectly
well compared to intimidation), are not such people sociable
in the highest degree? Are they not excellent copyists, *i. e.,*
devoid of any particular avocation or any controlling
ideas, and do they not possess the eminently Chinese or
Japanese faculty of speedily adapting themselves to their
environment? In their readiness to fall asleep, are they
not somnambulists of the first order? Intimidation plays
an immense part in society under the name of Respect.
Everyone will acknowledge this, and, although the part is
sometimes misinterpreted, it is never in the least exaggerated. Respect is neither unmixed fear nor unmixed love,
nor is it merely the combination of the two, although it is a
fear which is beloved by him who entertains it. Respect is,

primarily, the impression of an example by one person upon another who is psychologically *polarised*. Of course we must distinguish the respect of which we are conscious from that which we dissemble to ourselves under an assumed contempt. But taking this distinction into account, it is evident that whomsoever we imitate we respect, and that whomsoever we respect we imitate or tend to imitate. There is no surer sign of a displacement of social authority than deviations in the current of these examples. The man or the woman of the world who reflects the slang or undress of the labourer or the intonation of the actress, has more respect and deference for the person copied than he or she is himself or herself aware. Now what society would last for a single day without the general and continuous circulation of both the above forms of respect?

But I must not dwell any longer upon the above comparison. At any rate, I hope that I have at least made my reader feel that to thoroughly understand the essential social fact, as I perceive it, knowledge of the infinitely subtle facts of mind is necessary, and that the roots of even what seems to be the simplest and most superficial kind of sociology strike far down into the depths of the most inward and hidden parts of psychology and physiology. *Society is imitation and imitation is a kind of somnambulism.* This is the epitome of this chapter. As for the second part of the proposition, I beg the reader's indulgence for any exaggeration I may have been guilty of. I must also remove a possible objection. It may be urged that submission to some ascendency does not always mean following the example of the person whom we trust and obey. But does not belief in anyone always mean belief in that which he believes or seems to believe? Does not obedience to someone mean that we will that which he wills or seems to will? *Inventions are not made to order,* nor are discoveries undertaken as a result of persuasive suggestion. Consequently, to be credulous and docile, and to be so as pre-eminently as the somnambulist and the social man, is to be, primarily, imitative. To innovate, to discover, to awake for an instant from his dream of home and country, the individual must escape, for the time being, from his social surroundings. Such unusual audacity makes him super-social rather than social.

One word more. We have just seen that memory as well as habit, or muscular memory, as I have already called it, is very keen in the case of somnambulists or quasi-somnambulists, while their credulity and docility are extreme. In other words their *imitation of self* (memory and habit are, in fact, nothing more than this) is as remarkable as their imitation of others. Is there no connection between these two facts? "It cannot be too clearly apprehended," Maudsley says emphatically, "that there is a sort of innate tendency to mimicry in the nervous system." [1] If this tendency is inherent in the final nerve elements, we may be permitted to conjecture that the relations between the cells within the same brain have some analogy to the singular relation between two brains, one of which fascinates the other, and that this relation consists of a special polarisation in the latter of the belief and desire which are stored up in each of its elements. In this way, perhaps, certain curious facts might be explained, the fact, for example, that in dreams there is a spontaneous arrangement of images which combine together according to some inward logic, and which are evidently under the control of one of them which imposes itself upon the others, and gives them their tone through the superiority, undoubtedly, of the nervous element in which it was contained and from which it issued. [2]

---

[1] [*Mental Pathology,* p. 68 —*Tr.*]

[2] This view agrees with the master thought developed by M. Paulhan in his profoundly thoughtful work upon mental activity. (Alcan, 1889.)

CHAPTER IV

ARCHÆOLOGY AND STATISTICS

WHAT is history? This is the first question which presents itself to us. The most natural way for us to answer it and, at the same time, formulate the laws of imitation, is by turning our attention to two very distinct lines of research which have been highly honoured in recent days, the study of archæology and the study of statistics. I will show that as these studies have grown in value and fruitfulness, a point of view similar to mine in the matter of social phenomena has been unconsciously adopted in them and that, in this respect, the general conclusions and salient points of these two sciences, or, rather, of these two very dissimilar methods, are seen to be remarkably similar. Let us first consider the subject of archæology.

I

When human skulls and implements of various kinds happen to be found in some Gallo-Roman tomb, or in some cave belonging to the stone age, the archæologist keeps the implements for himself and hands over the skulls to the anthropologist. The anthropologist studies races, the archæologist, civilisations. It is useless for them to lock arms with each other; they are, nevertheless, radically unlike, as much as a horizontal line is unlike, even at the point of intersection, the vertical line which may be erected upon it. The anthropologist utterly ignores the biography of the Cro-Magnon or Neanderthal man whom he is examining. He cares nothing at all for this; his one aim is to distinguish the same racial character in one skull or skeleton after another. Although this very racial character has been reproduced and multiplied through heredity from some individual peculiarity, still it is impossible for the anthropologist to attempt to trace this back. The archæologist likewise ignores, three-quarters of the time, the names of the dead whose ashes remain to be deciphered like an enigma and looks for and sees in them only the artistic or industrial process, or the characteristic desires and beliefs, or the rites, dogmas, words, and grammatical forms that are revealed by the contents of their tombs. And yet all these things were transmitted and propagated by imitation from some single and almost always unknown inventor for whose radiant invention every one of the anonymous unearthed objects was but an ephemeral vehicle, a mere place for growth.

The deeper the past in which the archæologist buries himself the more he loses sight of personalities. Even manuscripts begin to be scarce prior to the twelfth century. Besides, manuscripts, which are, for the most part, nothing but official records, interest him primarily because of their impersonal character. Then, nothing but buildings or their ruins and, finally, nothing but a few remains of pottery and bronze, of flint weapons and implements, survive for archæological guess-work. And what a wonderful treasure of facts and inferences, of invaluable information, has been extracted in this humble shape from the earth's entrails wherever the picks of modern excavators have penetrated, in Italy, in Greece, in Egypt, in Asia Minor, in Mesopotamia, in America! There was a time when archæology, like numismatics, was only the servant of pragmatic history, when the only merit that would have been recognised in the present work of the Egyptologists was its confirmation of the fragments of Manetho. At present, however, the rôles are inverted. Historians are nothing more than subordinate guides, auxiliaries of those excavators who, revealing to us the things about which the former are silent, give us the details, so to speak, of the fauna and flora, of the hidden wealth of life and of the harmonious regularities of those lands that are so picturesquely described by historic landscapists. Through the archæologists we know what particular group of ideas, of professional or hieratic secrets, of peculiar desires, constituted the individual whom the annalists call a Roman or an Egyptian or a Persian. Below the surface, in some way, of the violent and so-called culminating events that are spoken of as conquests, invasions, or revolutions, the archæologists show us the daily and indefinite drift and piling up of the sediments of true history, the stratifications of successive and contagion-spread discoveries.

The archæological point of view, therefore, is the best from which to see that violent events which are in themselves dissimilar, and whose series are as irregular as mountain ridges, have merely served to aid or hinder, to restrict or enlarge, the quiet and even spread of various given ideas of genius in certain more or less badly defined territories. And just as Thucydides, Herodotus, and Livy become mere cicerones, faithful or false as it happens, to the antiquarians, so the heroes of the historians, their generals, statesmen, and legislators, may pass for the unconscious and, at times, refractory servants of the numberless and obscure inventors of bronze, of the art of weaving or writing, of oar and sail and plough, whose very date and birthplace cost the antiquarians even more effort to discover and locate than their names. Of course there is no doubt but that great warriors and statesmen have themselves had new and brilliant ideas, true inventions in the big sense of the word, but their inventions were *bound not to be imitated*.[1] They may be military plans or parliamentary measures, laws, decrees, or political revolutions, but they take no place in history unless they promote or retard other kinds of inventions which are already known and which are destined to be peacefully imitated. History would pay no more attention to the manœuvres at Marathon, at Arabela, or at Austerlitz than to so many skilful games of chess, were it

---

[1] If they are imitated, it is against the wish of their authors, as was the case, for example, with the turning movement of Ulm which the Germans copied so skilfully against the nephew of Napoleon.

not for the well-known influence which these victories had respectively over the development of the arts of Greece in Asia, and of French institutions in Europe.

History, as it is commonly understood, is, in short, only the co-operation or opposition of certain *non-imitable* inventions of merely temporary usefulness with or to a number of useful and imitable inventions. As for the *direct* causation of the latter by the former, it would be as impossible as the creation of a lizard or the development of the wing of a condor through an upheaval of the Andes or Pyrenees. It is true that the indirect action of the former is considerable, for, as an invention is, after all, merely the singular intersection of heterogeneous imitations in one brain,—an exceptional brain, to be sure.—everything that opens fresh outlets to the radiations of different imitations tends to multiply the chances of such intersections.[1]

Here I shall open a parenthesis in order to anticipate an objection. It may be urged that I am exaggerating the social importance both of the sheepish tendency to imitate and of the inventive imagination of mankind. Man does not invent for the pleasure of inventing, but for the satisfaction of some want that he experiences. Genius takes its own time to unfold. Consequently, it is the series of wants, not the series of inventions, which is the pre-eminently notable thing; and civilisation consists as much in the gradual multiplication and replacing of wants as in the gradual accumulation and substitution of arts and industries. On the other hand, man does not always imitate for the pleasure of imitating either his ancestors or his foreign contemporaries. Out of all those inventions, discoveries, or theories which solicit his imitation or adhesion (his intellectual imitation), he for the most part, or more and more, imitates and adopts only those which seem to him to

---

[1] As an example of the indirect influence of imitation upon invention, we know that as a result of the growing fashion in France of taking water-cures, the advantage (?) of discovering new mineral springs was realised, and between the years 1838 and 1863 the waters of two hundred and thirty-four new springs were discovered or collected.

be useful and true. It is, then, a search for utility and
truth, not a tendency towards imitation, which characterises
the social man, and it were much better to define civilisation
as the growing utilisation or verification of arts or ideas
than as the growing assimilation of muscular and cerebral
activities.

I answer by suggesting in the first place that, since the
desire for cannot precede the notion of an object, no social
desire can be prior to the invention by which the conception
of the commodity, or article, or service able to satisfy it,
was made possible. It is true that the invention was the response to a vague desire, that, for example, the idea of the
electric telegraph solved the long-standing problem of a more
rapid epistolary form of communication. But it is in becoming specific in this way that such a desire is spread and
strengthened, that it is born into the social world. Besides,
was it not developed itself by some past, or series of past, inventions, as in the given example, by the establishment of a
postal service and, later, of the aërial telegraph? Even physical needs cannot become social forces unless, as I have already had occasion to observe, they are made specific in an
analogous way. It is only too clear that the desire to smoke,
to drink tea or coffee, etc., did not appear until after the discovery of tea, or coffee, or tobacco. Here is another example among a thousand. " Clothing does not result from
modesty," M. Wiener justly observes (*Le Pérou*); " on
the contrary, modesty appears as a result of clothing, that is
to say, the clothing which conceals any part of the human
body makes the nakedness of the part which we are accustomed to see covered, appear indecent." In other words,
the desire to be clothed, in so far as it is a social desire, is
due to the discovery of clothing, of certain kinds of clothes.
Inventions are far from being, then, the simple effects of
social necessities; they are their causes. Nor do I think
that I have over-emphasised them. Inventors may, at given
times, direct their imagination in line with the vague desires
of the public, but we must not forget, I repeat, that these
popular desires have themselves been aroused by previous

inventors who were in turn indirectly influenced by still older inventors. This goes on until we finally find, on the one hand, as the primordial and necessary basis of every society and civilisation, certain simple, although very arduous, inspirations which are due, undoubtedly, to a very small number of innate and purely vital wants; and, on the other hand, certain still more important chance discoveries which were made for the mere pleasure of discovery, and which were nothing more than the play of a naturally creative imagination. How many languages, religions, and poems, how many industries even, have begun in this way!

So much for invention. The same answer may be made in regard to imitation. It is true that we do not do everything that we do through routine or fashion and that we do not believe everything that we believe through prejudice or on authority—although popular credulity, docility, and passivity are immensely greater than is usually admitted. But even when imitation is voluntary and deliberate, even when we do and believe that which appears to be the most useful and the most believable thing, our acts and thoughts are predetermined. Our acts are what they are because they are the fittest to satisfy and develop the wants which previous imitation of other inventions had first seeded in us; our thoughts, because they were the most consistent with the knowledge acquired by us of other thoughts which were themselves acquired because they were confirmed by other preliminary ideas or by visual, tactile, and other kinds of impressions which we got by renewing for ourselves certain scientific experiences or observations, after the example of those who first undertook them.¹ Thus imitations, like in-

---

¹ The character of our pre-existing wants and purposes does not alone influence or determine us in choosing the thoughts and acts, the creeds and careers, which we are always copying from others. The laws of respective countries, the prohibition of a certain industry, for example, or free trade, or obligatory instruction in a given branch of knowledge, are also factors. But laws act upon imitation in the same way, at bottom, as wants and purposes. They both rule over us, and the only difference in their rule is that the one is an outward master and the other an inward tyrant. Moreover, laws are only the expres-

ventions, are seen to be linked together one after the other, in mutual if not in self dependence. If we follow back this second chain as we did the first, we come, logically, at last, to *self-originating* imitation, so to speak, to the mental state of primitive savages who, like children, imitate for the mere pleasure of imitating. This motive determines most of their acts, all of the acts, in fact, which belong to their social life. And so I have not overrated the importance of imitation, either.

II

In brief, the picture of primitive society which rises before me is that of a feeble, wayward imagination scattered here and there in the midst of a vast passive *imitativeness* which receives and perpetuates all its vagaries as the water of a lake circles out under the stroke of a bird's wing on its surface. It seems to me that archæological researches fully confirm this view. Sumner Maine says in his *Early History of Institutions*: "Mr. Taylor has justly observed the true lesson of the new science of Comparative Mythology is the barrenness in primitive times of the mental faculty which we most associate with mental fertility, the Imagination. Comparative jurisprudence as might be expected from the natural stability of law and custom yet more strongly suggests the same inference."[1] This observation has only to be generalised. What is simpler, for example, than to represent Fortune with a horn of plenty, or Venus holding an apple in her hand? Yet Pausanias takes the trouble to tell us that the former emblem was originally conceived of by Bupalus, one of the oldest sculptors of Greece, and the latter, by Canachus, a sculptor of Ægina.

sion of the ruling wants and purposes of the governing class at a given time, and these wants and purposes may be always explained in the way that I have already indicated

[1] [*Lectures on the Early History of Institutions,* p 225, Sir Henry Sumner Maine, K. C. S. I, LL D, F. R. S, New York, 1875.—*Tr*]

From these insignificant ideas in the minds of these two men are derived, then, the innumerable statues of Fortune and Venus which are characterised by these emblems.

Archæological studies point to another fact which is just as important although it has been less observed. They show that in ancient times man was much less hermetically bound up in his local traditions and customs and was much more *imitative of the outside world* and open to foreign fashions in the matter of trinkets, weapons, and even of institutions and industries, than we have been led to suppose. It is truly surprising to find that at a certain period of antiquity such a useless thing as amber was imported from its original place of deposit on the Baltic to the extremes of southern Europe. The similarity in the decorations of the contemporary tombs of widely separated races is also a surprising fact. " At the same very remote period," writes M. Maury, on the subject of Euganean antiquities (*Journal des savants*, 1882), " the same art, whose productions we are now beginning to recognise, was spread through the littoral provinces of Asia Minor, through the Archipelago, and through Greece. The Etruscans seem to have held a place in this school. Every nation modified its principles according to its own genius " Finally, it is marvellous to find that, even in the most primitive of prehistoric ages, the types of flakes, of drawings, and of bone implements are the same almost all over the globe.[1] It seems as if every well-defined archæological period were distinguished by the preponderating prestige of some particular civilisation which illu-

[1] At first sight the striking similarity of the axes and arrowheads, and the other flint tools and weapons, which were discovered on both the old and the new continent, might seem to be the result of a mere coincidence, which the identity of human wants in war, hunting clothing, etc, would sufficiently explain But we already know the objections which could be raised against this explanation Moreover, we must note the fact that polished axes, arrowheads, and even idols of jade and jadeite, stones that were *absolutely unknown throughout the American continent,* have been found in Mexico Is not this a proof that *during the stone age* the germs of civilisation were carried over from the Old World to the New? The event of such an importation in later periods is doubtful (see M. de Nadaillac, *Amérique préhistorique*, p. 542).

minated and coloured all other rival or subject civilisations somewhat as every palæontological period is the reign of some great animal species, of some mollusk, reptile, or pachydermus.

Archæology can also show us that men have always been much less original than they themselves are pleased to believe. We come to overlook what we no longer look for, and we no longer look for what we have always under our eyes. For this reason, the faces of our fellow countrymen always impress us by the dissimilarity of their distinctive traits. Although they belong to the same race, we ignore their common racial traits. On the other hand, the people we see in our travels, Chinese, Arabians, negroes, all look alike. One might say that the truth lay between these opposite impressions. But in this instance, as in most, the method of averaging is erroneous. For the cause of the illusion which partly blinds the man settled down among his fellow citizens, the film of habit, does not dull the eye of the traveller among strangers. Therefore, the impressions of the latter are likely to be much more exact than those of the former, and they testify to the fact that among individuals of the same race inherited traits of similarity always outnumber traits of dissimilarity.

Well, for a like reason, in turning from the vital to the social world, we are always exclusively impressed, not by the analogies, but by the differences which are, in general, apparent between the pictures and statues and writings of our contemporary painters and sculptors and writers, and between the manners and gestures and witticisms of the friends and acquaintances in our drawing rooms. When, however, we glance over the works of Etruscan art in the Campana Museum, or when we pass for the first time through galleries of Dutch or Venetian or Florentine or Spanish art, containing pictures of the same school or period, or when we examine the mediæval manuscripts in our archives, or when, in a museum of historic art, we view the rifled contents of Egyptian tombs, it seems to us that we are beholding almost indistinguishable copies of a single model and that formerly, in the same country and at the same time, every style of writing, painting, sculpturing, building, every form of social life, in fact, was so much like every other as to be taken for it. This impression cannot be misleading, and it, too, should make us realise, by analogy, that we ourselves are infinitely more imitative than inventive. This is no mean lesson to draw from archæological studies. It is certain that within a century almost all the novelists and artists and, above all, the poets,—most of whom are the apes or rather the *lemurs* of Victor Hugo,—of whose originality we so naively boast, will justly pass for the servile copyists of one another.

In a preceding chapter I tried to prove that all or almost all social resemblances were due to imitation just as all or almost all vital resemblances were caused by heredity. This simple principle has been implicitly and unanimously accepted by modern archæologists as the guiding thread in the very obscure labyrinths of their immense subterraneous excavations, and, from the services which it has already rendered, we may predict those which it will still be called upon to give. Suppose that an ancient Etruscan tomb is discovered? How is its age to be determined? What is the subject of its frescoes? We can solve these problems by noting the slight and sometimes elusive resemblances between its paintings and others of a Greek origin; and in this way we may at once infer that Greece was already imitated by Etruria at the time when the tomb was constructed. It does not occur to us to explain these resemblances as fortuitous coincidences. Imitation is the postulate which serves as a guide in these questions, and which, under wise management, is never misleading. Scholars are, to be sure, too often carried away by the naturalistic prejudices of their times; they do not limit themselves to deducing imitation from facts of resemblance, but infer kinship from them likewise. From the fact, for example, that the vases, *situlæ*, etc., found in the excavations at Este, in Venetia, were curiously like those found at Verona, Belluno, and elsewhere, M. Maury inclines to think that the builders of these different tombs belonged to the same people. Nothing seems to justify this conjecture. To be sure, M. Maury takes the trouble to add that, "*at any rate,* they belonged to populations who observed the same funeral rites and who possessed a common industry"—a somewhat different matter. At any rate, it seems pretty certain that even if the so-called *Etruscans of the North,* of Venetia, had Etruscan blood in their veins, they mixed it very freely with Celtic blood. On this point, M. Maury remarks elsewhere upon the influence which a civilised nation has always exerted, even without conquest, over its barbarous neighbours. "Etruscan works of art were clearly imitated," he says, "by the Gauls of Cisalpine Gaul." And so likeness between artistic products is no proof at all of consanguinity, it points only to a contagion of imitation.

In order to connect the unknown with the known archæologists have been obliged to seek for the secret of past generations in the most remote and, to the lay eye, imperceptible analogies in the matter of form, style, situation, language, legend, dress, etc.; thereby training themselves to discover the unexpected everywhere. Some of these unexpected things are based on fact; others, on different degrees of likelihood according to a very extensive scale of probability. In this way archæologists have contributed in a wonderful degree to deepening and widening the domain of human *imitativeness* and to almost entirely reducing the civilisation of every people, even that which at first may seem to be the most original, into a combination of imitations of other peoples. They know that Arabian art, in spite of its distinctive features, is merely the fusion of Persian with Greek art, that Greek art borrowed certain processes from Egyptian and perhaps from other sources, and that Egyptian art was formed from or amplified by many successive Asiatic and even African contributions. There is no assignable limit to this archæological decomposition of civilisations; there is no social molecule which their chemistry has not a fair hope of resolving into its constituent atoms. Meanwhile, their labours have reduced the number of still indecomposable centres of civilisation to three or four, in the Old World, and to one or two in the New. In the latter, strange to say, they are all situated on plateaux (Mexico and Peru), and in the former, at the mouth or on the banks of great rivers (the Nile, the Euphrates, the Ganges, and the rivers of China), although great water courses, as M. de Candolle justly remarks, are neither more uncommon nor more unhealthy in America than in Europe and Asia, and although habitable plateaux are not lacking in these latter parts of the world. The arbitrary factor which influences the choice of the first makers or importers of civilisation in the pitching of their tents shows itself here. And, perhaps, the civilisations that come from them will bear to the end of time the ineffaceable mark of their primordial caprice!

Thanks to the archæologists we learn where and when a new discovery first appeared, how far and how long it has spread, and by what roads it has travelled from the place of its origin to its adopted country. Although they may not take us back to the first furnace which turned out bronze or iron, they do take us back to the first country and century in which the pointed arch, printing, and oil-painting, and, still much more anciently, the orders of Greek architecture, the Phœnician alphabet, etc., displayed themselves to a justly marvelling world. They devote all their curiosity[1] and activity to following up a given invention through its manifold disguises and modifications, to recognising the atrium in the cloister, the prætorium of the Roman magistrate in the Roman church, the Etruscan bench in the curule-chair, or to tracing out the boundaries of the region to which an invention has spread through gradual

---

[1] I know that the curiosity of the antiquarian is often vain and puerile. Even the greatest among them, men like Schliemann, seem more bent upon discovering something relating to a celebrated individual, to a Hector or Priam or Agamemnon, than upon following out the course of the principal inventions of the past. But the personal aim and motive of the workers is one thing, the net gain and specific fruit of their work, another.

self-propagation and beyond which, for yet to be discovered reasons (in my opinion they are always the competition of rival inventions), it has been unable to pass, or to studying the results of the intersection of different inventions which have spread so widely that they have finally come together in one imaginative brain.

In short, these scholars are forced, perhaps unconsciously, into surveying the social life of the past from a point of view which is continually approximating that which I claim should be adopted knowingly and willingly by the sociologist. I refer here to the pure sociologist, who, through a necessary although artificial abstraction, is distinguished from the naturalist. In distinction to historians who see nothing else in history than the conflicts and competitions of individuals, that is, of the arms and legs as well as of the minds of individuals, and who, in regard to the latter, do not differentiate between ideas and desires of the most diverse origins, confusing those few that are new and personal with a mass of those that are merely copies; in distinction to those poor carvers-up of reality who have been unable to perceive the true dividing line between vital and social facts, the point where they separate without tearing, archæologists stand out as makers of pure sociology, because, as the personality of those they unearth is impenetrable, and only the work of the dead, the vestiges of their archaic wants and ideas, are open to their scrutiny, they hear, in a certain way, like the Wagnerian ideal, the music without seeing the orchestra of the past. In their own eyes, I know, this is a cruel deprivation; but time, in destroying the corpses and blotting out the memories of the painters and writers and modellers whose inscriptions and palimpsests they decipher and whose frescoes and torsos and potsherds they so laboriously interpret, has, nevertheless, rendered them the service of setting free everything that is properly social in human events by eliminating everything that is vital and by casting aside as an impurity the carnal and fragile contents of the glorious form which is truly worthy of resurrection.

To archæologists, then, history becomes both simplified and transfigured. In their eyes it consists merely of the advent and development, of the competitions and conflicts, of original wants and ideas, or, to use a single term, of inventions. Inventions thus become great historic figures and the real agents of human progress. The proof that this idealistic point of view is the just one, lies in its fruitfulness. Through its happy, although, I repeat, involuntary, adoption, do not philologist and mythologist, the modern archæologist, under different names, cut all the Gordian knots and shed light upon all the obscurities of history and, without taking away any of its grace and picturesqueness, bestow upon it the charm of theory? If history is on the way to become a science, is it not due to this point of view?

III

Something is likewise due to the statistician. The statistician, like the archæologist, considers human affairs from an entirely abstract and impersonal standpoint. He pays no attention to individuals, to Peter or Paul; he concerns himself only with their works, or, rather, with those acts of theirs which reveal their wants and ideas, with the act of buying or selling, of manufacturing, of voting, of committing or repressing crime, of suing for judicial separation, and even with the acts of being born, of marrying, of procreating, and of dying. All these individual acts are related on some of their sides to social life, in as much as the spread of certain examples or prejudices seems to aid in raising or lowering the rates of birth and marriage, and to affect the prolificness of marriages and the mortality of infants.

If archæology is the collection and classification of similar products where the highest possible degree of similarity is the most important thing, Statistics is an enumeration of acts which are as much alike as possible. Here the art is in the choice of units; the more alike and equal they are, the better they are. What is the subject of Statistics unless, like that of archæology, it is inventions and the *imitative editions* of inventions? Only, the latter study treats of inventions which are for the most part dead, worn out by their very activity, whereas the former treats of living inventions which are often modern or contemporaneous and which are in actual process of growth and expansion, of arrest or of decay. The one is the palæontology, the other the physiology, of society. While archæology tells us that specimens of Greek pottery were transported in Phœnician vessels at a certain rate of speed to certain places on the shores of the Mediterranean and far beyond, Statistics tells us what islands of Oceanica, how near the North or the South Pole, the English vessels of to-day carry the cotton goods of England and what number of yards they annually export to foreign markets. We must admit, however, that the field of invention seems to belong more especially to archæology, and that of imitation, to Statistics. While the former endeavours to follow out the thread between successive discoveries, the latter excels in estimating their individual expansion. The domain of archæology is the more philosophic, that of Statistics, the more scientific.

To be sure, the methods of these two sciences are precisely opposite to each other, but this is because of the difference in the external conditions of their investigations. Archæology studies the scattered examples of the same art a long time before it is able to hazard a conjecture about the origin or date of the primary process from which it has developed. For example, all the Indo-European languages must be known before they can be related to a perhaps imaginary mother tongue, to Aryac, or to their elder sister, Sanskrit. Archæology laboriously travels back from imitations to their source. The science of statistics, on the other hand, almost always knows the source of the expansions which it is measuring; it goes from causes to effects, from discoveries to their more or less successful development according to given years and countries. By means of its suc-

cessive records, it will tell you that, from the time that the
invention of steam engines began to gradually spread and
strengthen the need for coal throughout France, the output
of French coal increased at a perfectly regular rate and that
from 1759 to 1869 it multiplied sixty-two and one-half
times.   In the same way you may also learn that after the
discovery of beet sugar, or, rather, after the utility of the
discovery was no longer doubted, the manufacture of this
commodity was increased at an equally regular rate from
seven millions of kilograms in 1828 (until then it was almost stationary for the reason implied above) to one hundred and fifty millions of kilograms thirty years later
(Maurice Block).

I have taken the less interesting examples, but do we not
witness by means of even these dry figures the birth and
gradual establishment and progress of a new want or fashion in the community?   In general, there is nothing more
instructive than the chronological tables of statisticians, in
which they show us the increasing rise or fall, year by year,
of some special kind of consumption or production, of some
particular political opinion as it is expressed in the returns
of the ballot box, or of some specific desire for security that
is embodied in fire-insurance premiums, in savings-bank accounts, etc.   These are all, at bottom, representations in the
life of some desire or belief that has been imported and
copied. Every one of these tables, or, rather, every one of the
graphical curves which represent them, is, in a way, an historical monograph.   Taken together they form the best historical narrative that it is possible to have.   Synchronous
tables giving comparisons between provinces or between
countries are generally much less interesting.   Let us contrast, as data for philosophic reflection, a table of criminality in the departments of France with a curve showing
the increase of recidivists during the last fifty years; or,
let us compare the proportion of the urban to the rural
population with that of the urban population year by
year.   We shall see in the latter case, for example, that the
proportion increased from 1851 to 1882 at a regular and

uninterrupted rate from twenty-five to thirty-three per cent, *i. e.,* from a fourth to a third. This fact evidences the action of some definite social cause, whereas a comparison of the proportions between two neighbouring departments, between twenty-eight per cent., for example, in the one, and twenty-six per cent. in the other, is not at all instructive. Similarly, a table giving the civil burials which had occurred in Paris or in the provinces for the last ten years would be significant; just as a comparison of the number of civil burials in France, England, and Germany at any given time would be relatively valueless. I do not mean that it would be useless to state that in 1870 the number of private telegraphic despatches amounted in France to fourteen millions, in Germany to eleven millions, and in England to twenty-four millions. But it is much more instructive to know that in France, especially, there had been an increase from nine thousand despatches in 1851 to four millions in 1859, to ten millions in 1869, and, finally, to fourteen millions in 1879. We cannot follow this varying rate of increase without being reminded of the growth of living things. Why is there this difference between curves and tables? Because, as a rule, although there are many exceptions, curves alone deal with the spread of imitation.

Statistics evidently follows a much more natural course than archæology and, although it supplies the same kind of information, it is much more accurate. Its method is preeminently the sociological method, and it is only because we cannot apply it to extinct societies that we substitute the method of archæology. How many trivial medals and mosaics, how many cinerary urns and funeral inscriptions, we should be willing to exchange for the industrial, the commercial, or even the criminal statistics of the Roman Empire! But in order that Statistics may render all the services which we expect of it and may triumph against the ironical criticism to which it is exposed, it must, like archæology, be conscious both of its true usefulness and of its actual limitations; it must know where it is going and where it should go, nor must it underrate the dangers of the road which will take it to its goal. In itself it is merely a substitute. Psychological statistics which would take note of the individual gains and losses of special beliefs and desires called forth originally by some innovator, would alone, if the thing were practically possible, give the underlying explanation of the figures of ordinary statistics.[1] Ordinarily Statistics does not weigh; it only counts, and in its reckoning it includes nothing but acts, acts of manufacture and consumption, purchases, sales, crimes, prosecutions, etc.   But it is only after it has reached a certain degree of intensity that growing desire becomes action, or that decreasing desire suddenly unmasks itself and gives way to some contrary and hitherto restrained desire. This is also true of belief. In looking over the work of statisticians, it is most important to remember that the things which are under calculation are essentially subjective qualities, desires and beliefs, and that very often the acts which they enumerate, although equal in number, give expression to very different *weights* among these things. At certain times during the last century, church attendance remained numerically the same, whereas religious faith was on the decline. When the prestige of a government has been injured, the devotion of its adherents may be half destroyed although their number may hardly have diminished. This fact is shown by the vote on the very eve of a sudden political downfall. It is a source of delusion to those who are unduly reassured or discouraged by electoral statistics.

Successful imitations are numerous indeed, but how few they are in comparision with those which are still unrealised ojects of desire! So-called popular wishes, the aspirations of a small town, for example, or of a single class, are

---

[1] According to the statistics of railroads, omnibuses, excursion steamers, etc., their receipts diminish regularly every *Friday*. This points to the very widespread, although much weakened, prejudice about the danger of undertaking anything at all on that day of the week If we followed the variations in this periodic diminution from year to year, the gradual decline of the absurd belief in question might be easily calculated.

composed exclusively, at a given moment, of tendencies, which, unfortunately, cannot at the time be realised, to ape in all particulars some richer town or some superior class. This body of simian proclivities constitutes the potential energy of a society. It takes only a commercial treaty, or a new discovery, or a political revolution, events which make certain luxuries and powers, which had before been reserved for the privileged ones of fortune or intellect, accessible to those possessing thinner purses or fewer abilities, to convert it into actual energy. This potential energy, then, is of great importance, and it would be well to bear its fluctuations in mind. And yet ordinary statistics seem to pay no attention to this force. The labour of making an approximate estimate of it would seem ridiculous, although it might be done by many indirect methods and might at times be of advantage to Statistics. In this respect, archæology is superior in the information which it gives us about buried societies; for although it may teach us less about their activities in point of detail and precision, it pictures their aspirations more faithfully. A Pompeiian fresco reveals the psychological condition of a provincial town under the Roman Empire much more clearly than all the statistical volumes of one of the principal places of a French department can tell us about the actual wishes of its inhabitants.

Let me add, that Statistics is of such recent origin that it it has not yet shot out all its branches, whereas its older collaborator has ramified in all directions. There is an archæology of language, comparative philology, which draws up separate *monographs* for us of the life of every root from its accidental origin in the mouth of some ancient speaker through its endless reproductions and multiplications by means of the remarkable uniformity of innumerable generations of men. There is in archæology of religion, comparative mythology, which deals separately with every myth and with its endless imitative editions, just as philology treats every word. There is an archæology of law, of politics, of ethnology, and, finally, of art and indus-

try. They likewise devote a separate treatise to every legal
idea or fiction, to every custom or institution, to every type
or creation of art, to every industrial process, and, in addition, to the power of reproduction by example which is
peculiar to each of these things. And we have a corresponding number of distinct and flourishing sciences. But,
hitherto, in the matter of truly and exclusively sociological
statistics, we have had to be content with statistics of commerce and industry, and with judicial statistics, not to speak
of certain hybrid statistics which straddle both the physiological and the social worlds, statistics of population, of
births, marriages, deaths, medical statistics, etc. In tables of
election figures we have merely the germ of political statistics.[1] As to religious statistics, which should give us a
graphic representation of the relative annual spread of different sects and of the thermometric variations, so to speak,
in the faith of their adherents; as to linguistic statistics,
which should figure for us not only upon the comparative
expansion of different idioms, but upon the vogue or decline,
in each one of them, of every vocable, of every form of
speech, I fear that, if I should say anything more about
these hypothetical sciences, I might bring a smile to the lips
of my readers.

However, I have amply justified the assertion that the
statistician looks at human affairs from the same point of
view as the archæologist and that this point of view coincides with mine. At the risk of distorting it, let me simplify
it in a brief summary before we continue. In the midst of
an incoherent mass of historic facts, a puzzling dream or
nightmare, reason vainly seeks for an order which it does

[1] It may be that universal suffrage is of no value except on one of its
sides, a side hitherto overlooked. It has decided value as *an intermittent study in political statistics,* through which a nation is made conscious of the changes in its desires and opinions in vital matters. To
work under the conditions which are required for the calculation of
probabilities, this study must be based upon very large numbers. Hence
the necessity for extending the franchise as much as possible, and,
especially, of absolutely universalising so-called universal suffrage. (On
this subject, see an article published in my *Études pénales et sociales*).

not find because it refuses to look in the right direction. Sometimes it imagines that this order has been found and, in its conception of history as the fragment of a poem which is unintelligible except in its entirety, it refers us for the solution of the enigma to the moment when the final destinies of humanity shall have been fulfilled and its most hidden origins absolutely revealed. We may as well repeat the famous phrase: *Ignorabimus.* But if we look beneath the names and dates of history, beneath its battles and revolutions, what do we see? We see specific desires that have been excited or sharpened by certain inventions or practical initiatives, each of which appears at a certain point from which, like a luminous body, it shoots out incessant radiations which harmoniously intersect with thousands of analogous vibrations in whose multiplicity there is an entire lack of confusion. We also see specific beliefs that have been produced by certain discoveries or hypotheses that also radiate at a variable rate and within variable limits. The order in which these inventions or discoveries appear and are developed is, in a large measure, merely capricious and accidental; but, at length, through an evitable elimination of those which are contrary to one another (*i. e.,* of those which more or less *contradict* one another through some of their implicit propositions), the simultaneous group which they form becomes harmonious and coherent. Viewed thus as an expansion of waves issuing from distinct centres and as a logical arrangement of these centres and of their circles of vibration, a nation, a city, the most humble episode in the so-called poem of history, becomes a living and individual whole, a fine spectacle for the contemplation of the philosopher.

IV

If this point of view is correct, if it is really the fittest from which to elucidate social events on their regular, numerable, and measurable sides, it follows that Statistics should adopt it, not partially and unconsciously, but knowingly and unreservedly, and thus, like archæology, be spared many fruitless investigations and tribulations. I will enumerate the principal consequences that would result from this. In the first place, sociological Statistics, having acquired a touchstone for the knowledge of what did and what did not belong to it, and having become convinced that the immense field of human imitation, and only that field, was its exclusive possession, would leave to naturalists the care of tabulating statistics so purely anthropological in their results as, for example, the statistics of exemption from military service in the different departments of France, or the task of constructing tables of mortality (I do not include tables of birth rates, for, in this case, example is a powerful factor in restraining or stimulating racial fecundity). This is pure biology, just as much as the use of M. Marey's graphical method, or as the observation of disease through the myograph and sphgymograph and pneumograph, mechanical statisticians, so to speak, of contractions and pulsations and respiratory movements.

In the second place, the sociological statistician would never forget that his proper task was the measurement of specific beliefs and desires and the use of the most direct methods to grasp these elusive quantities, and that an enumeration of acts which *resembled each other* as much as possible (a condition which is badly fulfilled by criminal statistics among others), and, failing this, an enumeration of like products, of articles of commerce, for example, should always relate to the following, or, rather, to the two following ends: (1) through the tabulation of acts or products to trace out the curve of the successive increases, standstills, or decreases in every new or old want and in every new or old idea, as it spreads out and consolidates itself or as it is crushed back and uprooted; (2) through a skilful comparision between series that have been obtained in this way, and through emphasising their concomitant variations, to denote the various aids and hindrances which these different imitative propagations or consolidations of wants and ideas lend or oppose to one another (according to the varying degrees in which the more or less numerous and implicit propositions of which they always consist, more or less endorse or contradict one another). Nor should the sociological statistician neglect the influence, in these matters, of sex, age, temperament, climate, and seasons, natural causes whose force is measured, at any rate when it exists, by physical or biological statistics.

In other words, sociological statistics have: (1) to determine the imitative power which inheres in every invention at any given time and place; (2) to demonstrate the beneficial or harmful effects which result from the imitation of given inventions and, consequently, to influence those who are acquainted with such numerical results, in their tendencies towards following or disregarding the examples in question. In brief, the entire object of this kind of research is the knowledge and control of imitations. Medical statistics may be cited to show how the latter aim has been reached. Medical statistics, as a matter of fact, are related to social science in as much as they compare the proportion, in the case of every disease, of sufferers who are cured by the use of the different methods and remedies of ancient or recent discovery. In this way it has contributed to the spread of vaccination, of the treatment of the itch by parasiticides, etc. Statistics which show that crime, suicide, and mental derangements are greatly increased through residence in cities would tend to moderate, very feebly to be sure, the great current of imitation which carries the country population to the cities. M. Bertillon assures us that even statistics of marriage would encourage us to make an even greater use than we do of that very ancient invention of our forefathers,—a more original invention, let me say, parenthetically, than it may seem,—in showing us the diminished mortality of married men in comparision with bachelors of a corresponding age. But I must not linger on this delicate subject.

The second of the two problems which I have just noted and which seem to me to impose themselves upon the statistician, cannot be solved before the first. It is perhaps well to note this fact. Are we not putting the cart before the horse when we try to calculate, as we often do, the influence of certain punishments, for example, or religious beliefs or of a certain kind of education upon criminal tendencies before we have measured the force of these tendencies in free play, in the days of mob rule, when the populations are uncontrolled by police or priest or teacher, and turn to arson, murder, and pillage, deeds which are at once imitated from one end of a country to the other?

The preliminary operation, then, would be the preparation of a table of our principal innate or gradually acquired desires, beginning with the social desire to marry or have children, and of our principal old or new beliefs; or, which is one and the same thing, of certain *families of acts,* belonging to a single type, and expressing, with more or less exactness, its intrinsic powers. In this connection, commercial and industrial statistics, statistics that become so interesting from the above standpoint, are of especial value. Does not every article which is made or sold, correspond, in fact, to some special desire or idea? Does not the progress of its sale and manufacture at a given time and place express its motor power, *i. e.,* its rate of propagation, as well as its *mass,* as it were, *i. e.,* its importance? Statistics of commerce and industry are, then, the main foundation of all other statistics. Better still, if the thing were practicable, would be the application, on a larger scale, to the living, of the method of investigation which archæology uses in relation to the dead. I mean a precise and complete house-to-house inventory of all the furniture in a given country and the annual numerical variations in all of its different kinds of furniture. This would give us an excellent photograph of our social condition; it would be somewhat analogous to the admirable pictures of extinct civilisations which the delvers into the past have made in their careful inventories of the contents of the tombs, the houses of the dead, of Egypt, Italy, Asia Minor, and America.

But in the absence of such an inquisitorial census as I have in mind and of the glass houses which it presupposes, complete and systematic statistics of commerce and industry, and, particularly, statistics of publications showing us the relative changes in the annual publication of different kinds of books, suffice to give us the needed data.   Theoretically, judicial statistics take a second place, and it must be admitted that, although in one way they are more profoundly interesting, in another, they are inferior.   Their units lack similarity.   If I am told that during the current year a certain furnace has turned out one million steel rails or that a given manufactory is in receipt of ten thousand bales of cotton, I have to deal with like units representing like wants.   But it would be idle to divide thefts, for example, or distraints into classes and sub-classes; we should never succeed in keeping distinct acts which are quite dissimilar, inspired as they are by different wants and ideas, proceeding from different origins and belonging, in this way, to many different classes of activity.   The most one could do would be to make a separate column for the assassinations of women by mutilation or poisonings by strychnine or other offences of recent contrivance which really fall into one group and constitute certain characteristic criminal *fashions*.   Felonies and misdemeanours should properly be classified according to their methods of execution.   Then the empire of imitation in such matters could be seen.   It would be necessary to descend to details.   If crimes could be classified according to the nature of the prize at stake, or of the hardship eliminated, we should have a different and yet a natural kind of classification which would reproduce under a new form a classification of the industrial articles or services whose purchase procures for honest people corresponding satisfactions.

V

When the field of sociological statistics has been clearly defined, when the curves relating to the propagation, that is to say, to the consolidation as well, of every special want and opinion, for a certain number of years and over a certain stretch of country, have been plainly traced, the interpretation of these hieroglyphic curves, curves that are at times as strange and picturesque as mountain profiles, more often as sinuous and graceful as living forms, has still to be made. I am very much mistaken if our point of view will not prove very helpful here. The lines in question are always ascending or horizontal or descending, or, if they are irregular, they can always be decomposed in the same way into three kinds of linear elements, into inclines, plateaux, and declines. According to Quetelet and his school, the plateaux would belong pre-eminently to the statistician; their discovery should be his finest triumph and the constant object of his ambition. According to this view, the most fitting foundation for a *social physics* would be the uniform reproduction, during a considerable period, of the same number, not only of births and marriages, but also of crimes and litigations. Hence the error (it no longer exists, to be sure, thanks, especially, to recent official statistics concerning the progressive criminality of the last half-century), of thinking that the latter figures have, in reality, been uniformly reproduced. But if the reader has taken the trouble to follow me, he will realise that, without detracting at all from the importance of the horizontal lines, the ascending lines, indicating as they do the regular spread of some kind of imitation, have a far higher theoretical value. The reason is this: The fact that a new taste or idea has taken root in a mind which is constituted in a certain fashion carries with it no reason why this innovation should not spread more or less rapidly through an indefinite number of supposedly like minds in communication with one another. It would spread *instantane-ously* through *all* these minds if they were absolutely alike and if their intercommunication were perfect. It is this ideal, an ideal that is happily beyond realisation, that we are fast approaching. The rapid diffusion of telephones in America from the moment of their first appearance there is one proof in point. This ideal is almost reached already in the matter of legislative innovations. Laws or de-crees which were once slowly and laboriously administered in one province after another are to-day executed from one end to the other of a state the very day of their pas-sage or promulgation. This occurs because in this case there is no hindrance whatsoever. Lack of communication in *social physics* plays the same rôle as lack of elasticity in physics. The one hinders imitation as much as the other, vibration. But the imitative spread of certain well-known inventions (railroads, telegraphs, etc.), tends to diminish, to the benefit of every other invention, this insufficiency of mental contact. As for mental dissimilarity, it likewise tends to be effaced by the spread of wants and ideas which have arisen from past inventions and whose work of as-similation in this way facilitates the propagation of future inventions. I mean of future non-contradictory inventions.

When wants or ideas are once started, they always tend to continue to spread of themselves in a true geometric progression.[1] This is the ideal scheme to which their curve would conform if they could spread without mutual obstruc-tion. But as such checks are, at one time or another, inevita-ble, and as they continue to increase, every one of these social forces must eventually run up against a wall which for the time being is insurmoutable and must through accident, not at all through natural necessity, fall temporarily into that static condition whose meaning statisticians in general

[1] At the same time, they tend to entrench themselves, and their prog-ress extensively hastens their progress intensively. Let us note, incidentally. that there is no past or present enthusiasm or fanaticism of historic importance that cannot be explained through this interaction of the imitation of self with the imitation of others.

appear to so little understand. In this case, as in all others, a static condition means equilibrium, a joint standstill of concurrent forces. I am far from denying the theoretic interest of this state, because these equilibria are equivalent to equations. If, for example, I see that the consumption of coffee or chocolate has ceased to increase in a certain country at a certain date, I know that the strength of the desire there for coffee or chocolate is exactly equal to that of certain rival desires which would have to remain unsatisfied, considering the average fortune, by a more ample satisfaction of the former. The price of every article is determined in this way. But does not every one of the annual figures in progressive series or *slopes* also express an equation between the strength, at a certain date, of the desire in question and the strength of competing desires which hindered its further development at the same date? Moreover, if progression ceased at one point rather than at another, if the plateau is neither higher nor lower than it is, is it not because of a mere accident of history, that is to say, because of the fact that the opposing invention, from which arose the antagonistic wants that barred the progress in question, appeared at one time and place rather than at another, or because of the fact that it actually did appear instead of not appearing at all?

Plateaux, let me add, are always unstable equilibria. After an approximately horizontal position has been sustained for a more or less prolonged time, the curve begins to rise or fall, the series begins to grow or diminish with the appearance of new auxiliary and confirmatory or antagonistic and contradictory inventions. As for diminishing series, they are merely, as we see, the result of successful *growths* which have suppressed some declining public taste or opinion which was once in vogue; they do not deserve the attention of the theorist except as *the other side of the picture* of the growing series which they presuppose.

Let me also state that whenever the statistician is able to lay hold of the origin of an invention and to trace out year by year its numerical career, he shows us curves which, for a certain time, at least, are constantly rising, and rising, too, although for a much shorter period, with *great regularity*. If this perfect regularity fail to continue, it is for reasons which I will shortly indicate. But when very ancient inventions like monogamy or Christian marriage are under consideration, inventions which have had time to pass through their progressive period and which have rounded out, so to speak, their whole sphere of imitation, we ought not to be surprised if Statistics, in its ignorance of their beginnings, represents them by horizontal lines that show scarce a deviation. In view of this, there is nothing astonishing in the fact that the proportion of the annual number of marriages to the total population remains about constant (except in France, I may say, where there is a gradual diminution in this proportion) or even in the fact that the influence of marriage upon crime or suicide is expressed each year by pretty much the same figures. Here we are dealing with ancient institutions which have *passed into the blood of a people* just like the natural factors of climate, seasons, temperament, sex, and age, which influence the mass of human acts with such striking uniformity (which has been greatly exaggerated, however, as it is much more circumscribed than is generally supposed) and with a regularity that is also remarkable, in quite a different way, again, in connection with vital phenomena like death and disease.

And yet, what do we find at the bottom of even these uniform series? Let us see; the digression will be brief. Statistics have shown, for example, that the death rate from one to five years of age is always *three times* greater in the littoral departments of the Mediterranean than in the rest of France, or, at any rate, than in more favoured departments. The explanation of this fact is found, it seems, in the extreme heat of the Provençal climate during summer. This season is as harmful to early infancy (another statistical revelation contrary to current opinion) as winter is to old age. At any rate, climate intervenes in this instance, as a constant and fixed cause. But what is climate but a nominal entity by which a certain group of realities is expressed, to wit: the

sun, a radiation of light which tends towards indefinite expansion in unbounded space and which the earth-obstacle
opposes and checks; the winds, *i. e.*, fragments of more or
less well demarcated cyclones which are continually striving
to swell themselves out and reach over the entire globe and
which are held in check only by mountain chains or counter
whirlwinds; altitude, the effect of up-pushing subterranean
forces which hoped for an endless expansion of the happily
resistant crust of the earth; latitude, the effect of the rotation of the still fluid terrestial globe in its vain efforts at
further contraction; the nature of the earth, that is, of
molecules whose but partially satisfied affinities are engaged
in fruitless activity and whose power of attraction, venting
itself over any distance, strives for impossible contacts;
finally, to a certain extent, the earth's flora, its various vegetal species or varieties, each of which, from discontent with
its own habitat, would cover the entire surface of the globe
except for the restraint imposed upon its avidity by the
rivalry of all the others.

I might just as well say of age, sex, and other influences
of nature what I have said of climate. In short, all external
realities, whether physical or vital, display the same infinite
unrealised and unrealisable ambitions, ambitions that reciprocally stimulate and paralyse one another. The thing
in them that we call the fixity or immutability of the laws of
nature, the supreme reality, is, at bottom, only their inability to travel further in their strictly natural course and realise themselves more fully. Well, this is also true of the fixed
(the momentarily fixed) influences which Statistics discovers
or pretends to discover in the social order; for social realities,
ideas and desires, are not less ambitious than others, and it
is into them that analysis resolves those social entities which
are called customs, institutions, language, legislation, religion, science, industry, and art. The oldest of these things,
those past adolescence, have ceased to grow; but the younger
are still developing. One proof of this, among others, is
seen in the incessant swelling of our budgets. They have
enlarged, and will continue to enlarge until some final catas-

trophe occur which will be, in turn, the point of departure for a renewed increase which will end in the same way, and so on indefinitely. Without going back of 1819, from that date to 1869 the amount of indirect taxes has arisen very regularly from 544 to 1323 millions of francs. When thirty-three or thirty-seven millions of men,—thirty-three in 1819, thirty-seven in 1869,—have increasing wants because they are copying one another more and more, they must produce and consume more and more in order to satisfy their wants, and it is inevitable that their public expenditures should increase in proportion to their private expenditures.[1]

If our European civilisation had long ago put forth, like Chinese civilisation, all that it was able to in the matters of invention and discovery, if, while living upon its old capital, it was exclusively composed of old wants and ideas, without the slightest new addition whatsoever, Quetelet's wish would probably, in accordance with what has preceded, be fulfilled.

If statistics were applied to every aspect of our social life, they would lead in all cases to certain uniform series, which would unroll horizontally and which would be quite analogous to the famous "laws of nature." It is perhaps because Nature is much older than we, and because she has had the requisite time in which to bring to this state of inventive exhaustion all her own civilisations—I mean her living types (true cellular societies, as we know)—that we ascribe to her the fixity and permanence that we praise so highly. This is the reason for that fine and so much admired periodicity of the figures given by sociologico-physiological Statistics, so to speak, which obstinately insists upon emphasising the constantly uniform influences of age or sex upon criminality or nuptiality. We could be certain in advance of such regularity, just as we could be sure, if

[1] This increase is not peculiar to the nineteenth century. M. Delahante says (*Une famille de finances au XVIIIe siècle*) that under the ancient régime "the *ferme générale* brought in to the government a steadily increasing revenue of from one hundred to one hundred and sixty millions. [I, 195, Paris, 1880 —*Tr*]

we classified criminals as nervous, bilious, lymphatic, or sanguine, or, who knows, even as blondes or brunettes, that the annual participation of each of these groups in the annual perpetration of crime would be seen to be always the same.

Perhaps I had better draw attention to the fact that certain statistical regularities which seem to be of another kind belong, at bottom, to the above-mentioned group. For example, why for the last fifty years, at least, have the convictions of police courts been appealed nearly at the rate of forty-five per thousand, whereas, during the same period, the public prosecutor has been steadily cutting down the number of his appeals to one-half? This decrease in the government's appeals is the direct effect of increasing imitation in the legal profession. But how can the numerical standstill in the matter of prisoners' appeals be explained? Let us observe that when the man who has been sentenced is considering whether or not he should carry his case to a higher court he is not usually influenced by what other men like himself are doing or would do under similar circumstances. He is generally ignorant about such examples. He pays even less attention to the statistics that would prove to him that courts of appeal are becoming more and more inclined to confirm the decisions of the lower courts. But, other things being equal (that is, reasons for hope or fear, based upon the circumstances of the case, having on an average the same *annual* weight), it is the degree of boldness in the man's nature which influences him either to fear failure or hope for success, thereby making him act in one way or the other. Here, again, as an additional weight in the balance is the definite quantity of daring and self-confidence which goes to make up the usual temperament of delinquents and which necessarily finds expression as such in the uniform proportion of their appeals.

The error made by Quetelet may be explained historically. The first attempts of Statistics were concerned, to be sure, with population, that is, with the birth. death, and marriage rates that prevailed among both sexes at different ages and in different places, and, as these effects of climatic and physiological or of very ancient social causes naturally gave rise to regular repetitions of almost constant figures, the mistake was made of generalising observations that subsequently proved false. And thus it was possible for statistics, whose regularity only expresses, at bottom, the imitative bondage of the masses to the individual fancies or conceptions of superior individuals, to be called upon to confirm the current prejudice that the general facts of social life are determined, not by human minds and wills, but by certain myths that are called natural laws!

And yet statistics of population should have opened our eyes by this time. The total of population never remains stationary in any country; it increases or decreases at a rate which is singularly variable among different peoples and in different centuries. How can this fact be explained on the hypothesis of social physics? How can we ourselves explain it? Here we have a need which is certainly very old, the need of paternity, the extent of whose rise or fall finds an eloquent expression in the annual birth rate. Now, statistics show that, old as it is, it is subject to enormous oscillations, and if we consult history, the history of France, for example, it reveals to us a succession, in the past, of gradual and alternating depopulations and repopulations of territory. The fact is that this attribute of age is purely fictitious. The natural and instinctive desire for fatherhood is one thing and the social, imitative, and rational desire, another. The former may be constant; but the latter, which is grafted upon the former at every great change of customs, laws, or religions, is subject to periodic fluctuation and renewal. Economists err in confounding the two, or, rather, in considering the former only, whereas, it is the latter which is alone important to the sociologist.

Now, there are as many new and distinct desires of the latter kind for paternity as there are distinct and successive motives because of which the social man desires to have children. And we always find certain practical discoveries or theoretic conceptions in explanation of the origin of each of these motives.   The Spanish-American or Anglo-Saxon is prolific because he has America to people.   If Christopher Columbus had made no discovery, what millions of men would have remained unborn!   The insular Englishman is prolific because he has a third of the globe to colonise, a direct consequence of the series of fortunate explorations, of the traits of maritime and warlike genius, and, above all, of the personal initiatives, not to speak of other causes, that won for him his colonies.   In Ireland the introduction of the potato raised the population from three millions in 1766, to eight million three hundred thousand in 1845   The ancient Aryan desired descendants in order that his altar-flame might never be extinguished, nor the altar ever fail to receive its sacred libation, for he was persuaded by his religion that its extinction would bring misfortune to his soul.   The zealous Christian dreams of being the head of a numerous family in docile obedience to the *multiplicamini* of his Bible. To the early Roman to have children meant to give warriors to the Republic, a republic which would never have existed but for that group of inventions, of military and political institutions of Etruscan, Sabine, and Latin origin, which Rome exploited.   To develop mines, railroads, and cotton mills is to give new hands to the industries that are born of modern inventions.   Christopher Columbus, Watt, Fulton, Stephenson, Ampère, Parmentier, can pass, whether celibates or not, for the greatest of all the multipliers of the human species that have ever existed.

Let me stop here; I have said enough to make myself clear.   It is possible that fathers will always regard their actual children from the same point of view, but they will certainly consider their potential children quite differently according to whether, like the ancient *pater familias*, they look upon them as domestic slaves without any ultimate rights, or whether, like Europeans of to-day, they think of them as the perhaps exacting masters and creditors to whom they themselves may some day be enslaved.   This is a result of the difference in customs and laws which wants and ideas have made.   We see that here, as elsewhere, individual initiatives and their contagious imitations, have accomplished everything, socially, I mean. Thousands of centuries ago the human species might have been reduced to a negligible number of individuals and, like bear or bison, have ceased to progress, had not some man of genius arrived from time to time, in the course of history, to stimulate its reproductive power, either by opening new outlets to human activity through industry or colonisation or, as a religious reformer, like Luther, by reviving or, rather, by rejuvenating in an entirely new form the religious zeal of the community and its general belief in Providence as the protector of all the birds of the air. Every stimulus of this kind may be said to have aroused a fresh desire, in the social sense, for paternity, and this desire was added to, or substituted for, preceding desires, the former more often than the latter, and then proceeded, in its turn, along its own line of development.

Now, let us take one of these purely social desires for procreation in its inception and let us follow its course. Such an example will serve as well as another to develop the general law which I am about to formulate. Suppose that in the midst of a population which has been stationary for a long time because the desire for children has been exactly counterbalanced by a fear of the greater misery which their multiplication would entail, the report is suddenly spread abroad that the discovery and conquest of a great island by a compatriot has secured to people a new means of enlarging their families without impoverishing themselves, with an increase of wealth, in fact, to themselves. As this news travels and is confirmed, the desire for paternity redoubles, that is, the pre-existent desire is redoubled by the addition of a new desire. But the latter is not satisfied at once. It has to contend with a whole tribe of rooted habits and antique practices which have given birth to a general belief that acclimatisation in such a distant land is impossible and death from famine, or fever, or homesickness, a certainty. Many years must elapse before this pervasive opposition can be generally overcome. Then a current of emigration sets in, and the colonists, set free from prejudice, begin to indulge

in extreme fecundity. At this time the tendency towards a
geometric progression which governs not merely the desire
to procreate, but all other desires as well, is actualised and,
to a certain extent, satisfied. But this period does not last.
The increase in the birth rate soon falls off because of the
very development of prosperity which accompanies it.
Needs of luxury, of leisure, and of a fancied independence
which it has itself created encroach upon it day by day.
When they reach a certain point the ultra-civilised man is
placed in the dilemma of choosing between the joys offered
by them and the joys of a numerous family. If he choose
the former, he renounces the latter. Hence an inevitable
arrest of the progression in question. Then, if an extreme
kind of civilisation continue, a depopulation sets in like that
which occurred in the Roman Empire, and like that
which modern Europe and even America are bound some
day to experience. But a depopulation like this never has
gone and never will go very far, because of the fact that if
it were to pass beyond a certain limit, it would bring about
a setback to civilisation and a diminution in the desire for
luxury which would again raise the level of population.
Therefore, if nothing new occur, the establishment, after
some oscillations, of a static condition will necessarily be
maintained until some new order of chance or genius takes
place.

We need not fear to generalise this observation. Since
it applies to such an apparently primitive desire as that for
paternity, how much more readily would it apply to the so-
called needs of luxury, all of which are plainly the result of
discovery, to the desire, for example, for locomotion by
steam. Although this desire was at first restrained by fear
of accidents and by the habit of sedentary life, its successful
development was not delayed until it came into contact, in
our own day, with the more redoubtable adversaries that it
had itself, in part, created and encouraged. I mean the need
for the thousand various satisfactions of civilised life but
for the satisfaction of which the pleasure of travel could not
fail to increase indefinitely. The same remark applies as

truly, although less obviously, to desires of a higher order, to the desire for equality, or for political liberty, or, let me add, for truth. These desires, the third included, are of fairly recent origin. The first arose from the humanistic and rationalistic philosophy of the eighteenth century; the second, from English parliamentarism. The sources and leaders of the first movement we know, and, without going back very far, it would not be difficult to name the successive inventors and promotors of the second. As for the desire for truth, this torment, if we are to believe M. Dubois-Reymond, was unknown to classic antiquity,—a lack which explains the strange inferiority in science and industry of that brilliant and otherwise eminently gifted period; it was the peculiar fruit of Christianity, of that spiritual religion which, in exacting faith even more than deeds, and faith in accredited historic facts, teaches man the high value of truth. Thus Christianity gave birth to its great rival, to science, the modern check upon its heretofore triumphant propagation. Science dates barely from the sixteenth century, when the love of truth, great as it was, was confined to a small band of devotees. It has been widening its boundaries ever since then. But already there are clear signs that the twentieth century will not be as absorbed in disinterested curiosity as the three centuries which preceded it. And it may be safely predicted that the day is not far distant when the need for well-being, which industry, the child of science, is developing without limitation, will suppress scientific zeal and will lead coming generations to a utilitarian sacrifice of their free and individualistic worship of hopeless truth to the social need for some common and, perhaps, state-imposed consoling and comforting illusion. And it is certain that neither our already much diminished thirst for political liberty nor our present passion for equality will escape a similar fate.

Perhaps the same thing should be said of desire for private property. Without adopting all the ideas of M. de Laveleye on this subject we must recognise the facts that this desire, one which arose from a group of agricultural inventions and which is a prime agent in civilisation, was preceded by a desire for common property (the North American *pueblos,* the Hindoo village-community, the Russian *mir,* etc.) ; that, as a matter of fact, it has not ceased to grow up to the present day at the expense of the latter desire, as is proved by the gradual division of undivided property, of our common lands, for example; that it is no longer growing, however, and that when it once enters into competition with desire for superior subsistence and for more general well-being, it will withdraw before the rival to which it itself gave birth.

Every new belief as well as every social desire passes, as it spreads, through the three phases that I have described, before reaching its final resting place. To sum up, then, every desire or belief has first to toil through a network of contrary habits or convictions, then, after this obstacle is overcome and victory won, it has to expand until new enemies are raised up by its triumph to hinder its progress and finally to oppose an insurmountable frontier to its further spread. In the case of a desire, these new enemies will consist mainly of habits which it has directly or indirectly established. In the case of a belief, which we know is always partly erroneous, they will consist of somewhat conflicting ideas which have been derived from it or whose discovery has been prompted by it, of heresies or of sciences proceeding from and yet contrary to the given dogma whose victorious and world-wide course is thereby arrested, and of scientific theories or of industrial inventions which have been suggested by antecedent theories whose application is limited and whose truth or success is hemmed in by them.[1]

[1] When a belief or desire has ceased to spread, it can nevertheless continue to send down roots into its circumscribed field Take, for example, a religion, or a revolutionary doctrine, after its period of conquest Besides, a gradual taking-root of this kind presents, like the gradual expansion which it follows or accompanies, certain well-defined and analogous phases In the beginning, when belief is still contested, it is conscious judgment; just as nascent desire is, for the same reason, purpose or volition. Subsequently, thanks to an unanimity which grows and which strengthens the convictions and volitions of each individual,

A slow advance in the beginning, followed by rapid and uniformly accelerated progress, followed again by progress that continues to slacken until it finally stops: these, then, are the three ages of those real social beings which I call inventions or discoveries.   None of them is exempt from this experience any more than a living being from an analogous, or, rather, identical, necessity.   A slight incline, a relatively sharp rise, and then a fresh modification of the slope until the plateau is reached: This is also, in abridgment, the profile of every hill, its characteristic curve.   This is the law which, if taken as a guide by the statistician and, in general, by the sociologist, would save them from many illusions.   They would no longer think, for example, that the populations of Russia, Germany, the United States, Brazil, will continue to grow at their present rates of increase.   They would no longer fearfully compute the hundreds of millions of Russians or Germans that France will have to fight one hundred years hence.   Nor, would they continue to think that the need of railroad travel, of letter-writing and telegraphing, of newspaper reading, and of political activity, will develop in France in the future as rapidly as they have done in the past.   These errors may be costly.

All these needs will cease, just as, without comparing them in any other way, the need of tattooing, cannibalism, and tent life, which appear in remote times to have been very quick-spreading fashions, came to an end.   In more recent periods, the passion for ascetic or monastic life is an example.   A moment arrives, to be sure, when an acquired desire comes, by reason of its growth, to vie with even innate desires, some of which are always stronger than it.   It is because of this fact that, as I have said before, the most original civilisations, at a certain point, and in

judgment passes over into principle or dogma or almost unconscious quasi-perception, and purpose, into pure passion or desire Finally, dogmatic quasi-perception, finding itself more and more jostled by the direct perceptions of opposing and stronger senses, ceases to gain in strength, and acquired desire, coming into greater and greater opposition with certain innate and more energetic desires, is arrested, in its turn, in its downward movement into the depths of the heart.

spite of their free development, leave off accentuating their differences It might almost be thought that they subsequently tended to narrow them down; but this illusion is easily explained by their frequent intercourse and by the preponderating influence of one civilisation over the other. A slow and inevitable assimilation through imitation and an apparent return to nature results, because the shock of two contending civilisations weakens in each of them the factitious needs in which they differ and conflict and strengthens the primordial needs in which they resemble each other. Does it follow that, in the last analysis, organic needs ultimately control the course of artistic and industrial progress just as external reality ends by controlling the course of thought? It does not, for let us observe that no nation has ever been able to push its civilisation far ahead and to reach its limit of divergence except on the condition of being eminently conservative and, like Egypt, China, or Greece, attached to the particular traditions in which the divergence is best expressed. But let us close this parenthesis.

Now, of the three phases of development which I have indicated, it is the second that is of the greatest theoretical importance; it is not the final static condition which is merely the limit of the third and to which statisticians appear to attach so much value. Between the rounded summit of a mountain and the gentle slope of its base there is a certain direction which marks better than any other the exact energy of the forces which raised it up before the denudation of its peak or the heaping up of its base. Thus the intermediate phase in question is the one best fitted to show the energy of the upheaval which the corresponding innovation has stamped on the human heart. This phase would be the only one, it would absorb the other two, if rational and voluntary imitation could be substituted in everything and everywhere for unreflecting and mechanical imitation. It is evident, moreover, that it requires less time for a new article of manufacture to find a market and that it also requires less time for its circulation to be cut off, according to the measure in which this substitution is effected.

It remains to be shown how through the application of the preceding law the most complex and, at first sight, the most puzzling curves can be readily deciphered and interpreted. There are few curves, to be sure, which plainly conform to the ideal type which I have outlined; for there are few inventions which, as they spread and encounter others, do not bestow upon or receive from one of the latter some success-accelerating improvement or which are not undermined by other inventions or checked by some physical or physiological accident like a dearth or epidemic, not to speak of political accidents. But, then, if our norm is not seen in the whole it is, at least, in the details. Let us ignore the disturbing influence of the natural accidents of war or revolution. Let us overlook any rise in the curve of thefts that may be due to the high price of wheat or any deflection in the curve of drunkenness that may be due to the phylloxera. After we have easily discounted the part played by these extraneous movements, we may be sure, upon inspecting a given curve, particularly if it has been plotted according to the rules that were given some pages back, that as soon as the first obstacles are overcome and it has assumed a well-marked upward movement according to a definite angle, every upward deviation will reveal the insertion of some auxiliary discovery or improvement at the corresponding date, and every drop towards the horizontal will reveal, on the other hand, according to our foregoing law, the shock of some hostile invention.[1]

---

[1] Or else the drop is only apparent. Under the ancient régime, the consumption of tobacco was continually increasing, just as it is at present. This fact was proved by the steady increase of the taxes collected under the *fermes générales*. From thirteen millions in 1730 there was a rise to twenty-six millions in 1758, when there was a sudden drop in the receipts. It seemed at first to point to a restriction of the consumption, but it was then shown that the revenue was simply the victim of a fraud that had been organised on an immense scale. See on this subject M Delahante's book, *Une famille de finance au XVIIIe siècle*, II. 312, and the following To return to the advance in the consumption of tobacco, it increased from thirteen millions in 1730

And if we study by itself the effect produced by each successive improvement, we shall see that it, too, has taken, according to the law in question, a certain time in which to make itself acceptable, that it has then spread very quickly, then less quickly, and that it finally has ceased to spread at all. Is it necessary to recall the gradual but prodigious extension that every improvement in the loom, in the electric telegraph, or in the manufacture of steel has given, after a certain period of probation, to textile industries, to telegraphic activity, to the production of steel? And is not each of these improvements due to some new inventor following upon the steps of earlier ones? When an unexpected outlet has been opened up to a local industry, to the iron industry, for example, through the suppression of internal taxation or through an international treaty which has doubled or tripled the sale of its products, again what do we see but the felicitous intersection of two great currents of imitation, the one starting from Adam Smith and the other, according to mythology, from Tubal Cain or from him, whoever he may have been, who was the forerunner of our metallurgists? If, at a certain date, we see that the curve of arson or of judicial separations is suddenly rising, we shall find, if we investigate, that the rise in the former is explained by the introduction, at the corresponding date, of the invention of insurance companies, and that the rise in the latter is explained by some immediately preceding legislative invention which permits poor people to litigate free of charge.

When, for example, an irregular statistical curve resists the preceding analysis and cannot be resolved into normal, or into segments of normal, curves, it means that it is in itself insignificant, that it is based on curious, but absolutely non-instructive, enumerations of unlike units and of arbitrary groups of certain acts or objects in which, however,

to seventy-four millions in 1835, and then to one hundred and fifty-three millions in 1855, and to two hundred and ninety millions in 1875 And yet this rate tends to slacken. It is remarkable that the American Indians who taught us the use of tobacco, have recently altogether lost the habits of tobacco and snuff.

order would suddenly appear if the presence of a definite underlying desire or belief were revealed. Let us consider the table of the annual expenditure on public works by the French government from 1833 to the present time. This series of figures is exceptionally irregular, although if it be taken as a whole it presents, in spite of its discontinuity, a remarkable progression. I will merely draw attention to the fact that in 1843 the figures took a sudden rise and remained at the high level of about one hundred and twenty millions until 1849, when they suddenly fell at a very rapid rate. This sharp rise was due, as we know, to the building of railroads at this period. This is equivalent to saying that at this time the imitative spread of railroad invention in France ran counter to that of the much more ancient inventions which make up the sum of other public works, such as highroads, bridges, canals, etc. Unfortunately for the regularity of the series, the state intervened and monopolised this new kind of work and so substituted for the continuous progression which unmolested private initiative could not have failed to produce, the discontinuity which characterises those intermittent explosions of the collective will called laws. But, after all, a real and incontestable regularity does exist, although hidden below these numerical gyrations which state intervention creates for the interpreter of statistics. How, in fact, did the law of June 11, 1842, which provided for the establishment of our first great network of railroads, come to be passed, unless it was because of the fact that before this date the idea of railroads had circulated abroad and that confidence, which was at first so feeble and unsettled in the utility of the new discovery, and desire for its realisation, which was at first a mere matter of curiosity, had been silently growing?

Here we have the constant and regular progression which the preceding table disguises, but by which it can alone be explained. For is it not because of the uninterrupted course of this twofold advance in confidence and desire, following its normal curve, that the Chamber has adopted the Freycinet plan in recent years, and that expenditure for

public works has again risen to alarming proportions?
Now is it not evident that had we undertaken to make an
approximate numerical measurement of this progress of
public opinion the idea of the above table would undoubtedly
have been the most inappropriate of means for this end? Of
course an estimate of the annual increase in the number of
voyages and voyagers and in the transportation of freight
by rail would be more valuable.

VI

Having given an account of the subject, the aim, and
the resources of sociological Statistics as an applied study of
the laws of imitation, I have now to discuss its probable
future. The special appetite which it has whetted rather
than satisfied, this thirst for social knowledge of mathematical precision and impersonal impartiality, is only incipient;
its development lies in the future. It is only in its *first phase*
and before reaching its predestined goal, it can, like every
other need, look forward with perfect propriety to immense
conquests.

Let us take any graphical curve, that, for example, of
criminal recidivists for the last fifty years. If its physiognomy is unlike that of the human face, is it not, at least, like
the silhouette of hills and vales, or, since it is a question of
movement,—for in statistics we speak quite properly of the
movement of criminality, of birth or marriage rates,—like
the sinuous lines, the sharp rises and sudden falls. in the
flight of a swallow? Let me stop a moment at this comparison and consider if it is specious? Why should the
statistical diagrams that are gradually traced out on this
paper from accumulations of successive crimes and
misdemeanours—whose records are transmitted in official
reports to the government, from the government in annual returns to the bureau of statistics at Paris and
from this bureau, in blue books, to the magistrates of
the different tribunals—why should these silhouettes, which

likewise give visible expression to masses or series of co-existent or successive facts, be the only ones to be taken as symbolical, whereas the line traced on my retina by the flight of a swallow is deemed an inherent reality in the being which it expresses and which essentially consists, it seems to me, of moving figures, of movements in an imaginary space? Is there really less symbolism in one case than in the other? Is not my retinal image, the curve traced on my retina by the flight of this swallow, merely the expression of a mass of facts (the different states of the bird) which we have not the slightest reason in the world to consider as analogous to our visual impression?

If this is so, and philosophers will readily grant that it is, let us continue our discussion.

The most appreciable difference, then, between statistical curves and visual images consists in the fact that the former are laborious to trace or even interpret, whereas the latter record themselves on our retinæ without any effort on our part and lend themselves with the greatest ease to our interpretation. The former, moreover, are traced long after the causation and appearance of the changes and events which they represent, and represent, too, in the most intermittent and irregular as well as in the most dilatory fashion, whereas the latter always show us regularly and uninterruptedly what has just occurred or what is actually occurring. But if each of these differences is taken by itself, they will all be seen to be more apparent than real and to be reducible to differences of degree. If Statistics continues to progress as it has done for several years, if the information which it gives us continues to gain in accuracy, in despatch, in bulk, and in regularity, a time may come when upon the accomplishment of every social event a figure will at once issue forth automatically, so to speak, to take its place on the statistical registers that will be continuously communicated to the public and spread abroad pictorially by the daily press. Then, at every step, at every glance cast upon poster or newspaper, we shall be assailed, as it were, with statistical facts, with precise and condensed knowledge of all the peculiarities of actual social conditions, of commercial gains or losses, of the rise or falling off of certain political parties, of the progress or decay of a certain doctrine, etc., in exactly the same way as we are assailed when we open our eyes by the vibrations of the ether which tell us of the approach or withdrawal of such and such a so-called body and of many other things of a similar nature. This information is interesting from the point of view of the conservation and development of our organs, just as the former *news* is interesting from the point of view of the conservation and development of our social being, of our reputation and wealth, of our power, and of our honour.

Consequently, granted that statistics be extended and completed to this extent, a statistical bureau might be compared to an eye or ear. Like the eye or ear, it would save us trouble by synthesising collections of scattered homogeneous units for us, and it would give us the clear, precise, and smooth result of this elaboration. And, certainly, under such conditions, it would be no more difficult for an educated man to keep informed of the slightest current changes in religious or political opinion than for a man whose eyesight was impaired by age to recognise a friend at a distance, or to distinguish the approach of an obstacle in time to avoid it. Let us hope that the day will come when the representative or legislator who is called upon to reform the justiciary or the penal code and yet who is, hypothetically, ignorant of juridical statistics, will be as rare and inconceivable a being as a blind omnibus driver or a deaf orchestral leader would be to-day.[1]

I might freely say, then, that each of our senses gives us,

---

[1] According to Burckhardt, Florence and Venice must have been the cradle of statistics "Fleets, armies, power and political influence, fall under the debit and credit of a trader's ledger" [*The Civilization of the Period of the Renaissance in Italy*, I, 97, Jacob Burckhardt. English translation by S G C. Middlemore, London, 1878 — *Tr.*]. We find detailed statistics in Milan dating from 1288 In reality, embryonic statistics must have always existed in even the most ignorant and negligent states, just as there are rudimentary senses in the very lowest animals.

in its own way and from its special point of view, the statistics of the external world. Their characteristic sensations are in a certain way their special graphical tables Every sensation—colour, sound, taste, etc.,—is only a *number,* a collection of innumerable like units of vibrations that are represented collectively by this single figure. The *affective* character of these different sensations is merely their distinctive mark, it is analogous to the difference which characterises the figures of our system of notation. How should we know the sounds of *do,* of *ré,* of *mi,* except for the fact that there is in the air about us, during a certain consecutive period of time, a certain proportionate number per second of so-called sonorous vibrations? What does the colour red, blue, yellow, or green mean except that the ether is agitated, during a certain consecutive period of time, by a certain proportionate number of so-called luminous vibrations?

Touch, as a sense of temperature, is nothing more than the statistics of the heat vibrations of the ether; as a sense of resistance and weight, it is merely the statistics of our muscular contractions. But the impressions of touch, unlike those of sight and hearing, follow one another without definite proportions; there is no tactile gamut. Hence the inferiority of this sense. Statisticians are lacking in the same way when they fail to give us the relative proportions of their crudely tabulated figures. As for the senses of smell and taste, if they are justly ranked as altogether inferior senses, is it not because, poor statisticians as they are, they do not conform to our elementary rules, but are satisfied with defective figures, with the expressions of faulty additions in which the most heterogeneous units, all sorts of nervous vibrations and chemical actions, have been thrown together in the same kind of disorder that we see in a badly made budget?

The reader may have noticed that some of our newspapers publish from day to day graphical curves, showing the fluctuations of the different securities of the stock-ex-

change, as well as other changes about which it is useful to
know. These curves are now relegated to the last page,
but they tend to encroach upon the others, and, perhaps, before long, at any rate, at some time in the future when people have been satiated with declamation and polemic, just as
very well read minds begin to be with literature, and when
they will read the papers merely for their multifarious state-
ments of exact and ungarnished fact, they will usurp the
place of honour. The public journals, then, will become
socially what our sense organs are vitally. Every printing
office will become a mere central station for different bureaus of statistics just as the ear-drum is a bundle of acous-
tic nerves, or as the retina is a bundle of special nerves each
of which registers its characteristic impression on the brain.
At present Statistics is a kind of embryonic eye, like that of
the lower animals which see just enough to recognise the approach of foe or prey. But this already is a great benefit
to have bestowed upon us, and through it we may be
kept from running serious dangers.

The analogy is plain. It is strengthened by a comparison of the part taken by the senses throughout the animal
world, from the lowest to the highest rung of the mental
ladder, with the rôle that has been played by newspapers
during the course of civilisation. In the case of mollusk,
insect, and even of quadruped, the senses are more than the
mere scouts of the intelligence—the more imperfect they
are, the more important they become. But their functions
diminish as they become localised, and the nearer the approach to man, the more subordinate the position which
they hold. Similarly, in growing and inferior civilisations
like our own (for our descendants will look down upon us
just as we do upon our lower brethren), newspapers do
more than furnish their reader with thought-stimulating
information; they think and decide for him and he is me-
chanically moulded and guided by them. A sure sign of advance in civilisation upon the part of a certain class of readers, is the fact that the newspaper which appeals to them
devotes a smaller portion of itself to phrases and a larger

portion to facts and figures and to brief and reliable information. The ideal newspaper of this kind would be one without political articles and full of graphical curves and succinct editorials.

It is obvious that I am not inclined to minimise the function of statistics. And yet, although I realise its future importance, I must point out, before concluding, a certain exaggerated expectation which is sometimes entertained in relation to it. When we see that these numerical results become more and more constant and regular as they come to refer to larger and larger numbers, we are at times inclined to think that if the tide of population continues to advance and great states to enlarge, a movement will come when in the distant future all social phenomena will be reducible to mathematical formulas. Hence the mistaken inference is drawn that the statistician will some day be able to foretell future social conditions with as much certainty as the astronomist of to-day predicts the next eclipse of Venus. In this event Statistics would be fated to plunge further and further ahead into the future as archæology has gone back into the past.

But from all that which has gone before we know that Statistics is hemmed within the field of imitation and that the field of invention is forbidden ground. The future will be made by as yet unknown inventors and no real law concerning their successive advents can be formulated. In this respect, the future is like the past. It does not fall to the archæologist to tell precisely what processes of ancient art or industry preceded those which had been substituted for them in the use of a given people at a certain period of its history. Why should the statisician be more fortunate in the opposite direction? The empire of great men, the eventual disturbers of prognosticated curves, cannot fail to increase, rather than diminish. The progress of population will only extend their imitative following. The progress of civilisation will but hasten and facilitate the imitation of their examples, while, at the same time, it will multiply for a certain period the number of inventive geniuses. It seems as if the further we progressed the more all kinds of new and unforeseen things flowed out from the class that governs, from the discoveries, and that among the class that is governed, the copyists, the things that are foreseen (which start, however, from the unforeseen) spread themselves out more and more uniformly and monotonously.

And yet, on closer view, progress would seem to have spurred on the ingenuity of invention-aping imitation rather than to have fertilised the inventive genius. True invention, invention which is worthy of the name, becomes more difficult day by day; so that, some time in the near future, it cannot fail to become more rare. And, finally, it must become exhausted; for the mind of any given race is not capable of indefinite development. It follows that, sooner or later, every civilisation, Asiatic or European, is fated to beat itself against its banks and begin its endless cycle over again. Then Statistics will undoubtedly possess the promised gift of prophecy. But this goal is far distant. Meanwhile, all that can be said is that in as much as the direction of future inventions is chiefly determined by prior inventions, and in as much as the latter are becoming more and more preponderating because of their accumulation, predictions based upon statistics may one day be hazarded with a certain degree of probability, just as it is also quite probable that archæology may come to throw light upon the origins of history.

VII

It is not superfluous to note, in conclusion, that as the preceding chapter was an answer to the difficult question " What is Society? " so this chapter is an answer to the question " What is History? " We have searched much and in vain for the distinctive marks of historic facts, for the signs by which we should recognise the natural or human events that were worthy the notice of the historian. According to the learned, history is a collection of those things that have had the greatest celebrity. I prefer to consider it a collection of those things that have been the most successful, that is, of those initiatives that have been the most imitated. An immensely successful thing may have had no celebrity at all A new word, for example, may slip into a language and become entrenched in it without arousing any attention; a new idea or religious rite may make its way, obscure and unnoticed, into a community; an industrial process may spread anonymously throughout the world There is no truly historic fact outside of those that can be classed in one of the three following categories: (1) The progress or decay of some kind of imitation. (2) The appearance of one of those combinations of different imitations which I call inventions, and which come in time to be imitated (3) The actions either of human beings, or of animal, vegetal, or physical forces, which result in the imposition of new conditions upon the spread of certain imitations whose bearing and direction are thereby modified. From this latter point of view, a volcanic eruption, the submerging of an island or continent, even an eclipse, when it occasions the defeat of a superstitious army, and, still more, the accidental illness or death of an important personage, can have the same kind and degree of historic importance as a battle or a treaty of peace or an international alliance The issue of a war in which the fate of a civilisation was at stake, has often depended upon inclement weather. The severe winter of 1811 affected the destinies of France and Russia as seriously as did the Napoleonic plan of campaign. From this point of view pragmatic and even anecdotal history regains the place which philosophers have so often refused to grant it. Nevertheless, *the career of imitations* is, on the whole, the only thing which is of interest to history. Therein lies its true definition.

CHAPTER V.

THE LOGICAL LAWS OF IMITATION

STATISTICS gives us a sort of empirical law or graphical formula for the very complex causes of the particular spread of every kind of imitation. We must now consider those general laws, laws which are really worthy the name of science, which govern all imitations, and to this end we must study, one by one, the different categories of causes which we have heretofore merged together.

Our problem is to learn why, given one hundred different innovations conceived of at the same time—innovations in the forms of words, in mythological ideas, in industrial processes, etc.—ten will spread abroad, while ninety will be forgotten. In order to solve this question systematically let us first divide those influences which have favoured or hindered the diffusion of successful or non-successful innovations into physical and social causes. But in this book let us pass over the first order of causes, those, for example, which make the people of southern countries prefer new words composed of voiced to those composed of whispered vowels, and the people of northern countries, the opposite. In the same way there are in mythology, in artistic or industrial technique, or in government, many peculiarities which result from a racial conformation of ear or larynx, from cerebral predispositions, from meteoric conditions or from the nature of fauna and flora. Let us put all this to one side. I do not mean that it has no real importance in sociology. It is of interest, for example, to note the influence which may be exerted upon the entire course of a civilisation by the nature of a new and spontaneous production of its soil. Much

depends upon the spot in which it springs; the conditions
of labour, and, consequently, the family groups and political
institutions of a fertile valley are different from those of a
moor more or less rich in pasture-land.   We must thank
those scholars who devote themselves to researches of this
character, researches which are as useful in sociology as
studies upon the modification of species by the action of
climate or general environment are in biology   It would
be erroneous to think, however, that because we had
shown the adaptation of living or social types to external
phenomena we had thereby explained them.   The explanation must be sought for in the laws which express the
internal relations of cells or of minds in association.   This
is the reason why, in this discussion of pure and abstract,
not of concrete and applied, sociology, I must set aside all
considerations of the above nature

Now, social causes are of two kinds, the logical and the
non-logical.   This distinction is of the greatest importance.
Logical causes operate whenever an individual prefers a
given innovation to others because he thinks it is more
useful or more true than others, that is, more in accord
than they are with the aims or principles that have already
found a place in his mind (through imitation, of course).
In such instances, the old or new inventions or discoveries
are themselves the only question; they are isolated from
any prestige or discredit which may have attached to those
circulating them or to the time and place of their origin.
But logical action is very rarely untrammelled in this way.
In general, the extra-logical influences to which I have
referred interfere in the choice of the examples to be followed, and often, as we shall see further on, the poorest
innovations, from the point of view of logic, are selected
because of their place, or even date or birth.

Unless these necessary distinctions are constantly borne
in mind, it is impossible to understand the simplest social
facts.   Language is a notable example.   It seems to me
that its present inextricable skein might be readily un-
ravelled by applying these ideas (if any professional philolo-

gist would pay me the compliment of adopting them).
Philologists seek for those laws which should govern the formation and transformation of languages. But, hitherto,
they have only been able to formulate rules which are subject to very many exceptions, in regard to both changes
in sound (phonetic laws) and changes in meaning, in regard to the acquisition of new words through the combination of old roots or of new grammatical forms through the
modification of old forms, etc. Why is this? Because only
imitation and not invention is subject to law in the true
sense of the word. Now, small, successive inventions have
always had to accumulate in order to form or transform
an idiom. Besides, in the service of language a large part
must be conceded, at the outset, to the accidental and
arbitrary.

It is because of these individual factors that, among
other peculiarities, there are a certain number of
roots in a language, that one root will consist of three consonants and another of a single syllable, or that one termination and not another will be adopted at the behest of a
given shade of thought. After this concession has been
made to invention and to influences of a climatic or physiological order, a great field is still open to the laws of
language.

There is, of course, apart from both the irrational
and important, not to say pregnant, motives of which
I have been speaking, a host of minor linguistic inventions which were suggested to their unknown authors by
way of *analogy*,[1] *i. e.*, through imitation of self or
others; and it is in this direction that linguistic inventions are subject to law. The first man to conceive
the idea of expressing capacity for respect by adding
the suffix *bilis*, which, according to hypothesis, was already used in the compound *amabilis*, to the root of
veneratio, or of creating *Germanicus* upon the model of
Italicus, was an unconscious inventor, but, to put it briefly,

---

[1] Philologists all recognise the immense rôle played by analogy in
their science. See Sayce in particular on this point.

he imitated at the same time that he invented. Whenever
terminations, or, similarly, declensions or conjugations, have
been broadened and generalised in this way, imitation of
self and of others has taken place, and precisely to this
extent is the formation and transformation of languages
subject to formulation into rules. But these rules, which
should explain to us why one among many almost synono-
mous forms of speech which are concurrently at the service
of the tribal, or civic, or national mind has alone fought
its way into general usage, fall into very distinct
groups.

In the first place, we see that the incessant struggle between minor linguistic inventions which always ends in the
imitation of one of them, and in the abortion of the others,
finally comes to transform a language in such a way as to
adapt it, more or less rapidly and completely, according
to the spirit of the community, to external realities and
to the social purposes of language. Enlargements of vocabulary correspond to increases in the number of human
beings and of their modes of life. Grammar, by means of
a more flexible conjugation of verbs or a clearer or more
logical arrangement of phrases, lends itself to the expression of more subtle relations in time and space.
The softening and differentiation of vowels (in Sanskrit
they are all sharp sounds in *a* or *o*; in Greek and Latin,
e, u, ou, and *i* have been added to the vocal key-board) and
the contraction and abbreviation of words render a language more and more pliable and expressive, and distinguished philologists like M. Régnaud [1] have raised to the
dignity of a law the vowel softening and the contraction of
words of the Indo-European family. In fact, in Zend,
Greek, Latin, French, English, and German, the *e* appears
" in an infinite number of cases as a weakened substitute
for *a*," whereas, " the opposite never, or hardly ever, takes
place " If, by the way, this rule could be accepted unreservedly, we should have here a pretty example of linguistic irreversibility.

[1] See his *Essais de linguistique évolutionniste,* previously cited.

But, on the other hand, even in the most perfect idioms, even in that Greek of which it may be said that its conjugation is a "system of applied logic,"[1] we see that many modifications effected in the course of time are far from being advances in utility or truth. Is the loss of *j* and *v* (digamma) or, in many cases, of an initial sibilant of any advantage to Greek? Is it not rather a cause of deterioration? In France have not certain expanded forms succeeded contracted ones contrary to the law of word contraction, as *portique* from *porche, capital* from *cheptal*, etc.? In such cases certain influences, in regard to which the need of logic and finality had no part, preponderated. We know that in the case of the last example certain writers of renown manufactured many words like *portique* and *capital* in servile imitation of Latin, and that they succeeded by means of their own prestige in putting them into circulation.[2]

But I do not wish to dwell at greater length upon the science of language. I am content with having indicated in these few observations the drift of the laws which we have still to formulate. In this chapter, the logical laws will occupy our attention exclusively.

I

Invention and imitation are, as we know, the elementary social acts. But what is the social substance or force

---

[1] Curtius, the historian, has borrowed this expression from his brother, the philologist. See his *History of Greece* [I, 24, ·English translation by A. W. Ward, M. A., London, 1868 —*Tr.*].

[2] We also know that when one of many rival dialects like those, for example, of Greece or of mediæval France, succeeds in supplanting its competitors and in crushing them back into the rank of *patois*, this privilege is not always and never altogether due to its intrinsic merits. It owes it primarily to political triumphs, and to the real or fancied superiority of the province in which it was first spoken. It was thanks to the prestige of Paris that the speech of the Isle of France became the French language. We may note, in passing, that the laws of imitation serve to explain both the inward transformations of a language and its outward diffusion.

through which this act is accomplished and of which it is merely the form? In other words, what is invented or imitated? The *thing* which is invented, the *thing* which is imitated, is always an idea or a volition, a judgment or a purpose, which embodies a certain amount of *belief* and *desire*. And here we have, in fact, the very soul of words, of religious prayers, of state administration, of the articles of a code, of moral duties, of industrial achievements or of artistic processes. Desire and belief: they are the substance and the force, they are the two psychological quantities[1] which are found at the bottom of all the *sensa-*

[1] I take the liberty of referring the reader, if he be a psychologist, to two articles which I published in August and September, 1880, in the *Revue philosophique* upon *belief* and *desire* and the *possibility of measuring them.* These articles were republished unrevised in my *Essais et mélanges sociologiques.* Since then my ideas on this subject have been somewhat modified. But let me state in what respects At present I realise that I may have somewhat exaggerated the rôle of *belief* and *desire* in individual psychology, and I no longer affirm that these two aspects of the ego are the only things in us which are susceptible of addition and diminution On the other hand, I now attribute to them a greater importance in social psychology. We may admit that there are other quantities in the soul; we may concede to the psycho-physicists, for example, in spite of M. Bergson's remarkable study on the *Données immédiates de la conscience*—which conforms so well in other respects to my own point of view on this subject—that the intensity of sensations, considered apart from their relation to reason, and apart from the amount of attention which is bestowed upon them, changes in degree without changing in nature, and that it therefore lends itself to experimental measurement. But it is nevertheless true that, from the social standpoint, belief and desire bear a unique character that is well adapted to distinguish them from simple sensation. This character consists in the fact that the contagion of mutual example re-enforces beliefs and desires that are alike, and weakens or strengthens, according to circumstances, beliefs and desires that are unlike, among all those individuals who experience them at the same time and who are conscious of so experiencing them Whereas, although a visual or auditory sensation may be felt in a theatre, for example, in the midst of a crowd attentive to the same concert or spectacle, it is in no way modified by the simultaneity of the analogous impressions experienced by the surrounding public. From certain astounding historical occurrences we may infer how intense a man's belief or desire may become, when it is also experienced by everybody else around him For example, even in the depraved but still credulous Italy of the Renaissance, *epidemics of repentance* burst out from time to time, which, as Burckhardt says, touched even the most hardened consciences These epidemics, of which the one at Florence of 1494-98, under Savonarola, is only one among hundreds,—

tional qualities with which they combine; and when invention and then imitation takes possession of them in order to organise and use them, they also are the real social quantities. Societies are organised according to the agreement or opposition of beliefs which reinforce or limit one another. Social institutions depend entirely upon these conditions. Societies function according to the competition or co-operation of their desires or wants. Beliefs, principally religious and moral beliefs, but juristic and political beliefs as well, and even linguistic beliefs (for how many acts of faith are implied in the lightest talk and what an irresistible although unconscious power of persuasion our mother tongue, a true mother indeed, exerts over us), are the plastic forces of societies. Economic or æsthetic wants are their functional forces.

These beliefs and desires which invention and imitation make specific and in this sense create, although they virtually exist prior to the action of the latter, originate far below the social world in the world of life. In like way, the plastic and functional forces of life that are made specific and turned to account by generation, originate beneath the animate in the physical world. In like way, the vibration-ruled molecular and motor forces of the physical world originate in turn in an inscrutable hypophysical world that some of our physicists call the world of noumena, others, Energy, and yet others, the Unknowable. Energy is the most widespread name for this mystery. By this single term a reality is designated which, as we can see, is always twofold in its manifestations; and this eternal bifurcation, which is reproduced under astonishing metamorphoses in each successive stage of universal life, is not the least of the

for one occurred after every plague or disaster,—revealed the deep and steady activity of the Christian faith Wherever souls are possessed of the same faith or ideal, intermittent outbursts of similar contagions are the result We ourselves no longer have epidemics of penitence, unless they are in the form of contagious pilgrimages—those unique manifestations of the power of suggestion,—but we do have epidemics of luxury, of gambling, of lotteries, of stock-speculation, of gigantic railroad undertakings, as well as epidemics of Hegelianism, Darwinism, etc.

common characteristics to be noted between life's stages. Under the different terms of matter and motion, of organs and functions, of institutions and progress, this great distinction between the static and the dynamic, in which is also included that between Space and Time, divides the whole universe in two.

It is important to state at the outset and firmly establish the relation between these two terms. There is a profound insight underlying the Spencerian formula of Evolution which states that all evolution is gain in matter with corresponding loss in motion, and that all dissolution is the inverse. Translated into a somewhat modified and less materialistic phraseology this thought means that every development in life or society is a growth in organisation offset *or, rather, secured* by a relative diminution in function. As an organism grows in weight or dimension, as it unfolds and differentiates its characteristic forms, it loses its vitality,[1] just because it has used it up in the process, a fact Mr. Spencer fails to mention. As a society enlarges and expands, as it perfects and differentiates its institutions, its language, religion, law, government, industry, and art, it loses its civilising and propelling vigour; for it has been using it up in its course. In other words, if it is true that the substance of social institutions consists in the sum of faith and confidence, of truth and security, in a word, in the unanimous beliefs which they embody, and that the motor power of social progress consists in the sum of the curiosities and ambitions and of the consistent desires which it expresses, if all this is so, then as a society advances it becomes richer in beliefs than in desires. The true and final object of desire, then, is belief. The only *raison d'être* of the impulses of the heart is the formation of high degrees of mental certitude and assurance, and the further a society has progressed the more is it possessed, like a mature mind, of stability and tranquillity, of strong

---

[1] The body of a child contains more vital activity, *in proportion to its size*, than that of a mature man. The *relative* vitality of the adult has diminished.

convictions and dead passions, the former having been slowly formed and crystallised by the latter.[1] Social peace, a unanimous belief in the same ideal or in the same illusion, a unanimity which presupposes a continually widening and deepening assimilation of humanity—this is the goal for which, irrespective of our wishes, all social revolutions are bound. This is progress, that is to say, social advancement along logical lines.

Now, how is progress effected? When an individual reflects upon a given subject first one idea comes to him and then another until from idea to idea, from elimination to elimination, he finally seizes upon the guiding thread to the solution of the problem and then, from that moment, passes quickly out from the twilight into the light. Does not the same thing happen in history? When a society elaborates some great conception, which the curious public pushes forward before science can correct and develop it, the mechanical explanation of the world, for example, or when it dreams in its ambition of some great achievement like the use of steam in manufacture or locomotion or navigation before it can turn its activity to exploiting it, what happens? The problem that is raised in this way at once prompts people to make and entertain all kinds of contradictory inventions and vagaries which appear first here and then there, only to disappear, until the advent of some clear formula or some suitable mechanism which throws all the others into the background and which serves thenceforward as the fixed basis for future improvements and developments. *Progress,* then, is a kind of collective thinking, which lacks a brain of its own, but which is made possible, thanks to imitation, by the solidarity of the brains

---

[1] Let us fully understand each other on this point too. In the course of civilisation desires increase in number, but decrease in strength, whereas truth and security are both multiplied and strengthened at an even more rapid rate. The contrast is a more striking one, if the condition of barbarity, and not that of savagery, be taken as the starting point of the evolution of civilisation. The latter state, according to our present means of observation, is the final term of a social evolution complete in itself, not the first term of a higher evolution.

of numerous scholars and inventors who interchange their successive discoveries. (The fixation of discoveries through writing, which makes possible their transmission over long stretches of time and space, is equivalent to the fixation of images which takes place in the individual brain and which constitutes the cellular stereotype-plate of memory.)

It follows that social like individual progress is effected in two ways, through substitution and through accumulation. Certain discoveries and inventions can only be used as substitutes, others can be accumulated. Hence we have logical *combats* and logical *alliances*. This is the general classification which we will adopt, and in it we shall have no difficulty in placing all historical events.

Moreover, in different societies discord between fresh desires and old, between a new scientific idea and existing religious dogmas, is not always immediately perceived nor perceived within the same period of time. Besides, when the discord is perceived, the desire to put an end to it is not always equally strong. The nature and intensity of the desire vary with time and place. In fact, *Reason* exists in societies as well as in individuals; and *Reason* in all cases is merely a desire like any other, a specific desire which like others is more or less developed by its own satisfactions as well as created by the very inventions or discoveries which have satisfied it; that is to say that systems, programmes, catechisms, and constitutions, in undertaking to render ideas and volitions coherent, create and stimulate the very desire for their coherence. This desire is a real force, located in individual brains. Its rise and fall and its direction and object vary according to given periods and countries. At times, it is a passing breeze; at times, a whirlwind. To-day it attacks the government of states; yesterday and the day before it attacked languages; to-morrow it may make an attack upon our industrial organisations, and another time upon our sciences; but it never pauses in its incessant labour of regeneration or revolution.

This desire, as I have said, has been aroused and recruited by a series of initiations and imitations.   But this is
equivalent to saying by a series of imitations, for an innovation that is not imitated is socially non-existent.   Consequently all those streams and currents of belief and desire which flow side by side or contrary to one another in society, quantities whose subtractions and additions are regulated by social logic, a kind of social algebra,—all, including
the very desire for this general reckoning and the belief in its
possibility,—all are derived from imitation.   For nothing in
history is self-creative; not even its own ever-incomplete
unity, the secular fruit of constant and more or less successful efforts.   A drama, to be sure, a stage play, a fragment in which the whole of history is mirrored, is a logical
and gradual and intricate harmony which seems to work itself out independently of anybody's design.   But we know
that this appearance is misleading and that the harmony
transpires as surely and rapidly as it does only because it answers to the imperious need for unity that is felt by the
dramatist as well as by the public to whom he has suggested it.

Everything, *even the desire to invent,* has the same
origin.   In fact, this desire completes and is part of the
logical need for unification, if it is true, as I might prove,
that logic is both a problem of a maximum and a problem
of equilibrium.   The more a people invent and discover, the
more inventive and the more eager for new discoveries they
grow. It is also through imitation that this noble kind of
craving takes possession of those minds that are worthy of
it.   Now, discoveries are gains in certitude, inventions, in
confidence and security.   The desire to discover and invent
is, consequently, the twofold form which the tendency to-
ward achieving a maximum of public faith takes on.   This
creative tendency which is peculiar to synthesising and assimilating minds often alternates, is sometimes concomitant, but in all cases always agrees with the critical tendency towards an equilibrium of beliefs through the elimination of those inventions or discoveries which are contrary

to the majority of their number.   The desire for unanimity of faith and the desire for purification of faith is each
in turn more fully satisfied, but in general their ebullitions
either coincide with, or follow closely upon each other.
For just because imitation is their common source, both of
them, the desire for stable as well as that for absolute
faith, have a degree of intensity proportionate, other things
being equal, to the degree of animation in the social life,
that is, to the multiplicity of relations between individuals.
Any fine combination of ideas must first shine out in the
mind of the individual before it can illumine the mind of a
nation; and its chance of being produced in the individual
mind depends upon the frequency of the intellectual exchanges between minds.   A contradiction between two institutions or two principles will not harass a society until
it has been noted by some exceptionally sagacious person,
some systematic thinker, who, having been checked in his
conscious efforts to unify his own group of ideas, points out
the aforesaid difficulty.—This explains the social importance of philosophers.—And the greater the amount of
mutual intellectual stimulation and, consequently, the
greater the circulation of ideas within a nation, the more
readily will such a difficulty be perceived.

In the course of the nineteenth century, for example,
the relations of man to man having been multiplied beyond
all expectation as a result of inventions in locomotion, and
the action of imitation having become very powerful, very
rapid, and very far-reaching, we should not be surprised to
see that the passion for social reforms, for systematic and
rational social reorganisations has taken on its present proportions, just as, by virtue of its previous conquests, the
passion for social, especially industrial, conquests over
nature has known no bounds.   Therefore it is safe
to predict that a century of adjustment will follow upon the
past century of discovery.   (Does not the nineteenth century deserve this name?)   Civilisation requires that an
afflux of discovery and an effort to harmonise discoveries
shall coincide with or follow one another.

On the other hand, when societies are in their uninventive phases they are also uncritical, and *vice versa*. They embrace the most contradictory beliefs of surrounding fashions or inherited traditions,[1] and no one notes the contradictions. And yet, at the same time, they carry within themselves, as a result of the contributions of fashion and tradition, much scattered thought and knowledge which would reveal from a certain angle a fruitful although unsuspected self-consistency. In the same way they borrow out of curiosity from their different neighbours, or cherish out of piety as a heritage from their different forefathers, the most dissimilar arts and industries, which develop in them ill-assorted needs and opposing currents of activity. Nor are these *practical antinomies,* any more than the aforesaid theoretical contradictions, felt or formulated by anybody, although everybody suffers from the unrest which they provoke. But at the same time neither do such primitive peoples perceive that certain of their artistic processes and mechanical tools are fitted to be of the greatest mutual service and to work powerfully together for the same end, the one serving as the efficient means of the other, just as certain perceptions serve as intermediaries in explaining certain hypotheses which they confirm.

The grindstone and the paddle-wheel were known about for a long time without the idea occurring to people that by means of a certain artifice, that is, by adding a third invention, a mill, to the other two, they might be made to co-

---

[1] M. Barth, for example, says that "Buddhism carried in itself the denial, not of the régime of castes in general, but of the caste of the Brahmans, and this without respect to any doctrine of equality, and without, for its part, having any thought of revolt Thus it is quite possible that the opposition which existed remained for long an unconscious one on both sides" [*The Religions of India,* pp. 125-26, A Barth, English translation by Rev J Wood, London, 1882 — *Tr*] Finally, it became flagrant, but, for all that. and here was another unconscious contradiction, "the name brahman remained a title of honour among the Buddhists, and in Ceylon it was given to kings" [*Ibid ,* p 127.— *Tr.*] somewhat as the titles of count and marquis are valued in our own democratic society, in spite of its stand against the principles of feudalism.

operate to an extraordinary degree. Back in Babylon, bricks were marked with the names of their maker by means of movable characters or stamps, and books were composed; but the thought of combining these two ideas, of composing books with movable characters, was not conceived of, although it was a very simple matter and one that would have precipitated the coming of printing by some thousands of years.

The cart and the piston likewise coexisted for a long time without giving rise to the idea of using the latter (through other inventions, of course) as a means of propelling the former. On the other hand, at the close of the decadent Middle Ages, for example, how many pagan and licentious tastes for luxury, importations or revivals from Arabia or from the ancient world, crept through castle loopholes and monastery windows to ingratiate themselves within and to form bold medleys, not at all disturbing, however, to the men of those times, with the existing practices of Christian piety and the rude customs of the feudal system! Even in our own days, how many opposite and contradictory objects our industrial or national activity is engaged in achieving! And yet, as the exchange and friction of ideas and the communication and transfusion of needs becomes more rapid, the elimination of the weaker by the stronger, when opposition arises, will be more quickly accomplished and, at the same time, and for the same reason, mutually helpful and confirmatory aims and ideas will be more prompt to encounter each other in the ingenious mind. In these two ways, social life must necessarily reach a degree of logical unity and power hitherto unknown.[1]

[1] Now we can see why the process of unifying the national faith by the expulsion of religious or political heretics (the revocation of the Edict of Nantes, every kind of religious persecution) is always far from accomplishing its object. It keeps a population, to be sure, ignorant of those contradictions which might undermine their beliefs, but, although it may maintain the latter, it also precludes additions to their number. For the ignorance of contradictions which dulls the critical sense also sterilises the imagination and dims the consciousness of mu-

I have now pointed out how the social need for logic, through which alone a social logic is formed, arises and develops. It is at present necessary to see how it sets about to obtain satisfaction. We already know that its two tendencies are distinguishable, the one creative, the other critical, the one abounding in combinations of old *accumulable* inventions and discoveries, the other in struggles between *alternative* inventions or discoveries. We shall study each of these tendencies separately, beginning with the latter.

II *The Logical*[1] *Duel*

Suppose that a discovery, an invention, has appeared. There are straightway two facts for us to note about it: its gains in faith, as it spreads from one person to another, and the losses in faith to which it subjects the invention which had the same object or satisfied the same desire when it intervened. Such an encounter gives rise to a logical duel. For example, cuneiform writing spread for a long time undisturbed throughout Central Asia, while Phœnician writing had the same career in the Mediterranean basin. But one day these two alphabets came into conflict over the territory of the former; and cuneiform writing slowly receded, but did not disappear until about the first century of our era.

Studied in detail, then, the history of societies, like psychologial evolution, is a series or a simultaneous occurrence of logical duels (when it is not one of logical unions). What happened in the case of writing had already happened in that of language. Linguistic progress is effected first by imitation and then by rivalry between two languages or

tual confirmations. Moreover, a time comes when, as Colins says, enquiry can no longer be repressed.

[1] I might just as well have said *teleological* as *logical,* just as, later on, the term logical union means teleological union as well. But it seemed well to identify the two points of view in this chapter at least.

dialects which quarrel over the same country and one of which is crowded back by the other, or between two terms or idioms which correspond to the same idea. This struggle is a conflict between opposite theses implicit in every word or idiom which tends to substitute itself for another word or grammatical form If, at the moment I think of a horse, the two words *equus* and *caballus,* borrowed from two different Latin dialects, come into my mind at the same time, it is as if the judgment "*equus* is a better designation than *caballus*" were contradicted in my thought by the judgment "*caballus* is better than *equus.*" If I have to choose between *i* and *s* to express plurality, for example, this choice is also conditioned by judgments which are intrinsically contradictory. During the formation of the Romance tongues thousands of like contradictions came into the brains of the Gallo-Romans, Spaniards, and Italians; and the need of adjusting them gave birth to the modern languages. What philologists call the gradual simplification of grammars is only the result of the work of elimination that is prompted by a vague feeling of these implicit contradictions. This is the reason, for example, that Italian always uses *i* and Spanish, *s,* whereas Latin sometimes made use of *i* and sometimes of *s.*

I have compared the logical struggle to a duel. In fact, in each of these separate combats, in each of the elementary facts of social life that pass through an edition of numberless copies, the opposing aims or judgments are always two in number. Have you ever seen a battle take place in ancient or mediæval or modern times between three of four parties? Never. There may be seven or eight, or ten or twelve, armies of different nationalities, but there can be only two hostile camps, just as in the counsel of war prior to a battle there are never more than two opinions at the same time, in relation to any plan of action, the one for it and the other made up of those united against it. And, obviously, the quarrel to be fought out upon the battlefield may always be summed up in a *yes* opposed to a *no.* Every *casus belli* is this, at bottom. Of course the adversary who

gainsays the other (in religious wars principally) or who
thwarts the plan of the other (in political wars) has his
own particular thesis or plan as well; but only in as much as
his thought or will is more or less directly or indirectly, implicitly or explicitly, negative or obstructive, does it render
the conflict inevitable.   Hence whatever political parties or
fragments of parties there may be in a country, for example,
there are never more than two sides in relation to any question, the government and the opposition, the fusion of
heterogeneous parties united on their negative side.

This remark applies generally.   At all times and
places the apparent continuity of history may be decomposed into distinct and separable events, events both small
and great, which consist of *questions followed by solutions.*
Now, a question for societies, as for individuals, is a waver-
ing between a given affirmation and a given negation, or
between a given goal and a given impediment; and a solution, as we shall see later on, is only the suppression of one
of the two adversaries or of their inconsistency.   For the
moment I shall speak of questions only.   They are really
logical discourses; one says yes, the other, no.   One desires
a yes, the other, a no.   It makes no difference whether we
are dealing with language or religion, with jurisprudence
or government, the distinction between the affirmative and
the negative side is easily found.

In the elementary linguistic duel which we were considering above, the established term or idiom *affirms* and the
new term or idiom *denies.*   In the religious duel, the orthodox dogma affirms, the heterodox denies, just as, later,
when science tends to replace religion, the accepted theory
is the affirmation that is controverted by the new theory.
Juridical contests are of two kinds.   The one occurs in the
bosom of a parliament or cabinet whenever it deliberates
upon a law or decree, the other, in the bosom of a court
whenever a case is tried before it.   Now, the legislator must
always choose between the adoption or the rejection of the
proposed law, *i e ,* between its affirmation or its negation.
As for the judge, we know that in every suit that is brought

before him,—a peculiarity that has been overlooked in spite of its significance,—there is always a *plaintiff* who affirms something and a *defendant* who denies it.   If the defendant puts in a counter claim, this means that a second suit is added to the first.   If other parties intervene, each of them takes on the character of plaintiff or defendant and thus multiplies the number of the separate questions between the litigants of the action.   In political contests a distinction should be made between foreign and intestine wars.   The latter are called civil wars when they reach their highest pitch of intensity and result in armed violence.   In ordinary times, they constitute the parliamentary or election contests of political factions.   In a foreign war is there not always an offensive and defensive army, one in favour of a fight and the other against it?   And, above all, is not the cause of war the advance of some claim, or, if it be a doctrinal war, of some dogma that is noised about and pushed forward by one of the belligerents and rejected by the other? In electoral or parliamentary wars there are as many separate combats as the number of measures or principles that are proposed or proclaimed on the one hand and condemned or contradicted on the other.   This process between an official plaintiff and one or more opposing defendants is renewed under countless pretexts, from the moment that a ministry or government is first formed; it is ended by the destruction of the opposition—as, for example, in 1594, by the defeat of the Catholic League—or by the downfall of the government or ministry. As for industrial rivalries, to conclude, they consist, if we consider them closely, in many successive or simultaneous duels between inventions that have spread and been established for a shorter or longer period and one or more new inventions that are trying to spread by satisfying more fully the same need. Thus there are always in an industrially progressive society a certain number of old products which defend themselves with varying fortune against new ones.   The production and consumption of the former embody a strong affirmation or conviction,—in the case of tallow candles, for example, we have the affirmation that this means of lighting is the best and most economical,—that is impugned by the production and consumption of the latter. We are surprised to find a conflict of propositions underlying the quarrel over shop-counters. The quarrels that are to-day past history between cane sugar and beet sugar, between the stage-coach and the locomotive, between the sailboat and the steamboat, etc., were once real social discussions or even argumentations. For not only two propositions, but two syllogisms, were here face to face, according to a general condition unheeded by logicians. The one said, for example, " The horse is the fastest domestic animal. Now, locomotion is possible only by means of animals; consequently the stage-coach is the best means of locomotion." To this, the other answered: " The horse is, to be sure, the fastest animal, but it is not true that only brute forces can be utilised in the transportation of men and merchandise, consequently, your conclusion is false." This observation should be generalised, and it would be easy for us to discover many syllogistic rebuffs of a similar kind in the above logical duels.

I may add that, in the case of industry, the contest is not merely one between two inventions meeting the same need or between the manufacturers or corporations or classes which have monopolised them separately. It is also one between two different needs. The one, some widespread and dominant desire that has been developed by a number of antecedent inventions, like the love of country, for example, among the ancient Romans, is supposed to be of superior importance; the other, aroused by some recent or recently imported inventions, like the taste for objects of art or for Asiatic effeminacy, implicitly impugns the superiority of the first, against which it contends. This kind of contest seems, of course, to be more closely connected with morality than with industry; but in a certain sense morality is only industry viewed in its high and truly political aspect. Government is only a special kind of industry that is able or is supposed to be able to satisfy the chief need and aim that the nature of long-prevailing systems of production and consumption or of long-ruling convictions has planted without a rival in the heart of a people and to which morality insists that all others be subordinated. One country clamours for glory, another for territory, a third for money; it all depends whether its people have done most of their work under arms or at the plough or in the factory. As nations or as individuals, we are ever unwittingly under the control of some guiding desire or, rather, some persistent resolution which, born itself of some past victory, has always fresh combats to wage. We are also under the control of some fixed idea or opinion which has been adopted after some hesitation and whose citadel is continually being attacked. This is called a state of mind in individuals, and a state of society in nations. Every mental or social state implies, then, while it lasts, an ideal. To the formation of the ideal which morality defends and preserves, all the military and industrial as well as all the æsthetic past of a society has contributed. And finally art itself has its own peculiar conflicts of theses and antitheses. In each of its domains there is always some prevailing school that affirms a certain type of beauty which is denied by some other school.

But here I should linger for a moment to emphasise the preceding points. We are considering social facts mainly from the logical point of view, that is, from the point of view of the corroborative or contradictory beliefs which they imply, rather than from that of the auxiliary or contrary desires which they likewise imply. It is difficult to understand how inventions and their aggregates, institutions, can either endorse or disavow one another, and this point I must make clear once for all. Invention only satisfies or provokes desire; desire expresses itself as purpose; and purpose, besides being a pseudo-judgment in its affirmative or negative form (I desire, I do not desire), includes some hope or fear, generally hope, that is, it always includes a true judgment. Hope or fear means affirmation or negation accompanied by a greater or less degree of belief that the thing desired will come to pass. Suppose that I wish to be a Deputy,—a desire which has been developed in me through the invention of universal suffrage and representation,—it means that I hope to become a Deputy by means of certain well-known methods. And if my opponents hinder me (because they *believe* that another will aid them more in obtaining the places which they desire, a desire which has been provoked in them by the old or new invention of the functions in question), it is because they have some quite contradictory hopes. I affirm that thanks to my good management I shall probably be elected; they deny it. If they should absolutely cease denying and lose all hope, they would no longer oppose me, and the teleological duel would end, as it always does end, in the logical duel—a proof of the capital importance of the latter.

What is social life but a continual turmoil of vague hopes and fears intermittently excited by fresh ideas which stir up fresh desires? When we dwell upon the conflict or competition of desires we get a social teleology, when upon that of hopes, a social logic. When two inventions satisfy the same desire, they clash together, as I have shown, because each implies on the part of its respective producer or consumer the hope or conviction that it is the better adapted to the end in view, and, consequently, that the other is the inferior of the two. But, even when two inventions satisfy two different desires, they may contradict each other, either because the desires are dissimilar expressions of a higher desire which each thinks itself the fitter to express, or because the satisfaction of either requires that the other shall remain unsatisfied and because each hopes that this will be the outcome.

We have an example of the first case in the invention of oil painting in the fifteenth century. This invention gainsaid the ancient invention of painting on wax in the sense that the growing passion for the former contested with the existing taste for the latter the right of considering itself the best form of the love of pictures. As an example of the second case we have the invention of gunpowder in the fourteenth century. In developing among sovereigns an ever-growing craving for conquest and centralisation, a craving which required the subjection of the feudal lords for its satisfaction, it found itself in opposition with the inventions of fortified castles and elaborate armour, inventions which had developed the need for feudal independence among the nobility; and if the latter persisted in their resistance to their king, it was because they continued to have as much confidence in their castles and cuirasses as the king in his cannon.

But in history the chief contradiction between two inventions arises from their satisfying the same desire. The Christian invention of the diaconate and the episcopacy certainly contradicted the pagan invention of the prætorship and consulship and patriciate, for both Christian and pagan thought that their desire for grandeur was satisfied by their respective dignities and denied that it could be satisfied by the dignities of the other. Consequently a social state which tolerated all of these opposite institutions at the same time contained a hidden evil; and, as a matter of fact, many contradictions of this kind contributed, after the advent of Christianity, to the break-up of the Roman Empire and to that absorption of Roman civilisation which at the Renascence forced the civilisation of Christendom to give way in its turn. In a way, too, the invention of the monastic rule of the first religious orders also gainsaid the ancient invention of the Roman phalanx, since each of these inventions, in the eyes of those who made use of it, satisfied, to the exclusion of the other, the desire for true security.

In like manner the Doric and Corinthian orders were gainsaid by the pointed style, and the hexameter and pentameter by the rhymed verse of ten syllables. The hexameter and the Corinthian order satisfied the Roman's desire for literary and architectural beauty; they failed to do this for the twelfth-century Frenchman, whom the ten-syllabled verse, dear to the trouvères, and the style of Notre Dame de Paris alone satisfied. The irreconcilable elements in such conceptions, then, are the judgments which accompany them. This is so true that when in modern times a more liberal taste attributes grandeur to both the patriciate and the episcopacy and beauty to both the hexameter and the heroic measure, formerly antagonistic elements are reconciled, just as long before this monasticism and militarism came into perfect harmony when it was seen that in the one lay security for the life to come and in the other, for life from day to day.

It is quite certain, therefore, that all social advances by means of elimination consist, at first, of duels between antagonistic affirmatives and negatives. But it is well to note that the negative is not entirely self-sustaining, that it must depend upon some new thesis which is itself gainsaid by the thesis of the affirmative. In times of progress, then, the elimination must always be a substitution, and I have merged these two ideas into the latter one. This necessity explains the weakness of certain political oppositions which have no programmes of their own, and whose impotent criticism controverts everything and affirms nothing. For the same reason no great religious heretic or reformer ever confined himself wholly to the negative side in any effective opposition to dogma. The cutting dialectic of a Lucian did less to shatter the statue of Jupiter than the lisping by slaves of the least of the Christian dogmas. It has been justly observed, too, that an established system of philosophy resists all attack until the day when its enemies have become its rivals in the establishment of another original philosophic system.

However ridiculous a school of art may be, it continues vigorous until replaced. It took the pointed style to kill the Roman style of architecture, and the art of the Renascence to kill the Gothic. Classic tragedy would have survived its critics but for the appearance of the romantic drama, hybrid though it was. A commercial article disappears from consumption only because another article satisfying the same want takes its place, or because the want that it satisfies has been suppressed by a change of fashion or custom, and this change can be accounted for not alone by the spread of some new distaste or objection, but by that of some new taste or principle as well.[1] In the same way a new legal principle or procedure must be formulated or adopted before inconvenient or antiquated principles or procedures can disappear. In Rome archaic civil processes would have persisted indefinitely but for the ingenious invention of the Formulary system. Quiritian law gave way only to the happy fictions and liberal inspirations of Prætorian law. In our own days the French penal code, as well as many other foreign criminal codes, is clearly old-fashioned and contrary to public opinion, but it will be maintained until criminologists agree upon some new theory of penal responsibility that will be generally adopted.

Finally, if a people retain the same number of ideas to be verbally expressed (if it loses some of its ideas without acquiring at least an equal number, its civilisation is declining instead of progressing), the words and grammatical forms of its language can be eliminated only through the spread of equivalent terms or idioms. When one word dies another is born, and, consequently, or analogously, when one language perishes, it means that another has been born within it or outside of it. Latin would still be spoken, in spite of the barbarian invasions, providing certain important linguistic inventions, the derivation of articles from pronouns, for example, or the characterisation of the future tense by the infinitive followed by the verb *to have (avoir) (aimer-ai)*, had not come to group themselves together somewhere or other to form a rallying point for the Romance languages. Here were new *theses* without which the *antithesis*, which consisted in opposition to the cases and tenses of the Latin declensions and conjugations, would never have succeeded.

Thus every logical duel is in reality twofold, consisting of two sets of diametrically opposite affirmations and nega-

---

[1] Under the inroads, however, of poverty, disease, or general misfortune a want may disappear without being replaced at all; or it may be replaced only by increased intensity on the part of lower wants which have become excessive and exclusive of all others. Then a decline or set-back instead of an advance in civilisation takes place.

tions. Still, although, at every moment of social life, one of the two hostile theses gainsays the other, yet it presents itself as pre-eminently self-affirmative; whereas the second thesis, although it likewise affirms itself, owes its prominence only to its contradiction of the first. It is essential both for the politician and the historian to distinguish in every case whether the affirmative or the negative side preponderates and *to note the moment when the rôles are reversed*. This moment almost always arrives. There is a certain time when a growing philosophy or religious or political sect owes all its popularity to the support which it lends to the controvertists of the accepted thesis or dogma or to the detractors of government; later, when this philosophy or sect has enlarged, we see that all the forces of the still resistant national church or orthodox philosophy or established government are called upon to serve as a protection against the objections, the doubts, and the alarms that have been aroused by the ideas and pretensions of the innovators, ideas and pretensions that have by this time become attractive in themselves. In the case of industry and fine arts, it is for the pleasure of change, of *not doing* the usual thing, that that part of the public which is influenced by fashion adopts a new product to the neglect of some old one; then when the novelty has become acclimated and appreciated for its own sake the older product seeks a refuge in the cherished habits of the other part of the public which is partial to custom and which wishes to show in that way that it also *does not* do the same thing as the rest of the world. In the struggle of a new form of speech with some old expression, the new form at first relies upon its chiefly negative charm for neologists who wish to talk out of the ordinary; and when the new form in turn becomes time-worn, the older expression finds support in its turn, but upon its negative side merely, among the lovers of archaisms who do not wish to talk like all the rest of the world. The same somersaults are turned in a duel between a new principle of justice and a traditional one.

It is now essential to distinguish between the cases in which the logical duel of theses and antitheses is individual and those in which it is social. The distinction could not be more clear-cut. The social duel commences only after the individual one has ceased. Every act of imitation is preceded by hesitation on the part of the individual, for every discovery or invention that seeks to spread abroad always finds some obstacle to overcome in some of the ideas or practices that have already been adopted by every member of the public. And then in the heart or mind of every such person some kind of a conflict sets in. It may be between two candidates, that is, between two policies which solicit his vote, or, if he be a statesman, between two perplexing lines of action. It may be between two theories which sway his scientific belief; or between religion and irreligion, or between two sects which contend for his religious adherence. It may be between two objects of art or commerce which hold his taste and his purchase price in suspense. If he be a legislator, it may be between two contrary bills [1] or principles that seem equally important; or, if he be a lawyer, between two solutions of a legal question over which he is reflecting, or between two expressions which suggest themselves at the same time to his hesitating tongue. Now, as long as a man hesitates in this way, he refrains from imitation, whereas it is only as an imitator that he is a part of society. When he finally imitates, it means that he has come to a decision.

Let us suppose, although it is an hypothesis that could never be realised, that all the members of a nation were simultaneously and indefinitely in a state of indecision like that which I have described. Then war would be at an end, for an ultimatum or a declaration of war presupposes the making of individual decisions by cabinet officers. For war to exist, the clearest type of the logical duel in society, peace must first have been established in the

---

[1] A greater number of bills may be up for consideration, but there are never more than two in conflict at the same time in the hesitating mind of the law-maker.

minds of the ministers or rulers who before that hesitated to formulate the thesis and antithesis embodied in the two opposing armies. For the same reason there would be no more election contests. There would be an end to religious quarrels and to scientific schisms and disputes, because this division of society into separate churches or theories presupposes that some single doctrine has finally prevailed in the previously divided thought or conscience of each of their respective followers. Parliamentary discussions would cease. There would be an end to litigation. A lawsuit, the presentation of a social difficulty for settlement, shows that each party has already settled in his own mind the mental difficulty that was presented to him. Industrial competition between rival establishments would cease because their rivalry depended upon each having its separate group of patrons, and now their products would no longer vie against one another in their patrons' hearts. There would be an end to the struggles and encroachments of different kinds of law, such as those between the Custom and the Roman law of mediæval France, for such national perplexity means that individuals have chosen one or the other of the two bodies of law. There would be an end to contests for pre-eminence between distinct dialects, between the *Langue d'Oc* and the *Langue d'Oïl,* for example, for a linguistic hesitation of this kind in a nation is due to the linguistic steadfastness of the individuals who compose it.

In brief, to reiterate, social irresolution begins when individual irresolution ends. Nowhere else can be seen to greater advantage the striking similarity and dissimilarity of the logic and psychology of society to the logic and psychology of the individual. I hasten to add that although the hesitation which precedes an act of imitation is merely an individual fact, yet it is caused by social facts, that is, by other accomplished acts of imitation. The resistance which a man always puts up against the influence, whether rational or prestigeful, of another man whom he is about to copy is always the outcome of some prior influence which he has already experienced. His delay in imitating is due to the intersection in his mind of a given current of imitation with an inclination towards a different imitation. It is well to note here that even the spread of an imitation involves it in an encounter and struggle with another imitation.

At the same time it may be seen that the necessity of there being only two adversaries in social oppositions is explained by the universality of imitation, the essential fact of social life. In fact, only two theses or judgments can be in opposition wherever this elementary fact occurs: the thesis or purpose of the individual-model and the thesis or purpose of the individual-copy. If we wish to look abroad over masses of human beings, the duel may be seen to be reproduced, magnified, and socialised under thousands of forms; but the more narrow and complete the order of the phenomena of human association in question, the more clearly will it be reflected in the total group of facts. It is very clear in military affairs as armies become disciplined and centralised and as it comes about that only one great combat is waged at the same time on the same battlefield instead of the multiplied single combats of the Homeric period. It is very distinct, too, in religions, as they grow more united and more hierarchical. The duel between Catholicism and Protestantism, or between Catholicism and free thought, implies an advance in the organisation of these cults and of that of free thought as well. The duel is less clear in politics, but it becomes more clear as parties advance in organisation. It is even less clear in industry; but if industry ever comes to be organised on a socialistic basis, the case will change. In language it is very vague, for language has become less conscious of nationality than any other human product. However, I mentioned above the struggle of the *Langue d'Oc* and·the *Langue d'Oïl,* and there are many other analogous examples. The duel became vague, too, in jurisprudence when the study of law ceased to be a passion, and law schools were no longer recruited by the trained and enthusiastic followers of famous professors, and ceased to witness anything comparable to the great contentions of the Sabiniani and Proculiani at Rome, of the Romanists and Feudists at the close of the Middle Ages, etc.

When social irresolution has been produced and accentuated it must be transformed in its turn into resolution. How? Through a fresh series of individual states of irresolution followed by acts of imitation. If several political programmes are splitting a nation up, one of them will spread, through means of propaganda or terror, until it has won over almost everybody one by one. The same is true of one among many rival churches or philosophies. It is useless to multiply examples. Finally, when a certain degree of the unanimity which is never absolute comes to be realised, all irresolution, whether individual or social, is very nearly over. This is the inevitable finish. Everything which we see anchored and rooted in our customs and beliefs of to-day began by being the object of ardent discussion. There is no peaceful institution which has not been mothered by discord Grammars, codes, catechisms, written and unwritten constitutions, ruling industries, sovereign systems of versification, all these things which are in themselves the *categorical* basis of society, have been the slow and gradual work of social *dialetic*. Every grammatical rule expresses the triumph of some habit of speech which has spread at the expense of other partially contradictory habits. Every article of the French Code is a bargain or treaty made after bloody street broils, after stirring journalistic polemics, and after rhetorical parliamentary tempests. No constitutional principle has ever been accepted except in the wake of revolutions, etc.[1]

The categories of the individual mind originated in the

[1] A distinction has been made between constitutions that are *made to order*, or, if you like, improvised, and *contract* constitutions that are formed little by little (see M. Boutmy). This distinction is elsewhere of importance. But, in the last analysis, constitutions that are made to order themselves result from a transaction between the opposing parties in the bosom of the parliament from which they spring Only in these cases, there is but one struggle, and one contract, whereas the English Constitution, for example, was the outcome of a great number of struggles and contracts between pre-existent powers.

same way.[1] Our slightly developed notions of time, space,
matter, and force are, according to the well-grounded conclusion of the new psychology, the result of the inhibi-
tions, inductions, and acquisitions that take place in the
individual during the first period of life. But, just as the
little child in the cradle possesses at an age which defies
analysis the germ of vague ideas on space and time, if
not on matter and force, so every primitive society presents to us a confused body of grammatical rules, of customs, of religious ideas, and of political forces about whose
formation we are absolutely ignorant.

The conclusion of society's logical duel occurs in three
different ways. (1) It quite often happens that one of
the two adversaries is suppressed merely by the natural
prolongation of the other's progress. For example,
the Phœnician writing had only to continue to spread
to annihilate the cuneiform. The petroleum lamp had
only to be known to cause the brazier of nut oil, a slight
modification of the Roman lamp, to fall into disuse in
the shanties of Southern France. Sometimes, however,
a moment arrives when the progress of even the favoured
rival is checked by some increasing difficulty in dis-
lodging the enemy beyond a certain point. Then, (2)
if the need of settling the contradiction is felt strongly
enough, arms are resorted to, and victory results in the
violent suppression of one of the two duellists. Here
may be easily classed the case in which an authoritative, although non-military, force intervenes, as happened in the vote of the Council of Nice in favour of
the Athanasian creed, or in the conversion of Con-
stantine to Christianity, or as happens in any important decision following upon the deliberations of a dictator
or assembly. In this case, the vote or decree, like the
victory in the other case, is a new external condition which

---

[1] In a treatise published in August and September, 1889, in the
Revue philosophique, under the title of *Catégories logiques et institutions sociales,* and reproduced in my *Logique sociale* (1894), I have
developed at length the parallel which I have here confined myself to
indicating.

favours one of the two rival theses or volitions at the expense of the other and disturbs the natural play of spreading and competing imitations somewhat as a sudden climatic change resulting from a geological accident in a given locality disturbs the propagation of life by preventing the multiplication of some naturally fertile animal or vegetal species and by facilitating that of others which otherwise had been less prolific. Finally, (3) the antagonists are often seen to be reconciled, or one of them is seen to be wisely and voluntarily expelled through the intervention of some new discovery or invention.

Let us consider for a while this last and, as it seems to me, most important case, for here the intervening condition comes from within rather than from without. Besides, the successful discovery or invention plays the same part here as that played in the preceding case by the happy inspiration of the general on the battlefield whose flash of military genius ensured the victory of his side. It took the discovery, for example, of the circulation of the blood, to put an end to the interminable discussions of the anatomists of the sixteenth century. It took the astronomical discoveries due to the invention of the telescope, at the beginning of the seventeenth century, to settle the question in favour of the Pythagorean hypothesis and contrary to those of the Aristotelians whether the sun revolved around the earth or the earth around the sun, as well as many other questions which divided the astronomists into two camps. Turn to any library and see how many sometime burning questions, how many belching volcanoes of argument and abuse, are now cold and extinct! And the cooling down has almost always been started, as if by a miracle, by some scholarly, or apparently, by some even erudite or imaginary, discovery. There is not a page of the catechism which is at present unchallenged by believers but whose every line embodies the outcome of violent polemics between the founders of its dogma, between the Church Fathers or the Councils

What was needed to end these at times bloody combats?

The discovery of some more or less authentic and sacred text, or of some new theological conception—unless some supposedly infallible authority cut short the controversy by force. In the same way, how many conflicts between men's wills and desires have been settled or singularly, calmed down by some industrial or even by some political invention! Before the invention of wind-mills or water-mills, desire for bread and aversion to the enervating labour of grinding by hand were openly antagonistic in the hearts of the master and his slaves. To wish to eat bread was to wish this atrocious fatigue for one's self or for others, and not to wish this fatigue for one's self, if one were a slave, was to wish that nobody should eat bread. When the water-mill was invented, it was an immense relief to slave-labour, and the aforesaid desires ceased to impede each other. Before the invention of the cart, one of the most wonderful inventions of antiquity, the need to transport heavy weights and the wish not to exhaust one's strength by carrying them on one's shoulder and not to prostrate beasts of burden with them fought together and blocked each other's way in people's feelings. In short, slavery was but a necessary evil for the accomplishment of painful and obligatory work the necessity of which was recognised by the slave as well as by his master. The master threw the burden of it upon the slave in order that, as far as he himself was concerned, at any rate, the conflict of contradictory desires might be settled; otherwise it would have been settled for nobody. This chronic antagonism of desires and interests gave way but gradually to comparative harmony through a series of capital inventions which provided for the utilisation of the inanimate forces of nature, of steam, of the winds and streams, etc., to the great and equal advantage of both master and slave.

Here each intervening invention did better than merely to suppress one of the terms of the difficulty; it suppressed their contrariety. This is what happens in the unravelling of a comedy (for an invention is a *dénouement*, and *vice versa*), when the contradiction in the wills of a father and son, for example, comes to a point that seems to be insurmountable, some unexplained disclosure shows that it is entirely fictitious and groundless.[1]   Industrial inventions may be compared, then, to the unravelling of a comedy, in other words, they are pleasing and satisfactory to all the world, whereas military inventions, with their perfected armaments and cunning strategy and eagle-eyed perception at critical moments, plainly suggest the unravelling of a tragedy where the triumph of one rival is the death of the other, where so much passion and prejudice is embodied in the actors, where the contradiction between their desires and their convictions is so serious that harmony becomes impossible and the final sacrifice inevitable.   Every victory is in this way the suppression, if not of the vanquished, at least of his national and resisting will, by the national will of the victor.   It is this rather than a mutual agreement, in spite of the treaty which follows and which is an involuntary compact.   In short, history is a tissue, an interlacing of tragedies and comedies, of horrible tragedies and cheerless comedies.   If we look closely, we can

[1] We sometimes have, or, rather, we think we have, these happy surprises in politics and religion as well as in industry. Renan makes a somewhat similar remark. " In great historic movements," he says (the early Church, the Reformation, the French Revolution), " there is a moment of exaltation when men, bound together by some common work (Peter and Paul, Lutherans and Calvinists, Montagnards and Girondists, etc.), *turn from or kill one another for some shadow of a difference,* and then there is a moment of reconciliation when *the attempt is made to prove* that the apparent enemies have been really working together in sympathy for the same end   After a time a single doctrine issues forth from all this discord, and perfect agreement reigns (or seems to reign) between the followers of those who had once anathematised one another " (*Les Evangèles*). In moments of exaltation the slightest shades of difference *must* lead to violence, for in the extraordinary light of an exalted conscience this shadow, *this partial mutual contradiction,* is perceived, and, since every man at such times embodies himself wholly in the thesis which he has adopted, and devotes himself absolutely to its unlimited propagation, the suppression of any thesis that contradicts his own involves the murder of him or them in whom the former is embodied. Later, when the first actors have disappeared and been replaced by less enthusiastic successors, the lukewarmness of opposite convictions lets us throw a convenient veil over their mutual contradictions. A mere lowering of the general plane of belief has brought about this change.

easily distinguish them.   This is perhaps the reason, I may say in passing, why, in our much more industrial than military age, it is not surprising to find that, on the stage, where real life is reflected, tragedy is becoming more neglected day by day and is yielding to comedy, which grows and flourishes, but which becomes sombre and gloomy at the same time.

III. *The Logical Union*

Now that we have discussed the inventions and discoveries which fight and replace each other, I have to deal with those which aid and add to each other.   It must not be inferred from the order I have followed that progress through substitution originally preceded progress through accumulation.   In reality, the latter necessarily preceded, just as it plainly follows, the former.   The latter is both the alpha and the omega; the former is but a middle term. For example, the formation of languages certainly began in a successive acquisition of words, of verbal forms, which, as they expressed ideas hitherto unexpressed, found no rivals to contest their establishment; and this circumstance undoubtedly facilitated their first steps.   In the beginnings of primordial religion the legends and myths with which it was enriched found in their character of answers to entirely fresh questions no prior solutions to contradict them, and it was easy for them not to contradict each other, since they gave separate answers to different questions.   It was probably difficult for primitive customs to graft themselves upon the waywardness peculiar to a state of nature; but as they answered to problems of justice which had until then been unpropounded and as they regulated individual relations which had until then been unregulated, they had the good fortune to have no pre-existing customs to combat, and it was an easy matter for them not to become embroiled with one another.

Finally, primitive political organisations must have been free to develop up to a certain point without any inward disturbance or military or industrial struggle.   The very first form of government was in answer to a demand for security which had until then received no satisfaction, and this circumstance was favourable to its establishment. When the art of war first arose, every new weapon or drill or tactic could be added to those already in existence, whereas, in our own day it is seldom that a new engine of war or a new military regulation does not have to battle for some time with others which its introduction has rendered useless.   In the beginnings of industry, in its pastoral and agricultural forms, every newly cultivated plant and every newly domesticated animal were added to the feeble resources of field and barn, of garden and stable, and did not, like to-day, replace other domestic plants and animals of almost equal worth.   At that time, likewise, every new astronomical or physical observation which lit up some hitherto obscure point in the human mind took an undisputed place side by side with anterior observations which it in no way contradicted.   It was a question of scattering shadows, not of overcoming falsehoods.   It was a question of exploiting unbounded and uncultivated lands, not of improving lands that had already been worked by other possessors.

But we should not overlook the fact that the kind of accumulation which precedes substitution by means of logical duels is different from that which follows it.   The first kind consists of a weak aggregation of elements whose principal bond lies *in not contradicting one another;* the second, in a vigorous group of elements which not only do not contradict one another, but, for the most part, *confirm one another*.   And this should be so, because of the continually growing need of strong and comprehensive belief . From what has preceded we can already see the truth of this remark; it will presently become still more apparent.   I will show that along all lines there are two distinct kinds of inventions or discoveries, those that are capable of indefinite accumulation (although they may also be replaced) and those that, after a certain degree of accumulation has been reached, must, if progress is to continue, be replaced. Now, the distribution of both kinds takes place quite naturally in the course of progress. The first both precede and follow the second, but in the latter instance, after the exhaustion of the second, they present a systematic character which they previously lacked.

A language may grow without limit through the addition of new words corresponding to new ideas; but although nothing may check the increasing bulk of its vocabulary, the additions to its grammar are restricted. Outside of a small number of grammatical rules and forms which are alike in character and which meet, more or less satisfactorily, *all* the needs of the language, no new rule or form can arise without entering into opposition with others and without tending to recast the idiom in a different mould. If the idea of expressing case by means of a preposition followed by an article comes into a language which is already possessed of declensions, either the article and the preposition must eventually eliminate the declensions, or the declensions must repel them. Now, let me observe, after the grammar of a language has become fixed, its vocabulary does not cease to grow richer; on the contrary, it increases still more rapidly; besides, from this time on, as every new term takes on the same grammatical livery, it not only does not contradict the others, but even indirectly confirms their implicit propositions. For example, every new word which came into Latin with the termination *us* or *a* seemed in its declension to reiterate and confirm that which was said by all the other words similarly terminated and declined, namely, the following general propositions: *us* and *a* are signs of Latinity, *i, u, æ, um* are signs of the genitive, the dative, the accusative, etc.

Religions have also, like languages, two aspects. They have their dictionary of narrative and legend, their starting point, and their religious grammar of dogma and ritual. The former is composed of Biblical or mythological tales, of histories of gods and demi-gods, of heroes and saints, and it can develop without stop; but the latter cannot be extended in the same way. After all the main conscience-tormenting problems have been solved according to the peculiar principle of the given religion, a moment comes when no new dogma can be introduced which does not partly contradict established dogma; similarly, no new rite, in as much as it is an expression of dogma, can be freely introduced when all the dogmas have already been expressed in ritual. Now, after the creed and ritual of a religion have been defined, its martyrology, hagiography, and ecclesiastical history never fail to grow richer, and this even more rapidly than before. Moreover, the saints and martyrs and devotees of a mature religion, not only do not contradict one another in the conventionality and orthodoxy of all their acts, thoughts, and even miracles, but mutually reflect and endorse one another. In this respect they differ from the divine or heroic persons, from the gods and demigods, from the patriarchs and apostles, as well as from the legends and prodigies, that succeeded one another before the making of dogma and ritual.

Here I must open a parenthesis for quite an important observation. If a religion is primarily narrative, it is highly variable and plastic; if it is primarily dogmatic, it is essentially unchangeable. In Greco-Latin paganism there is almost no dogma, and since ritual has, therefore, almost no dogmatic significance its symbolism is of the more distinctly narrative kind. It may represent, for example, an episode in the life of Ceres or Bacchus. Understood in this way there may be no end to the accumulation of different rites. If dogma amounted to almost nothing, narrative was almost everything, in ancient polytheism. Therefore it had an incredible facility for enrichment. This is analogous to the inflation of a modern idiom, like English, which, although it is grammatically very poor, incorporates all manner of foreign words by merely making a slight change in their termination, a kind of linguistic baptism. But although this capacity for un-limited enlargement is a cause of viability in a narrative religion, this does not mean that it is particularly well fortified against the attacks of criticism. It is quite a different thing from the solid theological system or body of self-consistent or apparently self-consistent dogma and dogmatic ritual that can rise up in a mass to confront any outside controversialist that may oppose them.

But to return. What is true of religion is also true of that which seeks to replace it, of science. As long as science merely enumerates and describes facts, sense-given data, it is susceptible of indefinite extension. And science begins in this way by being a collection of non-related as well as non-contradictory phenomena. But as soon as it becomes dogmatic and law-making, in turn, as soon as it conceives of theories that are able to give to facts the air of mutual confirmation instead of merely mutual non-contradiction, as soon, indeed, as it unwittingly synthesises the data of sensation under intuitive mental forms which are implicit general propositions called time, space, matter, and force, then science becomes, perhaps, the most incapable of extension of all human achievements. Scientific theories undoubtedly become more complete, but this happens through mutual substitution and through periodically fresh starts, whereas observations and experiments go on accumulating. Certain leading hypotheses that reappear from one age to another—atomism, dynamism (modern evolutionism), monadology, idealism (Platonic or Hegelian)—are the inflexible frames of the swelling and overflowing mass of facts. Only, among these master thoughts, these hypotheses or *inventions* of science, there are certain ones which receive increasing confirmation from one another and from the continual accumulation of newly discovered facts which, in consequence, no longer merely restrict themselves to not contradicting one another, but reciprocally repeat and confirm one another, as if bearing witness together to the same law or to the same collective proposition. Before Newton, successive astronomical discoveries did not contradict one another; since Newton, they confirm one another. Ideally, every distinct science should be reducible, like modern astronomy, to a single formula, and these different formulas should be bound together by some higher formula. In a word, there should be no longer sciences, but Science, just as in a polytheistic religion which has become monotheistic by means of selection there are no longer gods, but God.

And so in a tribe which passes from a pastoral to an agricultural and then to a manufacturing state, adding wheat fields and rice fields to its pasture lands, enriching its orchards and gardens, elaborating its textile fabrics, interests do not fail to multiply nor corresponding laws and customs to accumulate. But the general principles of law which finally shine out from such a medley are always limited in number, and for them progress means substitution. Now, after the formation of a legal grammar, the dictionary of law, in France called the *Bulletin des lois,* can, of course, visibly enlarge and redouble its activity as well; but from this time on, succeeding laws are garbed in the same uniform of theory, a uniform which adapts them to codification, to a rural code, to a commercial code, to a maritime code, etc. This systematisation would have been impossible before.

Finally, from the point of view of government (I use the word in its large sense to mean the *directed activity* of a nation in all its forms) analogous distinctions are exhibited. We may say that the directed national activity is either militant or industrial and that the former type of activity is divisible into military and politcal forces, according as it consists of the short and bloody warfare of armies or of the long and stormy warfare of parties, of the oppression of a conquered and tributary foreigner or of that of a home foe who has been crushed down by taxation. Now, it is remarkable that in both these subdivisions, the administrative side is continually unfolding and improving as its functions multiply, whereas the arts of war and statesmanship are always moving in a narrow circle of strategies and constitutions which may be gathered up into a small number of different and mutually exclusive types. But it is only after civil or military functions have been taken and multiplied by some constitutional or strategic plan, that they converge, instead of merely refraining from over-diverging, and that they form a true state or army, instead of a horde or federation of barbarians.

As for the industrial division of directed national activity, the same remarks are applicable, modified by certain observations. Industry, as I have already said, can be separated only in thought from the dominant ethics and æsthetics of any given period. If we hold to this idea as we should, we shall perceive that only a certain number of new industrial ideas or inventions are, as I have so often repeated, susceptible of indefinite progress, that is to say, of an almost endless amount of accumulation. The *industrial machinery* of course increases; but the *ends* of the service to which all these means are eventually put, follow one another only through mutual elimination. At first sight and taking the means and ends of industry collectively without distinguishing between them, it would seem as if the industrial systems of different periods had wholly replaced each other. Nothing is less like the industry of Greece or Rome than the industry of Assyria; the industry of the seventeenth century is quite unlike that of the Middle Ages and modern manufacture unlike the hand labour of our forefathers. In fact, each of these great groups of human actions is held together and inspired by some great dominant desire which completely changes from one age to another. It may be the desire to prepare for the life after death or the desire to propitiate one's gods or to honour and embellish one's city, or the desire to give expression to religious faith or kingly pride or the desire to equalise society. The change in this highest aim of all explains the sequence of those striking works in which a whole period is epitomised, works like the Egyptian tomb, the Greek temple, the Roman circus and triumphal arch, the mediæval cathedral, the palace of the seventeenth century, the railroad stations or city structures of to-day.

But, as a matter of fact, it is the civilisation and not the industry which has disappeared forever in this way, if by civilisation we mean the sum of a period's moral and æsthetic aims and industrial *means*. The junction of the former with the latter is always partially accidental. For the given ends exploited the given means because they happened to run across them, but they might have made use of others, and although the given means did serve the given ends, they stood ready to serve different ones as well. Now, the ends pass away; but the means, or what is essential in them, remain. An imperfect machine survives, by a sort of metempsychosis, in the more perfect and complex one which was in whole or in part the cause of its annihilation; and every primitive mechanism such as the rod, the lever, or the wheel reappears in our most modern implements. The long bow survives in the cross bow, the cross bow in the arquebuse and gun. The primitive cart survives in the carriage on springs and the latter in the locomotive. The stage-coach was not routed, but absorbed, by the locomotive, which added something to it, namely, steam and the capacity for a higher rate of speed. On the other hand, the Christian's desire for mystical salvation did not absorb, but actually routed the Roman's desire for civic glory, just as the Copernican theory banished the Ptolemaic system.

In short, the industrial inventions which have followed one another for thousands of years may be compared to the vocabulary of a language or to the facts of science. As I have said above, many tools and products are, in truth, dethroned by others, just as many inexact pieces of information have been driven out by more accurate knowledge, but, in the long run, the number of tools and products, like the sum of knowledge, has increased. Science properly called, a collection of facts that can be drawn upon to prove a given theory, is comparable to industry properly called, a store of processes and mechanisms that can serve to actualise a given system of morals or æsthetics. Industry, in this sense, is the *content* whose *form* is supplied by prevailing ideas of justice and beauty, by ideas concerning the criterion of conduct. And by industry I also mean art, in as much as it is distinct from the changing ideal which uplifts it and which lends to its manifold secrets and facilities their profound inspiration. Now, the resources of industry, including the artifices of artists and even of poets, go on multiplying both before and after the formation of well-defined moral and æsthetic systems, that is, of a hierarchy of wants consecrated by unanimous judgment, but, before this is formed, they are scattered, whereas, after it is formed, they are concentrated; and it is only then, when a single thought is implicitly affirmed in all the branches of national industry, that they present the spectacle of that mutual confirmation, of that unique orientation and of that admirable internal harmony which was known in Greece and in the twelfth century of our era and which our grandchildren may, perhaps, live to see.

For the time being, we must confess, and this remark leads us to new considerations, our modern contemporary epoch is in search of its pole. Its character has been rightly described as chiefly scientific and industrial. By that we must understand that theoretically a successful search for facts has predominated over preoccupation with philosophic ideas and that, practically, a search for the means has predominated over regard for the ends of activity. That means that our modern world has at all times and places instinctively precipitated itself in the direction of discoveries or inventions that can be accumulated without questioning whether the neglected discoveries or inventions that can be substituted for one another did not alone justify and give value to the others. But let us, at any rate, put this question to ourselves: Is it true that the sides of social thought and conduct that cannot be indefinitely extended (grammars, dogma, and theories, principles of justice, political policy and strategy, morals and æsthetics) are less worth cultivating than the sides that can be indefinitely extended (vocabularies, mythologies and descriptive sciences, customs, collections of laws, industries, systems of civil and military administration)?

Indeed, on the contrary, the side open to substitution, that which after a certain point cannot be extended, is always the essential side. Grammar is the whole of language. Theory is the whole of science, and dogma, of religion. Principles constitute justice. Strategy, war. Government is but a political idea. Morality is the sum of industry, for industry amounts to neither more nor less than its end. The ideal is surely the all of art. What are words good for but for building sentences, or facts, but for making theories? What are laws good for but to unfold or consecrate higher principles of justice? For what use are the *arms,* the tactics, and the different divisions of an army but to form part of the strategical plan of the general in command? Of what use are the multiple services, functions, and administrative departments of a state but to aid in the constitutional schemes of the statesman who represents the victorious political party? Of what use are the different crafts and products of a country but to co-operate in achieving the objects of its prevailing morality? Of what use are schools and works of art and literature to a society but to formulate and strengthen its characteristic ideal?

Only it is much easier to move forward in the direction of possible acquisitions and endowments than in that of necessary substitutions and sacrifices. It is much easier to pile up neologism upon neologism than to master one's own tongue and, thereby, gradually improve its grammar; to bring together scientific observations and experiments, than to supply science with theories of a more general and demonstrated order; to multiply miracles and pious practices than to substitute rational for outworn religious dogma; to manufacture laws by the dozen than to conceive of a new principle of justice fitted to conciliate all interests; to increase the complexity of armaments and tactics, of offices and functions, and to have excellent civil or military administrators than to have eminent generals or statesmen able to conceive of the proper plan at the desired moment and to contribute by their example to re-modelling and improving military art or statecraft; to multiply wants by virtue of an ever richer and more varied consumption and production than to substitute for some dominant want a superior and preferable want, one more conducive to order and peace; finally, to artistically unroll an inexhaustible series of tricks and ingenuities than to obtain the slightest insight into some fine new thing that was more worthy of exciting love and enthusiasm.

But modern Europe has been somewhat carried away by the deceptive charm of doing things easily. This is the reason of the especially striking contrast between the wealth of its legislation and the feebleness of its juridical system (compare it, in this particular, with Trajan's Rome or even with Justinian's Constantinople), or between its industrial exuberance and its æsthetic poverty (compare it, in this respect, to the great days of the French Middle Ages or of the Italian Renaissance). I might also bring forward to a certain extent the contrast between modern Europe's sciences and its philosophy of science. But I hasten to recognise the fact that although the philosophic side of its knowledge is comparatively neglected, it has been the object of a much more profound and extensive cultivation than the moral side of its activity. Industry, from this point of view, is notably behind science. It has aroused, on all sides, factitious wants which it satisfies indiscriminately without bothering itself about their arrangement or harmony. In this it resembles the ill-digested science of the sixteenth century which gave birth to a crop of incoherent and pedantic guesses and vagaries each of which was fostered by a certain number of facts. Contemporary activity, contemporary civilisation must straighten out this chaos of heterogeneous wants, just as the science of the sixteenth century had to bridle the imagination of its scholars, and prune away the majority of their conceptions in order to give others a chance to be transformed into theories. What are the simple and fruitful wants which the future will develop, and what are the sterile and smothered wants that it will cast aside? This is the secret. It is hard to find out, but we must make the attempt. All these wrangling or ill-adjusted wants which flourish at every point on the industrial field, and which have their passionate devotees, constitute a sort of moral fetichism or polytheism which seeks to branch out into a comprehensive and authoritative moral monotheism, into a great new and potent system of æsthetics.

Besides, it is industry far more than civilisation that has progressed in recent times. As a proof of this I might point to my embarrassment a while ago in trying to find some characteristic monument of our modern industry. It is a strange fact and one that has been lost sight of that, at present, the grandest works of industry are not industrial products, but industrial implements, namely, great factories, prodigious machines, immense railroad stations. How trivial are the things, even the most important things, which come out of our great foundries or factories; how trivial the fine houses and theatres and city halls compared with the giant laboratories themselves! How the petty magnificence of our private or public luxury fades away before our industrial expositions, where the sole usefulness of the products is self-display! Once the opposite was true, when the miserable huts of Pharaoh's fellahs, or the obscure stalls of mediæval artisans surrounded the gigantic pyramid or cathedral that was reared on high through the sum of their combined efforts. It seems in these days as if industry existed for the sake of industry, just as science exists for the sake of science.

Additional Considerations

We have seen that social progress is accomplished through a series of substitutions and accumulations. It is certainly necessary to distinguish between these two processes; and yet evolutionists have made the mistake, here as elsewhere, of merging them together. Perhaps the term evolution is badly chosen. We may call it social evolution, however, when an invention quietly spreads through imitation—the elementary fact in society; or even when a new invention that has already been imitated grafts itself upon a prior one which it fosters and completes. And yet why should we not use, in this second instance, the more precise term of *insertion?* A philosophy of universal Insertion would be a happy contribution to the correction of the theory of universal Evolution. Finally, when a new, invention, an invisible microbe at first, later on a fatal disease, brings with it a germ which will eventually destroy the old invention to which it attaches itself, how can the latter be said to evolve? Did the Roman Empire evolve when Christianity inoculated it with the virus of radical negations of its fundamental principles? No, this was counter-evolution, revolution perhaps, but certainly not evolution. At bottom, of course, in this case as in the preceding, there is nothing, elementarily, but evolution, because everything is imitation; but, since these evolutions and imitations struggle against each other, it is a great mistake to consider the sum formed by these conflicting elements as *a single* evolution. I thought it important to note this fact in passing.

Let us note another more important fact. Whatever method may be used to suppress conflict between beliefs or between interests and to bring about their agreement, it almost always happens (does it not always happen?) that the resulting harmony creates a new kind of antagonism. For contradictions and contrarieties of details, some massive contradiction or contrariety has been substituted, and this also seeks a solution for itself only to raise up still greater oppositions, and so on until the final solution is reached. Instead of quarrelling together over cattle or game, over utilitarian objects, a million of men will organise themselves into an army and work together for the subjection of a neighbouring people. This is the rallying point of all their avarice and activity. And, in fact, before com-

merce and exchange existed, militarism must have been for
a long time the only logical outcome of the problem raised
up by rival interests.   But militarism gives birth to war,
and war between two peoples is a substitute for thousands
of individual struggles.

In the same way a group of some hundred men will
cease from individual fights and plots and counterplots and
will set to labour together in one workshop.   Their acts
are no longer antagonistic, but from this very fact an unexpected contrariety arises, namely, the rivalry of their
workshop with others that turn out the same kind of goods.
This is not all.   The workmen in every factory are collectively interested in its prosperity; in any case their desires
in production, thanks to the division of organised labour,
converge towards the same end.   The soldiers of an army
have likewise a common interest in victory.   But, at the
same time, the struggle between so-called Capital and so-
called Labour, that is, between the total number of employers
and the total number of workmen,[1] as well as rivalry between different ranks in an army or between different
classes in a nation, is aroused by this imperfect agreement.
These teleological problems are inherent in the very progress of industrial or military organisation, just as scientific
progress raises problems of logic and uncloaks soluble and
insoluble antinomies of reason which an earlier state of
ignorance had concealed.

The feudal system on one hand and the ecclesiastical
hierarchy on the other were powerful in allaying the passions and consolidating the interests of the Middle Ages.
But the great and bloody conflict between the Papacy and
the Empire, between the Guelphs, the partisans of the Pope,
and the Ghibellines, the partisans of the Emperor (at first
a logical, later, a teleological, i. e., political, duel), arose

---

[1] This is so true that already in the sixteenth century we find
"opposed to syndicates of employers (corporations), syndicates of
organised labourers " (see Louis Guibert, *Les anciennes corporations en
Limousin*, etc.)   Combinations of workmen in Paris, in Lyons, and
elsewhere, "supply the printers, the bakers, the hatters, with resources
with which to resist their masters."

from the chock of these two harmonious systems which could not be mutually harmonised without the downfall of one of them. The question is whether or not the displacement of such contradictions or contrarieties is advantageous and whether the harmony of interests or of minds can ever be complete without being offset by discord. In other words, whether or not a certain amount of error and falsehood, of deception and sacrifice, will not always be necessary for the maintenance of social peace?

When the displacement of contradictions or contrarieties consists in their centralisation, an advantage is certainly gained. Although the organisation of standing armies may provoke cruel wars, that is better than innumerable combats of small feudal bands or of primitive families. Although the progress of the sciences may have disclosed profound mysteries, and although great chasms may divide different schools of philosophy because of the new questions over which they contend in arguments drawn from the same scientific arsenal, we are not able to regret the times of ignorance that were free from these problems. In short, science has done more to satisfy poignant curiosity than to arouse it, civilisation has done more to satisfy needs than to engender passions. Inventions and discoveries act as cures through the method of substitution. By stilling natural wants and arousing those of luxury, inventions substitute less urgent for more urgent desires. Discoveries replace the first very anxious states of ignorance by perhaps as many, but, at any rate, by less disquieting, *states of not-knowing*. And, then, can we not see the goal to which this protean transformation of contradiction and contrariety leads us? Competition ends inevitably in monopoly. Free trade and *laisser-aller* tends towards the legal organisation of labour. War tends to the hypertrophy of states;—it will go on producing enormous agglomerations until the political unity of the civilised world is finally consummated and universal peace is assured. The more the conflict between *masses* that is caused by the suppression of minor conflicts increases in emphasis and scale (until a point is even reached which makes us regret the latter), the more inevitable this peaceful outcome of it all becomes. When a royal army was substituted for provincial or feudal militia, it began by containing a much smaller number of soldiers than the effective total of the former militia, and consequently the amount of disaster involved in the conflicts of royal armies was far from equalling that which would have existed in the conflicts which they precluded. But this advantage has, as we know, been decreasing in proportion to the irresistible necessity that has forced each state to enlarge its military contingent to such a point that, at present, the great nations have drafted all their able-bodied men into their armies. Therefore, all the gain of civilisation in this respect would vanish, did not the very enormity of these armies betoken the imminence of some decisive upheaval followed by some colossal unity-and-peace-bringing conquest—unless our soldiers' weapons should become rusty from lack of service and end by dropping out of their hands.

CHAPTER VI

EXTRA-LOGICAL INFLUENCES

WE have now to study the non-logical causes of preference or aversion which are back of different kinds of rival imitations and which determine their victory or defeat.

Before entering upon these considerations, however, let me say a few words about certain modes which an imitation may assume. The modes, namely, of exactness or inexactness, of consciousness or unconsciousness.

1. In the first place, imitation may be either vague or precise. Let us enquire whether, as the acts or ideas to be imitated increase in number and complexity in the course of civilisation, imitation becomes more exact or more confused. We might think that every forward step in complexity brought with it additional inaccuracy. Just the opposite, however, may be observed. Imitation is to such an extent the primal soul of social life, that among civilised men skill and facility in imitating increases even faster than the number and complexity of inventions. Besides, it establishes resemblances that become more and more complete. In doing this, it bears out its analogy to reproduction and vibration. Vibrations of light are much more numerous and delicate than vibrations of sound, and yet the light of the stars is transmitted to us with a marvellous accuracy that is never reached by the latter. The equally numerous and complex vibrations of electricity are transmitted with incomparable and what would be incredible fidelity, but for the striking proofs given to us by the telegraph and telephone and phonograph. A noise is a series of unlike waves, whereas a sound is a series of waves

that are very much alike; nevertheless the latter with their linked harmonies are more complex than the former. Is it true that when heredity has to reproduce highly differentiated organisms it produces less exact resemblances than when it has to reproduce beings of a lower order? On the contrary, the type of a cat or orchid is at least as well conserved as that of a zoöphyte or mushroom. The faintest varieties in human races can, if they have the time in which to become fixed, be perpetuated with the utmost perfection by heredity.

From any point of view social life is bound to lead, in its prolongation, to the formation of etiquette, that is, to the complete triumph of conventionality over individual fancy. Language, religion, politics, war, law, architecture, music, painting, poetry, polite manners, etc., give rise to a conventionality that is the more complete, to an etiquette that is the more exacting and tyrannical, the longer it has lasted and the more undisturbed it has been in its development. Orthography or linguistic purism, the etiquette of language, and ritual, the etiquette of religion, possess about an equal degree of arbitrary precision, when their respective language and religion are alike very old and very original.[1]

[1] Nothing equals the strangeness of certain cults unless it be their persistence. But the same thing may be said of language. It is a fixed caprice, an established, everlasting disorder, like that of the starry heavens What is stranger or more irrational than the use of the word *cabinet* to designate a group of ministers, or of the word Porte as a name for the Ottoman government? What logical relation exists between the words *horse, equus, ἵππος,* and the animal they represent? And yet no law, however sensible and useful it may be, is followed with the same degree of readiness, constancy, and respect as the custom of using accepted words, however outlandish they may appear. In the same way, what resemblance is there, at bottom, between that chain of sacramental ceremonies which is called the Mass, and the sentiment of high morality and refined spirituality of which it is a means of expression among Catholic populations? *Mass* is another word in point; and we know the tenacity of this old word. The difficulty for a whole people to agree at the same time upon the choice of a better term, or to renounce their needs of expression, sacred or secular, is really insurmountable; for such an agreement would be possible only through the spread of imitation. and not through contact. For this reason, although religious persecutions which are directed towards the suppression or replacement of some cult appear to be highly rational, they are, in reality, most absurd;

Although Christianity has grown more complex, from century to century, it has shown itself from its very beginning more and more exacting in point of regularity, uniformity, and orthodoxy. Although savage languages are very meagre, they are, according to Sayce and Whitney, as variable and as carelessly transmitted as civilised languages, in spite of their richness, are uniform and persistent. Procedure, the etiquette of justice, is also very formal when the law is very old, however complicated it may have become. *Ceremonial*, the etiquette of worldly relations, is less strict among nations whose polite society is of later origin than their law or religion. The contrary is true in Chinese society for the opposite reason. Prosody, the etiquette of poetry, becomes more and more despotic as versification increases and, strange to say, as the poetic imagination expands. Red tape and administrative routine, the etiquette of government, increase day by day with differentiation in government. Architecture requires its followers to become more and more servile in the repetition of the consecrated types that are for the time being in favour. This is true also of music. Painting also requires its servants to reproduce with more and more photographic exactness the models of nature or tradition. Under the ancient régime, the military uniform was less general and less respected than it is to-day, and the farther back we go the greater individual variety do we find in the dress of military ranks. According to Burckhardt, at Florence, in the Middle Ages, everyone dressed to suit his fancy as if at a mask-ball. How we should be scandalised to-day by such license!

This need for conventionality is so natural to social man that after it has reached a certain degree of strength it becomes conscious of itself and adopts violent and expeditious means for its satisfaction. All old civilisations

---

about as absurd as *linguistic persecutions*. The latter never succeed in their aim to substitute one language for another, except, at times, through the spontaneous *imitation* of a *superior*, of a conqueror by the conquered.

have had their masters of ceremony, high functionaries who are charged with the perpetuation of traditional rites.[1] We find these chamberlains under different names not only in monarchical states, in Egypt, China, in the Roman Empire, in the Lower Empire, in the Escurial of Philip II and his successor, in the Versailles of Louis XIV, but in republics as well, in Rome, where the censor kept a strict oversight over old usages, and even in Athens, where religious life was subject to the most absolute formalism. We ridicule all of this, overlooking the fact that our smart tailors and dressmakers, our big manufacturers, and even our journalists, bear exactly the same relation to fashion-imitation as these masters of civil or religious ceremony bore to custom-imitation and that they are likely to take on the same comic importance that the latter did. The former cut out our clothes, our conversations, our information, our tastes, and our various wants according to one uniform pattern from which it is improper to depart. Its sameness from one end of the continent to the other passes for the most obvious sign of civilisation, just as the perpetuation for century upon century of certain legends, traditions, and customs was once taken, and much more wisely, for the foundation of a people's grandeur.[2]

2. In the second place, imitation may be conscious or unconscious, deliberate or spontaneous, voluntary or involuntary. But I do not attach great importance to this classification. Is it true that as a people becomes civilised its manner of imitating becomes more and more voluntary, conscious, and deliberate? I think the opposite is true. Just as with the individual unconscious habits were origi-

[1] Some of these rites are very strange. At the moment when, on the night of the wedding, the marriage of the Emperor of China is consummated, two great personages are present at the *solemnity,* and sing a love duet in the imperial alcove

[2] Everything that is true in Spencer's chapter on what he calls *ceremonial government* implicitly confirms the above The writer errs in thinking, as he seems to do, that ceremony is decreasing, and that its sway is strongest in the beginnings of societies But what he takes for primitive societies had already a long past behind them in which the so-called rule of ceremony had already been slowly formed.

nally conscious and self-determined acts, so in the nation everything that is done or said by tradition or custom began by being a difficult and much-questioned importation. I should add, to be sure, that many imitations are from the very beginning unconscious and involuntary. This is so of the imitation of the accents, manners, and more often of the ideals and sentiments peculiar to the environment in which we live. It is also plain that imitation of the will of others—I know no other way of defining spontaneous obedience—is necessarily involuntary. But let us observe that the involuntary and unconscious forms of imitation never become voluntary and conscious, whereas the voluntary and conscious forms are likely to take on the opposite characteristics. Let us distinguish, moreover, between the consciousness of imitating or the will to imitate someone in thinking or doing a certain thing and the consciousness of conceiving the thought or the will to perform the act. Consciousness or volition, in this latter sense, is the constant and universal fact which the progress of civilisation neither augments nor diminishes. In the former sense, there is nothing more variable, and civilisation does not seem to encourage consciousness or will understood in this way. Certainly the savage in whose eyes the ancient custom or religion of his tribe is justice or truth incarnate is no less conscious of imitating his ancestors and is no less desirous of imitating them in practising his juridical or religious rites, than is the modern labourer or even the modern bourgeois of imitating his neighbor, or employer, or editor, in repeating what he has read in his newspaper or in buying the piece of furniture which he has seen in the parlour of his employer or neighbour. But, in fact, in both cases, man is wrong in thinking that he imitates because he wishes to. For this very will to imitate has been handed down through imitation. Before imitating the act of another we begin by feeling the need from which this act proceeds, and we feel it precisely as we do only because it has been suggested to us.

After these remarks on the intrinsic characteristics of

imitations, let us turn our attention to the inequalities that they present in their career by reason of their content (according as the content is the sign or the thing signified, an inward or an outward model), or by reason of the alleged superiority or inferiority of the persons or classes or even places from which they issue or of the past or present epochs in which they originate. In this chapter I propose to show that, *the logical or teleological values being by hypothesis equal,* (1) the subjective model will be imitated before the objective,[1] and (2) the example of persons or classes as well as of localities that are thought superior will prevail over the example of inferior persons or classes or localities. In the following chapters I shall show that a like presumption of superiority attaches (3) at times to the present, at times to the past, and is a potent factor and one of considerable historic significance in favour either of the examples of our fathers, or of those of our contemporaries.

I. *Imitation from Within to Without*

This would be the moment, if I did not shrink from so difficult a task, to exploit an entirely unexplored field and compare the different functions of organic or psychological life from the point of view of their more or less pronounced tendencies, in the average case, to transmit themselves through imitation. This relative transmissibility varies greatly from one period or nation to another. It will be impossible to measure it with any precision until the day when Statistics shall have redeemed all its promises. A few words, then, on this subject must suffice.

Is not thirst more contagious through imitation than hunger? I think it is. This may explain the rapid strides of alcoholism. Although gourmandism has also increased, as we may infer from the more varied and abundant diet of

---

[1] This advance from within to without, from the thing signified to the sign, really answers an innate need of logic, and, therefore, the considerations based upon it might have found a place, up to a certain point, in the preceding chapter.

the middle classes, of the labourer, and of the peasant, its advance has certainly been slower. The same drinks may be in vogue over a great stretch of country (tea in one place, wine in another, beer here, maté there, etc.), whereas the greatest diversity may still prevail in local viands. Is thirst more or less contagious than sexual desires? I think less so. Debauchery is the first vice to develop, even before alcoholism, in large gatherings of men and women or in newly populated cities. Movements of the leg, and especially movements of the upper part of the body, are still more easily communicated. The impetus of marching together is one of the great military forces. The soldier's tendency to keep step and march with his fellows is innate before it is obligatory. It has been proved through careful tests that everybody in the same village walks on an average at the same rate of speed. As for characteristic manners and gestures, they are much more readily transmitted than peculiarities of gait among people who are accustomed to live together. This is partly the reason why in modern hospitals hysterical convulsions readily take on the character of an epidemic, like the diabolical possessions in the convents of the past. The vocal function, like all functions of intercourse, is eminently imitative, particularly on its intellectual side, in diction and pronunciation, not in the timbre of the voice.[1] Accent is also transmitted. But this happens gradually and during youth. Every city retains a characteristic accent long after its food and dress have become like those of other cities. Yawning, I mean the yawn of boredom, whch has a mental cause, is much more contagious than sneezing or coughing.

The functions of the higher senses are more transmissible through imitation than those of the lower. We are much more likely to copy someone who is looking at or listening to something than someone who is smelling a flower or tasting a dish. This is the reason why in large

---

[1] Children take the most lively pleasure in reproducing all the striking sounds, even more than in copying the gestures, in their environment.

cities a gathering is so soon formed around a lounging-place. We plunge into the waiting line behind the doors of a theatre much more eagerly than into the restaurant behind whose window panes we see its patrons enjoying their dinner.

All passions and needs for luxury are more contagious than simple appetites and primitive needs. But shall we say, as to passions, that admiration, confidence, love, and resignation are superior in this respect to contempt, distrust, hatred, and envy? In general, yes, otherwise society would not endure [1] For the same reason, and in spite of frequent epidemics of panic, hope is certainly more catching than terror. Indolence is likewise more so than ambition and avarice, the spirit of saving than avidity. And this is very fortunate for the peace of society. Is courage more catching than cowardice? I am much less certain of this. Here curiosity deserves a special, if not the chief, place of honour. All those throngs of people which end in bringing on revolutions in religion, government, art, and industry begin to collect under the sway of this sentiment. When a person is seen to be curious about what once may have appeared to be the merest trifle, we immediately desire to know about it. This movement spreads very quickly, and the intensity of everybody's desire increases in proportion to its spread, through the effect of mutual reaction. Whenever any novelty whatsoever, a sermon, a political platform, a philosophic idea, a commercial article, a poem, a novel, a drama, or an opera, appears in some notable place, i. e., in a capital city, it is only necessary for the attention of ten persons to become ostensibly fixed upon this thing in order that one hundred, one thousand, or ten thousand persons may quickly take an interest in it and enthuse about it. At times, this phenomenon takes on the character of hysteria. In the fifteenth century when Böhm, the German piper, began to preach his evangel of

---

[1] At any rate, during the ascendency of a people It is only in its decline that it sees judgments of disparagement spread more rapidly than judgments of admiration.

fraternal equality and community of goods, an epidemical exodus set in. "The journeymen hastened from their workshops, the farm maids ran with their sickles in their hands," reports a chronicler, cited by Jansenn, and in a few hours more than thirty thousand men had assembled in a foodless desert. Once general curiosity has been excited, the mob is irresistibly predisposed to be carried away by all the different kinds of ideas and desires which the preacher, the orator, the dramatist, and the novelist of the hour may seek to popularise.

M. Ribot has pointed out that the memory of sentiments is much more persistent than that of ideas. I should say the like of the imitation of sentiments compared with the imitation (*i. e.*, the spread) of ideas. Certainly morals and religious and moral sentiments which consist of reciprocal impregnations of affective states have a greater tenacity than opinions or even principles.

But now I have sufficiently glanced over a group of ideas that I do not wish to analyse more closely. Let us turn to a truth of more general import.

All imitations in which logic has no place fall into two great categories, namely, credulity and docility, imitation of belief and imitation of desires. It may see strange to call passive adherence to the idea of another, imitation; but if, as I have said, it matters little whether the reflection of one brain upon another be active or passive in character, the extension which I give to the usual meaning of this word is highly legitimate. If we say that the scholar imitates his master when he repeats his spoken words, why should we not say that the former has already imitated the latter as soon as he has adopted in thought the idea which he afterwards expresses in speech? It may also surprise the reader to find that I consider obedience a kind of imitation; but this assimilation, which can, at any rate, be easily justified, is necessary, and it alone permits the full significance of the phenomenon of imitation to be recognised. When one person copies another, when one class begins to pattern its dress, its furniture, and its amusements after those of another, it means that it has already borrowed from the latter the wants and sentiments of which these methods of life are the outward manifestations. Consequently it can and must have borrowed the latter's volitions, that is, have willed in accordance with its will.[1]

Is it possible to deny that volition, together with emotion and conviction, ·is the most contagious of psychological states? An energetic and authoritive man wields an irresistible power over feeble natures. He gives them the direction which they lack. Obedience to him is not a duty, but a need. That is the way every social tie begins. Obedience, in short, is the sister of faith. People obey for the same reason that they believe; and just as their faith is the radiation of that of some apostle, so their activity is merely the outgoing of some master will. Whatever the master wills or has willed, they will; whatever the apostle believes or has believed, they believe. And it is because of this that whatever the master or apostle subsequently does or says, they, in turn, do or say or are inclined to do or say. Those persons and classes, in fact, whom one is most inclined to imitate, are those whom one is most docile in obeying. The common people have always been inclined to copy kings and courts and upper classes according to the measure in which they have submitted to their rule. During the years preceding the French Revolution, Paris no longer copied court fashions, and no longer applauded the plays in favour at Versailles, because the spirit of insubordination had already made rapid strides. In all periods,

---

[1] Moreover, commands began by being set examples I have indicated the steps in the gradual transformation of example into command in the preface of my *Logique sociale*, p vii "In a band of monkeys, horses, dogs, or even bees or ants, the leader sets an example of the act which he mentally orders and the rest of the band imitate him. Gradually the imperative intention is separated from the initiative of the act which is commanded and with which it was at first merged. Finally the leader merely outlines the act: later on, he reduces it to a gesture and then to some sign, a cry, a look, an attitude, and, finally, to an articulate sound. But the word always calls up the image of the act to be performed,—a familiar act, of course, for a stroke of genius cannot be described in advance,—and this image is equivalent to the primitive example set by the leader."

the ruling classes have been *or have begun by being* the model classes. In the cradle of society, in the family, this close correlation between imitation, strictly speaking, and obedience and credulity is clearly shown. The father is, especially at first, the infallible oracle and sovereign ruler of his child; and for this reason he is his child's highest model.[1]

Imitation, then, contrary to what we might infer from certain appearances, *proceeds from the inner to the outer man.* It seems at first sight as if a people or a class began to imitate another by copying its luxury and its fine arts before it became possessed of its tastes and literature, of its aims and ideas, in a word, of its spirit. Precisely the contrary, however, occurs. In the sixteenth century fashions in dress came into France from Spain.[2] This was because Spanish literature had already been imposed upon us at the time of Spain's pre-eminence. In the seventeenth century, when the preponderance of France was established, French literature ruled over Europe, and subsequently French arts and French fashions made the tour of the world. When Italy, overcome and downtrodden as she was, invaded us in the fifteenth century, with her arts and fashions, but, first of all, with her marvellous poetry, it was because the prestige of her higher civilisation and of the Roman Empire that she had unearthed and transfigured had subjugated her conquerors. Besides, the consciences of Frenchmen were Italianised long before their houses or dress or furniture

[1] This must be so, let us observe, if the action at a distance of one brain upon another, which I call imitation, is to be classed with hypnotic suggestion, in so far, at least, as a normal and continuous phenomenon may be compared with a rare anomaly which it reproduces on a larger but much less intense scale. We know how credulous and docile the hypnotic subject becomes We know what a good comedian he is We know, too, how deeply the personality which is suggested to him becomes incarnated in him We know that at first it penetrates, or appears to penetrate into his very heart and character before it expresses itself in his posture or gesture or speech. His dominant characteristics are absolute credulity and docility.

[2] Bodin writes that " in the matter of dress he will always be rated dull and loutish who does not apparel himself in the prevailing fashion which has come to us from Spain with the farthingale."

through their habit of submission to the transalpine Papacy.

Did these very Italians who fell to aping their own Greco-Roman restorations begin by reflecting the externals of the ancient world, its statues, its frescoes, its Ciceronian periods, in order to become gradually filled by its spirit? On the contrary, it was to their hearts that their transplendent model made its first appeal. This neo-paganism was the conversion of a whole community, first its scholars and then its artists (this order is irreversible), to a dead religion; and whenever a new religion, it matters not whether it be living or dead, that is made fascinating by some compelling apostle, takes hold of a man, it is first believed in and then practised. It does not begin with mummeries. Mummeries do not lead to virtues and convictions. Far from that, it is the neophyte, above all, who is impressed by the *soul* of a religion independent of its external form, and formalism of worship does not become empty and meaningless until much later, when religion has lost its place in people's hearts although it may still survive in their usages. Thus the neophyte of the early Renaissance continues in his feudal or Christian habits of life, but in faith he is already pagan, as his excess of sensuality and his overruling passion for glory go to prove. It is only at a later period that he becomes a pagan in morals and manners, first in morals and then in manners. The same thing happened, if we go farther back, in the case of the barbarians of the fifth or sixth century, in the case of a Clovis for example, or a Chilperic. They forced themselves to bow down to the customs of Rome and decorated themselves with the consular insignia. But before becoming Latinised in that clumsy, superficial sense they had experienced a much more profound Latinisation in being converted to Christianity, for at that date the Roman civilisation which fascinated them survived only in Christianity.

Let us suppose that two peoples of different religions come into contact, pagans with Christians, Christians with Moslems, Buddhists with Confucians, etc. Each borrows from the other certain new rites to illustrate its own peculiar dogmas, and, at the same time, while each continues to practise its ancient rites it receives new dogmas which are more or less contradictory to the old. Now do rites spread more or less quickly than dogmas? The persistence of old rites in new religions shows that they spread less quickly. In the same way two peoples may borrow both each other's ideas and forms of speech, but they will borrow the former before the latter. If they borrow each other's legal procedure and ceremonial together with each other's principles of justice, the exchange of the latter will be much more rapid than that of the former. And so we have at Rome, in England, in France, etc., the persistence of legal form long after legal reform.

In this way imitation passes on from one people to another, as well as from one class to another within the same people. Do we ever see one class which is in contact with, but which has never, hypothetically, been subject to the control of, another determine to copy its accent, its dress, its furniture, and its buildings, and end by embracing its principles and beliefs? This would invert the universal and necessary order of things. The strongest proof, indeed, that imitation spreads from within to without is to be found in the fact that in the relations between different classes, envy never precedes obedience and trust, but is always, on the contrary, the sign and the result of a previous state of obedience and trust. Blind and docile devotion to the Roman patricians, to the Athenian eupatrides, or to the French nobility of the old régime preceded the envy, *i. e.*, the desire to imitate them externally, which they came to inspire. Envy is the symptom of a social transformation which, in bringing classes together and in lessening the inequality of their resources, renders possible not only the transmission, as before, of their thoughts and aims, not only patriotic or religious communion and participation in the same worship, but the radiation of their luxury and well-being as well. Obedience, the cause, engenders envy, the effect. Consequently, when, for example, the ancient plebeians or the middle class Guelphs in the Italian cities of the Middle Ages, came into power, their manner of using it was an evidence and a continuation of their preceding bondage, since the oppressive laws which they enacted against the sometime reigning aristocracies were suggested by the need which they felt to copy their ancient masters.

It will be observed that obedience and trust, the subjective imitation of a recognised superior, is prompted by a devotion and, so to speak, loving admiration, just as the objective imitation of a questioned or disowned superior results from envious disparagement; and it is clear that communities pass from love to covert envy or from admiration to open contempt in respect to their old masters, but that they never pass back, as far as the latter are concerned, at any rate, from envy to love or from contempt to admiration. To satisfy their persistent need of loving and admiring, they must continue to raise up new idols for themselves, from time to time, only to shatter them later on.[1]

It is a great mistake to say that populations are controlled by fear alone. On the contrary, everything points to the fact that in the beginnings of all great civilisations or, rather, of all religious or political institutions whatsoever, modern ones included, there have been unheard-of expenditures of love and of unsatisfied love at that. This fact explains everything; without it, nothing is explained. If the *king-god* whom Spencer has so strongly portrayed had not been loved as well as feared, he would have been straightway killed. And, to go back to the cradle of societies, are we

---

[1] After a certain point, the more superficial social inequalities become, the harder they are for inferiors to endure The cause of this is that after they have been softened down beyond a certain point, they fail to produce either admiration or credulity or obedience, all of which dispositions make for social strength, and they, therefore, lose their *raison d'être* Then they inspire envy, and envy helps to make them disappear. The demands of utility are analogous, in this case, to those of beauty. The beautiful rules out any compromise between an ellipse and a circle or between a parallelogram and a square As soon as the disproportion between the two axes of the ellipse or between the length and breadth of the parallelogram ceases to be sufficiently pronounced,

to believe that the patriarch of antiquity, the first of the *king-gods*, owed his absolute authority over his children and his slaves exclusively to their terror? His children, if not his slaves, certainly loved him. They probably loved him much more than he himself loved them; for here, as elsewhere, the unilateral seems to have preceded the reciprocal tie. Ancient documents lead us to think that there was far less paternal tenderness on the part of the fathers of antiquity than on the part of those of the present day. I am not speaking of mothers, for the causes of their affection are vital much more than social, and it is to this fact that it owes its relative depth and steadfastness. Filial love itself, then, must have begun as an almost one-sided unsatisfied affection. We may picture the head of the primitive family as king, judge, priest, and teacher all in one. Like a little Louis XIV, he failed to recognise that his subjects had any claims upon him and in perfect egotism offered himself to their adoration. In view of his own glorification he acknowledged, to be sure, the duty of protecting them. And they were as grateful to him, in return, as if he had bestowed a favour upon them Hence his apotheosis. It was necessary for the family-cult and for the perpetuation of the family, the basis of city and civilisation.

The Bible and all ancient legislation testify to the extent to which the patriarch was believed in and obeyed. His thought was divined and his will willed almost without a word, and it was because of this that his children had so keen an inclination to follow his example in all things, to reproduce his accent, his language, his gestures, and his manners. They would never have been led to believe in

our æsthetic sense desires its suppression altogether, and the smaller the disproportion, the stronger our wish or desire. Now as soon as an approximate equality is effected between the different classes of a society, envy itself, having accomplished its work of assimilation, tends to disappear; and then its work is endangered by this very extreme. The need of individual divergence, of *dissimilation,* or, as we say, of liberty, grows out of the equality which is born of resemblance; and society would return to the disintegration of savagery, providing new causes of inequality did not arise But arise they always do and obey him by futilely mimicking the outside man had they not first understood him by means of their faith and docility. The formation of a social tie by the first method was impossible. But let us go back still further, to that pre-historic dawn when the art of speech was unknown. At that time how was the secret content of the mind, its desires and ideas, transfused from one brain to another? That it was, in fact, effected we may infer from what happens in the societies of animals who seem to understand one another almost without signs, as if through a kind of psychological electrisation by suggestion. It must be admitted that in that age inter-cerebral action at a distance may have taken place with perhaps remarkable intensity, with an intensity which has diminished from that time on. Hypnotic sugges-tion can give us some vague idea of this in so far as a morbid phenomenon can resemble a normal one. This action is the elementary and fundamental problem which *sociological psychology* (which begins where physiological psychology leaves off) should undertake to solve.

The invention of language wonderfully facilitated, but did not originate, the inoculation of ideas and desires of one mind by another and consequently the progress of imi-tation *ab interioribus ad exteriora.* For had not this prog-'ress already existed, the birth of language would be in-conceivable. It is not difficult to understand how the first inventor of speech set to associating in his own mind a given thought and a given sound (perfected by gesture), but it is difficult to understand how he was able to *suggest* this relation to another by merely making him hear the given sound. If the listener merely repeated this sound like a parrot, without attaching to it the required meaning, -it is impossible to see how this superficial and mechanical *re-echoing* could have led him to understand the meaning of the strange speaker or carried him over from the *sound* to the *word*. It must then be admitted that the sense was transmitted with the sound, that it reflected the sound. And whoever is acquainted with the feats of hypnotism, with the miracles of suggestion, that have been popularised to so great an extent of late, should certainly not be reluctant to admit this postulate.

Moreover, observation of two- or three-year-old children who are beginning to talk adds great weight to this hypothesis. It is easily seen that they understand what is said to them long before they are themselves able to say the same things. How could this be possible unless they had already imitated older persons *ab interioribus ad exteriora?* Now, this point admitted, the establishment of language, marvellous as it seems, presents no further difficulties. Speech was not, in the beginning of history, what it has since become, namely, an interchange of knowledge and opinion. In accordance with the law which I have frequently formulated that the unilateral precedes the reciprocal in and for everything, speech must have been at first a purely one-sided lesson or command of a father to his children, a prayer to an unresponsive deity, *i. e.*, a kind of sacerdotal and monarchical function, eminently authoritative and accompanied by some *suggested* hallucination or action, a sacrament, an august monopoly. The ruler, like the modern schoolmaster, alone had the right to speak aloud in his domain. Besides, only a chosen few, objects of admiration and, then, of envy, knew how to speak.

Later the right of writing was also monopolised by the upper classes, and this fact explains the prestige that writing, according to *Sacred Scripture,* still held, in the past, in the eyes of the unlettered. If speech has wholly lost this same prestige, it is undoubtedly because it is much more ancient. That it once possessed it is proved by the virtue that attached to so-called *sacramental* expressions in old legal procedures, as well as by the magical power attributed to *Prayer* in its apotheosis in the Vedas of the Aryans and to the Word, the Logos, by the Byzantines and Christians. In another chapter I will show that the needs of consumption have in every order of facts preceded the needs of production and that this important phenomenon is related to the progress of imitation from within to without. If this is so, the need of listening must have preceded that of speaking.

When the action at a distance of a dominant mind over one that is dominated has once been facilitated and regulated by the habit of verbal communication it acquires an irresistible force. We can get some idea of what language was originally as an instrument of government from the power that it exerts to-day in its most recent form, the daily press, in spite of the fact that the latter has lost part of its power through its expansion and self-combativeness. It is due to speech that imitation in the human world has accentuated its leading characteristic of first attaching itself to the most intrinsic thing in its living model and of reproducing with incredible precision the hidden side, the thoughts and aims, before it seizes upon and reflects with less exactness the outward gestures, attitudes, and movements of its model. The opposite occurs among animals, where imitation is effected in a pretty inexact manner, and only in the reproduction of songs and cries and muscular acts and where the transmission of nervous phenomena, of ideas and desires, is always vague. Because of this animal societies stand still; for although some ingenious idea might gleam through the brain of a crow or bison, it would, according to hypothesis, die with him and be necessarily lost to the community. With animals, it is primarily and pre-eminently muscle which imitates muscle; with us, it is primarily and pre-eminently nerve which imitates nerve and brain which imitates brain. This is the chief contrast through which we may explain the superiority of human societies. In them no good idea is lost, and every exceptional thinker lives on in the posterity which he raises up to his own level. Good ideas may have been for a long time only the visions of a madman or the caprices of a despot. It matters not, for in passing from the leader to the multitude they at least produce the immense and fundamental benefit of that religious or political unanimity which alone makes collective discipline and military action possible, just as, in the future, when true ideas and useful applications shall have come to light, general participation in the same science and in the same morality will be an indispensable factor in any great florescence of art or industry.

Let us note in relation to the arts that their evolution does not proceed, as Spencer contends, from the more objective to the more subjective, from architecture through sculpture and drawing to music and poetry. On the contrary, it always opens with some great book or epic or poetical work of very remarkable relative perfection. The Iliad, the Bible, Dante, etc., are the high sources from which all the fine arts are fated to flow.

This progress from *within* to *without,* if we try to express it more precisely, means two things: (1) That imitation of ideas precedes the imitation of their expression. (2) That imitation of ends precedes imitation of means. Ends or ideas are the *inner things,* means or expressions, the outer. Of course, we are led to copy from others everything which seems to us a new means for attaining our old ends, or satisfying our old wants, or a new expression for our old ideas; and we do this *at the same time* that we begin to adopt innovations which awaken new ideas and new ends in us. Only these new ends, these needs for novel kinds of consumption, take hold of us and propagate themselves in us much more readily and rapidly than the aforesaid means or expressions.[1]

A nation which is becoming civilised and whose wants are multiplying consumes much more than it is able or than it desires to produce. That amounts to saying, in the language of æsthetics, that the diffusion of sentiments anticipates that of talents. Sentiments are habits of judgment and desire which have become very alert and almost un-

[1] I do not mean to deny that the outside of the model is sometimes imitated to the exclusion of the inside. But when we begin in this way, as women and children often do (less often, however, than one might think), with outward imitation, we stop short there; whereas, if we begin with inward imitation, we pass on from it to the other. Dostoïesky tells us that after some years of prison life he became like his fellow convicts superficially. "Their habits, their ideas, their dress, left their colour upon me and became mine on the surface, without penetrating at all into my inner nature."

conscious through repetition.   Talents are habits of activity which have also gained a mechanical facility by repetition. Both sentiments and talents, then, are habits; the only difference between them is that the former are subjective, and the latter, objective facts.   Now, is it not true that æsthetic sentiments form and spread long before the talents which are fitted to satisfy them?   And have we not a proof of this in the commonplace observation that the virtuosity of periods of decadence survives the exhaustion of their inspiration?

No art makes its own religion; style does not create the thought back of it; but a religion or an idea ultimately makes the art or style which expresses and illustrates it. Can we imagine the painting of Cimabue or Giotto being prior to the spread of Christianity?   Our law explains why the fusion of beliefs is always and everywhere accomplished long before that of arts or that of morals and why, consequently, even in the periods of small and hostile neighbouring states, a common religion can spread over a vast territory.   We know that the Greek games and oracles, particularly the Delphic Oracle and the Olympic games, at first created and then continued to strengthen the sentiment of Hellenic nationality in spite of the small states into which Greece was broken up.   But long before the games became a common centre, long before they gave people an opportunity to see and imitate each other from the point of view of the outward things of life, the authority of the oracles was recognised by all   Their origin is lost in a fabulous antiquity.   And so in the Middle Ages, also, a common faith dominated Europe long before the great monarchies with their brilliant courts and their exchanges of contagious luxury began to assimilate the outsides of their respective peoples.   There is not a single example of the contrary.

We know that if juridical or legislative changes are viable, they never precede, but follow at some distance the intellectual or economic changes to which they correspond. Our thesis requires this.   It also requires, as a corollary, that laws, which are the outer framework of society, should survive for some time their inner reason for existence, the wants and ideas which they embody. Coming later or proceeding less quickly, they must or may persist afterwards. This is also true of certain customs, as observation shows us, and this general phenomenon is alone able to explain the particular case to which I have referred. The *survivals* of custom, to use Lubbock's excellent term, have had so much light thrown upon them, that it is useless to cite many examples. Nevertheless, let us call to mind that after the matriarchal system was abolished and even forgotten, a simulation of it was perpetuated in the couvade, the attribution of a fictitious maternity to the father, and that after marriage by capture had fallen into disuse, marriage ceremonies preserved the fiction of it. Up to the marriage of Louis XVI, the custom of paying down thirteen deniers upon the conclusion of a marriage prevailed in France, in certain provinces at least, as a relic from the time of wife-purchase. Sects who rejected the dogma of the Eucharist have simulated the communion service and free-thinkers who opposed infant baptism have celebrated a civic quasi-baptism of their children. Moreover, what living religion has not borrowed its external observances, its rites and processions, from some dead religion? Is not the conservation of a linguistic root whose meaning has changed a survival of the same kind that is complicated, as in the preceding case, by the introduction of a new meaning which adapts an old organ to a fresh function? I have just spoken of juridical survivals. Our codes are full of them. Although feudal law has been dead for centuries, I defy a jurist to do without it in explaining the famous distinction between a possessory and a petitory action, the nightmare of our justices of the peace. Finally, in the sphere of art and poetry, there is nothing more usual than to see the cloak of a certain school whose soul is extinct pass on to some new genius.

What does this prove? In the first place it proves the tenacity, the energy, of the inclination which leads man to imitate the past. But, besides these æsthetic or ritualistic or purely mechanical simulations of vanished wants and beliefs, we also see the survival of the outward parts of imitation after the inward parts—a natural fact, if the latter are older or have evolved more rapidly than the former.

The survivals in question give us the counter-proof of our law. The following observation will remove any remaining doubt. As they spread abroad, honorary titles (*sieur* instead of *seigneur*), salutations (a slight inclination of the head instead of the bent knee of feudal times), compliments, and manners become abbreviated, diluted, and simplified. Spencer has shown this in a masterly way. This fact demands that others of a like kind be brought into relation with it. Words are contracted from being constantly used and vulgarised. They lose their edge and wear themselves out like a rolling stone. Religious beliefs lose their intensity, arts degenerate, etc. These facts seem to prove that imitation is the necessary weakening of that which is imitated and that new inventions or entirely fresh sources for imitation are therefore necessary for the timely reanimation of expiring social energy. And there is much truth in this, as we shall see later on. But is it always so? No; these resemblances occur only between the final periods of those different evolutions which we have been comparing. Before a word contracts, it must be formed and fostered and magnified by a series of ascendent and not yet decadent imitations. Before an etiquette is shaken, it must have established itself through the reinforcement of every imitation of which it has been the object. Before a dogma or a rite declines, it must have asserted and spread itself throughout the youth of its religion.

Whence comes this contrast? Does it not result from the fact that in the first period imitation was essentially from within and had to do with the spread of beliefs or desires, of beliefs and desires whose outward forms were merely their expression, were merely secondary objects, of beliefs and desires which gradually flared up by virtue of their own law through their very propagation and mutual reflection; whereas, in the second period, the outward forms continued to spread in spite of the gradual drying up of their inward source and had, consequently, to lose in strength? And so the phenomenon is explained on the ground that imitation passes from within to without, from the thing signified to its sign. Now, why does a moment come when it is not the inward side of the model, the faith or desire implicit in the act or speech in question, but the outward side which is reproduced? It is because another faith or desire which is entirely or partly irreconcilable with the former appears on the very scene where the other has already spread itself. Then, although the model continues to live on the surface, it is stricken to the heart. It goes on living in a state of self-mutilation and suicide until the moment when some new spirit succeeds it.[1] We know from the writings of Tertullian and the discoveries of archæology that in spite of the religious fervour and inward sincerity of the early Christians they continued, both men and women, to live externally, to *dress*, to *coiffe,* and even to amuse themselves like pagans, without regard to the anti-Christian indecency of the garments and amusements in question.

I cannot conclude this discussion of imitation *ab interioribus ad exteriora* without briefly calling attention to the analogy which imitation presents in this relation as well as in so many others to the other forms of Repetition.

It is obvious, from the very obscurity that is inherent in the study of life, that all the developments of life, from fecundation to death, proceed from some wholly internal and absolutely hidden action, from some vital faith or inspiration, so to speak, which is breathed into the germ by

---

[1] "Ceremonial is the great museum of history," observes M. Paul Viollet with much truth. If this is so, and we can hardly doubt it, it is time to dispose of Spencer's idea of ceremony as primitive government. A museum is far from being a primitive thing which is complete at birth and which shrinks in course of time. It takes a long time for it to be formed and enlarged. Besides, it replenishes itself from age to age.

its progenitors and which is anterior to its *manifestations*.
The evolution of the individual is the drawing out of this
germ. At the moment of conception the parents repeat
themselves in the child in their most essential vital characteristics before they repeat themselves, thanks to the
former transmission, in their more visible and external
traits; for in the fecundated germ the whole future growth
is potential. Similarly, at the moment when a catechumen
is converted, some apostle is repeating himself on his deep-
est social side, the side which is soon to be the source of
the religious prayers and observances of the catechumen,
where the apostle's own prayers and observances will be no
less faithfully reproduced. The analogy to physical phenomena of a like order is more conjectural. And yet we
know the fruitlessness of efforts to explain, for example,
the transmission or repetition of movements, either through
contact or at a distance, without presupposing the existence
of some preliminary communication of a hidden force or
attraction; and the attempts to explain chemical changes
and combinations as combinations of atoms without parts
or dimensions have been equally unsuccessful. Let us conclude that in nature, as in society, Repetition, *i. e.*, Action,
proceeds, I cannot repeat it too often, *ab interioribus ad exteriora*.

Will the reader perchance argue, among other objections which could be raised against this thesis, that women
are much more prompt to adopt foreign fashions in
clothes than foreign ideas? But in this instance the intrinsic thing, the thing signified, is either a woman's vain
affirmation of self,—when in order to raise herself a peg she
imitates the dress of a higher class whose pride and vices
and pretensions have already taken hold of her,—or the sexual desire to please,—when she imitates her fellows or equals
because she has first been persuaded, so often mistakenly,
that she will be beautified by the adoption of some new
style of dress or headgear. Moreover, the example of
womankind is an illustration not only of the law of the
spread of imitation from above to below, which I am about

to discuss, but likewise of the law which we are considering at present. Every woman we know imitates the man whom she loves or admires or to whose ascendency she submits. But we may also notice that the man's sentiments and ideas are communicated to her long before she has copied his mannerisms or literary knack, or adopted his forms of speech or accent. When a woman passes into a family or community which she considers superior to her own, she becomes at once impregnated with the ideas, the passions, the prejudices, the vices or the virtues which prevail in her new society, and she becomes saturated with them much sooner than a man under similar circumstances. If, at the beginning, woman is, in many respects, notably in matters of religious belief, unimpressionable to outside examples, it is because the principle of imitation from within to without is absolutely applicable in her case. As a corollary of this principle, the external manifestations of an ancient belief persist in the speech, gestures, habits, and manners of woman, much more than in the case of man, long after it has itself disappeared and been secretly replaced by another. The new cult must have won a stronghold in the soul of a woman long before she decides to adopt its outward garb. This has always been so, and it is still so. In the sixteenth century Marguerite de Valois and her feminine following were at heart converted to Calvinism,—in fact it was through them that the doctrine of Calvin, in spite of its being a doctrine so little suited to please them, began to spread through France, —but they continued to practice the Catholic religion, in part, undoubtedly, from fear of being butchered, but, primarily, because of the logical necessity which rules that the things signified should precede their signs.

II. *Imitation of the Superior by the Inferior*

The profoundly subjective character that is taken on from the earliest times by human imitation, the privilege which it has of binding souls together from their very centres, involves, as may be seen from what has preceded, the growth of human inequality and the formation of a social hierarchy. This was inevitable, since the relation of model to copy developed into that of apostle to neophyte, of master to subject. Consequently, from the very fact that imitation proceeded from the inside to the outside of the model, it had to consist in a *descent* of example, in a descent from the superior to the inferior. This is a second law that is partly implied in the first, but it needs separate examination.

Moreover, let us be sure that we understand the exact bearing of the considerations in hand as well as of those that have preceded. In the first place, we know that they are based on the hypothesis that the influence of prestige, of alleged superiority, is neither partly nor wholly neutralised by the action of logical laws. However lowly or even despised may be the author or introducer of a new idea of relatively striking truth or utility, it always ends by spreading through the public. Thus the evangel of slaves and Jews spread throughout the aristocratic Roman world because it was more adapted than polytheism to answer the main problems of the Roman conscience. Thus at a certain period in ancient Egypt the use of the horse was introduced from Asia in spite of the Egyptians' contempt for Asiatics, because for many kinds of work the horse was obviously preferable to the mule, which had been in use up to that time.   There are innumerable examples of this kind. Similarly, the most objective of examples, a word detached from its meaning, a religious rite from its dogma, a peculiarity of custom from the want which it expresses, a work or art from the social ideal which it embodies, may readily spread in a strange environment whose ruling needs and principles find it to their advantage to replace their usual methods of expression by this new one which is perhaps more picturesque, or more clear, or more forcible.

In the second place, even when the action of logical laws does not intervene, it is not only the superior who causes himself to be copied by the inferior, the patrician by the plebeian, the nobleman by the commoner, the cleric by the layman, and, at a later period, the Parisian by the provincial, the townsman by the peasant, etc., it is also the inferior who, in a certain measure, much less, to be sure, is copied, or is likely to be copied, by the superior. When two men are together for a long time, whatever may be their difference in station, they end by imitating each other reciprocally, although, of the two, the one imitates much the more, the other much the less. The colder body imparts its heat to the warmer. The haughtiest country gentleman cannot keep his accent, his manners, and his point of view from being a little like those of his servants and tenants. For the same reason many provincialisms and countrified expressions creep into the language of cities, and even capitals, and slang phrases penetrate at times into drawing rooms. This influence from the bottom to the top of a scale characterises all classes of facts. Nevertheless, on the whole, it is the generous radiation of the warm body towards the cold, not the insignificant radiation of the cold body towards the warm, that is the main fact in physics and the one which explains the final tendency of the universe towards an everlasting equilibrium of temperature. Similarly, in sociology, the radiation of examples from above to below is the only fact worth consideration because of the general levelling which it tends to produce in the human world.

1. Now let me endeavour to elucidate the truth which we are discussing. There is nothing more natural than that those who love each other should copy each other, or, rather, as this phenomenon always begins by being one-sided, that the *lover* should copy the *beloved*. But in proof of the depth which is reached by the action of imitation in man's heart we see people aping one another everywhere, even in their fights. The conquered never fail to copy their conquerors if only to prepare for their revenge. When they borrow the military organisation of their conquerors they are careful to say and they sincerely think that their sole motive is a utilitarian calculation. But we shall find this explanation inadequate, if we compare this fact with

a considerable number of correlated facts in which the sentiment of utility plays no part whatsoever.

For example, the conquered do not merely borrow the superior weapons, the longer range guns, and the more admirable methods of their conqueror; they also take from him many of his insignificant military peculiarities and habits, whose acclimatisation, granted that it were possible, would raise difficulties wholly out of proportion to its feeble advantages. During the thirteenth century Florence and Sienna, who were always at war with each other, arrayed troops against each other that were not only organised in the same way, but that were also preceded by that strange cart *(carroccio)* and singular bell *(martinella)* which were at first peculiar to Lombardy, that is, to what was for a long time the most powerful part of Italy (so much so that *Lombard* and *Italian* had the same meaning), and which were then imported with certain modifications to Florence, whence, thanks to the prestige of that flourishing city, they spread to its hostile neighbours. And yet the cart was an encumbrance and the bell a real danger. Why, then, should both Florence and Sienna have copied those peculiarities instead of keeping to their own customs? For the same reason that the lower classes of society, that is, the defeated, or the sons of the defeated, in civil wars, copy the dress, the manners, the speech, the vices, etc., of the upper classes. It will not be said, in this instance, that the imitation is a military operation in view of revenge. It is simply the satisfaction of a special fundamental need in social life the final consequence of which is the preparation through many conflicts of conditions of future peace.[1]

Whatever may be the organisation of a society, aristocratic or democratic, we may be sure, if we see imitation making rapid strides in it, that the inequality between its

[1] It seems that before the Japanese came into communication with China they possessed a syllabic writing, or several, in fact, of much greater usefulness and convenience than the Chinese writing; but as soon as this youthful and pre-eminently suggestible people felt the prestige of the superiority which they attributed to the mandarins, they adopted Chinese writing to the hindrance of their own progress

different levels is very great, besides being more or less apparent. And we have only to learn the set of its main current of examples, overlooking the unimportant *back eddies,* to discover the real social power. If the nation is on an aristocratic basis the thing is very simple. Given the opportunity, a nobility will always and everywhere imitate its leaders, its kings or suzerains, and the people, likewise, given the opportunity, its nobility. Baudrillart writes in his *Histoire de luxe* that at Constantinople under the Byzantine emperors, " the court looks up to the prince, the city looks to the court for its model, and the poor man gazes upon the rich man and wishes to share in his luxury." [1] The same was true in France under Louis XIV. Saint-Simon writes on the same subject of luxury: " It is a sore that once introduced becomes an internal, all-devouring cancer, for it quickly communicates itself from the court at Paris to the provinces and the armies." M. de Barante writes that in the fifteenth century " it was purposed to strictly forbid all those games, dice, cards, or rackets, which had found a way to the people in imitation of the court." The innumerable card players that we see in the inns and taverns of to-day are, then, unwitting copyists of our old royal courts. Forms and rules of politeness have spread through the same channel. Courtesy comes from the court, as civility comes from the city. The accent of the court and, later on, that of the capital spread little by little to all classes and to all provinces of the nation. We may be sure that in times past there were a Babylonian accent, a Ninevite accent, a Memphite accent, just as there are to-day a Parisian accent, a Florentine accent, and a Berlin accent. This transmission of accent, precisely because it is one of the most unconscious, irresistible, and inexplicable forms of imitation, very properly illustrates the depth of that force and the truth of that law which I am expounding. When we see that the influence of the upper classes upon the lower, of townsmen upon rustics, of colonial whites upon native blacks, of adults upon children, of upper

[1] [II, 340—*Tr.*]

classmen upon lower, is felt even in the matter of accent, we can no longer doubt that it is felt *a fortiori* in matters of writing, gesture, facial expression, dress, and custom.

The tendency to ape the hierarchical superior and the rapidity with which this inclination has at all times satisfied itself, at the slightest touch of public prosperity, deserve to be indicated.[1] The frequency of the sumptuary edicts during the entire period of the old régime is a proof of this, just as the multiplicity of a river's dykes bears witness to the impetuosity of its currents. The first French Court dates from Charles VIII; but we must not think that the imitative contagion of court manners and luxury took several centuries to reach down to the common people of France. From the time of Louis XII its influence was felt everywhere. The disasters of the religious wars arrested its development in the sixteenth century, but, in the following century, it started up again very rapidly. Then the miseries brought on by the last war of the Grand Monarch occasioned another setback. During the eighteenth century there was a fresh start; under the Revolution, another reaction. In the time of the First Empire the advance began again on a great scale; but from that time on it took a democratic form about which we need not trouble ourselves for the moment. Under Francis I and Henry II the spread of the luxury begun under Louis XII continued. At this period a sumptuary law forbade " all peasants, labourers, and valets, unless attached to princes, to wear silken doublets or hose overladen or puffed out with silk." From 1543 to the time of the League there were eight important ordinances against luxury. " Some of them," says Baudrillart, " apply to every French subject; they interdict the use of cloth of gold, of silver, or of silk." [2] Such was the general elegance

---

[1] The point to which this craze can go may be seen from the following example. In 1705, according to the Marquis d'Argenson, the very valets of men of high rank had servants.

[2] [*Histoire de luxe*, III, 440.—*Tr.*]

that prevailed on the eve of the religious wars.[1] To justify laws in restraint of trade "one of the reasons most frequently cited was the fact that France was ruining itself in the purchase of objects of luxury." Besides, the same fact is revealed in the prosperity of the industries of luxury which presuppose an extensive patronage.[2]

If we go still farther back to classical antiquity, the same law will be verified. We learn from a text of Sidonius Apollinaris that the speaking of Latin was begun in Gaul by the Gallic nobility and spread from them, together with Roman morals and ideas, into the bosom of the people.

Here is another example. Let us picture to ourselves

[1] Abundant proof that the same condition existed in Germany is given by Johannes Janssen. For example, "in Pomerania and the island of Rugen, . . . the peasants are rich They wear none but English garments or others as good Their dress is as fine as that *formerly worn by the burghers or nobles*" [*Die allgemeinen Zustande des deutschen Volkes beim Ausgang des Mittelalters,* p. 312, ninth edition, Freiburg, 1883 — *Tr.*].
These lines are quoted by Janssen from Kantzow, a Pomeranian historian of the time. We learn from sermons that silken garments were being worn by the peasants In Italy, according to Burckhardt, there was at the same period the same descent of luxury to all classes.

[2] This contagion of luxury has often been an instrument for the spread of useful things Our most useful species (animal), Bourdeau says in his *Conquête du monde animal,* were originally bred for amusement rather than for the then unforseen advantages which its domestication might procure The same motive leads us to-day to search for new and peculiar species, and in primitive times every animal that was conquered had this charm of novelty Formerly in Rome and Greece a duck or a goose was presented as a love-token to the beloved woman or child In the time of Cæsar the Britons kept chickens and geese for luxurious display, not for consumption   ; in the sixteenth century the Indian duck and turkey ornamented the parks of the nobility before they descended into the ranks of ordinary poultry to be banished to the barnyard   . *This movement is logical and necessary* Only the wealthy classes are able to have costly lessons and make hazardous experiments. But when success is assured the gain becomes general."
If the Gallic nobility began to adopt the speech and customs of Rome, after the conquest, it was because then, for the first time, they felt the superiority of Rome Why did the American Indians never adopt European civilisation ? Because their immense pride kept them from considering themselves inferior to Anglo-Americans. On the other hand, the negroes of America, who have been accustomed to recognise

the basin of the Mediterranean in the eighth century before Christ; at the moment of the great Tyrian or Sidonian prosperity, when the Phœnicians, the European carriers of the arts of Egypt and Assyria, were arousing among the Greeks and other peoples a taste for luxurious and beautiful things. These merchants were not like modern English traders in cheap and common fabrics; like the mediæval Venetians, they were wont to display along the seaboard fine products that appealed to the rich people of all countries, purple garments, perfumes, golden cups, figurines, costly armour, ex-voto offerings, graceful and charming ornaments. Thus all over, in Sardinia, in Etruria, in Greece, in the Archipelago, in Asia Minor, and in Gaul, the highest classes, the chosen few, might be seen wearing helmets, swords, bracelets, and tunics which were more or less alike from one end to the other of this vast region, while beneath them the plebeian population continued to be differentiated from one another by their characteristic dress and weapons. And yet, although these plebeians differed so much from their leaders on the outside, they closely resembled them in their ideas and passions, in their religious superstitions and ethical principles.

In the fourteenth or fifteenth century of our era, exactly the same spectacle would have struck the Arthur Young of that time in travelling through France and Europe. At this epoch the same Venetian products had spread everywhere and were inundating and assimilating palaces and chateaux and city mansions, whereas, although the same religion and morality prevailed in huts and cottages as in noble and sumptuous dwellings, the former still retained their distinct and original characteristics. Now, little by little, from above to below, assimilation has so advanced both in antiquity and in modern times, that finally a great carrying trade, not for the use of the few, but for that of the entire mass of a vast people, has become possible,

the supremacy of the whites, even after the abolition of slavery, have had a very strong and noticeable tendency to copy their masters, or their sometime masters, in everything.

—to the great advantage of the England of to-day, of the America of to-morrow.[1]

Therefore the apologists for aristocracy have, in my opinion, passed over its best justification. The principal rôle of a nobility, its distinguishing mark, is its initiative, if not inventive, character. Invention can start from the lowest ranks of the people, but its extension depends upon the existence of some lofty social elevation, a kind of social *water-tower,* whence a continuous water-fall of imitation may descend. At every period and in every country the aristocratic body has been open to foreign novelties and has been quick to import them,[2] just as the staff of an army is the best-informed part of the army on the subject of foreign military innovations, and the most apt in adopting them intelligently, thereby rendering as much service as by the discipline which it inspires. As long as its vitality endures, a nobility may be recognised by this characteristic. When, on the other hand, it throws itself back upon traditions, jealously attaches itself to them and defends them against the attacks of a people whom it had previously accustomed to changes, it is safe to say that its great work is done, however useful it may be in this complementary rôle of moderator, and that its decline has set in.[3]

---

[1] Let me anticipate an objection. It may be urged that in imitating foreign fashions in dress, armour, and furniture, the Mediterranean aristocracy in the time of the Phœnicians, and the European aristocracy at the time of the Venetian commerce, proceeded *ab exterioribus ad interiora;* but this would be a mistake. Both these aristocracies succumbed to the prestige of some dominating nation, of Egypt or of Assyria, of Italy or of Constantinople The literature of these countries had penetrated them before their arts; their glory had subjugated them. The social function of aristocracies is to initiate populations into an admiration and envy of foreign things, and thus to cut a way for fashion-imitation as a substitute for custom-imitation.

[2] Another example: it was through the Roman aristocracy, during the days of the Scipios, that Greek ideas and Greek speech and civilisation reached Rome

[3] It sometimes, or, even, often, happens that the conquerors pattern themselves after the conquered, borrowing their habits, their laws, and their language The Franks in Gaul became Latinised and spoke a Romance tongue. The same thing happened to the Normans in England, to the Varangians in Russia, etc. But in these cases it was

2. In this respect, in spite of appearances to the contrary, the ecclesiastical resembles the civil hierarchy. Certainly, had it not been for the strongly aristocratic constitution of the Christian clergy, the spread of the same dogmas and, later on, of the same rites, could never have covered such an immense space as it did, and produced, in spite of the disintegration of feudal society, that great unity of spirit and ritual called Christianity. It was because of the lack of such a pyramidal organisation that, although Protestanism appeared at an epoch of great national centralisation instead of disintegration, at an epoch, therefore, which was highly favourable for the diffusion of one uniform doctrine or cult, it was, nevertheless, split up into an endless number of sects. Now, as long as the pontifical court and the episcopal body of the Catholic clergy continued to be an active aristocracy, their special characteristic was their monopoly of religious initiatives; and the singular complexity of the dogmas and cult which were enriched and expanded at each council and synod testified to their initiating propensity. Through these numerous and frequently reform reunions, the bishops and abbots kept in touch with new fashions in theology, in casuistry, and in liturgy, and enabled these fashions to reach downwards.[1] Their taste for innovation went even farther; it was not confined to the religious sphere. The higher clergy became depraved at the end of the Middle Ages for the same reason for which, later on, the French nobility became enervated. It was because, at that epoch, it was the pre-eminently superior and controlling class, the first to be touched by the dawn of a new civilisation. If the ecclesiastical pinnacles of

because the conqueror felt the social superiority of the conquered, and the more real and appreciated this superiority the more faithfully was the latter reflected by the former. As the Anglo-Saxon was only slightly superior to the Norman of William the Conqueror, there was a fusion of two civilisations and, especially, of two languages, into one civilisation and into one new language, rather than a triumph of the Saxon element. Besides, we know that the Gallo-Roman nobility survived the invasion and continued to take the lead.

[1] In India, according to Barth, the Brahmans are at the head of all religious innovations, the source, in that country, of all changes whatsoever.

the Europe of that day had withstood the influence of new inventions and discoveries, and, consequently, of new manners and morals, the arrival of modern civilisation would have certainly been retarded for several centuries if not indefinitely postponed.

In a period of theocratic aristocracy, if the hovel copies the chateau, the chateau copies some church or temple, first in its style of architecture and then in the different forms of art and luxury which develop in it before spreading down to lower circles. In the Middle Ages the cathedral goldsmith and cabinet-maker set the standard for the secular artisans who filled the dwellings of the nobles with Gothic jewelry and furniture. Sculpture, painting, poetry, and music were secularised in the same way. Just as the royal courts created, under the form of flattery and of narrow and one-sided courtesy, the habit of reciprocal and general amiability and politeness, and just as the example of the command of one chief or of the privileges of a chosen few had only to spread to give birth to law, the command of each to all and of all to each, so we find in the beginning of every literature some sacred book, the Book of all others, the book of which all later secular books are merely sanctuary-stolen reflections, in the beginning of all writing some historic writing, in the beginning of all music some religious dirge or lyric, at the beginning of all sculpture some idol, at the beginning of all painting some tomb or temple fresco or some monachal illumination of the sacred book. . . . Temples, then, antedate palaces, in the right of being considered the secular, and, for a long time, the indispensable centres of the spread of civilisation in the extrinsic and superficial meaning of the word as well as in its intrinsic and deeper meaning, in matters of art and elegance as well as in those of maxim and conviction.[1]

---

[1] The instructive traveller, Abbé Pelitot, says that among the Esquimaux the men, *but not the women,* pray in the morning and evening. With us the opposite is the more frequent occurrence. In this connection the *Revue scientifique* (November 21, 1888) justly remarks that " among all primitive peoples, religion, like war and hunting, is the

3. It is during the periods when the sacerdotal rule is declining and when ecclesiastical teaching is becoming less and less the source of beliefs that the art and luxury of priestly examples come to be more and more closely followed, and that there is no fear of profaning the decorative sides of worship in secularising them. In the same way when aristocratic rule begins to weaken, and when less obedience is paid to privileged classes, people are emboldened to copy them in external things. We know that this conforms to advance *ab exterioribus ad exteriora,* but it is also in part explained by the application of another very general law, which should be combined with that concerning the imitation of superiors. If the latter were unconditional, the most superior thing would be the one to be most imitated; but, in reality, the thing that is most imitated is the most superior one *of those that are nearest.* In fact, the influence of the model's example is efficacious inversely to its *distance* as well as directly to its superiority. *Distance* is understood here in its sociological meaning. However distant in space a stranger may be, he is close by, from this point of view, if we have numerous and daily relations with him and if we have every facility to satisfy our desire to imitate him. This law of the imitation of the nearest, of the least distant, explains the gradual and consecutive character of the spread of an example that has been set by the highest social ranks. We may infer, as its corollary, when we see a lower class setting itself to imitating for the first time a much higher class, that the distance between the two had diminished.[1]

function of the men" From this fact, we may properly infer that if religion survives longer in the hearts and in the habits of women, it is because they originally adopted it from the example of their lords and masters. Another confirmation of our law.

[1] "How does it happen," queries M Melchoir de Vogüé, "that the negro fetich worshippers who are pursued by the man-hunting negro Moslems adopt with so much facility the Mahometan faith of their persecutors?" It is the imitation of a superior But it is necessary for the superior to be near; the superiority must not be great enough to discourage imitation That is the reason why Christianity makes little progress among negroes. Whereas the conquests of Islam among them are almost as rapid as the conquests of the days of Mahomet.

4. A period is called democratic as soon as the distance between all classes has lessened enough, through various causes, to allow of the external imitation of the highest by the lowest. In every democracy, then, like our own, where the fever of subjective and objective assimilation is intense, we may be sure of the existence of an established or incipient social hierarchy of recognised superiors, of superiors through heredity or selection. In our own case it is not difficult to perceive by whom the ancient aristocracy was replaced after the sceptre of the refinements of life had in large part slipped from its grasp. In the first place the administrative hierarchy has been growing more complicated, adding to its height by increasing the number of its grades and to its breadth by increasing the number of its functionaries. The same thing is true in the case of our military hierarchy because of the reasons which have forced modern European States to become military nations. Prelates and princes of the blood, monks and cavaliers, monasteries and chateaux have been suppressed to give place to publicists [1] and financiers, to artists and politicians, to theatres, banks, bazaars, barracks, government buildings, and to the other monuments that are grouped within the circumference of a capital. Here celebrities of every kind congregate. Now what are all the different kinds and degrees of glory or notoriety that are known to society, but a brilliant hierarchy of either filled or vacant places which the public alone is free, or thinks it is free, to dispose of?

Now, instead of becoming more simple and more humble, this aristocracy of place, this platform of brilliant stations, grows more and more impressive through the very effect of democratic transformations which lower national and class walls and give a more and more universal and international suffrage to the candidates for fame. The amount of glory that may be divided among the actors increases in proportion to the number of the spectators who are clapping or

---

[1] Tocqueville shows in a masterly way (*Démocratie en Amérique*) that "the sway of journalism must extend as men grow more and more equal"

hissing in the pit, and the distance between the most obscure onlooker and the most applauded player enlarges accordingly. The apotheosis of Victor Hugo, an impossible occurrence thirty years ago, revealed the existence of a high mountain of literary glory which has been recently raised up, like the Pyrenees in the past, from out of a vast and unbroken plain, and which, with its train of minor peaks, piled up at its base, offers itself henceforward to the ambition of future poets. Invisible mountains of this kind are ever springing up through the pavements of big cities, where they crowd upon each other like the roofs of houses. In the prodigious growth, in the hypertrophy of great cities and, especially, of capitals, where oppressive privileges take root and ramify, while the last traces of the privileges of the past are jealously effaced, is to be found the kind of inequality which modern life creates and which it finds indispensable, in fact, in managing and promoting the great currents of its industrial production and consumption, *i. e.*, of imitation on an immense scale. The course of a Ganges like this necessitated a Himalayas. Paris is the Himalayas of France. Paris unquestionably rules more royally and more orientally over the provinces than the court ever ruled over the city. Every day the telegraph or the railroad distributes its ready-made ideas, wishes, conversations, revolutions, its ready-made dresses and furniture, throughout the whole of France. The suggestive and imperious fascination which it instantaneously exerts over this vast territory is so profound, so complete, and so sustained, that it no longer surprises anyone. This kind of magnetisation has become chronic. It is called liberty and equality. It is futile for the city labourer to consider himself a democrat in working for the destruction of the middle classes (engaged as he is in rising into the middle class himself); he is none the less an aristocrat himself, the much admired and the much envied aristocrat of the peasant. The peasant is to the labourer what the labourer is to his employer. This is the cause of the emigration out of the rural districts.

Although the *sworn communes* of the Middle Ages grew,

out of a spirit of hostility against the local over-lord and against feudalism in general, nevertheless, as M. Luchaire informs us, their effect and *their aim* was to raise the city in which they were established to the rank of a *collective seigniory,* the vassal or suzerain of other seigniories, receiving or contributing feudal dues and having its own rank in the feudal hierarchy. The seals of the communes generally represented military emblems, a foot soldier, or an armed knight on a galloping horse, like the seals of the nobility. The same writer, in his exhaustive historical work on the subject, has proved that the emancipating movement of the communes of the twelfth century was not confined to the cities but that, *following their example,* the mere villages on their outskirts or beyond freed themselves in the same way, by confederation. The historians have hitherto ignored this fact, but it is nevertheless incontestable that, in the Middle Ages, there were first *urban* communes and then *rural* communes. It is a remarkable thing that the same order is followed even in the case of agricultural innovations. Roscher says, for example, that "it was in the town that the modern system of rent, of ground rent, was first substituted for feudal dues, as may be seen from the Charter, of Ghent of 1259 in the Warnkoenig." Let me add that contrary to the opinion of Augustin Thierry the emancipation of the communes was not caused by popular insurrection, by a spontaneous uprising of lowly artisan corporations, but, as recent historical research has shown,[1] by an originally very exclusive league of rich merchants who were already associated in guilds or religious brotherhoods and who formed the aristocracy of the city. "They were transformed into real leagues and *ranged behind themselves the rest of the inhabitants,* so that the commune started, in general, from a league of all the inhabitants grouped together under the oath of the middle-class aristocracy."

A capital, a great modern city, is the first choice, the cream, so to speak, of the population. While the numerical

[1] See *Histoire générale* of Lavisse and Rambaud, II, 431 and following.

importance of the two sexes is about equal in a nation taken as a whole, the number of men in great centres is notably larger than that of women. Besides, the proportion of adults is far greater in the cities than it is in the rest of the country. Finally, and above all, the cities attract to themselves from all directions the most active brains and the most nervous organisms, the fittest to utilise modern inventions. This is the way in which they form the modern aristocracy, a select, non-hereditary, but liberally recruited body; and yet this does not keep it in the least from being as scornful of the lower rural population as were ever the nobles of the old régime of the common people.[1] This new aristocracy is as selfish, as rapacious, and as destructive as the ancient aristocracy, and if, like all aristocracies, it did not speedily renew itself by the incoming of new elements, it also would quickly perish from the vices which eat into it, from tuberculosis and syphilis, its characteristic diseases, from poverty, its curse, from alcoholism, from all those causes which render its death rate unusually high in spite of its exceptionally distinguished constituency.

Modern capitals not only help to suppress and equalise all the subordinate parts of their nation, they also aid in the assimilation of the different communities lying between them, and from this point of view they again play the rôle of the ancient royal courts. Under the Plantagenets, the luxuries of France and England were, in spite of the infrequency of travel and international relations, strikingly alike. This similarity can be explained only as an outcome of the influ-

[1] At first it would seem as if the law of imitation from above to below were inapplicable to the propagation of Christianity in view of its original spread among the lower classes. It is true that its progress amounted to little until it won over the upper classes and even the Imperial court. But we should note, especially, that Christianity began to spread in cities, in large cities first, and that it was only later that it reached the country districts where the lowest class of peasants *(pagani)* made their home. Fustel de Coulanges *(Monarchie franque,* p. 517) draws attention to this urban propagation of Christianity. Early Christianity like modern socialism spread through the capitals. "This contagious evil," Pliny writes to Trajan, "has spread *not only in the cities, but also* in the towns and villages."

ence of the constant communication between the French and English courts. The courts were, therefore, mutual centres of light and colour. Through the constant interplay of their rays over national frontiers, they supplied people with their first examples of a certain kind of uniformity. To-day the capitals, the daughters of the courts, take their place. In them all eventually successful initiatives are concentrated, towards them all eyes turn, and as they are in constantly reciprocal relations, universal uniformity, offset by a perpetual variability, must be the result of their prolonged preponderance. Let me add that, in their reciprocal relations, the movement of imitation from above to below is also observed. There is always one capital after which the others are likely to pattern themselves both at heart and on the surface, just as formerly there was always one court which was the general model. It is the capital of the preponderating people, or of the people that had preponderated up to the time in question, just as formerly it was the court of the victorious king or of the king who had been long accustomed to victory in spite of recent defeats.[1]

In democratic countries, as Tocqueville remarks, majorities, as well as capitals, have prestige. " As citizens become more equal and more alike the tendency of each to blindly believe in a given man or class diminishes. *The disposition*

[1] Preaching, like all other branches of rhetorical art, had fashions in the past whose variety compensated for the relative immutability of dogma Here again the laws of imitation apply. When scholasticism came in at the Sorbonne, first the divines of Paris, then those of the provincial towns, and finally those of the rural districts, fell to preaching according to set argumentative forms, and we have to be familiar with the ordinary force of the currents of imitation to conceive how this dry and repellent manner of preaching could have been established Later, at the polished court of Louis XIV, the preachers, who were by this time courtiers and men of the world themselves, adapted the language of society to their Advent or Lenten or other kinds of sermons, and then this reform spread little by little from the Court to the Capital, from the Capital to the big and then to the smaller cities But at the time when La Bruyère wrote, this practice had only begun to spread abroad, as we may see from the following remark: " Scholasticism has at last been banished from all the pulpits of the large cities and relegated to towns and villages for the instruction and salvation of the labourer and wine-dresser."

to believe the masses increases and public opinion guides society more and more." Since the majority becomes the real political power, the universally recognised superior, its prestige is submitted to for the same reason that that of a monarch or nobility was formerly bowed down to. But there is still another reason. " In times of equality men have no faith in one another because of their mutual likeness; but this very resemblance inspires them with an almost un-limited confidence in the judgement of the public; for it seems improbable to them that when all have the same amount of light, the truth should not be found on the side of the greatest number." This appears logical and mathe-matical; if men are like units, then it is the greatest sum of these units which must be in the right. But in reality this is an illusion are based upon a constant oversight of the rôle played here by imitation. When an idea arises in triumph from the ballot-box we should be infinitely less inclined to bow down before it if we realised that nine hundred and ninety-nine thousandths of the votes that it polled were but echoes. Even the most careful historians are constantly misled by this and are inclined to enthuse with the crowd over the unanimity of certain popular wishes which the people's leaders have inspired, as if it were something marvellous. Unanimities should be greatly distrusted. Nothing is a bet-ter indication of the intensity of the imitative impulse.

Everything, even progress towards equality, is effected by imitation and by the imitation of superior classes. Be-fore political and social equality between all classes of so-ciety was possible or even conceivable, it had to be estab-lished on a small scale in one of them. Now, it was first seen to occur on top. From Louis XI to Louis XVI the different grades of nobility which had formerly, in the time of great vassals and of pure feudalism, been separated by such impassable distances were steadily levelled, and, thanks to the crushing prestige of royalty and to the com-parative multiplicity of the points of contact between all men of gentle birth, fusion was brought about even between the nobility of the sword and the nobility of the gown.

Now, strange to say, while this levelling was being accomplished on top, the innumerable sections of the middle classes and the common people continued to hold aloof from one another with even intensified class vanity until the eve of '89. Read Tocqueville for an enumeration, for example, of the different grades of upper, middle, and lower middle classes in a town of the ancient régime at this date. There was certainly more antagonism between the consuls and the petty merchants of the eighteenth century than between those of the Middle Ages. The apparent paradox may therefore be safely advanced that the real preparatory work in behalf of modern equality was carried on in the past, not by the middle classes, but by the nobility. In this respect, as well as in the diffusion of philosophic ideas and in the impetus that was given to industry through a taste for exotic fashions, aristocracy was the unconscious mother of modern times. Moreover, these causes are linked together. If the royal courts had not levelled the ranks of the nobility, the literary and, consequently, the philosophic, radiations of the seventeenth and eighteenth centuries would not have darted forth, and fashion-imitation, the love of foreign-bred innovations, would never have prevailed over ancestor-imitation in the bosom of the ruling and influential caste. Consequently, the original centre of all these centres is the king.[1]

[1] Political mania, like drunkenness, began by being the privilege of the upper classes. A century ago this passion thrived among great lords and ladies, and among the scholars of the land, whereas the people and even the lower middle classes remained comparatively indifferent to this kind of emotion. In our own day, the higher classes and people of education are apt to take relatively little interest in politics or to discuss them with unwarranted moderation. In the conversations of fashionable society such questions occur merely incidentally, in the course of gossip, as we may see from the insignificant place that they hold in the journals which picture "society." But as this passion for dangerous problems abates on top, it descends and spreads from one social level to another. The time will come when a combination of political mania and alcoholism will raise the folly of the masses to the highest pitch. Of course, I do not wish to associate religious or even superstitious faith or practice with the above aberrations. But I may be allowed to point out, as

Thus, whether the social organisation be theocratic, aristocratic, or democratic, the course of imitation always follows the same law. It proceeds, given equal distances, from superior to inferior, and, in the latter, from within to without. One essential point of difference, however, must be noted. When the standard-setting points of superiority are transmitted by heredity, as in the case of the ancient nobility and in the priesthood of a caste system, or communicated by consecration (a kind of fictitious heredity or adoption), as in the case of acquired nobility and of the Buddhist and Christian priesthood, they are inherent in the person himself considered under all his aspects. The supposedly superior individual is copied in all respects. He appears to copy no one below himself, and this is approximately true. The relation of the model to the copy is, consequently, almost one-sided. But when for this aristocracy based on the vital tie of real or fictitious affiliation an aristocracy of purely social factors, recruited by spontaneous choice, is substituted, prestige attaches only to the special aspect in which the individual is prominent. He is imitated in this respect only, all others are overlooked.

The man no longer exists who is imitated in every thing, and he who is most imitated himself imi-

one of the explanations of the religiosity of the masses of the people, that in very remote antiquity religion began by being the exclusive luxury of a few patricians before it became a general and vulgarised need of the plebeians.

Fortunately the passion for politics was not the only thing to spread in this way, the love of country was spreading at the same time. The sentiment of patriotism first arose in the ranks of the aristocracy, whence it afterwards passed down, little by little, through imitation, to the middle classes and to the common people. On this point the democratic historian, Perrens, may be credited "The sentiment of patriotism," he says, "was not popularised until after the Hundred Years War, but it had already had a long life among the gentry; it had already appeared in the twelfth century in the poems which they had inspired. *Douce France* is from that time on a favourite expression in the poetry of chivalry After the disaster of Poitiers, it burst out for a time among the middle classes and the common people."

tates, in some particulars, some one of his imitators. Thus imitation, in becoming generalised, has also become mutualised and specialised.

5. It is not enough, however, to say that imitation spreads from above to below; I must be more definite about the concept of the superiority in question. Shall we say that it is always the higher political or economic classes who set the standard? It is not. At those times, for example, when power, and with power enhanced facility for acquiring wealth, is in the hands of the people's representatives, the latter are *desired* to be rather than *estimated* to be superior by those who elect and elevate them. Now, the privilege of having one's self reflected on all sides belongs to the kind of superiority which is believed in, not to that which is merely desired. In fact, to desire a man's promotion is to realise that he is not already high up, and that fact alone often keeps him from having prestige. This is the reason why so many successful candidates have so little weight with their electors. But, in this case, the classes or persons who have real prestige are those classes that have had power and wealth up to a still recent period, even if they have actually been despoiled of them, or those persons who, through their eminent and timely talents, are on the road to fame and fortune. Again, when a man has been powerful or rich for a long time, he inevitably wins consideration through the conviction that gradually comes to people that he really deserves his advantages. So, in spite of everything, the two ideas of power and wealth are sure to be connected with that of social superiority.

They are connected, however, as effect to cause. It behooves us to go back to the cause, to learn what are the qualities which lead or have led men, or groups of men, to power and wealth and which make them the objects of the admiration, envy, and imitation of their neighbours. In primitive times they were physical vigour and skill, physical bravery; later, skill in war and eloquence in council; still later, æsthetic imagination, industrial ingenuity, scientific genius. In brief, the superiority which is imitated is the superiority which is understood;[1] and that which is understood is what is believed, or seen, to be conducive to benefits which are appreciated because they satisfy certain wants. I may say, parenthetically, that these wants are derived, to be sure, from organic life, but that their social mould and channel are made by the example of others. Sometimes these benefits are vast domains, great herds of cattle, numerous leuds or vassals seated around the immense tables of their over-lords, sometimes they are capital cities and a constituency of devoted electors. Again they may be men's hopes of heaven and the credit they are supposed to have with great personages beyond the grave.

If I am asked, What is the series of social superiorities which takes place in the course of civilisation? I shall answer that it depends upon that series of social goods which are successively pursued under so many changing forms by the majority of men of a given epoch and country. Now, what impels and directs this latter series? It is the sequence of both mutually helpful and mutually hindering inventions and discoveries which present themselves

[1] It has been noticed that all the Roman provinces west of the Adriatic (Italy, Sicily, Spain, Gaul, Germany, etc) were more or less easily Latinised, and had to adopt the laws, language, and customs of Rome; whereas in the East, even after the conquest of Greece, the Greek language and civilisation continued to hold their own and even to spread. This was because the superiority of the Romans was recognised by those whom they had conquered in the West, by the Celts, Iberians, Germans, etc, whereas Greek nationality refused, even after its downfall, to confess itself inferior to the barbarians of the Tiber, and preserved its proud sentiment of intellectual pre-eminence. For a like reason, the Gallo-Romans, who were conquered at a later date, refused to assimilate with the Germans. An entirely analagous thing occurs whenever the common people come into power and set to imitating the manners and customs of a fallen aristocracy whom they have always recognised as holding the sceptre of the refinements of life. The prestige of Rome and Constantinople, as well as of Athens, was magnified by their very downfall.

It is evident that all the external history of Rome is explained by the law of imitation from upper to lower. Its internal history is explained in the same way. The Roman plebs raised itself up only through copying the customs and then the prerogatives and privileges of the patricians, beginning with legal marriage.

one after the other to the human mind, in the irreversible, to a certain extent, and inevitable order that is indicated by social logic. The discovery of the advantage of cave dwellings, the invention of stone weapons, of bows and arrows, of bone needles, of fire from the friction of wood, etc. kindled for the first troglodytes their ideal of happiness,— a lucky hunt, fur garments, game (human, at times!) eaten in the recesses of a smoke-filled cave. Later on, the discovery of certain ideas of natural history and the important and immensely fruitful invention of domesticating animals brought a change of ideal; great herds of cattle under patriarchal supervision was the new dream. Then the discovery of the first elements of astronomy, the invention of domesticating plants, *i. e.*, of agriculture, the discovery of metals and the invention of architecture made possible a dream of great domains peopled by slaves and dominated over by a palace, the model of houses to come. Finally, the discovery of the sciences,' from the nascent physics of the Greeks and the babbling chemistry of the Egyptians up to our own learned treatises, and the invention of arts and industries, from the hymn to the drama or from the grindstone to the steam mill, made possible the gradual building up of the happiness of our millionaires, the piling up of their bank accounts or of their government or real-estate securities. So much for wealth. As for power, the same considerations apply in the succession of its historic forms.

In view of these facts, a definite answer shapes itself to the question we are concerned with. The qualities which make a man superior in any country and at any period are those which enable him to understand the group of discoveries and to make use of the group of inventions which have already appeared. Sometimes, quite often, in fact, it is some accidental or objective condition rather than personal qualities which enable an individual to make use of, or, for a time, monopolise the leading inventions of his day; and, in general, these two factors are in combination. Although the tribe or city where a progressive idea or a superior industrial process or a more powerful military engine happens to appear, may be inferior in race and culture, yet it will retain a monopoly of the novelty for a long time. It may have been due to such a change as this that the Turanians had the advantage throughout remote antiquity of being almost the only people to practise metallurgy. The prosperity of the Phœnicians is partly explained through the discovery on their shores of the little purple-producing shell-fish. From this a great maritime export-trade arose which was most timely in encouraging the natural bent of these Semitic peoples towards navigation. The first people to domesticate the elephant or horse must have derived immense advantage from them in war. Formerly, the mere fact of being the son of a father who was possessed of the natural qualities demanded by the civilisation of his day was an advantageous condition which stood in lieu of those qualities. The idea of hereditary nobility came about in this way.[1] Finally, when a given locality has long held the privilege of attracting to itself those individuals who are the best endowed from the point of view of contemporary ambition, a presumption of superiority attaches, as I have said before, to residence in that place, and this is one of the most favourable circumstances for the happy employment of the resources furnished by the civilisation of the time. In our own day, when science and industry are the great bodies of discoveries and inventions which we must appropriate in order to grow rich, it is advantageous to live in the great cities where scholars, inventors, and capitalists are concentrated. This is so much the case that it is often enough for a woman who is a newcomer in a provincial town, to be a Parisian, to set the style in the place. During the feudal period, when

---

[1] Let me add that the idea of nobility arose at a time when the physical and moral qualities that were necessary to make use of the very simple military engines and methods of the period were readily developed by proper training and were easily transmitted by inheritance, much more easily than the subtle characteristics of modern times. And so the son of a powerful warrior generally came to have a well-founded reputation of his own.

the art of war, which was then the unique source of territorial wealth, was the customary privilege of the lord of
the castle, the castle inmate, however lowly his station,
far outranked the citizen. This was not so in Italy, however. There the cities learned how to organise bodies of
militia to keep the neighbouring castles under control.
When the royal court came to be formed, the courtiers
of Versailles totally eclipsed, for like reasons, the Notables
of Paris, the royal favour having become the supreme prize.

We must see that social superiority always and everywhere consists of objective circumstances or of subjective
traits which aid in the exploitation of existing discoveries
and inventions. Now let us remove to one side the first
of these two sources of superiority and turn our attention
to the matter of subjective traits. Here, undoubtedly, the
qualities which make a man, or a group of men, superior,
are always bodily characteristics or personal qualities;
nevertheless, the character of their superiority is wholly
social, since it consists in their pre-eminent aptitude to carry
out the objects of social thought. From the very beginnings of humanity, when physical force is supposed to have
ruled superior, the successful savage was not the most vigorous one; he was the most agile one, the one most skilful in handling bow and club and sling, in cutting stone.
Nowadays it is useless for a man to be muscular and well-
proportioned; unless he also possesses that cerebral hypertrophy which was once abnormal and disastrous, but
which is now normally exacted by the exigencies of our
civilisation, he is condemned to defeat. Between these
two extremes there is, perhaps, no peculiarity of race or
temperament, no morbid or monstrous trait which has not
had its day of glory and expansion. Were we not surprised
by the bestial although royal and authoritative type of the
recently unearthed Rameses the Great? How many of
our instinctive criminals would have been heroes in other
days! How many madmen would have had statues and
altars erected to them!

But through this oscillating multiformity, which explains

the *partly* fortuitous character of inventions and discoveries, it is easy to remark, on the whole, the gradual decline of aptitudes that are muscular rather than nervous and the concomitant progress of aptitudes that are nervous rather than muscular. The countryman is muscular; the citizen is nervous; the same distinction exists between the civilised and the uncivilised man. Why is this? There are two reasons. In the first place, social logic eliminates a smaller number of contradictory discoveries and inventions than the number of the consistent ones which it accumulates; and the resulting excess of complexity necessitates a more highly developed cerebral capacity and a more perfect cerebral organisation. In the second place, the accumulation of mechanical inventions puts an increasing number of animal, chemical, and physical forces at the disposition of man and frees him day by day from having to reinforce them with muscular labour.[1]

Racial or individual differentiation is, we see, like a musical instrument upon which inventive genius is free to play under the general guidance of social logic. This has an important corollary for historians. If you are seeking the cause of a people's prosperity or decay you must look for it in the peculiarities of its organism which rendered it particularly fit to make use of contemporaneous knowledge, or in the appearance of new knowledge which it was not physically able to utilise as it had its old knowledge. If the elements of a civilisation are given and you wish to describe with accuracy its parent race, on its mental side, at any rate, the same principle will serve as a guide. In this way we have been able, instinctively, to describe the psychology of the primitive Etruscan or Babylonian A

[1] From this it follows that everywhere, at any given moment in history, the superior classes belong to races that are more mixed and complex and artificial than those of the inferior classes. In Egypt, the fellah has remained like the ancient Egyptians, whereas his masters have fallen away from the ancient type The higher the class, the more extensive its matrimonial market The higher you mount in the ranks of the old French nobility, the more scattered do you find its marriages The royal family was at the top and it had all Europe for its matrimonial domain.

people who were marvellously gifted for the chase and whose very agility and more brilliant parts unfitted them for pastoral occupations, had inevitably, in spite of their vigour, to succumb in a pastoral period, just as nowadays, in our industrial cities the old-fashioned poetic or artistic temperament succumbs. In general, the advent of some new race corresponds to every fresh influx of important, civilisation-shaping inventions. It may be because the established race was born without the traits required in the exploitation of the rising ideas, or, because, although it may once have have had these traits, it has come to lose them while it was controlled by its old ideas. Every established civilisation ends by creating its own race. Our own civilisation, for example, is engaged in shaping for itself the American of the future.

Let me conclude with the observation that the social peaks, the classes or nations which are most imitated by others, are those within which the greatest amount of reciprocal imitation goes on. Great modern cities are characterised by the intensity of their imitation of internal things; it is proportionate to the density of their population and to the multiform multiplicity of the relations of their inhabitants. This, as M. Bordier justly remarks, accounts for the " epidemic and contagious " nature of their fashions and vices, as well as of their maladies and of all the striking phenomena which occur in them. Formerly, the aristocratic classes, especially the royal courts, were distinguished by this same characteristic.[1]

6. The law which I have been developing is certainly very simple; but I think that if we do not lose it from view certain points of history which have hitherto been obscure may be cleared up. To cite one only, what is more shadowy than the formation of the feudal system during the Merovingian and Carolingian period? In spite of the service of Fustel de Coulanges in throwing light upon this subject by revealing the Roman origins of many alleged German institutions, many sides of the question are still

[1] See *Vie des sociétés*, p. 159.

obscure, and I certainly do not pretend to scatter all their shadows But I take the liberty of pointing out to historians who are throwing light upon these dark places that among other things they may have failed to sufficiently reckon with the examples set by the Merovingian king and the inevitable radiations of these examples. The majority of historians have not taken the trouble to notice that the feudal tie of the lord to his vassal as it was constituted and generalised in the ninth and tenth centuries is strangely like the relation between the king and his antrustions as it existed in some of the royal palaces during the fifth and sixth centuries If historians have noted this fact, they have not classified it properly. The antrustion is devoted body and soul to his king, like a vassal to his lord, in return for the protection which shields him. In the beginning, to be sure, the antrustionship is temporary, but it soon becomes hereditary and proprietary as well. M. Glasson writes that " land grants were at an early time attached to the antrustionship, and this dignity was transmitted from father to son long before the capitulary of Kiersy recognised the hereditary character of benefices and offices." Thus, the two main features of feudalism, inheritance and land-tenure, existed in the case of the antrustion before existing in the case of the beneficiary. Is it not natural to see in the latter a manifolded copyist of the former, and for the same reason to consider the beneficiaries of beneficiaries, the petty vassals of a great vassal, as new imitative editions of the same model?[1] It is a controverted question," as M. Glasson puts it, " whether the king alone had antrustions or whether the great nobles were

[1] This attempt to solve the problem of feudalism must not be confounded with an hypothesis which has been put forth concerning the origin of the nobility. It has been queried whether the Frankish nobility is not derived, physiologically, from the antrustions M Glasson denies this, and, apparently, with reason. Nobles are born (in the vital meaning of the word) from royal functionaries whose functions have become hereditary. This does not preclude the fact that in gaining the inheritance they must have thought of the antrustions and desired to have them themselves.

also entitled to have them. In my opinion no decisive
reason can be given on one side or the other." But how
can we admit that the nobles could have withstood the desire to have the same kind of body-guards as those of their
monarch? Call to mind La Fontaine's line: "Every petty
prince has his ambassadors." The oath of homage and allegiance is another characteristic of the feudal tie; and is
it not a multiplied copy of the oath of fidelity pledged to
the Merovingian kings by their subjects? There is nothing
analogous to this oath under the Roman Empire. It would
have been very surprising if this peculiar custom had not
made an impression, and if, later on, when suzerains had
come to exact the same kind of an oath from their followers,
it had not been the thing to suggest this idea to them.
Finally, is not the origin of most of the feudal rights explained quite naturally by certain of the imposts or rents
that were the dues of the Merovingian monarch? M.
Glasson says, for example, that "the custom of making
gifts to the king under certain circumstances, notably on
the occasion of fêtes or *marriages,* already existed under
the Merovingians. . . . The first Carolingians regulated
this custom and changed these gifts into a direct tax." [1]
Now, later on "under feudalism, *the nobles exacted similar
gifts from their vassals,*" [2] on precisely the *same* kind of
occasions. Is not this significant? Why should not these
royal examples have been imitated when it is known that so
many others were imitated, especially those which help to
explain to us the characteristics taken on by mediæval serf-
dom? It has been asked how it was that the serf of the
Merovingian period, from whom his master could exact
almost arbitrarily any service whatsoever, came to evolve
into the serf of the eleventh century from whom only a
fixed quit-rent could be demanded? The answer has been
made in drawing attention to the fact that this substitution
of a fixed for an arbitrary arrangement began by being an

[1] [*Histoire du droit et des institutions de la France,* II, 482. E.
Glasson, Paris, 1888 —*Tr.*]
[2] [*Ibid.,* II, 483.—*Tr.*]

innovation in the royal and ecclesiastical domains. To quote again from the learned author I have already cited, " the nobles imitated the Church, the abbeys, and the king in all their acts, and the quit-rent tended to become a fixed charge everywhere."

Fustel de Coulanges is too clear-sighted to have altogether misinterpreted the importance of the antrustions. In his *Origines du système féodal,* where he studies minutely the Roman, Gothic, and German sources of feudalism, he dedicates a few pages, but only a few, to the king's *trust* in the midst of long chapters upon the Roman *precarium,* upon *benefices, patronage,* etc. It is a pity, in my humble opinion, that he puts the first of these subjects in the same or, in fact, in a considerably lower rank than the others, and I think that he would have escaped this error had he reckoned upon the universal tendency of men to copy one another, and, above all, had he considered the particularly contagious nature of royal example in all periods of history. To be sure, the Roman *precarium* and even the various kinds of benefice and patronage, Germanic, Roman, or Gallic, are merely modes of land appropriation and of personal subjection; they are without any military character and, in general, they lack the religious sanction of the oath. Those customs are undoubtedly the conditions and even the very roots of the feudal tie, but they do not constitute it. They are too trivial and too widespread among the most diverse nations to explain adequately one of the most original forms of society that the world has ever seen. Only when these different sources met in a single current in the court of the Merovingian king, in a military and sacramental setting, did the germ of feudalism really expand. Our eminent historian seems to almost recognise this in the following remarkable passage (p. 332): " We already find here," he says, in concluding his over-short chapter on the *royal trust,* " certain features which will persist in feudalism. In the first place we find as essentials, the *oath* and the *contract;* we also find that *the oath is taken in its characteristic form, upon the hand of the chief, sword at side.* Finally, we find certain terms which are also characteristic, the terms trusty man [*fidèle*], friend, peer, and, in particular, the Germanic term which corresponds to the term man [*homme*]." The italics are mine. Truly, I cannot conceive why the author did not attach more importance later on to such striking analogies. We shall reread his book in vain to find anything in all his careful analyses of other institutions which is anywhere near as closely suggestive of feudalism.

Only one feature, I repeat, is lacking in this picture of perfect resemblance. The title of antrustion is purely individual, it is not inherited. A man becomes a king's antrustion by spontaneous agreement. The title of vassal in the tenth century is, on the contrary, hereditary, and although the necessity of new investiture with every generation, through the plighting of a new oath of homage and allegiance, is recognised, as a matter of fact it merely testifies to the original voluntary and contractual nature of a tie which has eventually come to be innate and hereditary. This difference is explained by another law of imitation which we are about to discuss, the law by which fashion entrenches itself as custom, *i. e.*, the hereditary consolidation of what began by spreading itself contagiously from contemporary to contemporary.

After all, the preceding historical hypothesis is only offered as a specimen of the services which, in more skilful and scholarly hands, might be rendered by the application of the general ideas which we have been developing.

CHAPTER VII

EXTRA-LOGICAL INFLUENCES (CONTINUED)

Custom and Fashion

THE presumption of superiority which recommends one among a thousand examples of equal logical value, attaches not only to the persons, classes, and localities from which the example emanates, but to the time of its origin as well. I intend to devote this chapter to a consideration of this last-named order of influences. It is, we see, only a consequence of the law of the imitation of the superior, looked at under a fresh aspect. Let us begin by laying down the principle that even in societies which are, like our own, the most over-run with foreign and contemporary (thus doubly accredited) literature, institutions, ideas, and turns of speech, ancestral prestige still immensely outweighs the prestige of these recent innovations. Let us compare some of the few English, German, and Russian words that have recently been popularised, with the foundations of our old French vocabulary; some of the fashionable theories on evolution or pessimism with the mass of our ancient traditional convictions; our present-day reform legislation with the bulk of our codes, whose fundamental points are as ancient as Roman law; and so on. Imitation, then, that is engaged in the currents of fashion is but a very feeble stream compared with the great torrent of custom. And this must necessarily be so.[1] But, however slender this stream may be, its

---

[1] Just as from the social point of view, or, at least, from the point of view of temporary, if not lasting, social peace, it is much more important that beliefs should be held in common than that they should be true,—hence the supreme importance of religions;—so, from the

work of inundation or irrigation is considerable, and it behoves us to study its periodic rises and falls in the very irregular kind of rhythm in which they occur.

In all countries a certain kind of revolution is gradually effected in people's minds. The habit of taking on faith one's priests and one's ancestors is superseded by the habit of repeating the words of contemporary innovators. This is called substituting the spirit of investigation for credulity. Actually, it is merely a welcoming of foreign and persuasive ideas following upon a blind acceptance of traditional and authoritative affirmations. By persuasion is meant the apparent agreement of these foreign ideas with those that are already established in dogmatic minds, that is, with dogmatic ideas. The difference, we see, does not lie in the voluntary or non-voluntary nature of the acceptance If traditional affirmations are accepted, I will not say more freely, but more quickly and vigorously, by the mind of the child, and are imposed upon it through authority, not through persuasion, it means that the mind of the child was a *tabula rasa* when the dogmas came into it, and that to be received they had neither to confirm nor contradict any

---

same point of view, the important thing in the matter of public instruction is the common, much more than the useful, nature of knowledge; or, rather, the principal utility of knowledge consists in its being common property, consists in its very diffusion. It is certainly easy to prove that the teaching of Greek and Latin is not the most useful thing in relation to human wants (aside from the want which we are about to discuss), any more than such and such religious dogmas are among the things of which we have the best proofs. The only advantage, but it is a big one, of maintaining this instruction, is in not breaking the chain between generations, in not cutting ourselves off too sharply and too utterly from our forefathers and from each other; in conforming ourselves as members of an educated class to one another and to our forebears in order that, united by the tie of imitating the same model, we shall not fail to form one single society Although a youth might possess much truer and much more valuable knowledge than our collegiate students, if he did not know what they knew, he would be socially estranged from them This is, at bottom, the real and inner reason, whether avowed or unconscious, why, even in spite of unanimous criticism, respect for so many archaic things persists. There is no stronger confirmation than this of the conception of the social tie that has been brought out in this book.

idea that was already established there. They had only to arouse fresh curiosity, and to give it indifferent satisfaction. This is the whole difference. It follows that the authoritative form of impression must have necessarily preceded the persuasive form, and that the latter is an outcome of the former.

Similarly, in every country, a like revolution occurs in the case of people's *volitions*. Passive obedience to ancestral orders, customs, and influence, comes to be not replaced, but neutralised in part, by submission to the pressure, advice, and suggestions of contemporaries. In acting according to these last-named motives, the modern man flatters himself that he is making a *free choice* of the propositions that are made to him, whereas, in reality, the one that he welcomes and follows is the one that meets his pre-existent wants and desires, wants and desires which are the outcome of his habits and customs, of his whole past of obedience.

The epochs, and societies in which the prestige of antiquity rules exclusively are those where, as in ancient Rome, *antiquity* means, in addition to its proper sense, some *beloved object*. *Nihil mihi antiquius est,* nothing is dearer to me, said Cicero. In China and Siberia[1] you tell the passer-by, to please him, that he *looks aged,* and your interlocutor is deferentially addressed as *elder brother.* The epochs and the societies which are, on the contrary, controlled by the prestige of novelty are those where it is proverbial to say that everything new is admirable. And yet the traditional and customary element is always, I repeat, preponderant in social life, and this preponderance is forcibly revealed in the way in which the most radical and revolutionary innovations spread abroad; for their supporters can further them only through oratorical or literary talent, through superior handling of language, not of scientific, or philosophic, or technical language, all bristling with new terms, but of the old and antique language of the people, so well known to

---

[1] See Dostoïesky's *Maison des morts* And so in Siberia, in speaking of a man twenty years old, they say: " My respects to old man so-and-so "

Luther and Voltaire and Rousseau. The old ground is always the vantage-point from which to tumble down old edifices and to rear up new ones. The established morality is always the basis for the introduction of new political ideas.

It seems as if I ought to cross-classify the foregoing distinctions between imitation of a native and ancient model and imitation of a new and foreign model. Is it not possible for both the ancient and the novel models to have prestige, although the former is neither native, nor the latter foreign to either family or city? This may be so, of course, but it is such a rare occurrence that it is not worth the trouble of making the distinction. Those epochs whose byword is " everything new is admirable " are essentially *externalised*—on the surface, at least, for we know that in reality they are more deeply penetrated than they think for by ancestral religion; and those epochs whose unique maxim is " everything antique is good," live a life wholly from within. When we no longer venerate the past of our family or city we cease, *a fortiori,* to venerate every other past, and the present alone seems to inspire us with respect. Inversely, when it is only necessary to be blood-kindred or compatriots, to be considered equals, the stranger alone seems to produce as a rule that impression of respect which leads to imitation. Remoteness in space acts here like the remoteness in time in the former case. In periods when custom is in the ascendant, men are more infatuated about their country than about their time; for it is the past which is pre-eminently praised. In ages when fashion rules, men are prouder, on the contrary, of their time than of their country.

Is the revolution to which I have referred universal and necessary? It is, for the reason that independently of any contact with alien civilisation, a given people within a given territory must inevitably continue to grow in numbers, and must no less inevitably progress in consequence towards urban life. Now, this progress causes the nervous excitability which develops aptitude for imitation. Primitive rural communities can only imitate their fathers, and so they acquire the habit of ever turning towards the past, because the only period of their life in which they are open to the impressions of a model is their infancy, the age that is characterised by nervous susceptibility, and because, as children, they are under paternal rule. On the other hand, the nervous plasticity and openness to impressions of adults in cities is in general well enough preserved to permit them to continue to model themselves upon new types brought in from outside.

In contradiction to this view may be cited the example of nomadic peoples like the Tartars, Arabs, etc., who appear for many centuries past to have been irrevocably tradition-bound. But perhaps, or, rather, undoubtedly, their present state of immobility is the end of the historic cycle which they had to traverse, the equilibrium which they have reached at the close of the anterior stages in which their semi-civilisation was formed by means of successive importations. In fact, the corresponding involution of the revolution we have discussed is no less necessary. Man escapes, and then but partly, from the yoke of custom, only to fall under it again, that is, to fix and consolidate, in falling under it again, the conquests due to his temporary emancipation. If he is full of genius and vitality, he escapes again and makes new conquests, only to pause for the second time, and so on. These are the historic somersaults of the great peoples of civilisation. There is a notable proof of this in the fact that the progress of urban life is not continuous; after accesses of fever like that which is now raging through Europe, it suffers intermittent setbacks and lets rural life develop again at its expense. This development takes place in all manner of ways, not only in the numerical increase of scattered rural and village communities, but, likewise, in the increase of wealth and welfare and enlightment outside of the great centres. A mature civilisation like China, for example, or ancient Egypt, or the Peru of the Incas (?), or feudal Europe in the twelfth century, is always essentially rural in the sense that the general level

of its cities remains static, while that of its country districts
continues to rise. Our own Europe, according to all probabilities, and in spite of the apparent unlikelihood of this
hypothesis, is bound towards a like goal.

But this final return from the spirit of fashion to that of
custom is in no sense a retrogression. In order to thoroughly understand it, it is necessary to throw some light on
the analogies presented by animate nature. Let us note that
each of the three great forms of universal repetition, vibration, reproduction, and imitation, is at first tied up with and
subservient to the form from which it sprang, but that it
soon tends to escape and, then, to subordinate the latter to
itself Among the vegetal and the lowest animal species we
see that reproduction is the slave of vibration. Their vitality, in its alternating periods of torpor and revival, follows
closely upon changes of season, upon solar light and
heat, whose ethereal vibrations stimulate the vibrating molecules of organic substances. But as life evolves, it consents
less docilely to turn like a top under the whip of the sun's
rays; and, although it can never escape from the enforced
flagellation, it gradually transforms it into a regulative
thing. Thanks to various processes which permit it to store
up the products of solar radiation, it succeeds in holding in
reserve certain internal explosives and combustibles which
are always ready for the nervous system to use. Life sets
them off and burns them up at its own pleasure, not at that
of the seasons, in order to give itself the vibratory stimulus
that is indispensable to muscular effort, to flying, to jump-
ing, to fighting. A moment comes when life not only does
not depend upon physical forces, i. e., the great currents of
ethereal or molecular vibrations and the combustions which
generate them, but, in large measure, controls them. Man,
who even in the most extreme types of civilisation, remains
a simple living being, changes night into day, winter into
summer, the north into the south, with his street lights, his
furnaces, and his locomotives, and renders subject to himself, one after the other, all the vibratory energies of nature,
heat, electricity, and even the light of the sun.

Generation seems to me to hold analogous relations to imitation. In the beginning, it is likewise fitting that the latter should timidly attach itself to the former, like a child to its parent. And we see that in all very primitive societies the privileges of being believed in and obeyed, and of setting the example, are connected with the function of procreation. The father is imitated because he is the procreator. If an invention is to be imitated, it must be adopted by the *pater familias,* and the domain in which it can spread terminates with the limits of the family. The family must multiply for it to continue to spread. Because of the same principle or the same connection of ideas, the transmission of sacerdotal or monarchical power is conceived of, at a less remote period, as possible only by way of inheritance, and the vital principle regulates the course of the social principle. Then every race has its own language, its own religion, its own legislation, and its own nationality. Parenthetically, I may say that the desire in our own day to give an exorbitant historical importance to the idea of race is a sort of anachronism—a naturalistic point of view which can only be explained by the remarkable progress of the natural sciences.

But, from the very beginning, every discovery or invention feels itself cramped within the limits of the family or tribe, or even within those of the race, and seeks expansion by a less lengthy method than the procreation of children; and, from time to time, some invention will burst its bounds and cause itself to be imitated outside, thereby making a road for others. This tendency of imitation to free itself from reproduction hides, at first, under the ingenious mask of the latter, under the fiction of adoption, for example, or naturalisation of foreigners, adoption by the nation. It manifests itself more boldly in the admission of aliens to national worship (the admission of the Gentiles, for example, to the Jewish and Christian rites after the time of St. Paul), in the appearance of so-called proselyting religions, in the substitution of an elective or *consecrated* priesthood for an hereditary priesthood or of an elective presidency for hereditary rulership, in the power accorded to the lower classes to participate in the honours of the upper classes (the honour accorded to the plebeians, for example, of becoming prætors or consuls like the patricians), in people's growing eagerness to learn foreign languages or to learn the ruling dialect of their own country to the neglect of the local *patois,* and to copy every striking peculiarity in the customs, arts, and institutions of foreigners.

Finally, the social principle becomes despotic in turn, and dominates, in its emancipation, the vital principle. At first a feeble body of inventions, an embryonic civilisation, depended upon the pleasure of the race in which it had appeared for a chance to spread. It could hope to spread only as its race spread. Later on, on the contrary, after a conquering civilisation has made the tour of the world, no race can survive or propagate itself unless it be apt, and only in the measure that it is apt, in developing that potent body of discoveries and inventions that is organised in sciences and industries. Then, too, practical Malthusianism is introduced into the habits of society. This may be taken as a negative form of the subjection of reproduction to imitation, since it consists in restraining the power of the former within the estimated limits of production, *i. e.,* of labour, an essentially imitative thing.[1] We have the positive form not only, as I have said, in the choice of the fittest race to further the civilising idea, but also in the gradual formation of new races for this purpose, races born of age-long habits and of chance or deliberate intercrossings. The day may already be foreseen when civilised man, after having created so many vegetal and animal varieties to satisfy his own wants or whims, and after having kneaded at will the lower forms of life, as if to train himself for some higher purpose, will dare to approach the problem of directing his own development, of scientifically and delib-

[1] The most exaggerated expression of this negative subjection of generation to imitation is found in the monastic orders which exact, together with the vow of obedience (or, rather, of both obedience and conformity in belief), the vow of chastity.

erately transforming his own physical nature in the direction most consistent with the ultimate intent of his civilisation.

But, while we wait for this living masterpiece of human
art, for this artificial and superior human race which is
destined to supplant all known races, we can say that each
of the national types that has been formed since the dawn of
history is a fixed variety of the human type, due to the
long-continued action of some particular civilisation which
has unwittingly created it for its mirror.   In less than
two centuries we have seen the birth and establishment in the United States of an Anglo-American type.
This original product serves many sides of our European
civilisation as an admirable means for their propagation
and progress.   The same thing has always happened in the
past.   English, Spanish, French, Roman, Greek, Phœnician, Persian, Hindoo, Egyptian, and other living or
dead products of social domestication are merely modified offshoots of the ancient Aryan or Semitic trunk.

I have purposely omitted the Chinese type, although it
probably realises the most complete adaptation of a given
race to a given civilisation in the fact that each has become
inseparable from the other.   In this case, the civilisation
seems to have been moulded by the race as much as the race
by the civilisation, to infer from the essentially familial
character which this people has retained in spite of its
prodigious expansion.   The complete harmony of these two
elements without any very apparent subordination of either
of them to the other, is not the least peculiarity of this
unique empire.   It has known how to make much out of
little in all things; in it the national is only the domestic
on an immense scale.   This is true, too, of its civilisation
taken as a whole.   Like its other features, it has remained
rudimentary in spite of its refinement and even high at-
tainments.   Its language has grown rich and cultivated
without ceasing to be monosyllabic.   Its government is
both patriarchal and imperialistic.   In its religion
animism and ancestor-worship persist under the purest

form of spiritualism. Its art is as awkward and childish as it is subtle. Its agricultural system is simple and yet finished. Its industry is backward, and yet it thrives. In a word, China has been able to stop, all along the line, in the first of the three stages which I have indicated, and its example proves to us that, although the order of their succession is irreversible, a people is not obliged to pass through all of them to the end.

Now, what happens when a certain original form of civilisation has arisen and spread within a tribe for centuries *through custom,* and has then passed beyond and spread in neighbouring related or unrelated tribes *through fashion,* developing itself all the while, what happens when it ends by welding together all the tribes in which it has spread into a new human variety which is called a nation? When this physical type is once fixed, the civilisation attaches itself to it; it seems to have created it only to settle down in it. Ceasing to look beyond its own frontiers, it thinks only of its own posterity, and forgets the foreigner—as long, at least, as he does not force it to pay attention to him by some rude external shake-up. At this time everything in it takes on a national garb. It is to be observed that sooner or later every civilisation tends towards this period of drawing in upon and consolidating itself. Although our own European civilisation is following in all directions and through all varieties of races its own line of expansion, yet even it already shows plain signs of an inclination to choose out or fashion for itself some universally invading and exterminating race. Which will be this chosen and privileged race? Will it be Germanic or neo-Latin? And what part, alas! will be played by French blood in its definite formation? An anxious question for a patriotic heart! But "the future is no man's," says the poet. However this may be, imitation which was at first custom-imitation and then fashion-imitation, turns back again to custom, but under a form that is singularly enlarged and precisely opposite to its first form. In fact, primitive custom obeys, whereas custom in its final stage commands, generation. The one is the exploitation of a social by a living form; the other, the exploitation of a living by a social form.

This is the general formula which sums up the whole development of every civilisation, at least of all those which have been able to go the length of their course without sudden annihilation. But this formula applies even better to each of the partial developments of a society, to the little secondary waves which fringe, as it were, and constitute its full onward sweep, that is to say, to the evolution, as we shall show in the following sections of this chapter, of each of its separate elements, to language, religion, government, law, industry, art, and morality.

If the distinction between custom epochs and fashion epochs is not clearly defined in history, if it does not seem salient to historians, it is because epidemics of foreign imitation and sheeplike innovation very rarely flourish in all, or almost all, the regions of social activity at the same time. To-day they may make a revolutionary attack upon religion, to-morrow, upon politics or literature; another day, upon language, etc. Communities are like individuals; they are often revolutionary in politics and at the same time set and orthodox in religion, or innovators in politics and conservative purists and classicists in literature.

And the periods of these crises vary greatly in length in different cases. When by exception many of them do occur together, as, for example, in the Greek world in the sixth and fifth centuries before Christ, or as in Europe in the sixteenth or eighteenth centuries of our era, or as in contemporaneous Japan,[1] it is then impossible to misunderstand the eminently revolutionary character of the times or not to note their contrast to the ages which immediately preceded or followed them. But such synchronisms are rare.

---

[1] The frenzy for foreign imitation which reigns at present in Japan is exceptional, but not as much so as one might think. I hope, in this chapter, to dispose my reader to surmise that similar fevers have appeared here and there from the most remote period of antiquity, and that this hypothesis can alone explain many obscure events.

With the benefit of this observation, let us apply our three-fold division to the different aspects of social life and examine the facts which it explains.

I. *Language*

Different families or clans originally speak each its own separate tongue,[1] until the day comes when they begin to form a tribe; then the advantage of speaking a common idiom is appreciated, and, during a more or less prolonged period, one of the idioms, that generally of the ruling family, suppresses all the others.

The members of ruling families who have known and who have wished to know only the language of their fathers, come to learn, as a matter of fashion or taste, that of their foreign masters. Then, when the fusion of blood is completely effected, the tongue of the tribe, the great new family, first spreads and then takes root. It is a language that, after having begun by being foreign to the greater number of those who speak it, has, in turn, become a native

---

[1] I agree entirely with those philologists who assert that language did not appear *spontaneously* in an infinite number of places and families at the same time. However natural the desire of communicating one's thoughts to one's fellows may *have become,* it was certainly not able to bring the invention of speech into existence everywhere at the same time. Besides, let me remark that this desire was developed through the very speech which satisfied it, and did not exist before it, so to speak. It is extremely likely that it was experienced exceptionally violently by some savage of genius, and that through him the first manifestations of language took place in a *single* family. From this family, as from a centre, the example of this fruitful innovation spread very rapidly, and straightway brought to speaking families so great an advantage over non-speaking families, that the latter speedily disappeared; so that from that time on the faculty of speech became the characteristic of the human species. Only, —and on this point we must uphold M. Sayce and other eminent philologists who oppose the monogenists,—it was not so much the first crude products of linguistic invention which were imitated as this new direction of the inventor's spirit. All ingenious members of primitive families were more inspired when they heard spoken words for the first time to invent articulations like those, or pretty much like those, which they had heard, than to reproduce the very same articulations.

tongue, and one exclusively dear to all its speakers, who despise and reject all other foreign idioms. This is not all. It is well to observe that from now on the family, I mean the artificial as well as natural, patriarchal family of kinsfolk, slaves, and adopted strangers, is not the only primitive social group. By the side of it must be considered as the yeast of all ulterior progress, the inevitable reunion of the unclassed, of all the family outcasts, who are forced to organise into hordes for conquest or self-protection. The number of these outcasts increases with the increasing despotism of domestic law under patriarchal rule. If imitation is the true social life, these physiologically heterogenous elements will have no difficulty, even in the most primitive times, in merging together socially. From a linguistic point of view, this fusion will result in the creation of a composite language like the hybrid idioms of certain seaport towns. There has been, then, not only in periods of decay, but from the very beginning, a kind of philological as well as a kind of religious syncretism.

But let us continue. Later on, when tribes themselves

This must have been the great occupation of the nascent imagination. Sayce also says very truly: " It is perfectly plain that at a certain period of social life the tendency to express one's self in articulate language must have been irresistible Man must have rejoiced, like the savage or like the child of to-day in exploiting his newly acquired power The child never tires of repeating the words which it has learned; the savage and the primary scholar of imitating new ones." Hence the originally infinite multiplicity of tongues That unity of language which is imagined by the partisans of monogenism cannot be attributed to the beginning, but only to the end, of philological evolution. " Modern races are only the chosen remainder of an innumerable variety of vanished species. As much can certainly be said of languages. . . . Here and there certain languages have been stereotyped and spared by some happy selection; here and there the fragments of certain others may be found; but the largest number have perished as utterly as the animals of geological antiquity. . . . Pliny tells us that in Cocylium there were more than three hundred dialects Sagard reckoned in 1631 that among the Hurons of North America the same language was rarely found in two villages or even in two families within the same village" And this is not surprising, if we call to mind the permanent hostility which separates all families in primitive times. The following statement is still stranger: " In the island of Tasmania, a population of fifty persons had no less than four dialects."

seek to mingle together and form a confederation, the same phases are repeated on a larger scale. From the diffusion of one of the characteristic tribal languages and the suppression of the others, we pass on to the first foreign and, then, in turn, maternal, language of the city. Later on there is a new series in the same rhythm. The languages of cities and provinces which have concentrated into states vanish before the fatuous adoption[1] of one among them, and the resulting triumphant language finally becomes a national tongue which is as jealous and exclusive, as custom-bound and traditional, as those which preceded it. We ourselves are at this stage. But do we in Europe, where the need of international alliance and confederation is so manifest, do we not feel the anticipatory signs of the opening of a new period? Our mania for borrowing from the vocabularies of neighbouring peoples and our craze for teaching our children foreign languages are clear indications of this. Neologism flourishes everywhere, just as archaism once flourished. A certain language which is spreading with gigantic strides—I do not mean *Volapük,* I mean English—is tending to become universal. The day may come when this language, or some other, a language which will be the universal mother-tongue and which will be as familiar, as fixed, and as lasting as it is cultivated and widespread, will merge the whole human species into a single social family.

Within every separate nation, large or small, we may observe analagous effects. Tocqueville has very justly remarked that in aristocratic societies—where, as we know, everything is hereditary or customary—each class has not only its own habits, but its own tongue, a tongue which it has carved out of the common idiom for itself. It " adopts by choice certain words and certain terms which afterwards

[1] And how rapidly this takes place at times! The following is one example among a thousand Friedlander tells us that " not *more than twenty years* had elapsed after the entire submission of Pannonia, when Velleius Paterculus wrote his history, and when knowledge of the Latin language and even that of its literature had spread to a host of places in the wild and rough and wholly barbarous region which included Hungary, together with the eastern part of Austria."

pass from generation to generation like their estates. The same idiom then comprises a language of the poor and a language of the rich, a language of the plebeian and a language of the nobility, a learned language and a vulgar one," and, let me add, a sacred language and a secular language, the language of *ceremonial* and the language of everyday speech. On the contrary, when " men, being no longer restrained by ranks, meet on terms of constant intercourse," that is to say, when fashion-imitation begins to act openly, " all the words of a language are mingled and *patois* disappear. There is no *patois* in the New World."[1]

A language can spread in two ways by means of fashion. Thanks to conquest or to its own recognised literary superiority, it may be studied voluntarily by the aristocracies of neighbouring nations; they will be the first to renounce their own barbarous tongues and, later on, to inspire the lower classes with either a vain or a utilitarian desire to renounce them also. In the second place, it may exert a very sensible influence over those nations which it has not succeeded in subjugating in this way. Although the former may preserve their own maternal idiom, yet they copy the latter in their literature, they borrow from it the construction of its phrases, the harmony of its periods, its refinements, its prosody. This second kind of external imitation, this so-called literary cultivation of a language, frequently occurs in history and often coincides with the first kind. Thus at Rome, in the time of the Scipios, the young nobles not only studied Greek, they Hellenised the style of their own tongue. In France, in the sixteenth century, the nobility first learned to speak Spanish and Italian and then adapted French to Spanish and Italian phraseology. To go farther back into the past, it is probable that the Persian *Persianised* in this way neighbouring tongues, that the Arab *Arabianised* them, etc.

Now, in the one form or other, linguistic fashion

---

[1] [*Democracy in America*, II, 82, Alexis de Tocqueville English translation by Henry Reeve, Cambridge, 1863, 2d edition.—*Tr.*]

leads to custom. The foreign tongue that is studied and substituted for the maternal idiom, becomes, as I have said, the mother-tongue; the foreign culture which is introduced into a national language becomes national itself before long. In less than a century the Greek periods, the Greek metres, and the Greek constructions that were borrowed by Latin incorporated themselves in the genius of the Latin language and came to be transmitted as national products.

But throughout the above remarks I have attributed to imitation of foreigner and contemporary many changes which are due in large part to imitation of superior. It is, in fact, very difficult to distinguish between these two kinds of contagion. The former, however, does sometimes appear to be experienced by itself, notably in that badly demarcated period where, in the night, in the vast forest of the early Middle Ages, the Romance languages were born, like so many philological cryptogams, with such rapidity and in such obscurity. The linguists, like the old-time naturalists, have been in great haste to explain this apparently miraculous phenomenon on the hypothesis of true spontaneous generation. I confess that I am not satisfied by their explanation, and I think I can affirm that the supposed miracle will continue to be mysterious until we come to take another idea as our starting point, the idea, namely, that towards the ninth century of our era, the spirit of invention, having turned a little capriciously in the direction of language, perhaps because every other outlet was closed to it by circumstances, the breath of fashion, so to speak, began to blow, and for a long time drove and scattered to the four corners of Latin Europe and even beyond the new germs that had appeared somewhere or other, it matters little just where. If, as we are assured, the Romance idioms were born on the spot from the spontaneous decomposition of Latin in consequence of the breaking off of all pre-existing communication between the disintegrated populations of the Empire, it would be astonishing to find that Latin had been corrupted everywhere at the same time and in equal degree, and that nowhere, in no little isolated region, had the old Latin tongue survived with its declensions, its conjugations, and its syntax.

Such simultaneousness, such universality of corruption, in a time of such distraction and in the case of such a tenacious and such a live thing as language, may well astonish us. Moreover, if this were so, what should we think of the uniformity of structure which is to be observed between all the dialects and languages which germinated together from the rotten trunk of Latin? Certain "close and profound analogies exist" between the Langue d'Oc, the Langue d'Oil, Italian, Spanish, Portuguese, Walloon, and between their provincial variations, analogies which Littré justly admires, but about which he errs when he sees in them the effect of some general necessity. Was it a necessary and predetermined thing that everywhere, at all points at the same time, the article should spring up and be derived from the pronoun *ille,* or that the perfect indefinite should be added to the Latin preterite to form with the aid of the verb *avoir* placed in front of the past particle *j'ai aimai, ai amat, ho amato, he amado,* or that the word *meus* should be arbitrarily taken as a new suffix to constitute the new adverb, *chère-ment, cara-men, caramente. . . .* ? It is clear that each of these ingenious ideas sprang up in some place or other from which it radiated everywhere. But the sweep[1] and rapidity of this radiation would be inexplicable unless we admitted the existence of some special current of fashion in relation to the facts in question.

It would be inexplicable just because of that very territorial disintegration, and of that very rupture of ancient communications which has falsely appeared to furnish an

---

[1] It seems to have passed even beyond the limits of the Empire I find the proof of this in the fact that about the same period German and even Slavonic experienced transformations that were quite like those in the transition of Latin to the Romance tongues. Cournot observes that "according to Grimm and Bopp, the use of the auxiliary verb for the conjugation of the perfect tense did not begin to appear in the Germanic languages before the eighth or ninth century." Let him who can explain this coincidence on any other ground than that of imitation.

explanation of the phenomenon in question. Contrariwise, there is no better proof than this example of the reality and intensity of those special, intermittent currents which I feel compelled to hypothecate. Thus, in the sixteenth century, the teaching of Luther spread across the many bristling frontiers of those times with an unheard-of speed that was due to a similar hurricane, a religious one this time It vent itself throughout the whole of Europe; only, as the force of its blasts diminished, it assumed in each province or region a special physiognomy, comparable to the diversity of the Romance dialects in the eleventh century, after each province had reassumed its linguistic isolation. It must not be said, then, that in the ninth and tenth centuries Latin decomposed of itself. It no more decomposed of itself than did Catholicism at the time of Luther's sermons. In both cases the introduction of unexpected and really fresh microbes was necessary to bring about the decomposition that has been advanced as the cause itself This decomposition followed, but did not precede, the grammatical or theological innovations which transformed the language or religion in question. To spread these seeds far and wide, a kind of an epidemic disposition to welcome foreign novelties was necessary.

Ordinarily, every community brings this hospitable opening out of itself to an end by shutting itself up into its customs. Compare the extreme slowness with which even a conquering language spreads beyond its habitual area with the above-cited linguistic conversion of the masses of the Romance populations! Or compare the usual amount of time it takes to snatch a few catechumens away from their native religion, with the extraordinary success of the Catholic apostolate throughout the Greek and Roman worlds, and throughout Germany and Ireland during the first centuries of our era, or with the amazing triumphs of Luther at the time of the Reformation!

These great revolutions cannot be credited, or can be credited only in part, to the prestige of a superior. The Romance revolution in language, like the Christian revo-

lution in religion, in its first centuries, at least, arose and
spread in the bosom of the common people and of conquered nations. Nor could intrinsic superiority, in the
birth of Romance speech, at any rate, account for its triumph over Latin, although the logical laws of imitation do
apply here. When the embryo of Romance speech was
once substituted for the Latin language, it was undoubtedly
by means of logical substitution and accumulation, as I said
above, that this embryo grew and matured. But the preference which led in the beginning to the adoption of this
still rudimentary language had certainly nothing rational
about it, and if in the innumerable *logical duels* which occurred at that time between the Latin and the Romance
forms the latter had always the advantage, it was precisely because they had the wind of fashion behind them.
And yet an attempt has been made to justify this fact by
observing that because the article, the conditional, and the
perfect indefinite were lacking in Latin, Romance stepped
in to fill up the gap. And so the admirable instrument
which served the great writers of Rome was inadequate for
the barbarian colonists! Besides, if the innovation to
which I refer had been favoured merely on the ground of
improvements, Latin, whose genius was in no way contradicted by them, would only have been enriched by them.
But, as a matter of fact, it was destroyed by them, for the
same spirit which prompted them also prompted certain
substitutions, substitutions which I cannot think of as progressive, that of the preposition for the case of the declension, for example. Let no one say that the *delicate feeling*
of the inflections of the declension was necessarily lost as a
result of intellectual coarsening. Nothing penetrates gross
minds better than the subtleties of language. The populations of this period were far from having a dulled philological sense; it was so acute that they put themselves use-
lessly to the effort of invention for the mere pleasure of
invention, it seems to me, and because the human imagination must take some direction or other. And let us admire
the imaginative luxury of these primitive people! Littré,

who accuses them of having lost the key to Latin through
rusticity, does not perceive that he refutes himself in the following lines: " Every student of language will realise how
much delicacy and grammatical discrimination was developed *at the beginning of our language,* how lacking modern
French is in these particulars, and how false the opinion,
as I shall not cease to reiterate, which makes grammatical
barbarity our starting point."

No philologist will have difficulty in upholding this assertion. It applies to the formation of the Aryan languages
as well. The preceding considerations make a fitting introduction, I think, to certain insights into the social conditions
which presided over their prehistoric appearance, into the
debauch of invention and the zeal of imitation from which
they proceeded. This need of irrational linguistic revolution is one of the first epidemics of fashion which rages
among the adolescent, as we may see in our colleges. And
it affects the adolescence of nations as well.

The effects produced in the domain of language by the
alternate transition from custom to fashion, and from fashion to custom, are both many and plain. In the first place,
when imitation of the foreigner is combined with that of
the superior, a great progress is always to be seen, because
of a gradual enlargement of the territory that belongs to
the triumphant languages, and because of a reduction in the
total number of the languages that are spoken. But even
when fashion works alone, it is effective in the same direction; for the linguistic disintegration of feudal Europe,
compared with the Roman Empire, must not be attributed
to fashion. It was the fault of the custom which was forced
to grow up after it; and it is very likely that if fashion had
not helped to spread the budding Romance tongues, Latin,
left to itself in each distinct canton, would have evolved
without revolution in a thousand different directions, and
given rise to a still more lamentable disentegration.

Now, in view of the fact that language is the most potent
and indispensable means of human communication, it is safe
to affirm that the social transformations which are brought

about on a given territory in the direction of a levelling assimilation of all classes and localities by the introduction
of locomotives as substitutes for wagons are as nothing
compared with the same kind of social changes that are due
to the overflow of one great dialect over several petty ones,
of one language over several dialects. Linguistic similarity is the *sine qua non* of all other social similarities, and,
consequently, of all those noble and glorious forms of
human activity which presuppose the establishment of those
similarities and which work on them as on a canvas. The
transient period, in particular, in which a language spreads
on the surface through fashion alone, makes possible the
advent of what is called (for everything is relative) great
national literature. The maximum of value, or, what
amounts to the same thing, fame, to which literary works
can attain, is limited to the number of those who can understand them. Consequently, in order that they may raise
themselves to a far greater height of value or glory than
what has ever been reached before, their language must
flow out far beyond its old-time banks—irrespective of the
fact that the perspective of a more brilliant prize will stimulate genius. And yet this is not enough. Although a
given language might be unified if it were visibly transformed from generation to generation by a series of fashion-
spread grammatical vagaries without any strict fidelity to
usages or rules, yet its people would favour the blossoming
of ephemeral shows, the masterpieces of a day, applauded
to-day, forgotten to-morrow; they would refuse to consecrate those august and enduring reputations, whose majesty
grows in the course of ages because every new generation enlarges their public. Brilliant literature, there might
be, but there would be no classic literature. A classic writer
is an ancient literary innovator who is imitated and admired by his contemporaries, and then by following generations, because his language has remained unchanged.
Living, he owes his incomparable celebrity to the recent
diffusion of his language; dead, he owes his lasting authority to the fixation of his language by custom.

Successive crises of fashion also tend, other things being equal, to make prominent those linguistic innovations which are the fittest to direct language into a certain channel which it is difficult to define, but which is characterised, notably in English. by the simplification of grammar and by the enlargement of vocabulary, and by a utilitarian advance towards clearness and regularity, which is not without injury to poetic qualities.[1]   Let us bear in mind these characteristics; they will soon repeat themselves under other names. .

II. *Religion*

Religions have often been divided into two great classes: those that proselyte and those that do not.   But the truth is that at first even the most hospitable religions began by being jealously closed to the foreigner.   We shall find this so, at least, if we go back to their true origins.   Buddhism, to be sure, appealed from its very birth to men of every race; but Buddhism is only a detached branch of Brahminism, and Brahminism admits of no means of propagation, in principle at least, but transmission through blood.[2]   As for Christianity, it did not spread before the time of St. Paul beyond the Jewish race.   Besides, it sprang out of the Mosaism which had always repulsed the Gentiles.   It is only a *Jewish heresy,* as a child of Israel once proudly said. Before Islamism conquered so many nations, it remained for a long time an exclusively Arabian thing, and its armed pontificate was hereditary among the descendants of Mahomet.   Before the advent of Apollo, in Greece, every tribe

---

[1] Even in the substitution of the Romance tongues for Latin, and in spite of the grammatical refinements of these nascent tongues, this tendency is satisfied by their analytical character and simplified construction.

[2] It is true, according to Lyall's recent and direct observations, that through the aid of numerous fictions ancient Hindoo cults have succeeded in assimilating, by way of conversion, many non-Aryan peoples in India. But the latter have the name of having been Aryanised. And, besides, those very fictions by which they elude the rigour of the ancient regulation testify to the degree of its former severity.

had its own gods. The rapidly propagated cult of Apollo was the first bond of union between the Hellenic cities. Exclusive religions always precede non-exclusive religions, for the same reason that castes always precede classes, monopolies, commercial freedom, and privileges, equality before the law. In brief, this famous distinction between proselyting and non-proselyting religions merely means that the need of expansion *that is common to all alike* is satisfied in the one case by the transmission of useful maxims of piety to the posterity of the same race, a posterity that is always becoming more and more numerous,—this is the cause of the ardent desire of the Hebrew and Aryan of antiquity for a numerous offspring,[1]—whereas in the other case, the same need seeks an easier and a quicker satisfaction in the transmission of its rites and dogmas to contemporaries of other race and blood. In the first case the propagating agent is custom; in the second, that which I call fashion. And the passage from the first to the second is only an extraordinary advance of imitation; it has passed from pedestrianism to flight.

But the most expansive and hospitable worships end early or late by reaching their natural limits, and in spite of their vain efforts to pass beyond them, and in spite, even, of the accidental breaks which they sometimes effect in them (just as Mahometanism has been proselyting again of late on an immense scale in the heart of Africa), they resign themselves to confessing that a given nationality or group of

[1] Let me add that in the most exclusive religions, the desire to imitate the foreigner, the inclination to be in keeping with certain dominating international fashions, even in matters of religion, is experienced much more than one might suppose. For example, Israel, before the time of Samuel, was troubled and embarrassed in the midst of other nations because it had no national god *"in the manner of other peoples"* (See Darmesteter, *Les Prophètes*.) It needed both a god and a king upon the model adopted by its neighbours. "Give us a king to judge us, *as other peoples have*," says the Hebrew people to Samuel. It is certain that a like sentiment resulted upon a hundred other occasions, and for a hundred other peoples, in unifying the types of divinity and monarchy which obtained in regions of more or less vast dimensions.

kindred nationalities is their unique and, henceforward, impassable domain. Here they draw back and implant themselves, and here they generally break up into fragments. From now on, their chief care is not to spread themselves among distant peoples by means of conquest and conversion, but to prolong and perpetuate themselves for future generations through the education of childhood. All the great religions of our own days have reached this stage of withdrawal, a stage which is at first, before the decline which follows it, not lacking in fruitfulness.

But the three periods which I have pointed out as existing in each of the great religions had already been traversed by the lower types of religion on which they were based, and so on until we come to the lowest rung of the religious ladder, where we find ancestor or fetich worship, purely familial cults.[1] In the most ancient times, then, proselytism must have been known and practised, since a common worship, the worship of the god of the city, succeeded in establishing itself and in slowly crushing out the different domestic cults of different families. But it must also have always happened that the vogue of an exotic god, of a god outside of the household, was followed by a static period, when the exotic god became established as a patriotic god, because we find that these city gods became as hostile to, and as exclusive of, one another, as the household gods of a more remote age. Thus the historic rhythm of religions is an alternating transition from proselytism to exclusivism and *vice versa,* indefinitely. The statement that exclusivism was the first link in the chain could not be made without some hesitation.

The opposite view could be maintained. In India, where in the depths of Hindooism the birth of some very low form of religion is actually an everyday occurrence, Lyall informs us that their starting point lies in the preaching of some exalted reformer, of some ascetic or celibate, who

---

[1] For the original universality of the patriarchal family among those peoples, at least, who were destined for civilisation, see the extensive proof given by Sumner Maine in his *Ancient Law.*

has completely broken with his family and caste. He gains adherents on all sides, and then, from his followers' habits of eating and marrying among themselves, the sect becomes a caste in its turn, and ends by localising itself as a family. But we should be exaggerating the bearing of this contemporaneous fact if we saw in it a complete representation of what must have occurred at the origin of religions. It is valuable, however, as confirming the hypothesis according to which the family is not the unique source of societies. A band, or horde, or group of those who are called indifferently family exiles or emigrants, would be the first term of a social evolution differing very much from the preceding, although interwoven with it and modelled upon it. Besides, everything is a witness to the fact that all religions began in animism, that belief in deity was originally fear of spirits; and it is very probable that one of the first and principal manifestations of animism was the deification of dead ancestors, and that the souls of dead kinsmen were the first spirits that were feared. As for spirits of a different origin, the personified forces of nature in anthropomorphism, or, rather, at first, as we shall see, in spontaneous zoömorphism, was it not necessary to get the authority of the head of the family, of the chief, to have them adopted unanimously? The really primitive religion, then, could only be transmitted through blood.

In this connection let us note the strange character of ancestor apotheosis, and, especially, of its universality. For it seems very difficult to understand this worship and veneration of the dead, this obedience to the dead, in those crude times when one is accustomed to think of the adoration of power as ruling alone. I think that this phenomenon, to be understood, must be brought into relation with another equally general and primitive fact, the fact of *gerontocracy*. All primitive societies, however unendowed and unprogressive they may be, have veneration and fetich worship for old age. But how can this fresh fact be reconciled with the rule of brute force? How does it happen that in a young world, in the midst of perpetual conflicts, old men are not relegated to the rear? The likeliest explanation, in my opinion, is the following: In the primitive family, which is very self-centred and very hostile to even neighbouring families, the examples of the father must have a potent and irresistible influence over his children, his wives, and his slaves. In fact, the need of direction which they experience in view of their utter ignorance and lack of external stimulus, can be satisfied only through imitation of some one man, and he must be the man whom they have been in the habit of imitating from their cradles. The prestige of the example of the father, the king-priest of his small state, equals the sum of all that prestige to which our modern civilised Europe is subject, for the most part unconsciously, but whose influence is dispersed by a thousand different channels of docility and credulity, under the influence of teachers, comrades, friends, or strangers, instead of being concentrated in a single basin of paternal customs and traditions. Given this fact and the fact that the paternal magnetisation, as it were, is the more complete in the beginning the greater the age of the father, it having had more time to act in, the fact which Buckle has brought forward may be very well explained, the fact, namely, that the more prodigious the size and strength and intelligence that are attributed by primitive peoples to their superhuman giants, and heroes, and geniuses, the more remote is the past to which they tend to assign them. This is an optical effect, an orientation of admiration, which parental prestige is able to account for. The children know that their own father trembles before the shadow of his ancestor. The idol, then, of their idol must seem a superior kind of god to them.

But Buckle might also have observed that even in the most remote period of antiquity the worship of the foreigner appears alongside that of the ancestor. The distant in space is no less prestigious to barbarians and savages than the distant in time. And the wonders of the world they dream of, their Edens and Hells, in particular, and the beings they endow with supernatural power are localised by their legends on the borders of the known universe. The Aztecs thought that they were fated to be conquered by a divine race hailing from the shores of the far East. The Peruvians held an analogous belief. It is impossible not to recognise, moreover, that several of their gods were the alien reformers or conquerors who had charmed or subjugated their forefathers. The same fact may be observed in all old religions. The reason of it is that, from the most remote period of antiquity, parental prestige must have often been arrested by the sudden appearance of some external and superior prestige. From time to time some unknown chief of invincible fame rises up out of the distant horizon; all are prostrate before him, and the Penates are for the moment forgotten. A newcomer, a bringer of secret and admirable knowledge, is conceived of as an all-powerful sorcerer before whom the whole world trembles. The multiplication of such apparitions is all that is needed to turn men towards a new form of adoration, to substitute the fascination of the distant for that of the past.[1] Moreover, it is likely that the despotic authority of foreign masters and civilisers was copied from that of the *pater familias*, and the apotheosis of these epochs, whether filial or servile, displays itself to us as the highest degree of *reverential fear*. It is, therefore, not astonishing that the most despotic gods are also the most revered. To-day, families which are ruled by authority show us the same state of things. The terrifying character of ancient deities and the humiliating nature of ancient cults are not due to a source for which man need blush. And we can understand the persistence of such beliefs in ancient societies from the fact of their

---

[1] Hence the apotheosis of inventors which is such an important source of mythologies "Among the Phœnicians, as among the Iranians, the invention of fire and the beginning of a divine worship seem to be closely related. In reading the Biblical, Phœnician, Babylonian, and Iranian cosmogonies, side by side, we recognise in them *the intention to represent* in the succession of generic, instead of individual personages, *the succession of the inventions* and developments which had guided the human race up to the time when the cosmogones were written" (Littré *Fragments de philosophie positive*) [p 311 Paris, 1876 —*Tr.*].

dependence upon the social principle without which the so-cieties themselves could not have been possible. For this reason, although atheism would certainly have been a great relief to the hearts of devout people as an emancipation from their chronic state of terror, atheism could not spread at a time when it would have been social suicide.

Nevertheless, in the beginnings of mankind, the isolation of human families that were scattered in a growling wilder-ness of animal life must have been great enough to have prevented them from encountering or fighting one another very often. The cause, then, to which I have referred could not have gained its full importance until later. On the other hand, another class of strange charmers must have played, it seems to me, a preponderating, although overlooked or inadequately appreciated, rôle in the forma-tion of very ancient mythologies. These were, at first, wild beasts and venomous serpents; and then domestic animals. And I lay stress upon this side of mythologies, because here we have, in the most remote ages, the isolated action of fash-ion, independent of any such imitation of superiority as we had in the kind of progress which we have already dis-cussed.

To-day we hunt wild beasts, but our first ancestors *fought* them. It was with wild beasts, primarily, that they were forced·to be constantly at war, either for food or self-defence. "As often pursued as pursuer." Primitive man was undoubtedly far from feeling the contempt which we feel for the hare and quail of our plains, or even for the wolves and boars of our lingering forests, for the lions, the cave bears, the rhinoceros, and the mammoths against which he fought day after day with thrilling turns of for-tune. The end of the tertiary period and the beginning of the quartenary period, that is, of the age when man began to count for something, is characterised by a formidable "emission of flesh eaters." Such a deadly and such a cun-ning fauna had never before appeared on the earth. Ele-phants, rhinoceroses, tigers twelve feet long, lions, hyenas, etc., all belonged to extinct species of which extant ones are but pale reflections, and all habitually preyed upon man. Before these terrible belligerents, much more than before the great men of prey of neighbouring tribes, he trembled with that sacred fear which is the beginning of all devotion. And afterwards, when he found himself in the presence of any great phenomenon, a tempest, the phases of the moon, the rise or setting of the sun, etc., and when he *animated* the phenomenon in order to understand it, his spontaneous personification of it was more animal-like than human. For him to personify was to animalise, rather than to humanise. If all primitive gods, from the Scandinavan Pantheon to the Aztec Olympia, are saturated with blood and are unmerciful in exacting a periodic tribute of human lives, a tribute which comes to be rendered to them later on in an equivalent of animal lives, until only its shadow and mere vegetable symbol survives in the Christian host, if all these archaic divinities are cannibals, is it not because man conceived of them, not precisely in his own image, but in the type of those great superhuman monsters, reptiles or carnivora, which often devoured him?

This hypothesis allows us to rate primitive man as superior to his deities, since it explains their ferocity, not on the ground of his alleged wickedness, but on that of the hard conditions of his precarious and anxious and perilous existence. Now, nothing supports the ordinary hypothesis according to which man has modelled his gods after himself. The resemblance is so slight! They are immortal and invulnerable, he so ephemeral! They are caprice incarnate, he is routine itself. They command surrounding nature as its masters; he falls prostrate before the pettiest meteor. My conjecture, on the contrary, is based, as we have seen, on serious considerations. I may add that the universality of sanguinary deities is naturally explained by the universality of ferocious beasts; and the fact that all races have the same starting point explains, in turn, the similarity of the phases traversed by religious evolution: human sacrifices, animal sacrifices, fruit offerings, spiritual symbolism.

Moreover, if our point of view is true, it follows that

when, in a subsequent age, the ebb tide of animality and the rising tide of humanity enhanced the importance of war between man and man, and diminished that of the war between man and beasts, the gods of human form must have decidedly prevailed over the beast-like gods. This is just what happened; this gradual humanising of deities is one of our most substantiated facts. The Egyptian deities, with a man's face on an animal's body, or with an animal's face on a man's body, show us the most ancient transition that is known from the prehistoric *zoömorphic* gods to the purely *anthropomorphic* gods which the Greeks gradually elaborated. It was a profound transformation, whose accomplishment could not fail to revolutionise the divine idea. Originally, deity was pre-eminently *destructive;* whereas with us it is primarily *creative.* Warlike gods were necessarily triumphant, and in war to triumph was to destroy.

Incidentally, it seems to me that the habitual or ritualistic anthropophagy of primitive peoples is explained by the foregoing considerations. When man was overcome, and this frequently happened, in his combats with monsters, he was always devoured. Consequently, when he happened to overthrow them, he took it as his duty to kill and eat them, however unedible they might be, not only for food, but, following the everlasting custom of military retaliation, for the sake of reprisal as well.[1] On this supposition, what should happen when two tribes made war against each other? Such chance combats wedged themselves in between the familiar combats with the great carnivora, and bore the same relation to them as species to genus. And so it naturally came to be a rule for captives, and even for the corpses of the conquered, to be treated like animals that had been trapped or beaten; they were sacrificed and solemnly eaten at a triumphant feast. The first triumph must have been a banquet. Thus cannibalism must have arisen, originally, from imitation of the primitive chase, although

---

[1] This undoubtedly is the reason why, in prehistoric coves, we never find among their flint implements any complete animal skeleton, not even those of cave bears.

it might have been maintained later on for motives of a mystical or utilitarian nature.[1]

It may be seen how proper the preceding considerations are to explain a fact which greatly astonishes mythologists and which has called forth the most contradictory hypotheses from them, the fact, namely, that everywhere in the world the most ancient gods of mythology have been animals, savage and often ferocious beasts, and that if in the progress of the ages their zoömorphic, their *theriomorphic* character has gradually changed into anthropomorph-

---

[1] Let me add to this a consideration of a more sentimental nature, which will present in a still more favourable light the primitive adoration of animals. Originally, the social group is so small that it is unable to satisfy the greed of sociability which it has itself developed. *This want grows more rapidly, much more rapidly, than the group.* Consequently, those sentiments which find difficulty in venting themselves in the relations of man with his fellows, scattered as they are, and, especially in his relations to his friends and associates, the only ones that he can be with to any extent, must pour themselves out upon the creatures of nature, and especially upon the animals that are in constant contact with primitive man. This is perhaps the *partial* explanation of the great part which both wild and domestic animality plays in the life of the savage and the early troglodyte. The drawings of mammoths, of whales, of lions, etc, upon their ivory plates or staffs of command testify to their zoölatry, or, rather, to their theriolatry.

Goblet d'Alviella is quite right in seeing in these first attempts at art a response to the needs of deity, rather than to still undeveloped æsthetic needs. These mysterious gods, these god-beasts, must have inspired a strange kind of terror, a terror as strange as their monstrous shapes, as well as a singular kind of piety, a servile admiration which, in spite of its servility, was a touching and true form of adoration. Whatever terrifies always ends by being adored. But this animal idolatry is only part of the semi-social relations which primitive man created between himself and animal nature. On the other side, the domestic animals probably inspired in him a certain genuinely paternal or filial tenderness. There is still a trace of this in the affectionate care that the peasant daily bestows upon his cattle; he is never separated from them without regret. An animal slave, like a human slave, is easily taken into the family.

It is probable, therefore, that in the beginning the cords of the heart that were set in vibration by nature and, especially, by animal nature, were of much greater importance compared with those that were stirred by human society than their actual relative importance. An attempt was made to gain real social intercourse with animals; hence *the attribution of language to animals,* as Goblet d'Alviella reasonably surmises.

ism, it is never impossible to discern the deified beast under the humanised god.[1] The animal companion of a god has begun by being the god himself. This was true of the goose of Priapus, of the cuckoo of Hera, of the mouse of Apollo, of the owl of Pallas, as well as of the humming-bird of the Aztec god Huitzilopochtli. It has been proved that, prior to the invasion of the Shepherd Kings, " whenever the gods [Egyptian] appeared on monuments they were represented by animals." Shall we explain with Lang this universal deification of the surrounding fauna (and, at times, of the flora), as the result of totemism, of the universal custom among savages and primitive peoples of recognising some animal as their first tribal ancestor? And then shall we proceed to connect animal worship with ancestor worship? On the contrary, I think that, in this case, the effect is taken for the cause. Totemism does not explain the deification of animals; this deification can alone give a reasonable explanation of totemism.[2] The animal is not reputed to be an ancestor until after it has been deified. Now, why has it been deified? Because the sight of it inspired terror or admiration, or merely because it once chanced to create a lively feeling of surprise as the result, undoubtedly, of a mistaken observation on the part of some ignorant observer. The first animal, the first natural being which appealed to the savage's curiosity, opened out a new world to him, a world outside of his family, or, rather, made a new opening for him into that world which the never-ending growling of savage creatures had never allowed him wholly to ignore. Seen through his dreams or fears, either the commonplace or the terrible

[1] On this point I refer my readers to the *Mythology* of Mr Andrew Lang [Published in the *Encyclopædia Britannica.—Tr*]

[2] On the other hand, I readily admit that the interdiction, which is so frequent in ancient religions, against eating the flesh of certain animals, is explained by totemism and not at all by motives of hygiene. These motives were trumped up afterwards, like those of the somnambulist, who is quick to act on suggestion, to justify himself in his own eyes for the unconscious act of obedience which he is about to commit.

animal revealed to him something outside of himself or his people that was worthy of his interest. This animal, then, this stranger, whose prestige he feels and yields to, tears him away from the exclusive prestige of his divine ancestors and despotic masters. And if the deified animal comes to take higher rank than that of the latter, it is none the less true that, far from this new cult being derived from the family cult, it must have been in opposition to it. In the beginnings of mankind, when animality dominated, the stranger after whom man must have sought to model himself, and to whose fascination he must have yielded after he had escaped from that of his forefathers, must have been, ordinarily, an animal, although, from time to time, and later on more frequently, encounters with other tribes allowed the human stranger to play a like part. It is certain that two prominent kinds of myths are to be found side by side in all old mythologies, myths about animal-gods and myths about divine or heroic civilisers. This curious juxtaposition would be most incomprehensible unless my point of view were accepted. According to it, these two classes of myths are merely varieties of one genus. Both witness from the most remote periods to the action of external and contemporaneous prestige, the source of fashion, as contrasted with paternal prestige, the source of custom.

Let us continue. I have not yet finished my enumeration of the principal sources of primordial religions. To conclude this conjectural and somewhat digressive investigation, I may say that after the deification of fierce beasts, domestic animals should have been and were deified. Thus good gods came to take a place next to bad gods, forming in this way a transitory phase that it is well to notice between *theriomorphism* and anthropomorphism, in addition to the transitions already referred to. Conceive, indeed, of the immense and beneficent change which was wrought when, in the midst of some small human colony, which lacked all forms of industry or agriculture and all means of supply but the bow and harpoon, some savage genius dreamed of domesticating a dog, a sheep, a reindeer, a cow, an ass, or a horse.[1] What do all our modern inventions amount to in comparison with this capital invention of domestication? This was the first decisive victory over animality. Now, of all historic events, the greatest and the most surprising is, unquestionably, the one which alone made history possible, the triumph of man over surrounding fauna. Moreover, the farther back one travels into the past, the greater the value of cattle appears to be. Cattle were the most precious part of spoil, the most coveted kind of treasure, and the first form of money. Hence, the deification of bulls, oxen, and cows in the Old World and of llamas in America. This was a great advance upon the apotheosis of carnivorous animals. Egypt is a witness to this fact in the pre-eminence which she accorded to her Apis over the tiger, lion, and cat-like deities of her more ancient mythology. Archaic Greece gave a great impetus to the development of this already civilised form of animal worship. We have the proof of this, among other facts, in the myth of the centaurs, half men, half horses, which undoubtedly expresses the gradual humanisation of a primitive horse-worship, and to correspond in this new phase of the divine idea to the human-faced tiger-gods of Egypt. In his excavations in Argolis, Schliemann discovered thousands of very ancient idols in which a similar metamorphosis from a cow-goddess to a woman-goddess[2] could be traced through its many phases up to the point when two almost invisible little horns was the last sign of the originally bovine nature of the divinity. This explains the little-understood Homeric epithet of *boôpis*. It is unnecessary to remind the reader of the cow-worship of India.

---

[1] Inventions in matters of domestication are so significant that, like those relating to the conquest of minerals, they have seemed adequate to characterise different civilisations. Just as ages are marked out as the rough stone age or the polished stone age, as the age of bronze, as the age of iron, so the peoples possessing oxen and cows (the primitive Aryas), or horses (Turanians, Arabs), or asses (Egyptians), or camels (the desert Nomads), or reindeer (Laps), etc, are, or may be, distinguished accordingly.

[2] They were " either in the form of woman with horns on both sides of the breast, or in the form of cows."

But man celebrated the wonders of domestication not merely by his worship of different kinds of cattle; he also celebrated it in the nature of the cult which he paid to gods of various origins. After he had domesticated animals and had appreciated the immense advantage of their exploitation, he must have asked himself whether he could not also domesticate some of those gods, of those great spirits which he had already conceived of as the hidden springs of the great mechanisms of nature, of sun and moon, of rain and tempest, and which he had pictured under the lineaments of men and animals. Once these conceptions had been taken and developed into an innumerable *divine fauna,* the domestication of divinities must have been the great preoccupation of men of ability. It was a question of having one's own spirits attached to one's dwelling, like sheep, or dogs, or reindeer. These were the Lares; and they were not always, as a matter of fact, the souls of ancestors. But how were these wild deities to be overcome and humanised? By methods strangely like those which had served in the subjection of tame animals, namely, by caresses and flattery, by offering them the advantage, rare in those times, of a regular and abundant nourishment which would entirely relieve them of the effort of searching for an uncertain and intermittent one. Here we have the origin of sacrifices. This view will cease to appear odd if we try to conceive of what domestication must originally have been. To us the trained horse that is docile under its bit is merely a certain muscular force under our control. But to the savage of bygone ages, just as, to a certain extent, to the Arab of to-day, the horse possessed a hidden power which could not be managed without a certain superstitious fear of, or respect for, its latent mystery. Therefore, it is less surprising for worship to have been an attempt at domestication, if domestication was really a kind of worship.

In support of these speculations, I will add another which completes them and which seems to me to be equally probable. The idea of reducing men to slavery, instead of killing and eating them, must have arisen after the idea of training animals instead of feeding on them, for the same reason that war against wild beasts must have preceded that against alien tribes. When man enslaved and domesticated his kind, he substituted the idea of human beasts of burden for that of human prey.

But the preceding speculations on the probable origin of the earliest religions is, to be frank, a digression for which I crave the reader's indulgence. Let us return to our special subject and let us seek out, as we have already done in the case of language, the consequences which are involved in the transition, in questions of religion, from custom to fashion, and from fashion to custom, that is to say, in the development of a worship following upon its establishment in an enlarged domain. In the second place, let us ask ourselves what are the inner characteristics which the expansion of a cult presupposes and which enable it to be successful? I answer, in a word, to the first point of view, that a widespread religion is a prerequisite of every great civilisation, and that a stable religion is the no less necessary condition of every strong and original civilisation. As its cult, so its culture. To the second point of view I answer that the most spiritual and philanthropic religion has the greatest chance of expansion, and that, on the other hand, a religion which spreads beyond its source tends to become spiritualised and humanised.

This tendency of religions to become spiritualised in their onward movement is well known. The worship of Apollo, for example, which is so pure and noble a worship in comparison with the gross cults which it succeeded, Hebrew prophecy, which is spiritual, compared with the Mosaism which preceded it, Christianity, which is still more spiritual, and the particularly refined forms of Christian spirituality, Protestantism and Janseism, all these are so many successive steps in religious evolution. But now we know the reason of this progress. The idea of deity, which was at first bestial or physical in the times when the relations of men with beasts and nature were more frequent and important than their relations with their non-related fellows,

becomes gradually spiritualised, or, to put it better, humanised, in the social sense of the word, as man comes into
closer touch with both related and non-related man and as
his direct contact with nature diminishes. And we have
seen how the animal character of ancient gods came to be
effaced and replaced by human traits, which have themselves ended by vanishing, transfigured, into a sublime
dream of infinite Wisdom and Power. This change was
wrought in the divine idea at the same time that religion, of
which it is the soul, passed beyond the limits of its cradle
in the family. These two transformations must have been
parallel, for they emanated from the same cause: the preponderance that was acquired by the social and, consequently, by the spiritual side of human things over their
natural and material side. Imitation was emancipated
from heredity for the same reason that mind was disen-
gaged from matter.[1] On the other hand, the latter progress
facilitated the former. The god who is the least corporeal
and the most spiritual is the one who has the most chance
of subjugating foreign peoples; for men of different races
differ less from one another intellectually than physically,

[1] In Greece and Rome, especially, the more or less advanced spirit-
ualisation of a religion which had been hitherto materialistic was accompanied by the substitution of a priesthood, recruited by voluntary
consecration, by election or by lot, for an originally hereditary priesthood. This innovation took place at Athens about 510 B C., through
the reform of Cleisthenes, who completed the work of Solon and suppressed the four ancient tribes, which were religious corporations based
upon consanguinity, and replaced them with new tribes composed of
demes, a purely territorial division. Sacerdotal functions became, in
consequence, elective. A similar change was effected at Sparta and
in many other Greek cities at the same epoch, just when philosophy
had begun to creep into dogma. At Rome the fight between the
patricians and the plebeians turned largely on the question whether
the functions of the flamens, the salians, the vestals, and the sacrificial king should continue to be hereditary or should be passed on
through election A moment came, towards the end of the Republic,
when the light of Greece had begun to shine upon it, when the plebs,
who had already gained access to the different magistracies which
had before that been reserved to the patricians, likewise obtained a
right to aspire to the sacerdotal dignities which the superior caste
had kept to itself and transmitted as a privilege of birth. This was
one of the last conquests of the plebs.

or, at any rate, their physical differences are less rigid and unmalleable and more easily effaced through gradual assimilation than their physical differences. For the same reason the most systematic mythology is the one that is fated to win territory.

The springing up of a religion beyond its native race involves, we may suppose, another important progress. Is it because its founder has proclaimed the brotherhood of men of all races that a religion is apt to overflow, or does its founder profess this regenerating dogma to create in it this aptitude? It matters not. It is clear that the proclamation of such a truth greatly favours the propagation of the beliefs which are united to it. Christianity and Buddhism are proofs of this. When the spirit of Custom is in full sway, religious sentiment is directed towards the past or the future, man's great preoccupation is centred about his ancestors and his posthumous life, as in China or Egypt, or about his posterity, as in Israel. In a word, the devout spirit is supported by the thought of the infinite in time. On the contrary, where the spirit of Fashion is fully triumphant, religious sentiment receives its liveliest inspirations and its most spontaneous impulses from the thought of the immensity of the earth and heavens, from the conception of a universe whose boundaries are forever receding and of a great omnipresent God, the common father of all beings scattered throughout the infinity of space. Are not the sympathy, the pity, and the love which are engendered in the hearts of the devout by this belief the very source of moral life? It follows that the most moral religions are necessarily the most contagious. And, as I fail to see how any high standard of morality can arise and spread by any other means than an all-conquering religion, I think I am justified in accepting the conclusion of history that no great civilisation could ever have existed without religious proselytism.

I may add that without a stable religious institution, one resting on its conquests, a strong and original civilisation is impossible. By this I mean a profoundly logical social

state, from which, by means of a long and painful elaboration, all important contradictions have been banished, a state
where the majority of elements are in agreement, and where
almost everything proceeds from the same principles and
converges towards the same ends.   It takes a long time for
a religious faith to recast in this way, in its own image, the
small or large society which it has been invading.

We do not know, to be sure, how long it took the religion
of Egypt, before the old empire, after the indigenous gods
of Memphis, or of some other city, had spread the entire
length of the Nile Valley, to give birth to Egyptian civilisation.   We are also ignorant of the duration of the incuba-
tion of Babylonian civilisation by the primitive religion
of Chaldea, once its gods had radiated throughout the sweep
of that once thickly peopled and highly fertile valley.   But we
do know that the cult of the Delphic Apollo, the first religion
that was common to all the Doric and Ionic branches of
Greece, dates from the tenth century, B. C., and that " the
climax of maturity and beauty " in the art and poetry and
philosophy and statecraft of Greece was reached about the
sixth century.   We also know that the literature, architecture, philosophy, and governmental system of the Christian Middle Ages had just begun to flourish and grow
into harmony with the law of Christ in the eleventh century
of our era, four or five hundred years after the spread of
Christianity through Europe.   Arabian civilisation, born of
Mahomet, required a shorter period of gestation, but we
know how long it lasted.

It is not true, then, that the progress of civilisation results in the side-tracking of religion.   It is the essence of
religion to be everything or nothing.   If an established
religion falls behind, it is because another religion has
slipped silently and unperceived into its place, and has lent
itself to the setting up of a new civilisation which will end
by being just as religious as the prior civilisation in its best
days.   If, in the beginning of societies, everything in the
most trivial thoughts and acts of man, from the cradle to
the tomb, is ritualistic and superstitious, mature and consum-

mate civilisations present the same conditions. It has been said that the peculiarity of Christianity has been its aloofness from statecraft, in contrast to the intimate alliance of the cults of antiquity with the power of the state. But this feature is only apparent. In the spiritual and missionary religions of modern days, as well as in the gross and exclusive religions of antiquity, morals and dogma are inseparable; there is a higher law for conduct as well as for thought. Only, in consequence of the external expansion which results, as we know, from its internal developments, a religion ceases to be able to regulate of itself all the small details of practical thought and will. Like a ruler whose kingdom has grown more extensive, and whose administration has become more complicated, it delegates to its subalterns a part of its twofold authority of teacher and ruler, leaving a certain amount of independence to its delegates, who are pretty badly supervised by it because they are so far below it.

On one side, then, religion abandons to kings and statesmen, to whose personality it is quite indifferent, providing they are true believers, the care of commanding armies, of levying taxes, and of making laws, on the condition that they attempt nothing contrary to the general precepts of its catechism, a sort of supreme constitution. Thus religion becomes the sovereign ruler of souls and the final court of appeal for anyone who has been abused by secular power. On another side, it also allows inquisitive and enquiring minds to discover and formulate certain theories and natural laws, but it allows this, of course, on the condition of teaching nothing which openly contradicts the verses of its sacred books or the conclusions drawn from its texts.

In short, the god of the Christian or Moslem was, during the whole of the Middle Ages, at least, the sole teacher and master of Christianity or Islamism, occupying, in this particular, the same position as the divine Lars of the primitive family; and the pope or caliph, the organ of deity, taught and commanded as a sovereign. The only difference between the omnipotence of savage or barbaric religions and that of civilised religions lies in the fact that the former expresses itself through ritual, the formal equivalent of that period of morality; and the second, through morality, the spiritual equivalent of ritual. Ritual becomes more profound as it disguises itself. Was it not primitively the supreme statecraft of the ancients, the pre-eminent military and civil art of diplomacy? The armies of antiquity went into action only after they had been stimulated by the ceremonies of the war heralds, by sacrifices, and by the sacramental observations and experiments of the augurs. It is no exaggeration to say that the thrusts of lance and sword that followed seemed to the men of those times to continue as accessories the rites which had preceded them, a sort of sanguinary sacrament. Nor, for the same reason, did any deliberative assembly in these same epochs enter into any debate without the sacrifice of some victim or the offering up of some prayer or the performance of some rite of purification. Voting, as well as fighting, was only one way of worshipping and praying to one's gods, of placating and glorifying them.

Later on, when different cities and peoples come into communication with one another and endeavour to impose their rites, become more simple in their expansion, upon one another, a moment arrives when a purely spiritual cult, *i. e.,* morality as it is understood by Christians, Moslems, and Buddhists, seems to be the only cult worth the name. Then people say that morality should dominate politics and even soar over war. They also say, and with no less reason, that it should rule over art and industry. As a matter of fact, religion has always been implicitly conceived of in the bosom of every religious people, not only as a higher form of statecraft and diplomacy, but as the first of all arts and the most important of all industries. Architecture, sculpture, painting, poetry, music, metal-working, and cabinet-making, all forms of art, arise from the temple and issue from it, like a procession, to continue outside the solemnities occurring within. To the citizens of the Greek cities the great hecatombs were undoubtedly great productions of

wealth and value, of security and power. This was in part
imaginary, but not wholly so, for it is certain that faith is
power. What was the petty labour of a slave or an
artisan in comparison with those mystical works? And, besides, there was no important act in the life of a husbandman,
or even of an artisan, which did not begin with the offering
up of a prayer to the gods, or with a procession of the
Arval Brethren, or with the sacrifice of a lamb, so that every
industrial or agricultural task was merely a prolonged
prayer or sacrifice. In a more advanced and spiritual civilisation the same thing is expressed, at bottom, in saying that
work is a form of duty, and that the economic side of
societies, like their political and artistic sides, is merely a
development of their moral side.

Moreover, on the day when a scholar, like Galileo, undertakes to formulate the simplest scientific law or fact that
is contrary to the shortest verse of Sacred Scripture; or on
the day when a ruler publishes the pettiest decree that is
contrary to the most subordinate precept of an established
religion, an authorisation, for example, to sell meat during
a fast or to work on Sunday, or on the day, finally, when
a branch of industry or art begins to flourish in a given
country, although it is deemed immoral and impious by the
local religion, a profane theatre, for example, or a free-
thinking journal—on this very day, a germ of dissolution
has entered into the social body, and there is the most
urgent need either for this germ to be expelled, notably by
an inquisition, or for it to grow through philosophic or
revolutionary or reform propagandism, and extend itself
to the point of reconstructing the social order upon new
foundations. This is the point we are at in Europe. It is
a problem in social logic that is set before us by this redoubtable dilemma.[1] We do not know how it will be solved.
But we may be certain that when the order of the future is
once consummated, unanimous belief in an indisputable
truth, in an incontestable Good and Right will become again

[1] May we wait long for its solution! For the sake of freedom of
thought may the inappreciable intellectual anarchy which Auguste
Comte deplored be prolonged!

what it once was, intense and intolerant. And science, transfigured by a vast synthesis and supplemented by a highly
æsthetic morality, will be the religion of the future, before
which all professors and statesmen, all minds and wills,
will humbly bow.

The omnipotence and omnipresence of religion in all
functions of society justify the exceptional place which religion has been accorded in this chapter. But this consideration must not prevent us at present from examining rapidly
and separately the fragmentary and secondary governments
that rule with the consent of religion,—although not without a threatening kind of independence,—namely, the philosophy of certain periods on the one side and, on the
other, the government, in the usual sense of the word,
and the legislation and custom of all periods. When
an accredited philosophic system arises in a serious-
minded nation, it stands in the same relation towards
religious dogma as a form of government, a body
of law, or the sum of people's wants stands in any
country towards its religious morality. The one is the
foundation-stone of thought, the other of conduct. But this
does not prevent the frequent occurrence of conflicts between the suzerain, or so-called suzerain authority, and
those authorities that are vassal to it. Struggles between
philosophies and theologies correspond to those between
empires and priesthoods. Besides, if it is true that religion
controls civilisation in its entirety and moulds it after itself,
it is no less certain that the temporarily prevailing ·philos-
ophy directs and develops its own science, or that the
established government directs and develops its own politics
and war, or that legislation and custom determine the course
and character of industry. Let us see whether the transition
from custom to fashion and *vice versa* occurs here as above,
and whether it produces like effects. In any case, let us
refrain, for lack of space, from touching upon the philosophic and scientific sides of societies, an undertaking that
would require a separate volume. Let us pass on to the
practical side.

III. *Government*

All the foregoing remarks amount to saying that in the beginning the family, or the pseudo-family that grew up by the side of it, was the only social group, and that every subsequent change resulted in lessening its importance in this respect by constituting new and more ample groups which were formed artificially, at the expense of the social side of families, and which reduced them to mere physiological expressions; but that, finally, such dismembered families tended to aggregate into a kind of enlarged family that was both natural and social like the original family, except that the physiological characteristics, which were transmitted through heredity, existed mainly to facilitate the transmission through imitation of the elements of civilisation, and not *vice versa*. In fact, we have already seen from the linguistic point of view that in very remote prehistoric times every family must have had its own language, and that later on a single language embraced thousands of families who finally, because of the greater facility for *connubium* between speakers of the same tongue, gave birth to one race. Thus every tongue eventually had its own race, *i. e.*, its own great family, whereas, primitively, every family, as I have said, possessed its own tongue. We have also seen how, in the question of religion, every family had originally its own cult and was a church in itself, but who, later on, the same cult united thousands of families who, finally, through the more or less strict interdiction of marriage with infidels and the exclusive practice of *connubium*, combined into one race that was expressly created for its religion.

We can now see from the point of view of government an analogous series of transformations. In the beginning every family formed a distinct state; then followed a state which contained thousands of families, welded together by a purely artificial tie, and, finally, every state made its own nation, *i. e.*, its particular race or sub-race, its own family.

On this point, I might repeat what Fustel de Coulanges and Sumner Maine have said so well about the gradual transformation of the *patria potestas* into the *imperium* of the Roman magistracy, about the primordial union and the progressive separation of the power to *procreate* and the power to *command*. But I will not bore the reader with this. I prefer to observe that it is proper to round off this point of view by admitting that from the commencement of history, or even pre-history, artificial states were formed through a general infatuation for some renowned chief or brigand, and enlarged by those who had broken loose from surrounding families. Cities of refuge, like early Rome and the *free cities* of the Middle Ages, can give us some idea of these primitive aggregates. They were, perhaps, or rather undoubtedly, the first cities, properly speaking. And, as a matter of fact, the urban element, which has co-existed from the earliest time with the rural element, has always been distinguished by its predominant and widespread spirit of innovation, compared with the conservative spirit of the latter. We may infer that these original collections of undisciplined people have been the most active centres for war and conquests and that, consequently, although all the scourges born of war may be imputed to them, yet theirs is the honour of having created great national agglomerations, the eventual guarantee of wealth and peace.

In addition, we may see that custom and fashion are everywhere embodied politically in two great parties whose alternating strife and triumph explain all political advances. In fact, there are never more than two opposing parties, however subdivided they may be. Their names differ in different countries and at different times, but the one may be called, without impropriety, the party of conservatism, and the other the party of innovation. Among seaboard populations, their rivalry is usually expressed through that between agricultural interests, such as Aristides, the conservative, personified at Athens, and maritime interests such as were embodied in the innovator, Themistocles.

Among continental populations, the rivalry is between commerce and agriculture, between towns and country districts, between artisans and peasants. Now, it is fairly clear that the strife between conservatives and liberals, which is as ancient as history and which had already begun in the bosom of the primitive family or tribe, always leads back to that between custom and fashion. The progressive party welcomes with its whole heart the new ideas, the new rights, and the new products that are imported over land or sea and imitated as foreign models, whereas the party of tradition resists them with all the weight of the ideas and customs and industries which it has inherited from its forefathers. More specifically, the party of innovators desires to modify the political constitution of its country, in conformity with the theories which have been suggested to it by the sight of outside governments and which, in spite of, or by reason of, this very suggestion, a more or less unconscious one, seem applicable, through imitation, to all the peoples of the earth. The *Tory* party, on the contrary, desires people to respect and maintain unaltered the form of government which prevailed in the past.[1] We know that

---

[1] At any given period there will always seem to be, among the most prominent communities, one to embody the spirit of conservatism, and another, the spirit of novelty. But if we go back to the past of each, we shall see the contrast reversed. In our own days, the antithesis has been represented until recently by England and France, just as in ancient Greece it was represented by the conservative Dorians and the innovating Ionians. This has been repeated *ad nauseam.* Boutmy writes in his *Études de droit constitutionnel,* that "in France a natural and immediate authority is given to those ideas (political) which are sentimentally based upon the unity of mankind in general. In England it is given to those ideas that are sentimentally based upon ties with preceding generations. We are content only with a broad and extensive conception which everybody may share with us, and before whose articles of universal legislation all will bow. The English are satisfied with a narrow and intensive conception in which the centuries of their national life are seen in perspective, one after the other."

In other words, we enthuse over ideas which are capable of spreading through free and external imitation, since we have generally received them ourselves through this kind of imitation; whereas, our neighbours care only for those ideas which are and which can only be transmitted through an exclusive and hereditary form of imitation.

whenever and wherever a conflict arises between these two parties, it is because a liberal party that has been stimulated or awakened by contact with an outer and a more brilliant world has reappeared in the midst of a people who have been unwittingly traditional, and has aroused the conservative party, *i. e.,* the immense majority, to self-consciousness. This means that at first custom held sway here alone, or almost alone, but that at this point fashion has begun to replace it.

Meanwhile fashion grows, and the party which represents it and which was at first defeated ends by getting the innovations which it extols, accepted. The result of this is that the world makes a step in advance towards international political assimilation. This assimilation goes on even when political agglomeration, which is a different thing, is static or retrogressive. Indeed, even during antiquity and the Middle Ages, the uniformity of government which accompanies or heralds governmental unity was always brought about on any given territory—the territory being at one time very small and then becoming more and more extensive—by the triumph of some innovating party. Dating

But, it may be said in passing, that English parliamentarism is not precluded by its original character from communicating itself from one people to another, travelling by means of the freest and most general kind of contagion that has ever been seen. Then, we know that in the seventeenth century, England personified the spirit of revolution in comparison with monarchical France; and, now, after a rest of two centuries, do we not feel that the revolutionary yeast is working on British soil, thanks to the germs of radical or socialistic ideas that have been introduced from the Continent? It may easily happen that when this crisis is raging among the islanders across the Channel, the foundation of a national government will be finally laid in France

Let me add that the distinction which M. Boutmy draws between those constitutions which explicitly aspire to universality and those which are content to last during the life of a given race or nation, suggests the distinction between open and proselyting religions and exclusive and non-proselyting religions According to this analogy, the French system holds the future in its hands, since proselyting religions always have the advantage of their rivals. But just as the most expansive cult finally settles down and closes its doors, the most cosmopolitan system of government ends, as we shall see, by becoming, in its turn, an ancestral custom.

from the heroic period of Greece we can find certain traces of the breath of fashion blowing from time to time across communities who were supposed to be among those most custom-bound. It is very surprising, for example, to find the Dorians, who are such a tradition-bound race at the moment when history throws her light upon them, governed by certain institutions which were imported from Crete by the foreigner Lycurgus, and subject, moreover, to non-Dorian royal families. Can these facts be otherwise explained than by presupposing some anterior age in which foreign prestige swayed this nation, a nation which subsequently succumbed again to the prestige of its forefathers?

The second fact referred to is in no sense exceptional; on the contrary, it frequently occurs. The Greek historian Curtius cites, in this connection, the government of the Molossians by the Oacidæ, of the Macedonians by the Temenidæ, of the Lyncestæ by the Bacchiadæ, of the Ionians by the Lycians, etc., just as the Swedes are governed in our own day by the successors of Bernadotte. This prestige of the foreigner, therefore, has been general at times from the most remote periods. It must have gone very deep if we admit, with the learned author whom I have cited, that belief in the divine extraction of kings is explained by their foreign origin. Since their home vanishes into a distant unknown region, "they might be accounted sons of the gods, an honour which natives could scarcely have received from their countrymen." [1] Besides, wherever we see primitive families loyal subjects to one of their own number, or even to one of their own race, we must infer that this privileged family owes its supremacy to a more or less ephemeral infatuation by which admiration of ancestors has been momentarily eclipsed. But, although family sentiment may be broken for a time by the advent of some dynasty in this way, it is subsequently awakened and magnified under the name of civic spirit or patriotism.

If we find that in the tenth century Europe was covered with thousands of little states, called seigniories, that were

---

[1] [Ward's translation, I, 147.—*Tr.*]

all pretty much alike in their feudal constitution, whose originality was as striking as their resemblance in the midst of their diversity, we cannot doubt that the typical fief, wherever it originated, was copied by the intelligent liberals of the time and imposed by them upon recalcitrant reactionaries like the Gallo-Roman senators or others. The fief was at that time the great fruitful novelty, the model to which the royal power itself came to conform after, as we have seen already it had likewise suggested it. Before that the king had vaguely associated his authority with that of the ancient Roman emperors, the traditional type of sovereign power in the popular mind. It seemed as if the very essence of this supremacy lay in universal dominion or in the dream of it. But Hugues Capet was inspired with what might be called an idea of genius, a very simple idea withal. Instead of looking behind him in the Roman Empire for his ideal, he took it from his own neighbourhood. According to Sumner Maine, he is the prototype and the initiator of strictly feudal, non-imperial royalty. " Hugues Capet and his descendants were kings of France in an entirely new sense; they had the same relations to the soil of France as the baron held towards his fief and the vassal towards his land." The invention, in short, consisted merely in modelling sovereignty upon suzerainty and in extending over the entire territory of a great nation the feudal relations which had hitherto been confined to the petty limits of a canton. Witness, nevertheless, its success. " All subsequent sovereignty was based on this new model. The sovereignty of the Norman kings, copied from that of the kings of France, was positively territorial. Territorial rulers were established in Spain, in Naples, and in all the Italian principalities which were founded upon the ruins of municipal liberties."[1]

In modern times the contagion of another masterthought, of one which was in contradiction to the preceding, and which was forced to dethrone it in order to propagate

[1] Similarly, ecclesiastical administration took on an imperial garb during the Empire, and a feudal one during the Middle Ages

itself, has spread still more rapidly, namely, the idea of the state as we understand it to-day. Where was modern statecraft born? In the petty Italian republics, and, first of all, in Florence, whence the modern type of political activity spread to France and Spain and Germany and even to England. Spain and France, in particular, who disputed for such a long time over Italy, "began," says Burckhardt, "to resemble the centralised Italian states, and, indeed, to copy them, only on a gigantic scale." [1] Upon this fashion is grafted in the eighteenth century [2] a fashion which does not contradict it in any way, but which completes it. Anglomania becomes the rage. The parliamentary constitution of England began to be copied before its general diffusion in the nineteenth century, under two original forms, first by the United States, which made a simple republican translation of it, as Sumner Maine has shown in his *Popular Government,* and then by revolutionary France, which hastened to drive parliamentarism into Rousseau-inspired radicalism. This last transformation, whose dawn was greeted as a marvellous creation, called forth I do not know how many ephemeral republics in South America, overwhelmed the Old World and reacted even upon British soil.

One of the most remarkable traits of the liberal party and, consequently, of those times in which that party rules, is the cosmopolitan character of its aspirations. Cosmopolitanism, indeed, is not the exclusive privilege of our own time. It flourished in all those periods of antiquity and mediævalism in which fashion-imitation held sway. "Cosmopolitanism," says Burckhardt, "is . . . a sign of an

---

[1] [Middlemore's translation, I, 128 —*Tr.*]

[2] The eighteenth century inaugurated the reign of fashion on a large scale. This fact is very evident in the particulars of morals and institutions of this century. At this time, for example, the secret ballot came into use in municipal elections, and M. Albert Babeau tells us (in his work on the city of the old régime) that this was a fashion He adds that already in the sixteenth century—another age of invading fashions—the corporation of Angers had adopted this manner of voting, justifying itself by the usages at "the elections of senators at Venice, Genoa, Milan, and Rome" "So alert and eager for models was the municipal spirit at this time!"

epoch in which new worlds are discovered and men feel no longer at home in the old. We see it among the Greeks after the Peloponnesian War;[1] Plato, as Niebuhr says, was not a good citizen. . . . Diogenes went so far as to proclaim homelessness a pleasure and calls himself, . . . ἄπολις.[2] The Italians of the Renascence were cosmopolitan even before the fifteenth century, not merely because they had become habituated to their exile, but because their epoch and their country abounded in innovations of every kind and because people's minds were turned towards foreign and contemporary things even more than towards the domestic and patriotic things of their past. The weakening of French patriotism in the sixteenth and seventeenth centuries is notorious. Let us call to mind the monstrous foreign alliances that were made by the different parties during the religious wars and the compliments of Voltaire to the King of Prussia after Rosbach. Even Herder and Fichte, who became such ardent patriots under the heel of the conqueror, began by holding the idea of fatherland in contempt. In contemporary Germany and France it has taken the evident necessity of armed defence to restore to national sentiment some part of its old-time vigour.

But does everything terminate in the victory of fashion over routine? Not at all. This victory is itself incomplete until the conservative party, resigned to its defeat and to taking a subordinate place, transforms itself into a national party and set itself to making the sap of tradition circulate in the new graft of progress. This nationalisation of foreign elements is the completion of the historical drama which contact with different or superior neighbouring civilisations unfolds. Thus the feudal kingdoms which were founded by fashion on the model of the Capetian monarchy became national and traditional in the highest degree.

The stream of custom returns, then, to its channel—singularly enlarged, to be sure—and a new cycle begins. It

---

[1] In reality it must have appeared many times long before this.
[2] [*Ibid.*, 187, footnote 3.—*Tr.*]

spins itself out and ends like its predecessors. And this will undoubtedly continue until the political uniformity and unity of the whole human genus are achieved. The innovating party plays, then, in all of this, only a transitory, although an indispensable, part. It serves as a mediator between the spirit of comparatively narrow conservatism which precedes it and the spirit of comparatively liberal conservatism which follows it. (Consequently, traditionalism should no longer be opposed to liberalism. From our point of view the two are inseparable.) *Without hereditary imitation,* without conservative tradition, any invention or novelty that was introduced by a liberal party would perish still-born, for the latter is related to the former like shadow to substance, or, rather, like a light to its lamp. The most radical revolutions seek to be traditionalised, so to speak, and, reciprocally, at the source of the most rigid traditions we find some revolutionary condition. The object of every historic transformation seems to be to debouch in an immense and potent and final custom, where free and vigorous imitation will finally unite the greatest possible intensiveness to the greatest possible extensiveness.

Let me continue this subject in order to remark that the pursuit of this ideal is accomplished along the line of a rhythmical repetition of the same phases upon a scale of increasing size. In the transition from the primitive government of the family to tribal government, societies must have passed through exactly the same periods as contemporary societies are painfully traversing in order to pass from their systems of national government to the continental government of the future. Meanwhile, the foundations of municipal government and, then, of the government of small states or provinces, and, last of all, of the government of nations, all required the same series of efforts. To understand how each of these successive and intermittent enlargements of the political aggregates of the past took place, we should observe the manner in which modern political aggrandisements are effected. The little American republics which were to become the United States, lived separate and independent. One day a common danger brought them together and their union was proclaimed. The war which was the occasion of this great event was merely an historic accident, like the wars for conquest or independence which, during the course of history, have occasioned, have hastened, or retarded, but in no sense caused, the really stable extensions of the state from the family-state to the nation-state. The American Union, then, was decreed; but what made it possible and lasting? What was the cause that not only necessitated this federal tie, but that still works to make it closer, day by day, a cause that will eventually bring forth unity out of union? Tocqueville will tell us. "In the English colonies of the North, more generally known as the States of New England, the two or three main ideas which now constitute the basis of the social theory of the United States were first combined. The principles of New England spread at first to the neighbouring states; they then passed successively to the more distant ones; and, at last, if I may so speak, they *interpenetrated* the whole confederation. They now extend their influence beyond their limits, over the whole American world. The civilisation of New England[1] has been like a beacon lit upon a hill, which, after it has diffused its warmth immediately around it, also tinges the distant horizon with its glow."[2] It is certain that if each of the United States had remained faithful to the constitution of its fathers, if it had not welcomed the two or three foreign ideas which were formulated by a small group of neighbouring states, the political similarity of all these states, which alone made possible their political fusion, would never have existed. Fashion-imitation was, then, the cause of this progress. I may add that the ideas which were imported in this way into a majority of the United States were so fully acclimatised

---

[1] The author gives us the reason of its pre-eminent contagiousness. The colonists of New England, the Puritan immigrants, were the only people to cross the ocean to work for an idea

[2] [Reeve's translation, I, 37.—*Tr.*]

in them as to become part and parcel of their primitive customs. The final result was a collective patriotism which was
not less intense or less traditional or self-assertive than their
original forms of patriotism.

If the great American federation has just originated
in this way. under our very eyes, we ought to believe that
the origin of the little Greek federation was not very different. The innumerable municipal republics scattered
through Greece and the Archipelago were almost exact
copies of the two principal types, the Dorian and the
Ionian. Evidently the resemblance which prompted them
to unite on all occasions could not be explained by the mere
fact of colonisation by common mother-cities; such a propagation through *heredity* must have been followed by a propagation through imitation, and it was this that inaugurated
a new era of Greek civilisation. Then Sparta and Athens,
like fires lit up in lofty places, as Tocqueville says, radiated
abroad. Here was fashion-imitation; and when fashion
became settled and imbedded, it represented to all the cities
a common national custom which inspired the liveliest and
most hereditary patriotic sentiment that had ever been seen.
But, if we consider each of these little cities apart in its
deep attachment to its original institutions, before the assimilation of which I am speaking, and question how the
different tribes of which it was composed came themselves
to federate and form a city, we shall find no other reason
but that of their pre-existing similarity, a similarity which
had been effected by the radiant brilliancy of one of
their number, voluntarily or coercively copied by the
others.

These periods of brilliancy towards which the eyes of the
historians turn of their own accord, the age of Pericles, the
age of Augustus, the age of Louis XIV, are characterised,
in common, by the introduction, after an era of sudden
innovations and rapid annexations and assimilations, of a
new form of society and the inauguration of a new tradition. After language has been subject to change for a
long time, it becomes fixed in a mould which is hencefor-

ward respected. After many changes have been produced in religion by an over-hospitable welcoming of alien ideas, it is re-established and reorganised. After great upheavals, political institutions, remodelled and reorganised, take root anew. After innumerable gropings in the dark, art, in all its branches, finds its classical direction, and henceforward maintains itself in it. After a chaos of ordinances, decrees, and laws, legislation codifies and ossifies itself, so to speak. In this respect, Pericles, although he was the head of a democratic state and of the most stirring one of ancient peoples, resembles Augustus and Louis XIV. Under him, all those elements of Athenian civilisation, which were disorganised in consequence of the great current of fashion-imitation which had preceded him, and which, moreever, was never interrupted for long in the Greek world, given over, as it was, to an intermixture of commercial and maritime civilisations, came into logical agreement like that of the elements of Latin and of French civilisation, under the two great emulators of Periclean glory, subsequently to the troublous times which had disorganised the Roman Republic, before the advent of the one, and French society before that of the other. Then the Attic dialect began to spread everywhere, and to impose its colonial empire upon every one; and in its spread and consolidation it became fixed as the immortal language of the whole of subsequent antiquity. Then, too, sculpture and dramatic poetry attained their apogee, their *exemplary perfection*. And then, finally, government and finance took a truly permanent and conservative stand. For, although Pericles inclined towards intellectual novelties and welcomed foreign writers and thinkers, he was as *conservative* as Augustus and Louis XIV, each of whom was the patron and abettor of the intellectual and artistic life which he welcomed in order to appropriate it to himself.

Now, it is clear that if a return is made to tradition during these epochs of great men, or of great reigns, it is to an enlarged tradition, to a tradition that has been enlarged in two ways, by the extension of the territory over which it rules, and by the elaboration of the elements of which it is composed. Before Pericles, Athens was merely a greater and more illustrious city than the other Greek cities. During his time it became the capital of a fairly vast empire, whose life depended upon its life, and the intensity and complexity of this life was quite a different thing from that of the early centuries of Athens.

We have seen how the great centuries of which I am speaking may be considered under two aspects; in the first place, as the time when a new *logical equilibrium* is reached through what I have called the *grammar* in contrast to the *dictionary* of the elements of civilisation; in the second place, as the point of departure for a new era of *traditional* life. But these two aspects are bound together, for it is because innovations, introduced by the breath of fashion, have become harmonised, that they have subsequently become imbedded as customs. The proof that they have been harmonised is visible in the symmetrical and even artificial air which all the creations of such memorable epochs take on. In them, political administrations are uniform and centralised. In them, the streets and squares of cities are transformed into geometric symmetry. For example, when Pericles rebuilt Sybaris under the name of Thurii, Curtius tells us that the city " was laid out on the plan of the Piræaus," that " four principal roads ran from end to end and three from side to side." We can read in Babeau, *La Ville sous l'ancien régime*, of the transformations *à la* Haussmann, which were effected in all the cities of France under Louis XIV, and we can compare all of this with what Roman archæology teaches us about post-Augustan cities. Besides, although the austere and autocratic Pericles, the descendant of an illustrious family, a kind of republican Pitt, desired maritime grandeur and imperial expansion for Athens, he jealously opposed the introduction of the alien into the city as a member of the civic body. On this point, he reverted, Curtius tells us, " to antique, severe, and archaic legislation." He governed democratically, but he suppressed all democratic principles, *i. e.*, " rotation in office, division of authority, and even responsibility in public office." Like Augustus, he concentrated in his own person all the functions of the Republic, and out of them he made himself a sovereign power.

However, he had nothing in common with the ancient *tyrants* but appearances. The tyrant was far from representing or favouring the conservatism of custom; in spite of his despotism, he favoured those currents of foreign fashion which dissolved national traditions, his great stumbling block. Pericles, on the contrary, inaugurated a return to the life of tradition, because it was to his interest.

I do not mean to say that Pericles, in imposing his authority and in stamping his seal upon the institutions of his country, created that desire of a more national and traditional life by which he profited for the time being—too short a time, unfortunately. The Persian wars, like all warlike crises, had revived the sentiment of nationality (but of an aggrandised nationality) which had, in the preceding centuries, notably in the sixth century, been weakened by the drain upon it of cosmopolitan life. " Whereas, in the time of Solon," says Curtius (II, 476), " the facile life of the Ionians (of Asia) flourished at Athens, whose wealthy citizens took pleasure in displaying their purple and gold and perfumes, their horses, their hounds, their favourites, and their banquets, it is incontestable that with the Persian wars a more serious view of life penetrated the nation." There was a return to the customs of the Athenian forefathers. " The victory of Marathon brought back into honour the old Attic race of the *cultivators of the soil;* and the more the core of the Athenian people came to consider themselves superior to the *maritime* populations of Ionia [a form of pride, let us note, which is always dependent upon custom-imitation], the more they desired independence in language, customs, and dress." Dress became simpler in a return to primitive austerity. " Here was a purely objective difference between the Asiatic Ionians and the Athenians; but their customs and habits of life had already varied *for a long time." This is a proof of the priority of subjective over objective imitation*

There are many signs to show that the time immediately preceding Pericles, the beginning of the fifth century, and, especially, the sixth century, were periods in which the wind of foreign imitation blew throughout the Archipelago, in all the civilised or to-be-civilised basins of the Mediterranean. This was the epoch of Polycrates and the other Greek tyrants, all of whom were opposed to the ancient morality, all of whom were propagators of foreign customs and precursors of modern *administrative* government. Moreover, *tyranny* plainly showed by its rapid spread from island to island, at this epoch, the impressionability of the period to extraneous examples. A still better indication of this was the unheard-of spectacle that could be seen in Egypt, under the Psammetichi and under Amasis, in their imitation of the life of Greece and in their efforts to introduce it into the classical land of tradition! Amasis " was married to a woman of Cyrene; his boon companions were Greeks, and Greek princes were his friends and guests; like Crœsus [the innovator of Lydia], he honoured the gods of the Greeks." It was in this way, in the eighteenth century of our era, that Frederick the Great attempted to Gallicise his kingdom Darius may be considered to have shared in this movement of Hellenisation, but under more hidden and general forms. At any rate, he opened the way to the great *administrative* empires which followed him. Persia was " utterly transformed by him. A new spirit of administration took the place of its ancient customs."

Hence the *individualism* which appeared at this time. " An entirely new sentiment of personality was awakened." People dared to think for themselves; from this audacity philosophy was born. The Sophists were the agents of the intellectual freedom of the individual. Hence, too, the cosmopolitanism of this epoch.

Have I said enough to show the leading rôle which is played in political history by the alternation in the levels of the two great currents between which imitation unequally divides itself? Undoubtedly not, but I will conclude this exposition by studying more closely the political consequences which result from the occurrence of this simple rhythmical change in the direction of a single force and the characteristics which must be taken on by any form of government to fit itself to expand or to implant itself in the way that I have described.

The consequences are, in brief, as we already know, the progressive enlargement and consolidation of the political agglomeration, and, then, as we shall see, a continually growing administrative and military centralisation, the increasing opportunity given to a personal government to make itself universal and later on to perpetuate itself through becoming traditional. The characteristics are a relatively rational and democratic air in the case of constitutions that are expanding and an air of relative originality and authority in the case of constitutions that have already spread and that are already established. All this will become clearer through a comparison of our antithesis with two different but kindred antitheses, upon which two eminent although unequal thinkers are agreed.

Both Tocqueville and Spencer have had a lively appreciation of the great social transformation which is the slow and irresistible movement of our age. They have both endeavoured to formulate it in terms in which they thought they saw a general law of history. Spencer was especially impressed by the industrial development of our time. In this he saw the dominant trait which explained all the other traits of our societies, notably, the emancipation of the individual, the substitution of constitutional rights for natural rights, of the *régime* of contract for the *régime* of status, of justice for privilege, and of free and voluntary association for hereditary and state-imposed corporations. In generalising this view he considered the directing of activity towards depredation or production, towards war or peace, a major fact which sufficed to characterise two ever-conflicting types of civilisation: the militant type, which is approaching extinction, and the industrial type, which is destined to an idyllic and grandiose future of peace, liberty, morality, and love [1]

Tocqueville was profoundly and religiously impressed, as he tells us, by that levelling of conditions which is precipitating the peoples of Europe and America towards the inevitable slope of democracy. In his eyes, desire for equality is the highest motor power of our times, just as desire for privilege was the highest motor power of the past, and upon the opposition of those two forces he bases the contrast between aristocratic and democratic societies which have at all times differed in everything, in language, in religion, in industry, in literature, and in art, as well as in politics. Without alarm—on the contrary, with evident sympathy, but without superfluous illusions or, at least, without any dose of optimism that could be compared with that of Spencer's—he foresees the results of the equalisation that is to be consummated in the future of democracy, and he depicts them in a way which is at times prophetic.

On many points the antitheses of Spencer and Tocqueville agree, for it seems as if Spencer's militant societies were precisely, in many respects, the aristocracies of Tocqueville, and as if the industrial societies of the former tended to identify themselves with the democracies of the latter. Spencer tells us, however, that militancy engenders obligatory co-operation and the oppression of the individual under administrative centralisation, and that industrialism makes for voluntary co-operation, individual independence, and de-

---

[1] Comte, and not Mr Spencer, was the author of the antithesis between the industrial and the militant types of society. Comte did more than merely point out this antithesis; he often developed it; he even exaggerated it. He established, for example, an indissoluble tie between industrial evolution and artistic evolution, a tie that practically belied classical antiquity. Still, there is much truth at bottom in this point of view.

Only, even while exaggerating the merits of industrial activity and its superiority over the activity of war, Comte was careful not to carry this distinction to the point of considering it the *line of cleavage*, so to speak, in sociology. He knew that religious evolution, the succession and differentiation of theological and scientific forms and ideas, has a far-reaching control over these secondary considerations And this is what Mr. Spencer failed to see.

centralisation.   Tocqueville, on the contrary, in pages where
the most solid erudition is joined to the most thoughtful
and sincere insight, is forced to conclude, at the last and
against his wish, that democratic equality, born of general
uniformity, leads us almost inevitably to oppressive centralisation and excessive paternalism, and that local franchises
and personal guarantees were far more surely protected
in times of aristocratic differentiation and inequality.   This
avowal must have cost him dear, and I do not see how he
reconciles his passionate love for liberty, a love which far
outweighs his love for equality, with his sympathy for the
conventional and intolerant state, in a word, for the socialistic state, which he so clearly foresees.   And yet his liberalism is not more inconsistent than that of the great English
evolutionist.   At any rate, which of the two is in the
right?   Must we agree with Tocqueville in holding that an
aristocratic rule is decentralising, differentiating, and, in
a sense, liberal, and that a democratic rule is centralising,
levelling, and authoritative; or must we accept Spencer's apparently inverse proposition?

I think that Tocqueville's thesis contains a greater
amount of truth, but that he was wrong in not bringing out
more clearly a certain side of his thought which has remained in the shade.   At bottom, he generally means by
aristocratic rule the dominance of custom, and by democratic rule, the dominance of fashion, and, if he had expressed his thought in these terms, he would have been in-
contestably in the right.   But his expression was inexact,
for it is not essential to aristocracy to be bound to the spirit
of tradition, and every democracy is not hospitable to novelties.   Nevertheless, his merit consists in his having dis-
criminated between the hereditary and non-hereditary origin
of powers and rights, of sentiments and ideas, and of not
having misconstrued the capital importance of this distinction, a distinction which is wholly neglected or barely
touched upon by Spencer.   Spencer does not distinguish
between the hereditary and customary, i. e., feudal, form of
militancy, and its voluntary, legislative, and outwardly imi-

tative form, a form which is peculiar to our contemporaries. To him the important fact is whether the nature of ordinary activity is bellicose or industrial. But to say that obligatory co-operation is peculiar to every nation under the domination of an army, under the pretext that military organisation is essentially coercive, is to forget the fact that a great workshop is governed just as authoritatively as a barbarous horde, or as a modern fleet or regiment. Was not the Peru of the Incas a great phalanstery rather than a great barracks? At any rate, no military despotism was ever more dictatorial than this agricultural despotism. This was because obedience to custom was never more rigorously enforced, except, perhaps, in China. China is the least warlike and the most laborious country in the world; but in spite of this, co-operation there is as obligatory as it can possibly be, intolerance is absolute, and administrative centralisation is carried as far as the absence of railroads and telegraphs allows of in such an extensive stretch of territory. For there the yoke of custom and ancestral domination weighs everybody down, beginning with the Emperor.[1]

Spencer attributes to the militancy of France, whose development, as he says, surpasses that of England, because

[1] Is it by any chance the habit of fighting which strengthens authority and makes it hereditary? It is not; a victorious war might, of course, lead to the extension of a pre-existing nobility, or it might even create a new nobility, but only on the condition that the given society lived under the rule of custom and was thus predisposed to make all power hereditary. Otherwise, it would not have this effect at all. Could twenty years of continual warfare create a feudal system in modern Europe? It might create a dictatorship, based upon an even more insolent plutocracy than that of to-day; nothing more. In fact, every nobility is, originally, rural, patriarchal, and domestic. Aristocracies are particularly vigorous and unchangeable when they are not belligerent. The Swiss aristocracy is an example. In spite of its republican and federal form, it was perpetuated up to our own times long after the rest of the continent had set towards democracy. If, in spite of this, the idea of militancy is generally associated with aristocratic control, it is because the territorial disintegration which is produced by the aristocratic preponderance of custom multiplies the occasions of armed conflicts. Industrialism is so little incompatible with militancy that the city that was perhaps the most warlike city of the Middle Ages, Florence, was at the same epoch the most industrial region of Europe. Ancient Athens is another example.

of the more frequent wars of the former, the dictatorial and
centralising character of the old French régime (completed,
in this respect, as we know, by the Revolution).   But let
us observe that this character was accentuated in proportion
to the encroachment of the royal power, which, in its dependence upon the communes, that is, upon the industrial
classes of the nation, extended itself to the detriment of the
warrior caste of feudal lords.   If it did not result in preventing foreign and intermittent wars, it did, at least, prevent steady and intestine warfare, much to the advantage
of labour.   The King of France was essentially a peace
bringer.   England remained in a state of comparative de-
centralisation, because she continued to be an aristocratic
country.   Her industrial wealth, which, up to the end of the
eighteenth century, was not superior to that of France,
counted for nothing in this result.   As for the entirely recent tendency of contemporary nations towards state socialism,—so strong an argument against the liberalising influence that is attributed by Spencer to industrial development, and such a formal refutation of his views upon the
political future,—is it permissible to interpret it as an accidental and momentary effect of the exaggerated armaments which the Franco-Prussian war imposed upon
Europe?   And would it not be more exact to attribute to
this profound and invincible and, to all appearances. lasting
movement, an internal and permanent, instead of a fortuitous and external, cause, one which would closely connect
the progress of the modern state with the progress of modern
industry and democracy ? [1]

[1] Even in the United States, in spite of the essentially peaceful
character of its people, a universal tendency towards centralisation
may be observed.   The *Journal des économistes* says (July, 1886) that
in the March number of the *Political Science Quarterly,* an American
review published in Boston, an article of Mr. Burgess' tends to prove
that " an internal process is going on to reduce the importance of the
States to that of provinces or departments and to augment the
importance of the Union.   Moreover, the author proves that the Union
has always had precedence over the States."   See also on this subject the interesting and instructive work of M Claudio Jannet upon
the *États-Unis contemporains.* (Fourth edition, 1888).

This cause lies in the habit, which is becoming daily more general, of taking examples that are near at hand, in the present, instead of those that belong exclusively to the past. It is remarkable that from the time this habit began to prevail, nations have been urged, either by war or peace, in the direction of extreme centralisation and unification, and of the broadening and deepening of democracy, just as when the opposite habit prevailed, war and peace, chateaux and guilds, contributed to the maintenance of feudal disintegration. Why is this? / Because external imitation produces that great uniformity of ideas and tastes, of usages and wants, which makes possible and then necessary, not only the fusion of the assimilated peoples, but the equalising of their rights and conditions, i. e , juridical similarity between members of communities who have become alike in so many other respects. Because, in addition, this uniformity makes possible for the first time, and then necessary, both wholesale industry, machine production, and wholesale war, machine destruction. And, finally, because this same uniformity, which makes one man equal to another, necessarily leads to the treatment of men as like units, to the mechanical consideration and calculation of their desires by means of universal suffrage and of their actions by means of statistics, and to the restraining of them all under a uniform system of discipline by means of those other mechanisms that are called administrative bureaus or departments. Here the truly essential and causal thing is the multiplication of external relations among classes and peoples. This is so true that the social transformation in question set in immediately after the comparatively modern inventions in printing, in locomotion, and in communication, that it develops parallelly with the propagation of these inventions and that, in those places where it has not yet begun, the laying of railroads and the setting up of telegraph poles suffice to inaugurate it. If American democracy shows in a remarkable degree the features which M. de Tocqueville has attributed to democracies in general, and, notably, to European democracies, whose portrait he has drawn for them in advance, it is because North America has anticipated Europe in its bold and extensive use of new methods of transportation, in its steamboats and railroads, it is because nowhere else has there been so much or such rapid travelling, nor so great an interchange of letters and telegrams.

Moreover, may we not suppose that in the future, when our democracies are firmly established, they will differ in many points from the picture that Tocqueville makes of them? Is it true that a democratic rule essentially implies the empire of what I call fashion? Must its opinions and practices be in consequence unstable, as well as chaotic and domineering? Must the short-sightedness and capriciousness of its majorities equal their omnipotence? I see no reason to think this. The social being, after all, however social he may be, is a living being, born through the power of generation and born for it. He wishes to perpetuate his social body, and he knows no better way of doing this than to attach it to his physical body, and transmit it with his blood. Every civilisation which has run its course, Egypt, China, the Roman Empire, has presented the spectacle of a more or less extensive society, drawing back through the promptings of filial piety, after its *conversion* through a kind of beneficent epidemic to a given body of ideas and institutions, and shutting itself up in these ideas and institutions for ages at a time. I have already referred to China. In the last centuries of the Roman Empire we find a society which is not democratic, which is, on the contrary, pretty aristocratic, but which is very uniform, and at the same time very stable and mechanical, and which is ruled over by a highly centralised administration Ancient Egypt, which was to a certain extent democratic, was no less striking in its uniformity from one end to the other of the Nile basin, in its administrative centralisation, and in its prodigious immutability as well. All these examples and arguments suggest the thought that our own contemporaneous society may be unwittingly gravitating, in spite of its transient mobility and momentary bias for individual liberty (just as the fluctuations of the sea give a free air to a vessel), towards

an age of fixed custom in which the present work of rendering all things uniform will be completed. Towards the end
of his work Tocqueville had a presentiment of this. Once
a democratic state is established, he says, far from favouring
revolutions, it is antagonistic to them; and, he adds: "I
can easily discern a state of polity which, when combined
with the principle of equality, would render society more
stationary than it has ever been in our western part of the
world." [1]

[1] [Reeve's translation, II, 315-6.—*Tr*]

In an attentive reading of Tocqueville it may be perceived that although he never troubles himself to formulate the principle of imitation he is always running across it, and curiously enumerating its
consequences But if he had expressed it clearly and placed it at the
head of his deductions, he would, I think, have been spared many
minor errors and contradictions He justly remarks that "no society
can prosper without like beliefs, or, rather, there is none that subsists
without them; for without common ideas, there is no common action,
and without common action, men there may be, but not a social body."
This means, at bottom, that the true social relation consists in imitation, since similarity of ideas, I mean of those ideas which are needed
by society, is always acquired, never inborn. It is through equality
that he justly explains the omnipotence of majorities—the redoubtable
problem of the future—and the singular potency of public opinion in
democratic states, a sort of "immense pressure" which is brought to
bear by the spirit of all upon the spirit of each On the other hand,
he explains equality by means of similarity, of which, truly speaking, it
is only one aspect. He says that only when men resemble each other
to a certain extent do they recognise each other's mutual rights What
is there to add to this? Only one word, but it is indispensable: the
fact that imitation must have and has caused this similarity, a similarity which was not in the least innate. Imitation, then, is the essentially social action from which everything proceeds.

"In democratic centuries," Tocqueville says again, "men's extreme
mobility and their impatient desires cause them to move continually
from one locality to another, and cause the inhabitants of different
countries to intermingle, to see and hear each other and borrow from
each other. And so it is not only the members of one nation who
grow alike; nations themselves are assimilated" Under the term of
democratic revolution, the effects of a preponderance of fashion-imitation could not be better described. He offers an ingenious and, I
think, valid reason for that tendency of democracies towards general
and abstract ideas which makes them lose sight of living realities;
namely, that as men grow more alike, they find less difficulty in looking at themselves collectively, in summing themselves up, and they
thereby acquire the habit of seeing everything in this way This is
another effect of imitation I have taken these examples among a

IV. *Legislation*

The above consideration concerning government may be applied to legislation.[1] Legislation, like political and military systems, is only a particular development of religion. And, as a matter of fact, law was originally as sacred a thing as kingship. The most ancient collection of laws, Deuteronomy, the Irish codes of the ancient Brehons, the code of Manu, are inextricably mingled with legendary lore and cosmogonic explanations. This fact shows that the prophet who dogmatises and is deified after death is one with the legislator who commands and the king who governs. In the beginnings of history the father of the family, as well as the leader of the social group, is all that in one. His essential quality is that of pontiff, and, as such, he is, in consequence, both chief and judge. He is chief, in as much as he directs the collective action of the group for the common interest of all its members. He is judge when he interposes his authority between these members to settle their differences. If his method of settling them is continuous and self-consistent, if he possesses a system of jurisprudence, as our jurists would say, he comes to prevent their occurrence. And from that time on law exists in his little society; the memory of his past decisions implies the prevision of his future judgments. Then legislation is in the beginning and always, at bottom, nothing more than accumulated, generalised and capitalised justice, just as a constitution is merely accumulated, generalized, and systematised politics. Legislation is to justice, a constitution is to politics, what the Lake of Geneva is to the Rhone.

In general, there is between common law which is passed down by tradition and statute law which is born of some current of reform opinion the same difference as between

thousand similar ones. Again he writes. "It is not so much the rational desire to remain united which keeps a great number of citizens under one government, as the instinctive and, in a way, involuntary agreement which results from a similarity of sentiments and opinions"

[1] For the rôle of imitation and of social logic in the formation of law, see my *Transformations du droit.*

natural and rationalistic constitutions, or between exclusive and proselyting religions, or even between dialects and cultivated languages. Dialects, local cults, original systems of government, and customs, seek to transmit themselves from generation to generation; cultivated languages, open-armed religions, ready-made constitutions, and new codes, seek to spread themselves from man to man, either within the circumference of a single country or beyond it. This does not prevent the most widespread language from having been originally like any other dialect; or the most penetrating kind of religion from having germinated in some narrow sect; or the most triumphant and ambitious constitution from having been suggested by some petty, local government, like that of Lacedæmon, with which our conventions were so much taken, or, at any rate, by some traditional government, like that of England, over which our parliamentarians are still so enthusiastic; or, finally, the most contagious kinds of legislations like Roman law, or its hybrid derivative, modern French law, from having their source or sources in such humble customs as the primitive *jus quiritium* or the Frankish laws. Nor does this prevent the most widespread language, religion, constitution, or piece of legislation from contracting after its expansion, from becoming localised after its diffusion, and from tending to become in its turn a dialect, a local cult, a peculiar constitution or custom, but all this upon a much greater scale and with a higher degree of complexity. There are, then, I reiterate, three phases to be considered; and from the legislative point of view, just as in all other aspects, their characteristics are well marked. In the first, Law is extremely multiform and extremely stable, very different in different countries, and immutable from age to age. In the second, it is, on the contrary, very uniform and very changeable, as is the case in modern Europe. In the third, it endeavours to combine its acquired uniformity with its refound stability. A cursory glance will show us that this is the rhythm in which the whole history of Law is played.

There was a time when every family or pseudo-family

possessed its own peculiar law,—then every clan and tribe,
—then every city,—then every province. " In order to understand how each of these successive steps towards the
prospective unity of the legislative domain was accomplished, let us study the transitions from provincial to national law. For a long time every province of France possessed its own distinct customs, but gradually a body of
royal ordinances came to be superposed upon these customs.
Moreover, it should be noted that every parliament and tribunal interpreted new laws in its own way, and created its
own separate system of jurisprudence. This juristic
habit reduced legislation to the original provinciality
whence it seemed unable to escape in a time that was still
dominated by hereditary imitation. But, finally, contagious
imitation, the tendency to copy the legislative and juristic
innovations of Paris, having definitely prevailed, the edicts
of the Parisian legislators of the Revolution and of the Empire were readily obeyed throughout the France whose provinces had ceased to bow down before the authority of
their own ancestors and of native jurists. What is more,
the jurisprudence of every court or tribunal was modelled
(by compulsion, someone may say, but why, unless the need
of territorial conformity had become imperative?) upon the
jurisprudence of the court of cassation at Paris. Let me
add that already our national jurisprudence, established in
this way by fashion, is tending to become transfixed by tradition and to carry legislation with it into its own state of
immobility. The law of the Twelve Tables, which ended by
being the venerable tradition and sacred custom of Rome,
began by being a foreign importation that a fine outburst of
fashion-imitation caused to be adopted.

While this movement is transpiring, a still more majestic
change is inaugurated. The same cause which rendered
necessary first the superposition and then the substitution
of national law upon or in place of provincial laws, compels
the different national laws to reflect one of their own number,
and to prepare for the legislative unification of the future. It
was in the sixteenth century, unsettled period though it was,

a time of contagious innovations, that Roman Law arose
from its scattered ashes and spread throughout every state,
while in each one of them the progress of the royal power
was making their legislation uniform. Yesterday it was
the Napoleonic Code that crossed the frontiers of the
French Empire. (To-day, unfortunately, no prestigious
authority is arising potent enough to construct a new monument of law to dazzle the eyes from afar; but everything
leads us to think that if it did appear somewhere or other,
it would be copied with unheard-of rapidity everywhere—
witness the comparative success of the *Torrens act*. In the
absence of really new juristic solutions, the new problems
of law which occur, in connection, for example, with industrial accidents and labour legislation, are barely formulated
in any corner of the world before they violently rebound to
every other corner.

Well, if it is true that the disposition of the modern public towards free imitation of outside things has alone
made possible the diffusion of the French Code, for example, is it not likely that in past ages, when the same provincial law came to prevail over a certain number of cities,
and the same municipal law over a certain number of
tribes, etc., a like disposition characterised the public of
those times, and that without it none of these gradual extensions of the juristic sphere would have occurred? When
in the twelfth and thirteenth centuries we see in France and
Germany a certain number of cities which had been previously governed by very distinct customs, presenting a comparative similarity of legislation, we know that in France
this uniformity was established through the imitative spread
of the first charter granted to a commune, a document
which fascinated the eye of the public of the period, and we
know that the idea of mutual imitation in this respect came
to cities which already had multiple relations with each
other by way of commerce or treaty, or through language
or kinship. The customs of Lorris, for example, spread
with great rapidity in the royal domain and in Champagne.
The same thing happened in Germany. " Almost all the

municipal laws of the Rhine towns are like those of Cologne," writes M. Schulte, in his classical work upon the history of German law.[1] The Rhine towns lived a common life through that continuous stream of mutual imitation which was sustained and symbolised by the current of their river. " The law of Lübeck," says the same author, " was the model for that of Holstein and Schleswig, and the majority of the cities on the Baltic Sea." The law of Magdeburg was parallelled and developed, too, by Halle, Leipsic, Breslau, and other "sister cities," and from Breslau it " spread to Silesia, Bohemia, Poland, and Moravia, so that it was pretty closely followed through the entire East."[2] Nevertheless, after any municipal law or charter has spread in this way through fashion, after it has been somewhat modified, it soon becomes one of the most cherished of customs in the hearts of its administrators.

In letting this thought sink into our minds, we shall save ourselves from the error of differentiating between ancient and modern law, of digging a factitious abyss between them, and of supposing that the *bridging-over* from one to the other, in so far as it is genuine, has only been effected once in the world's history. That eminent thinker who has penetrated so profoundly into the law of the past, Sir Henry Sumner Maine, is not free from illusion of this kind. According to him, the great, the capital revolution which has been accomplished in law is that which took place, as he supposes, when the idea of common territory was substituted for that of consanguinity as a basis for poitical and juridical union. There is much truth in this view, but if we endeavour to particularise it, we shall see that it ought to be expressed in other terms, and that it would gain by such a translation. It is certain that the family was for a long time the narrow domain to which moral obligations were confined, and that all the rest of the

---

[1] [*Histoire du droit et des institutions de l'Allemagne*, p. 159 Frédéric de Schulte. French translation by Marcel Fournier. Paris, 1882.—*Tr*]

[2] [*Ibid*, p. 162.—*Tr*.]

universe was field for prey. Consequently, the ancient *pater familias* had power over life and death in his household; he could condemn to death his wife, his children, and his slaves. But what was this hermetically sealed family life but a profession of complete disdain on the part of its members for all external examples? It is obviously difficult to maintain such exclusiveness; little by little domestic barriers are broken down and foreign influences are added to paternal traditions. It is then, when different families have begun to lend and borrow to and from one another, that relations of neighbourhood combine with those of kinship in the creation of legal ties. But as the only recognised type of solidarity was habitually the tie of blood, ties of friendship were at first fictitiously classed under this tie by adoption or otherwise. Later, in Christian countries, spiritual fatherhood, the relation of godfather to godchild, with the rights and duties which accompany it, must be classed with paternity by adoption, just as the relation of spiritual nurse, that is, of spiritual preceptor, to disciple must be classed with that of foster-father to foster-child (the *fosterage* of Ireland). In Ireland, for example, the preceptor had the right to succeed to the fortune of his disciple. In this same country, I am still citing Sumner Maine, the very ecclesiastical organisation, the bulk of the monasteries and bishoprics, simulated a true tribe. It is perhaps because of a like fiction that the names of father, brother, mother, and sister are given to the inmates of convents and monasteries, in spite of their obligatory celibacy.

But, little by little, as non-related individuals came to intermingle and to assimilate with one another more and more, the impossibility of extending similar fictions to their new relations insured the rejection of these fictions, and the simple fact of living together in the same country sufficed to bind men legally to one another. Why was this? Because in the great majority of cases compatriots had become very much alike through their habit of reciprocal imitation. When, as an exception, a particular group was different from the others, like the Jews in the Middle Ages,

or the American negroes, or the Spanish Moors under
Philip II, or like the Catholics in Protestant countries, or
the Protestants in Catholic countries, during the sixteenth
century, participation in the law of the land was refused, or
with great difficulty conceded to them, in spite of their
common territory. So true is it that the real foundation
and first condition of law is the existence of a certain kind
of preliminary similarity between the men that it is to
unite. When blood relationship was a requisite, it was
because it alone presupposed this degree of resemblance,
whereas, at present, the possession of a common territory
suffices to give birth to this presumption. Besides, the
tie of a common territory aspires to strengthen itself
through the addition of the tie of kinship. In modern nations, where distinct races have had time to fuse together
through their prolonged submission to the same laws, the
national party are convinced that they have common ancestors, although the apparently territorial character of their
law disguises their faith in their common kinship. Seeley
justly places foremost among the conditions of national
unification, " community of race, or, *rather, belief in such
community.*" In the most modern as well as in the most
ancient times, then, the important thing is not so much real
consanguinity as fictitious or reputed consanguinity. Thus
we see that the action of fashion-imitation has produced,
not once, but very often, the important juridical revolution
to which Sumner Maine refers. But from the expression
of this author it would seem as if physiological or physical
causes, generation, or climate, or soil, were the factors of
this transformation, whereas an essentially sociological
force, imitation, has done it all.

In the preceding remarks it is true that imitation of superiors appears to be confused with imitation of contemporaneous innovators. But there are cases in the domain
of jurisprudence, as well as elsewhere, in which it is differentiated. The history of penal law furnishes us with
many striking examples of this. I will merely indicate
them here, as I have already spoken of them at some length

in another work.[1] It is stupifying to find with what rapidity certain odious and absurd criminal procedures, like torture or certain inadequate and unintelligent ones like the jury system, have, at certain epochs, been propagated. Torture was in fashion in Europe from the time of the unearthing of Roman law at Bologna, and up to the sixteenth century it spread like an inundation of blood. In the eighteenth century people fell in love with the jury system, without understanding it, upon the word of a few anglomaniacs; so much so that in 1789 all the official instructions of the electors to the deputies at the States-General were unanimous on this, as on so many other points. And we know how far prepossession for this lame and blind kind of justice has spread in our century of equality and enlightenment. Are we not forced to surmise from these two examples that the method which preceded torture, judicial combat, was itself propagated by means of some similar infatuation?

At any rate, it is notable that these foreign fashions were not slow to plant themselves as cherished customs in the hearts of the people. At present, the jury is a national and inviolable institution in France. But in the seventeenth century torture was honoured in the same way. Several times the States-General of the sixteenth century, and even those of 1614, declared themselves in favour not only of the maintenance, but even of the extension, of this method of proof, thereby bearing witness to the far-reaching extent of its popularity.

Let me hasten to add that the fevers of fashion here, as elsewhere, rarely produce such bad effects, and that since they are in general merely auxiliary to imitation of superiority and to social logic, they ordinarily favour the progress of legislation. As much could be said of the new customs which follow upon these crises. Let us enquire, then, into the characteristics which are apt to be taken on by a legislation which seeks first to extend itself and then to implant itself upon the vaster territory, and into the

[1] See my *Philosophie pénale* (edited by Storck, 1890).

consequences of both this extension and this entrenchment.

These characteristics are, in general, greater richness of content and greater simplicity of form. In expanding law, greater weight is attached to contracts, to reciprocal engagements, to equity, to humanity, and to individual reason; and in law which is being fixed and codified, in addition to these qualities, an air of learned casuistry and despotic regulation. Roman law, as it was spontaneously formed under the influence of the *jus gentium* and the prætorian modifications and as it was codified and transfixed during the Empire, is a remarkable example of this twofold type. Wherever it was propagated by the jurists, it was received for justice and logic incarnate, and this fact partly accounts for the annihilation under it of all the other original legislations of antiquity or the Middle Ages. Wherever it was established it became the potent instrument of despots. Let us note at this point that although we oppose equity to privilege and justice to custom, equity and privilege, justice and custom, have the same origin. Custom appears just to primitive men because, whether it favour or sacrifice the individual, it treats him in the same manner as it does the only persons to whom he is wont to compare himself, namely, his ancestors and the members of his caste. His desire to be treated like others is satisfied in this way in spite of the juridical disparities and dissimilarities which custom establishes between those who are already dissimilar in every respect. But when the individual begins to care more for this juristic likeness to his fellow-countrymen and to his contemporaries in general than for his likeness to his ancestors and kinsfolk, because his resemblance to the former has become marked in other respects, the equality of treatment to which he makes claim is what we call justice or equity. It matters little to him, then, if he is treated quite differently from his forefathers, provided he is treated like his neighbour.

To a certain extent the distinction between real and personal property, the social preponderance of which seems to alternate, is connected with that between custom-imitation and fashion-imitation. In times of custom and tradition ancestral heritages, lands, houses, offices, business houses, etc., are considered, and justly so at this time, much the most important part of a fortune. What the individual can acquire in the course of his ephemeral life through his particular little industry, through his commerce or through his spontaneous initiative or through the initiative that he has imitated from his contemporaries, does not in general add much to this hereditary fund, the fruit of accumulated savings produced by the exploitation of ancient inventions, of inventions in agriculture, in finance, in industry, in art, etc.

It is natural in these epochs to consider the *patrimony* as the most sacred piece of property, worthy of being safeguarded in its integrity by tutelary.laws, by successoral or feudal repurchase, by substitution or by religious respect for testamentary disposition. The habit of imitating one's forefathers first of all, of turning to the past for the choice of one's models, leads to the habit of obeying one's ancestors and of respecting their wishes above everything else. On the contrary, when imitation of contemporaries rages, that is to say, when the latter are remarkably inventive and when their inventions throw ancestral ones for the time being into the shade, the facility for growing rich in exploiting contemporaneous innovations is so great, that a patrimony is likely to be considered more and more as a mere outfit, initial capital to be either promptly dispersed or increased tenfold through bold speculation or labour or enterprise. Consequently, a patrimony loses its prestige and acquired property takes on a nobler character. At such times no property seems more respectable than that which is gained through personal effort, through the intelligent use of new industrial or agricultural ideas, etc. This is where we stand to-day in France and everywhere else. Consequently, it is not astonishing that there is some little talk everywhere, mistaken talk, I think, of making an attack upon the old laws of succession, of suppressing or limiting the right of bequest and the capacity to inherit and of basing the right of holding property exclusively upon personal labour.

Obviously, *here as everywhere else* the influence of fashion-imitation is exerted in an *individualistic* sense. Parenthetically, I may observe that this opposition between real and personal property is at the bottom of the opposition between the juristic and the economic points of view. It is notable that *political economy* was born in Greece, in Florence, and, in the eighteenth century, in England, *during their ages of fashion.*

The consequences which are involved by the progress of Law, first in extension and then in stability, are of several kinds; for legislation is concerned with all the directions which individual activity can take, and these directions far outnumber those of *collective* activity which are controlled by the constitution of the government. All that a national party can do collectively consists of military or diplomatic action in relation to other states or of internal political reform, the production of power or glory, or of national liberty, a more highly rated occupation. Moreover, a political reform is only the manipulating by legislation of matters which bear upon the acts and interests of private life, upon individual rights and duties. But the acts which individuals may perform *separately* are innumerable: they relate to rural or urban occupations of every nature, to all kinds of agricultural and industrial work, to all kinds of crime, to all forms of adjusted or conflicting interests. We must distinguish here between activity that is contrary to and activity that is in accordance with the laws. Activity which is contrary to law and which must be anticipated by law in order to be suppressed, is the sum of those occurrences which lead to civil or criminal actions; since the former, no less than the latter, presuppose a violation of justice by one of the contestants, only it is a violation that is supposed to have been committed by mistake and not by bad will. Activity in accordance with law is primarily the sum of all the works of civil or criminal justice, the production of peace and security, a special kind of industry, as well as the peaceful and legal exercise of all callings, the production of multiform wealth, industry strictly speaking. Now, in matters of justice, the uniformity of legislation which follows upon a diversity of legislation results in centralising and regulating, I was about to say in making mechanical, the administration of justice and in enlarging systems of jurisprudence; and stability of legislation results in consecrating and consolidating such enlarged systems of jurisprudence. This is particularly true of civil justice, although the penal system is subject to analagous changes. To a customary and mechanical penal system, one abounding in strange and atrocious as well as in absurd forms of torture, a methodical and rational system succeeded. This was undoubtedly too slow in coming, but it has already led to a singular contrast between the penitentiaries of to-day and the jails of the past. Indeed, every revolutionary access of fashion, in any order of facts whatsoever, introduces a higher degree of rationality into our society, just as every reversion to custom introduces a higher degree of wisdom.

In relation to any industry whatsoever, the substitution of uniform legislation for legislative disintegration is a *sine qua non* of all production on a large scale, of all production requiring machinery or concentration of capital, in questions of railroads, of manufactures, or of extensive farming. Thus uniform legislation is indispensable if we care to have brilliant prosperity; and stable legislation is indispensable if our prosperity is to be lasting. At any rate, as industrial development is still more directly dependent upon variations in such fundamental and implicit laws as the laws of want and habit than it is upon law technically speaking, it is proper to relegate considerations of this kind to the following section. But among industries, there is one, namely, agriculture, which is more immediately dependent upon legislation. We know, indeed, how much the progress of agriculture, which is carried on by machines and which has extensive markets at its command, can be hindered by a multiplicity of customs having the force of law, in questions of apprenticeship, of usufruct, of different kinds of ownership, of mortgages, of successions, of sales, of rent, of prescribing for title, etc. When these barriers are cast aside by the optional or obligatory, but in either case contagious, adoption of a single body of laws that has emanated from some prestigious court or capital or from some contemporaneous celebrity, the impetus is finally given to agriculture on a great scale.

V. *Usages and Wants.—Political Economy*

Usage is the most despotic and the most circumstantial of governments, the most rigorous and the best-obeyed kind of legislation. By usage I mean those thousand and one traditional or recently established habits which regulate private conduct, not abstractly and from a distance, like law, but close at hand and in every detail, and which include all the artificial wants, all the tastes and distastes, and all the peculiarities of morals and manners which characterise a given country or a given period. It is for the satisfaction of this group of special desires in the special forms which are determined by them and in conformity to the more or less badly formulated laws of political economy that industry exerts itself. In this sense, usage, like government and law, is connected with religion. It is an offshoot of ritual. Who would guess, for example, that our habit of writing from left to right has a sacerdotal origin? And yet this is absolutely so. The Greeks originally followed the example of the Phœnicians and wrote from right to left; but later on, following the example of their priests, who wrote down the oracles in the opposite direction because the direction towards the right was of good augury, the east lying to the right of the sacrificer who watches the sky with his face towards the north, they made an entire reform in this particular in their old habits. " Because people turned towards the right to pray," says Curtius, " the sacrificial cup, the casque which held the lots, the harp that was to celebrate the gods, were all passed on from left to right."

In view of this explanation of the direction in which we
write, it is curious to find anthropologists explaining it on
physiological grounds. Moreover, even in supposedly irre-
ligious societies, usage never fails to express the true and
deep cult, the chivalric or materialistic, the aristocratic or
democratic, ideal which dominates and directs them. The
mere form of the seats and chests of the twelfth and eighteenth centuries is enough to reveal the mysticism of the
first period and the epicurism of the second.

To-day, the same kind of comfort in food, in dwellings,
and in clothing, the same kind of luxury, the same forms of
politeness, bid fair to win their way through the whole of
Europe, America, and the rest of the world. We no longer
wonder at this uniformity, a condition which would have
appeared so amazing to Herodotus. It is, nevertheless, a
capital fact, and although it was itself developed through
the progress of industry, without it our immense industrial
wealth would be impossible. A traveller through Europe
in the twelfth century would not have failed to observe that
at every step, from one canton to another, communities who
were possessed of the same religion and, often, of the same
language and law and form of government, differed
strangely from one another in their methods of nourishment,
lodging, clothing, personal adornment, and amusement.[1] But
had the traveller passed through the same places one hundred years later, he would not have perceived any marked
difference in these same particulars between the different
generations of a given canton. On the contrary, the modern
continental tourist will find, particularly in large cities and
among the upper classes, a persistent sameness in hotel fare
and service, in household furniture, in clothes and jewelry,
in theatrical notices, and in the volumes in shop windows.
But let him return ten or fifteen years later and he will find
many changes in all these things. New dishes will figure

[1] Thus ideas and dogmas spread more easily than usages, and the
latter were assimilated but slowly in the train of the former. This
fact is an example of what I have said above about the progress of
imitation from within out.

on the bill of fare; an entirely different style and perhaps a new kind of utility will characterise the furniture; new-fashioned costumes will have sprung from the imagination of the fashionable dressmakers, and new forms of jewelry from the phantasy of the jeweller's brain; new comedies and operas and novels will be in vogue. This contrast, one which I have referred to before, is more striking in this case than in any other.

Does this mean that the gradual and general or regular substitution of diversity in space for diversity in time and of similarity in time for similarity in space which is due to the progress of our civilisations must be considered as an inevitable law of history, and as an entirely irreversible order of things? No. Only the normal transition from geographical diversity to geographical similarity is really irreversible; for we cannot imagine, unless as a consequence of some social cataclysm, the return of usages to a state of disintegration once their unity was established. But we can well conceive, without any mental somersault, of a chronological reversal of the transition from identity to differentiation; we can well conceive that after a period of capricious changes or rather of hasty experiments, usages might become fixed. Steadfastness in the case of habits is far from contradicting in any respect their universality; it completes it. Europe, which is still so stormy, but which was not always so, is unconsciously making for this peace-bringing port. The fever of civilisation which torments it is not an entirely new and unheard-of thing in history; and we know how it ends. We may be sure that the entire basin of the Nile or Euphrates, or the whole of the Middle Empire, or all India, was not made partially uniform in more or less remote or obscure epochs without feverish agitation, seeing that this involved the destruction of a great number of local peculiarities. These were blotted out by a current of contagion whose transitory violence is evidenced to by this very effect. But this current, having done its work, has disappeared. And behind it, upon the great Asiatic territories over which it must have flowed, we are surprised to find not only an amazing resemblance in dress, in furniture, etc., but an immutable fidelity to ancient usages as well. This is so marked that the type of dwelling, for example, and of interior arrangements that is still made use of in Oriental palaces, enables us to reconstruct the plan of the ancient palaces of Assyria in spite of the shapeless character of their ruins.

It is infinitely likely that the alternating play of the two kinds of imitation was alone able to transform the world to the point of gradually effacing all traces of the primitive checker-board of local usages. But I must anticipate an objection. Because archæologists of prehistoric times find in every cave-dwelling about the same types of flakes, of knives, of very simple utensils, they hastily conclude that their savage possessors did not differ at all from one another in their clothes or morals or methods of life, and that this resemblance was due to the spontaneous appearance of the same ideas and wants among primitive men. But this conclusion is absolutely arbitrary, and the only one that is authorised by logic is that the production or consumption of flint arms or tools, of pottery, etc., was propagated by fashion-imitation over vast regions at those remote periods during which we are often led to think that tribal imitation played an insignificant part. When I call to mind that the Incas, in spite of their high degree of civilisation, never had any notion of a wagon or wheel, nor of illumination by means of a lamp or candle, thereby utilising the oleaginous substances which were right under their hands, I cannot doubt but that the majority of savage peoples would have always been ignorant of the art of pottery if they had not been taught it from outside. Consequently, it seems a fallacy to me to see in the almost universal diffusion of this art proof of the necessity of the innateness of certain discoveries.

I realise, however, that the life of savages on the lowest rung of the human ladder is almost as much lacking in originality as in variety, and that they resemble each other in many particulars without having imitated each other the least in the world. But their similarity in this respect is in no way social. It is entirely vital, for the only wants which they know are natural wants with a very slight impression of the special characteristics of the family.[1] Let us pass on to the point when the family has become more artificial than natural and begins to be and to wish to be a society, not solely a physiological group. Then true usages, fictitious wants which overlie or swell out physical wants, begin. They arise as distinct things in the several groups, and as they become more precise and more numerous in each group they become differentiated in them. But their internal precision and richness continues without let, whereas their external differentiation is soon checked by the inmate tendency to copy the foreigner famous for invention or conquest. Now and then this tendency has free scope and, thanks to this intermittent spirit of introducing foreign wants and to its combination with the steady spirit of conserving traditional wants, every tribe, and then every city, and then every province, and then every large nation, and finally almost the whole of the civilised globe, presents the spectacle, in respect to usages, as in so many other respects, of advances in similarity joined with increasing degrees of complexity.

If one wished to explain the architectural style and fashion of a given locality merely on the ground of the exigencies of its climate, one would be greatly handicapped. In Asia Minor, for example, all the houses on the slope of the Black Sea are roofed with tiles, whereas on the slope towards Cyprus their roofs are terraced, "whatever may be," says M. Élisée Reclus, "the difference of climate." It

---

[1] Besides, this similarity is far from being complete. M Émile Rivière, who has given much study to the fauna of prehistoric caves, remarks upon the extreme rarity of the remains of fish in the grottoes of Mentone. He is suprised by this fact, and has difficulty in explaining how it was that a seaboard people and one whose sea was so abounding in fish were so little or not at all addicted to fishing Is not the most simple explanation of this curious phenomenon the fact that these cave dwellers had not yet had the idea of inventing adequate or fitting means of catching the fish off their coasts?

is a question of fashion or custom, or, rather, of an ancient
fashion that has become a custom. From one end to the
other of the United States, from top to bottom, throughout
all classes, even among good-looking women (and there is
certainly no more striking example of the power of imitation
than this) we find the repugnant habit of tobacco chewing,
—a fact that explains the universal presence of the spittoon,
the most indispensable piece of furniture in America.[1] Is
this a habit that is made necessary by the exigencies of race
and climate? Not at all; it is another case of fashion and
custom.

Let me dwell a little upon this point, if only to emphasise
a distinction which might have been expressly indicated in
the preceding sections, but which finds a more natural place
here, the distinction between production and consumption.
In that beginning of society of which I have been speaking,
every family or every horde began by being a workshop
and a storehouse of all kinds of useful things, besides
being both church and state. In other words, it produced all that it consumed and consumed all that it produced either in the matter of private and individual utilities
or in that of beliefs or in that of collective utilities. This
means that exchange, economic solidarity, did not exist between families any more than political or religious solidarity.
Certain families did not produce wheat or rice, linen or
cloth, for the consumption of other families in exchange
for the different products or services, political or military
services, for example, of the latter, any more than certain
families taught or ruled over others, furnishing them with
an intellectual or volitional direction which the latter believed in and followed, in return for the latter's services
or products. Now I must show how production became
differentiated from consumption all along this line, and
it is incumbent upon me to prove that the law of the

[1] [It is unnecessary to point out to American readers the infelicity
of this illustration; but it may be well, for the benefit of English readers of Mrs. Trollope or Charles Dickens, to state that it is not founded
on fact —*Tr.*]

alternation of the two kinds of imitation applies both to
the spread of productive acts and to that of the desires of
consumption.

When the family is an exclusive and self-sufficient workshop, the secrets and processes of fabrication, of domestication, and of cultivation are transmitted from father to son,
and imitation functions only through heredity. At the same
time the wants which this embryonic industry satisfies are
transmitted in the same manner. But when the family
learns of better processes in use elsewhere, and copies them,
forsaking its old mistakes, then the new products, which
are always a little different from the old, must be desired
and called for simultaneously on the part of consumers.
Consequently, new needs of consumption must have themselves been transmitted by fashion. Finally, it always happens that after an influx of industrial innovations has been
freely welcomed on the part of an inheritance- and custom-
bound imitation, the desire to fix them as customs on a
larger scale appears. In this way corporations are born.
Parallelly, corresponding desires of consumption end by
taking root and becoming national habits.[1] Then this process begins anew. On the other hand, an era of free competition, that is, of free external imitation, succeeds to the close
corporations of the old régime, and this new era invariably
winds up with a return to the ancient monopoly on a vaster

[1] Periods of fashion-imitation may be recognised by the effacement
of certain characteristics which had previously distinguished the different professions. This means, in fact, that each individual looks
about him and seeks to copy people in other occupations instead of
choosing his *patron*, his *chief*, the head of his professional family, for
his unique model.

Voltaire writes, for example, in his *Siècle de Louis XIV:* " Formerly
all the different conditions of life could be recognised by their characteristic defects. Military people and young men who were about to
enter upon the profession of war had an exaggerated vivacity, and
members of the legal profession, a forbidding gravity, to which the
habit of always wearing their robes, even in the royal court, contributed not a little. This was also the case in the medical profession
and in the universities. Merchants still wore mean attire when they
met together, and when they called upon ministers of state. In those
days the greatest merchants were but common men. But as soon as

scale, under the name of great companies or professional syndicates. On the other hand, a rule of general caprice and all-pervasive fashion succeeds to the old usages of past times until the appointed hour comes for the quiescence of people's souls in wants that are alike stable and uniform.

Here we must take note of an apparently simple fact, but one, however, which has had great consequences in history. |Desires of consumption are in general much more rapidly and much more readily communicated than the desires of production which correspond to them. The first time that a primitive tribe sees any objects of war or adornment in bronze, it straightway desires to possess similar articles. But it is not until much later that it desires to make such objects for itself. Meanwhile, and the wait may be a long one, it appeals to the fabricators of some foreign tribe, and thus commerce arises. It has been noted with surprise that among the Semites, the Cushites, and the Aryans (not among the Chinese) the composition of prehistoric bronze was always the same, in spite of the possibly arbitrary proportion of its elements. M. Lenormand says this is "an important fact and one which proves that the same invention was passed on from one to another over a region whose geographical limits have been accurately determined by M. de Rouge-mont." This means that at a certain prehistoric period the desire to acquire this newly discovered metal spread from

citizens began to meet together in public buildings, at public spectacles and promenades, in order to enjoy the amenities of life, the outward appearance of them all became little by little almost identical Now-adays, we perceive that polite manners have made their way through all conditions of life. All these changes gradually reacted upon the provinces "

Broca used to say that memory is not a simple faculty. Every cerebral function has its particular memory and its own habits. I shall say as much of imitation, the social memory Every social function, and, especially, every pursuit, has its own particular style, that is, its own proper channel and current of imitation. *Professional imitation* deserves a special study. It should be subdivided into two chapters, one upon the *prejudices* and the other upon the *customs* that characterise every profession. At certain times, professional imitation runs in a narrow channel, at other times, it spreads at large. and different kinds of pro-fessional imitation connect with one another.

people to people like a powder train, and that the majority of tribes or peoples bought it long before they knew how to make it. Otherwise, its composition would have varied very materially in different places. Many other facts confirm this point of view, notably the spread of amber, in prehistoric ages, to very great distances from the place in which it was discovered. Thus the same condition held in the past as in the present. To-day, the nations which are entering upon civilisation are the markets for the old nations of Europe, because they have caught the contagion of new wants without being as yet stung to emulation by the sight of new industry. England's worldwide commercial conquests, so fruitful of immense consequences, result from this.[1]

Although this phenomenon is or appears to be very simple, the contrary phenomenon would be, *a priori,* much more conceivable. Desires of production have to spread only in a small group of men in order to be realised, whereas, if desires of consumption are to be viable, they must propagate themselves through a large mass of people. It is consequently surprising to find that when a whole people are charmed into wearing certain stuffs and jewels, and into living in houses which are built on certain plans, no member of the community is inspired with a lively desire to produce these stuffs and jewels and houses. So imitative is man, in general, and so passive besides, in his manner of imitating. However this may be, the fact that we have noticed may be observed in every order of social facts. The taste for reading poetry, for looking at pictures, for listening to music or plays, comes to all peoples through the imitation of some neighbour long before the taste to versify or to paint, or to compose operas or tragedies. Hence the universal radiation and the international character of certain

[1] " The Bushmen, who have been decimated by hunger, are surrounded by pastoral peoples. And, for centuries, they have preyed upon their neighbours' herds, only to destroy them; the idea of breeding animals themselves has never occurred to them " (Zaborowski, *Revue scientifique,* December 17, 1892.) In this case, *desire for consumption* has so far preceded *desire for production,* that the latter has not yet shown itself.

great literary and artistic reputations.[1]   In the same way, the need to be governed by intelligent and adequate legislation comes to a people long before the desire or the capacity to elaborate a judicial system.   Hence the spread of Roman law among the Visigoths and other barbarians and, after the Renascence, in almost all of feudal Europe.   In this same way, too, the need of religious sentiment precedes that of religious as well as that of philosophic genius, *i. e.*, theoretic invention.   Hence the very rapid conversion of young or aged peoples to a new religion.   Similarly, communities love military and patriotic glory through imitation before they possess the genius for war or statecraft which makes for a glorious army or fatherland.   This circumstance favours the annexation of large territories by illustrious conquerors; it favours the formation, for example, of the Roman Empire.   Finally, communities experience, through contact with foreign peoples, the desire to speak a rich and cultivated language before they are either capable or desirous of that cultivation which alone enriches and perfects an idiom.   I may say the same thing of the lower classes, who in their contact with the educated classes are eager to copy the polite language of the court or drawing room before they make any pretence of reproducing fashionable life.   Hence the rapid progress that is made by certain languages or dialects throughout a continent or country.   The spread of Greek throughout the Eastern Empire, of the dialect of the *Isle-de-France* throughout France, and of English throughout North America and the world in general, are examples in point.[2]

This priority along all lines of the needs for consumption

---

[1] In his interesting work, entitled *Politique internationale,* M. Novicow seems to think that a nationality that is worthy of the name should produce the arts and literature that it consumes.   This is a mistake, I think.   According to this, as long as we in modern Europe were principally fed upon Greek and Latin literature, there was no such thing as French, or English, or Spanish, or German nationality.

[2] The fifteen- or eighteen-months-old infant cannot talk, but he can understand his mother's speech.   According to Houzeau, certain animals, monkeys and dogs, come to guess the meaning of their masters' words.   They, too, consume language before they produce it.

over those for production may be deduced as an important corollary from the course of imitation *ab interioribus ad exteriora, i. e.,* from the thing signified to the sign. Here the sign is the productive act which actualises the idea and aim of the thing which is to be consumed. This idea and this aim are the hidden content of which the consumed product is the form. Now, in periods of change, the form, as we know, always lags behind the content. Guyau remarks very justly, for example, that "the political revolution of the first half of this century [in France] was accomplished in thought before it took shape in action: philosophic, religious, and social ideas which had been previously unknown to the poets burst forth in the beautiful setting of the tranquil alexandrines of Delille." The change to romanticism in verse was the making of the literary product appropriate to meet the demand of the new soul of poetry. Does not this inability of innovators to find at once suitable metres and processes and symbols of art for their ideas and sentiments suggest the impossibility on the part of countries which have been but just initiated into new desires for luxury and comfort to create industries adapted to the satisfaction of these desires ?

No social phenomenon has had greater consequences than the one in question. It has been a potent factor, as we have seen, in breaking down the barriers of nationalities before the torrent of civilising examples which escaped from it or which entered into it. International exchange arose in that way. Suppose that the need to reproduce, in every order of things, the new object that had been seen abroad had preceded or accompanied the need to consume this article, what would have happened? Primitive families would have copied one another without uniting together; they would have remained as much aloof from, if not as hostile to, one another after every act of borrowing as they were before it, like the monads of Liebnitz, which reflect but do not influence one another. It is true that this heterogeneity combined with this similarity, this disintegration in this uniformity, implies a kind of contradiction which cannot be indefinitely prolonged. And so the imitative passivity of mankind has had the happy result of multiplying the commercial and political and intellectual ties of human groups and of effecting or preparing their fusion. When, after it has been passive for a long time, imitation finally becomes active, when a people who have for a long time imported from abroad the books and paintings, the articles of luxury and the statesmen and legislators which it needs, undertakes to supply its own literature and art, its own luxuries, its own diplomacy, the greater part of its attempts fail. Or, if they do succeed by means of a high tariff, or by means of other methods of protection which tend to re-establish the community's previous state of isolation, its acquired habits are too strong to be entirely broken off, and they will regain their hold some day or other, to the advantage of all concerned.

In reality, when new desires for production break forth in a people, long after the establishment of new desires for consumption, they do not consist in simply and solely copying the literature, the arts, the industries, and the strategy of the nation whose products have heretofore inundated the aforesaid people. But an original system of production appears, which in its turn endeavours, and usually with success, to open up a market for itself among the original foreign producers. Moreover, in the preceding sections I concluded that the widespread propagation of a single language, of a single religion, of a single governmental authority, or of a single body of laws, was the first and preliminary condition of a great literature or civilisation or statecraft or system of security. And now I shall have no difficulty in showing that the widespread propagation of the same number of wants and tastes, or, in a word, of the same individual *usages,* is the first and preliminary condition of great wealth and of a great industrial system as well as of a great art (to anticipate the following section on this latter point).

Here, as before, we must distinguish the influence which the transition from custom to fashion in matters of usages and, later on, the return from fashion to a more extensive custom, exercises upon the characteristics of industry.

It is clear that in an age when custom imposed different kinds of food and clothing and furniture and houses in different localities, in localities where they remained fixed for several generations, machine production on a large scale would be, even if it were known, without a market. The artisan of such an epoch is bent upon making only a small number of very solid and durable articles,[1] whereas, later on, in periods when the same fashion holds sway over more than one country, although it changes from year to year, the quantity and not the stability of the product is the aim of industry. A builder of American trading vessels told Tocqueville that on account of the frequent change there in naval fashions it was to his interest to construct vessels of little durability. In ages of custom, the producer seeks the narrow and long-drawn-out market of the future, in ages of fashion he seeks the vast ephemeral market of the outside world. As far as products whose essential quality is permanency are concerned, such as buildings, jewelry of gold or precious stones, furniture, bookbindings, statues, etc., the insufficiency of contemporaneous patronage in times of custom may be compensated for up to a certain point by the prospect of the future patronage to which each generation will contribute. And so, the Middle Ages, in spite of the disintegration of their [2] local usages, possessed

[1] "The woollen industry of Rome," says Roscher, "is distinguished by the solidity of its products, for which monastic dress, *whose fashion does not change,* has set the standard."

[2] This does not mean that the Middle Ages were unacquainted with the charms of fashion. From the time of the thirteenth century, according to Cibrario, the nobility delighted "to dress in germents borrowed from the most distant nations, like the Saracens and Sclavonians." Florentine women wore the "crude green" of Cambria. Changes of fashion in everything bearing upon dress were pretty frequent among the nobility and the wealthy middle classes. They were much less frequent, however, than they are to-day in all articles whatsoever, and among all classes "The dress of the common people," says M. Rambaud, "changed very little during the Middle Ages." This is because it remained a matter of *tradition* "On the other hand," he adds, "the wealthy classes had a capricious variety of fashions." This is

its great architects and goldsmiths, its remarkable cabinet-makers and binders and sculptors. But for products destined to more or less immediate destruction, for those whose consumption is speedy, this compensation does not exist. Consequently, we must not be surprised to find that horticulture and even agriculture, that ordinary glass work and pottery and cloth-making, prospered or progressed so little during the feudal period. Inversely, if the fickleness of taste in times of fashion hinders the development of such arts and industries as architecture and statuary, things that must look to the future, a uniformity of taste over a vast territory highly favours, in spite of their instability, the progress of all manufacture which is essentially ephemeral, such as paper-making, journalism, weaving, landscape-gardening, etc. Nevertheless, if renewed stability were ever added to the acquired uniformity of usages, a third period of incomparable prosperity would open out to industry. Already such a period may be foreseen. China arrived centuries ago at this happy goal. We know how surprising her industrial wealth is in view of the slender treasury of inventions that she exploits.

Have I in any of this been exaggerating the rôle of imitation? I think not, for it is remarkable that when a great system of industry is introduced into a country it at first applies itself to objects of luxury, to tapestry, jewels, etc., and it is only later that it includes objects of *secondary* and then of *prime* necessity. Why is this? Because usages are assimilated in the upper classes, the consumers of objects of luxury, before this assimilation is accomplished among the common people. Therefore Colbert was very unjustly blamed for having encouraged the manufacturer of silks and other aristocratic industries. In his time, this was the only

because they experienced the influence of fashion. At all periods, in antiquity as well as in the Middle Ages, it is notable that the rule of fashion accompanies the brilliant and ascendant phases of civilisations. " The Persians," says Herodotus, " are most curious concerning foreign usages. In fact, they have copied the dress of the Medes . . . and in war they use Egyptian cuirasses. They have borrowed pederasty from the Greeks."

course open to him. And yet Roscher, in pointing out the apparently fantastic order of the successive forms of industry, does not seem to me to have perceived its reason. " In ancient times," he says, " the greatly inferior means of transportation, the manners and customs of different countries, and, finally, lack of machinery, resulted necessarily in a much greater dispersion of industry." Here the cause which I have pointed out as unique is not even mentioned Those which have been substituted for it are merely, in my opinion, its consequences. Was not inadequacy of transportation, for example, as well as difference of character, of customs, and manners, the result of putting a too feeble emphasis on foreign imitations on the part of consumers? If different localities had desired to buy the same articles, the need of common routes would have been experienced and, before long, satisfied. But roads [1] which were opened out by the bridge-building friars (a religious body which was expressly created in the Middle Ages for the construction of roads and bridges, a kind of clerical administration for bridges and highways) went to ruin for lack of use. Under the Roman Empire, too, excellent roads existed; but, in spite of the impetus given to universal assimilation by the prestige of Rome,[2] as the particular usages of the different provinces remained pretty dissimilar, industry on a large scale was little known at this period.[3]

[1] See Jusserand, *La Vie nomade*, in the Middle Ages.
[2] There is one astonishing fact which reveals both the prestige of Rome, and man's tendency to imitate his conqueror, namely, the fact that so odd and inconvenient a habit as that of eating in a reclining position became general throughout the Empire, or, at least, throughout the higher classes From this usage was derived a luxury with which we are no longer familiar, the eating as distinguished from the sleeping couch; and, I may add, from the nuptial couch, which differed from both.
[3] There were, however, thanks to the spread of Roman models, even in the barbarian world, exporting industries. The barbarians insensibly became Latinised in their wants and tastes, and, "little by little," says Amédée Thierry, "the use of Roman merchandise became so general, that the garments of the Sarmatian and the German were made either out of goods produced in the neighbouring provinces, or in Italy" *(Tableau de l'empire romain)*.

As for the lack of machinery, the same explanation applies. For, as a matter of fact, the germ of machinery that was fit to start or develop a great system of industry was latent in antiquity in all the branches of production that were scattered through Egypt and Phœnicia and Greece and Babylonia. If it had been propagated by fashion-imitation among producers, it could not have failed to suggest rapid improvements. The great lack, then, was the lack of a tendency to imitate the foreigner. Thus everything comes back to this. The first condition for the viability of paper-making on a large scale is, undoubtedly, a sufficiently general habit of writing. Besides, machinery, strictly speaking, is not indispensable to industry on a large scale. There is *manufacture* as well as *machine-facture*. In Rome, before the days of the printing press, there were great workshops of copyists who manufactured editions of Virgil and Horace and other classics. Here was an exceptionally extensive industry, because it appealed to the scholars of the whole Empire, scholars who were possessed of the same education, who spoke the same language, and who were inspired by the same literary tastes.[1]

We must not overlook the following fact. The mere existence of a similarity of wants and usages is not sufficient to make industry on a large scale possible. Recognition of the similarity is also necessary. In the Middle Ages, according to Jusserand, none but kings and their suites, none but great nobles, pilgrims, fugitive criminals, a few

---

[1] The slow progress of industry during the Middle Ages, and even in the beginning of the modern era, has also been attributed to the absurdity of sumptuary laws, and the narrow and mechanical organisation of corporations. But here again we have but the consequences of my explanation. Sumptuary laws checked or deadened the tendency to imitate one class on the part of other classes; and corporate monopoly prevented outside producers from copying the processes in use by members of the corporation. It has been said that the industrial prosperity of Germany, even before 1871, was due to its *tariff union* or *Zollverein*. But suppose that those petty principalities, those free towns, those hundreds of past fragments of present-day Germany, had kept their several characteristic wants and luxuries, would any tariff union have been possible? Certainly not.

wandering workmen, minstrels, preaching and begging friars, and hawkers of relics and indulgences, passed over the bad roads of the periods. From this enumeration it appears that the sole or principal industry of exportation that was popular at this epoch was the sale of relics and indulgences. As for the minstrels, they worked only for a few castles and for one or two royal courts. Does this mean that the people had only one desire in common, namely, that of buying relics and indulgences?[1] No, but this similarity, derived, as it was, from a common religion, was known to all, whereas the other resemblances, in general, were not. Nevertheless, pilgrims and other wanderers helped to spread, little by little, the originally vague consciousness of these resemblances. They even helped to increase the number of the already numerous points of resemblance. In this respect, they paved the way for the industry of the future. The preaching friars unconsciously contributed to the same end in assimilating people's minds, in spreading democratic ideas under an evangelical guise, or evangelical ideas under a democratic guise. In this way they moved souls, and this is always the right road, even to material well-being. The ardent homilies of innumerable Savonarolas, the preaching of Luther and his followers, the passionate theories of our Encyclopedists, were all necessary factors in causing almost all classes and nations to consciously and openly dress and live in approximately the same way. It is this condition which permits industry to unfold its wings.

Among the usages whose similarity is essential to extensive industry there is one which it is important to consider above all, because the assimilation of all the others would amount to very little, unless it, too, were assimilated. I mean that which is concerned with the regulation of price. I freely admit that some logical rule, although not that,

[1] This gave rise to an entirely new luxury, let me say in passing, to one which the most luxurious Romans never dreamed of, to the luxury of shrines and reliquaries.

to be sure, of *supply and demand,* as applied by dogmatic
economists, but one more precise and more complete, pre-
sides over the formation of price *when for the first time
any specific price is formed.* But when a price has once
been established as a result of an openly discussed calculation or contract, it spreads through fashion far beyond the
places where those special conditions which rationally determine it prevail; or else, it persists in a place through
custom long after the first conditions of its establishment
there have disappeared. But although this persistence
through custom or diffusion by fashion be or ought to be
considered by classical economists as an abuse or trans-
gression of their laws, it is certain that without this persist-
ance or diffusion, according to the period, industry would
have been hindered from its very start. Would our great
commercial houses be possible if each of the towns to
which they express their innumerable stores wished to pay
for them according to its traditional price and refused to
conform to their uniform price? And could our great factories carry on their business for long if each one of them
insisted upon always paying the same customary wages to
its work-people in disregard of the rise or fall of wages in
the general market? Formerly, on the other hand, when
every artisan worked with a view to the future, when every
perspective in the narrow circumference of contemporaneous
time was closed,[1] when he could not count for his livelihood
or fortune upon the extension of his patronage and his returns, when he could count only upon their permanency,
when rigid ties bound him for years at a stretch to his
patron, and when the patrons themselves were bound together in a perpetual association, what security could there

---

[1] On this subject, I take the liberty of referring the reader to two
articles which I wrote for the *Revue philosophique,* in September and
October, 1881, under the title *La Psychologie en économie politique.*
See, especially, p. 405 and the following in that volume of the *Revue.*
I dealt more comprehensively with the same subject in 1888, in the
Revue économique of M. Gide, under the title *Les deux Sens de la
valeur.* (These studies were reproduced with additions in my *Logique
sociale,* 1894)

have been for either consumers or producers if future prices
had not been fixed and assured in advance?   Thus the customary fixation of prices in the past compensated for their
local variation, just as in the present their uniformity com-
pensates for their changeability.   Some day, perhaps,
they will end by being both fixed and uniform, and by furnishing a scope and steadiness of outlet to production which
will increase its audacity tenfold.

In fact every new fashion endeavours to become rooted in
custom; but only a few are successful for the same reason
that many germs are abortive.   However, the introduction of only a few foreign wants, or of novel means of
satisfying them, suffices to complicate the consumption of a
given country; for pre-existent wants and luxuries do not
give way or disappear without prolonged resistance.   In
Europe the habit of eating bread was not encroached upon
by the importation of Asiatic rice, any more than in Asia
the habit of eating rice suffered to any serious extent from
the introduction of European bread.   But the dietary in
both places became complicated by a new element.   " The
mistake was made in France,[1] at the time of the signing
of the commercial treaty of 1860, of thinking that French
wines were going to replace beer in the United Kingdom.
We fancied that we could make our wines reach a class
of consumers that was supposed to have abstained from them
because of their high tariff and consequent high price.
This forecast was ill-founded.   If French wine has made
some progress in British markets, it is only among a
very limited circle of patrons, of which neither the working
classes nor even the majority of the middle classes [2] form
a part.   Although our alcoholic products are better appreciated to-day, *this has in no way come about at the cost of
beer.*   The consumption of beer has always increased in
very different proportions from that of foreign wines."

[1] *Journal des économistes*, February, 1882.
[2] In this case, as everywhere else, we see that the higher up we go in
the social scale, the slighter the attachment we find to native habits, and
the greater the openness to contagions of foreign things

Thus wine has been added to beer in England, but it has in no respect replaced it.

The characteristics which the rule of fashion in the matter of usages inspires in industry are easy to guess. In order to spread through a kind of conquering epidemic, language must become more regular and more prosaic, it must take on a more logical and a less animated air, religion must become more spiritual, more rational and less original, a government must become more administrative, less prestigious, legislation must shine through the reason and equity rather than through the originality of its forms, finally, an industrial system must develop its mechanical and scientific side at the expense of its spontaneous and artistic side./ In a word, the apparently singular fact is that the rule of fashion is tied to that of reason. I may add, to that of individualism and to that of naturalism. This is explained when we consider that imitation of contemporaries has to do with models individually considered, detached from any parent stock, whereas imitation of ancestors emphasises the tie of hereditary solidarity between the individual and his forebears. And we may also readily perceive that all epochs of fashion-imitation—Athens under Solon, Rome under the Scipios, Florence in the fifteenth century, Paris in the sixteenth and, later on, in the eighteenth century—are characterised by the more or less triumphant invasion of so-called natural law (as well read individual law) against civil law, of so-called natural against traditional religion, of art which I shall also call natural, that is to say, of art which is faithfully observant and reflective of individual reality, against hieratic and customary art, of natural morality, as we shall soon see, against national morality. The Italian humanists and Rabelais, Montaigne, Voltaire, personify this naturalistic and individualistic character under divers aspects. Since nothing is more natural to the individual human being than reason, since nothing is better able to satisfy individual reason than the substitution of a symmetrical and logical order for the mysterious complications of life, we must not be surprised to find rationalism, individualism, and naturalism hand in hand. The rule of fashion is distinguished in every order of things by the blossoming of certain great and free individualities. It is at such times that, in language, grammarians, like Vaugelas, have free play; even the wholesale makers of idioms, of Volapük, for example, can hope for some success, providing, of course, their reforms have the stamp of regularity and symmetry. In religion, it is the era of great reformers, of great heretics and philosophers, who succeed, providing they simplify and rationalise religion. In statecraft, in legislation, it is the epoch of illustrious legislators and founders of empire, of men who perfect codification and administration. Economically, it is the period of the great industrial inventors who perfect machinery. Æsthetically, I may add, it is the time of glorious creators of art who carry to the highest point of mechanical perfection the *tricks* and devices of composition. Besides, wherever we see that great reputations have been made, we may affirm that there the contagion of fashion has raged, although each of these glories may have been the point of departure of some traditional fetichism that is as exclusive and tenacious as the preceding forms of fetich worship which it destroyed. The Molièrites, for example, with their prior attachment to the petty traditions of the *théâtre français,* must not make us forget that their idol, Molière, was, in his innovating century of art, the most open-minded man to innovations, the worst enemy to fetiches. These followers of Molière can make us understand the followers of Homer. We may be sure that Homer, like Molière, appeared in an age of imitative expansion, when all the Archipelago and the whole of Asia Minor were beginning to open out to the radiations of Ionia.

To sum up, the rôle played by custom and fashion in the economic sphere closely corresponds to the action exerted in the other spheres of the social world by these two always co-existent, but alternately increasing and decreasing, forms of imitation. It falls without any difficulty into the general law which I have formulated. But, in addition, the reason of this law, of this vacillating struggle between custom and fashion which lasts until the ultimate triumph of the former, is at present suggested to us. Since every invention is the centre of some particular imitation which emanates from it, the desire to imitate must always be directed, by preference, towards the side where the richest galaxy of inventions is shining, that is to say, sometimes, exclusively towards the past, if one's ancestors were inventive or if they were more inventive than one's contemporaries, and sometimes, and this more and more frequently, towards the contemporaneous and the foreign, if one's contemporaries are more inventive than one's own ancestors. Now, these two situations will inevitably alternate for a long time, for, as soon as some mine of discoveries is disclosed, all the world exploits it, and it does not take long for it to become, for the time being, exhausted, thereby swelling the legacy of the past until some new vein be found; and when the last of these mines shall have been discovered, we shall have our ancestors alone to appeal to for examples.

There is a certain reciprocity of stimulation between the rule of fashion and the progress of contemporary invention which should not make us fail to recognise the priority of the latter. Undoubtedly, as I have said already, once the current of fashion has been set free, it excites the inventive imagination along the lines that are the fittest to accelerate its overflow; but what set it free, if it was not the impetus that was given to it by contact with some neighbouring country whose fruitful novelties had been more or less spontaneously struck out? We cannot doubt that this is so in our own century in whatever has to do with industry; for certainly the first cause of that fascination which causes all European peoples to imitate one another was steam machinery, which led to production on a large scale, and of railroads, which led to the distant transportation of products— not to speak of telegraphs. It is especially in the matters of industry and science that the modern imagination has had full swing; and it is especially on its economic and scientific side that it has broken down the barriers of custom. In matters of art, on the contrary, just as the creative imagination has often been lacking in them, so the spirit of tradition has subsisted in them, taken as a whole. The details are significant. In architecture we have invented almost nothing; our epoch has slavishly copied Gothic, Roman, and Byzantine models. In this respect the nineteenth century was as much given over to tradition—at least until the advent of what might be called architecture in iron—as the twelfth century was given over to innovation.

In fact, in spite of the partly accidental character of inventions, inventors themselves are so imitative, that there is in every period *a current of inventions* which is in a certain general sense religious or architectural or sculptural or musical or philosophical. There are certain currents of imitation which must through force of habit precede others. For example, the mythological genius must have habitually —I will not say, with Comte, necessarily—exerted itself before the metaphysical genius. The creative genius of language was most certainly prior to either. And this was the one to be exhausted first of all; so we should not be surprised if in the most progressive societies, societies which are the most scornful of custom in other respects, the empire of custom in what has to do with language prevails more and more, day by day, through a more exaggerated respect for orthography and a growing spirit of philological conservatism. It seems to me that many apparent peculiarities in history could be explained by considerations drawn from the same source. But the reader will be able to make for himself such applications as I have not indicated here.

VI. *Morality and Art*

Tastes which are formulated into principles of art and morals which are formulated into principles of morality, alike variable according to time and place, direct two important parts of social activity and, consequently, form part, like usages, laws, and constitutions, of the government of societies, in the large and true meaning of the word. This is so true that the more moral or artistic a people become, the less need they have of being governed. Consummate morality would make the coming of a-n-archy possible. But in order to avoid the commonplaces which I might indulge in in this twofold subject, I wish to limit myself here to a very brief discussion. I need not prove, I think it is enough to merely point out, the religious origin of art, of which I spoke in a previous chapter,[1] or of morality, whose duties were at first understood as divine commands. /Moral sentiments and artistic tastes emanate, then, from religion. Let me add, from the family. At the time when every family and tribe had its own language and worship, it had, when it was artistically well endowed, its particular art, which was piously transmitted from father to son, and when it was supplied with sympathetic instincts it had its particular morality where its own group of moral, often immoral, prejudices and of odd and difficult sacrifices had been scrupulously observed from time immemorial. How often must these walled-up arts and exclusive morals have broken down their barriers! How often, after their overflow outside, must they have shut their doors and secured themselves behind their new frontiers, only to push them forward again from time to time and from age to age! All this had to be done before it was possible to see on this earth the unheard-of sight of many vast nations feeling, at the same time and in about the same way, the beautiful and the ugly, good and evil, admiring or mocking at the same pictures, the same novels, the same dramas, the same operas, applauding the same acts of virtue or becoming indignant over the same crimes, crimes that are made public by the daily press in the four corners of the globe at the same time.

---

[1] Up to the last days of the Roman Empire, public spectacles and celebrations in which all the forms of art were displayed, made part of the solemnities of religion Moreover, the ancients were not at all familiar with the entirely modern distinction between secular and sacred music.

Under this new aspect the world shows us again the contrast which I have pointed out so often. Formerly, in those times when custom predominated in art and in morals as in religion and in politics, every nation and, to go back still further, every province was distinguished from neighbouring nations and provinces and cities by its original products of jewelry, chiselled weapons, ornate furniture, figurines and poetic legends as well as by its characteristic virtues, so that often, in different places, the beautiful and the good appeared quite different, but, on the other hand, from one century to another, in each country, the beautiful and the good were unchanging, and the same virtues, the same objects of art, were invariably reproduced. Nowadays, on the contrary, in our era of widespread and penetrating fashions, artistic works and virtuous acts are about the same everywhere, upon two continents at least, whereas, from decade to decade, not to say from year to year, the styles and schools of painters, musicians, and poets are transformed along with the public taste, and moral maxims are themselves worn out and changed and renewed with alarming facility. Nevertheless, we must not be over-alarmed by this extraordinary mutability, if it be true that, in connection with a corresponding universality, it is related to a whole series of rhythmical oscillations which grow bigger and bigger and whose consequences, from the point of view of morality, especially, have been most salutary, and if it be true that the experience of the past justify us in counting upon a return, in the more or less immediate future, to a reassuring fixity of ideals, joined, at last, to peace-bringing uniformity.

However simple moral duties may seem to those who have practised them for a long time, they were all in their beginnings individual and original inventions, inventions which, like all others, appeared and spread one after the other.[1]

---

[1] Buckle, as we see, was strangely mistaken when he contrasted the immutability of morality with the progressive character of intelligence and science. The immutability is only one of degree; and in this relative sense the antithesis is true.

They were instigated and helped to succeed, at times by the dogmas of a new religion whose practical and, usually, extremely strange consequences they were logical in scorning, at times by the new conditions of social life with which they found themselves in agreement. It is in this way that successive inventions of art owe their appearance and their fortune to changes either in ideas or in morals. Respect for old age, blood-feud, hospitality, bravery; later on, labour, honesty, respect for the cattle, or fields, or women of others; still later, patriotism, feudal loyalty, almsgiving, the emancipation of slaves, the relief of unfortunates, etc., were ushered in in the different ages of humanity, like the Egyptian tomb, or the Grecian temple, or the Gothic cathedral. It was therefore necessary for the breath of fashion, so to speak, to blow and scatter the germ of every new duty as well as that of every new thing of beauty that had duly blossomed forth somewhere or other, throughout the world, over the forbidding walls of tribes and cities shut up in their traditional art and morality. Hence the contradictions which arose so frequently between ancient customs and imported examples, and this partly explains the so frequently negative character of moral proscriptions as well as of canons of taste. Thou shalt not kill thy conquered enemy to devour him, thou shalt not sell thy children or kill thy slaves without a motive, thou shalt not kill or beat thy wives except for infidelity, thou shalt not steal thy neighbour's ass or ox, etc.—these are the highly original and much-discussed prohibitions which, in their respective epochs, composed the major part of the moral code of every people. Their æsthetic code is, likewise, full of prohibitions instead of positive directions for the guidance of taste.

I do not mean to say in what has preceded that the sentiment of fraternity as well as of equality and liberty and justice, that is to say, the germs and soul of moral life, is a modern discovery. That which is modern is the enormous compass of the human group where this superior sentiment is supposed to rule. This sentiment has always existed as a matter of fact, but it exists in groups which become more and more narrow the further back we go in the course of history. This potent and exquisite sentiment is, in fact, the very sweetening of social life, its peculiar charm and magic, the sole counter-balance to its inconveniences, and these inconveniences are such that, if this unique advantage had ever ceased to show itself in any society, that society would have fallen straightway into dust. They who have seen nothing in primitive humanity but combats and massacres, but the cannibalism and other horrors that were committed by one tribe upon another, they who have seen nothing but the lashes of the whip upon the slave, or the sale of little children by their fathers, these people have not understood primitive societies. They have looked at them only on the outside, they have not penetrated within. The inner side, the essence, the content of these societies is the relation which existed in them between the equals which composed them, between the family heads of the same tribe or clan, between the citizens of Sparta or Athens in the agora, between the nobles of the old régime in a drawing room. . . . . Always and everywhere, passing quarrels excepted, we see that union and peace and politeness prevailed in the reciprocal relations that were established between these equals, who in themselves exclusively composed the social group, to the exclusion of slaves, of minor sons, and of women, not to mention strangers. Strangers are, in comparison with the common interest of the equals, the *obstacle* to be overcome. Minors, women, and slaves are, in comparison with the same interest, a mere *means* of service. But neither the latter nor the former are associates.

Only, in the long run, contact with these peers inspires inferiors with a lively desire to be admitted into their magic circle, to force the circumference of their fraternal intimacy to widen out. This desire is realised but gradually and not without difficulty, not without revolutions. How is it realised? By the mere play of long-continued imitation [1]

[1] The Roman plebeians were assimilated with the patricians through imitation. According to Vico, the Roman plebs began by demanding

When we attribute a preponderating share in this result to
the preaching of philosophers or theologians, be they Stoics or
Apostles, we take the effect for the cause. A moment always
comes when, from having copied the superior in everything,
in thought, in speech, in prayer, in dress, and in general
methods of life, the inferior inspires him with the irresistible
feeling that they both belong by right to the same society.
Then this feeling finds expression, ordinarily in an exaggerated form, in some philosophic or theological formula which
strengthens it and which favours its expansion. When Socrates, in his dialogues, raised somewhat the dignity of
women and even of slaves, when Plato, going still further,
dreamed, in his *Republic,* of the complete equality of man
and woman and of the suppression of slavery, it was because,
in contemporaneous Athens, women had begun to cross the
thresholds of the gynecia, and because the slave was already
assimilated with the free man.[1] " The common people of
Athens do not differ from the slaves in dress or in general
bearing or in any other particular," says Xenophon. Besides, before his twofold Utopia could be realised, it was
necessary that for many more centuries the distance between
man and woman, between the citizen and the slave, should
continue to diminish until it reached the point that was attained under the Antonines. Aristotle was much more consistent with the practical morality of his time when he justified slavery; and the contrary opinion of the first masters of
Stoicism on this point remained practically unechoed until
the day when the world was ripe for the words of Epio-
tetus.

Unfortunately, friendship, as well as society, is " a circle

" not the right of contracting marriages with the patricians, *but of contracting marriages like those of the patricians, cunnubia patrum,* and
not *cum patribus*"

[1] Another cause which may have contributed to softening the lot of
the Athenian slaves, was, I think the inferiority in which women
were kept at Athens, and in all the rest of Greece. We see in the
Alcestis of Euripides, in Xenophon, and elsewhere, that Greek women
inspired their slaves with an affectionate attachment, due, undoubtedly,
to their common life and common subjection. They strove side by side
for emancipation.

which deforms itself in *stretching out too far*," and this serious objection has instigated the resistance of conservatives of all periods to the wishes of subject classes who aspired to equality. But it is necessary for this objection to fall away and for the social circle to widen itself out to the limits of humankind. We may query whether the gradual extension of the field of the sentiment of which I am speaking has not been bought at the price of its intensity, and whether there is not reason for thinking that in the past, in the remote past even, it was much more intense, *where it existed*, than it is at present. Has the word *pietas* the same force and fulness of meaning, has it the same divine unction, for us that it had for the ancients?

It has been very justly observed that just as foreign wars, the Persian Wars, for example, tend to strengthen the morality of the belligerents, so civil or quasi-civil wars, the Peloponnesian War, for example, are demoralising. Why so? The same means are used, there is always the same trickery and violence. But, in the one case, it is directed against a group of men who were strangers to one another to begin with and who, after the struggle and in consequence of the contact of war, become so much less strange to one another than they were before that they usually fall to copying one another; whereas, in the other case, they are directed against a group of men who were before that one another's social brothers and relations, one another's friends and compatriots. Thus, in the one case, in that of foreign war, the social *field* has not been curtailed, it even tends to enlarge itself, and the social *tie* is strengthened; in the other case, the social field is diminutised and the social tie is weakened. Here, then, everything is social loss; and that is why we properly talk of demoralisation. There is no better illustration of the eminently social character of morality.

At any rate, it is certain that from century to century the moral public, like the artistic public, has not ceased to extend itself, not by constant, but by intermittent, aggrandisement. By this I mean that the group of persons to whom the individual recognises that he owes certain duties and whose opinion influence his morality,[1] just as the circle of persons for whom the artist works and whose judgments count for something in his eyes, has gone on enlarging. This enlargement has been twofold; on the surface, by the incessant pushing forward of the urban and provincial and national frontiers across which the virtuous man of the city or of the province or of the nation saw no one to whom he felt under any obligation of pity or justice and across which the artist or the poet saw none but barbarians;[2] and, in depth, by the lowering of the barriers which separated classes and limited the horizon of duty and of good taste for each of them. This was a progress which was already immense of itself, but which was in addition accompanied necessarily by an internal remodelling of morals and arts. Now, how was this progress accomplished, how must it have been accomplished? We have first to answer that all the outbursts and overflowings of external imitation that had been brought about from the religious, political, industrial, legislative, or linguistic point of view, indifferently, were potent contributions to this result, through assimilating day by day an increasing number of men. If, from the beginning of the sixteenth century, popular rights forbid the sacking of captured cities, the enslavement of the conquered or the confiscation of his goods, if, from the same epoch, the right of succession to the estate of a deceased alien *(droit d'aubaine)* was no longer claimed,

---

[1] See on this subject my *Criminalité comparée,* p. 188 and the following, and my *Philosophie pénale.*

[2] We can follow, in certain epochs, the stages of this development. Up to Socrates, only the *spirit of the city* reigned in the little Greek republics; from Socrates to Plato, after the Persian wars and the work of fusion which followed them, the spirit of Greek nationality appeared (like French patriotism after the Hundred Years' War). Even Plato thinks of the Greek and of the Barbarian as two distinct beings, although his theory of ideas ought to have had the good effect, at least, of bringing them together in his thought under the idea of man. The conquests of Alexander extend Greece to the middle of Asia, the distinction between Greece and Persia, "those two sisters," is wiped out, and the moral field is singularly enlarged; but outside of the combination of Persian and Greek, man is not recognised as a brother. Under the Roman conquest, Greece, Italy, Spain, Gaul, Africa, and even Germany, come into the charmed circle.

if, in a word, duties towards the stranger, at least towards
the European and Christian stranger, came to be recognised,
it is largely due to the fact that this innovating century gave
a remarkable impetus to fashion-imitation on our continent
and was pre-eminently distinguished by the wide paths which
it opened out to this form of imitation. If Racine wrote for
some thousands of people of good taste in France, and if Victor Hugo has written in our day for some millions of admir-
ers in France and Europe, a great part of this extension of
the literary public is due to the fresh inundation of the
general current of examples, which, after the conservative
seventeenth century, was brought about in the eighteenth
century and which still flows under our eyes. Let us suppose that the steam machine, the loom, the locomotive, and
the telegraph had not been invented, that the principal facts
of modern chemistry and physics had not been discovered,
Europe would unquestionably have remained broken up in
an endless number of little dissimilar provinces, a state of
things as incompatible with a broad system of art or
morality as with an extensive system of industry. Thus all
the good ideas which have civilised the world may be considered auxiliary inventions and discoveries of art and
morality.

But, in matters of morality, at least, this general cause
would not have sufficed to bring about the overthrow of the
obstacles which were in the way of the enlargement of its
domain. To the ideas which indirectly effected this progress, must be added those which had it for its direct and
more or less conscious object. In this class I place in the
first rank all those fictions which in those primitive times
when it was necessary to be related by blood in order to be
social and moral compatriots created artificial systems of
consanguinity and extended to them the advantages of
natural kinship. Among many barbarian peoples the custom
prevails of cementing an alliance by mixing together a few
drops of the blood of the different contracting parties, who
thereby become in a sense consanguineous. Such a usage
could only have been imagined in an epoch when men judged

themselves under moral obligations only within the limits of the ties of blood; and Tylor has reason to celebrate this as " a discovery of a solemn means of extending beyond the narrow limits of the family the duties and affections of the fraternity." Adoption with its many strange forms was another no less ingenious means that worked towards the same end. Finally, the practice of hospitality might well have been based upon some analogous idea. The fact of entering into a house, into the domestic temple, might well have been regarded as a fictitious incorporation into the family, remotely comparable to adoption or to the mingling together of drawn drops of blood. But of all such ingenuities, the most marvellous and the most fruitful is undoubtedly the word of Christ: " Every man is thy brother, ye are all the sons of God." By virtue of this all men were included in one blood-relationship.

When, through these processes or others like them, or simply as a result of the levelling of civilisation, a more ample opportunity is given for the doing of upright acts or for the making of æsthetic things, we see peoples or classes who had before been cooped up by their own peculiar arts and morals inclined to interchange them; and from this common tendency results the triumph of a higher art or morality, which is, in turn, inevitably transformed. There is the same difference between imported morality and inbred, domestic morality, between a fashion-morality and a custom-morality, as between an art that is exotic, that is acclimating itself, and an art that is indigenous. The inspiration of the latter, in spite of its relative age and immutability, has much more freshness and force and originality. We have no cause to wonder at this; any more than at the oddly youthful energy which is inherent in the duties that are imposed by antique customs, in the duty of family vengeance, especially. But there are other points which I prefer to emphasise.

There are two points to note on the subject of art. In the first place, art, in the ages of custom, when it is born spontaneously, without any wholesale importation, springs up from handicraft, " like a flower from its stem," under the warmth of religious inspiration. This was the case in Egypt, in Greece, in China, in Mexico and Peru, and in Florence.[1] Architecture, Gothic or otherwise, is born of the builder's craft; the painting of the fourteenth century, of illuminating, and illuminating, of the craft of the copyists; sculpture, of mediæval cabinet-making, of the tombs of Egypt; modern music, of the ecclesiastical habit of intoning; eloquence, of the professions which involve speaking, of bench and bar; poetry and literature, of the different ways of speaking, of narration, of instigation, of persuasion. In the second place, at the same epochs, the work of art answers, not to the need of knowing something new, which is peculiar to the ages of fashion where curiosity is excited by the very stimulants which come in from outside, but to the truly loving need of seeing again, of finding again with tireless and ever keener eagerness, that which one has already known and loved, admired or adored, divine types of ancestral religion, divine legends, the history of the saints, epic tales of national history, the familiar scenes of life which conform to old customs, in a word, the traditional emotions which are summed up, for the artist and for his public, in a profound love for a remote past and in a profound hope in a long future on earth or in the posthumous future that is promised by religion. We do not demand the expression of fleeting impressions from architecture or music, impressions that are borrowed from foreign or from dead and artificially restored civilisations; we demand from them a vivid expression and reproduction of the impressions that are wrought into our life. We do not ask sculpture or painting to invent exotic or imaginary groups and scenes and landscapes, but to reproduce vividly and expressively the twelve apostles, St. Michael, St. Christopher, Christ, the Virgin, or family portraits or pictures representing the city of our birth with the dresses and celebrations and idiosyncracies which we think will last forever. We do not ask the epic or drama to inter-

---

[1] At Florence, the trades which were called the arts, and which deserved this name, were, indisputably, the cradle of the fine-arts.

est us by keeping us in ignorance of its climax or by the novelty of its subject, we ask it to vividly reproduce the legendary lore that we have known from childhood, the death of Prometheus or Hercules, the misfortunes of Œdipus, the drama of the creation from Lucifer to Christ or Anti-Christ, the death of Roland, etc.

These are the two principal characteristics of art proper in the ages of tradition. It may be seen that they are linked together. The art of these ages is, I will not say industrial, but professional, because it is formed by a slow accumulation of æsthetic processes which are transmitted with useful directions from father to son, and the cause which has produced this effect, that is to say, the habit of having one's heart and mind always turned towards the past, towards one's forebears and their subjective models, also makes it necessary for art to be the living and magical mirror of a past that is itself still living, of a past, in other terms, that is full of faith in its own future existence, instead of being the factitious resurrection of some extinct past or the translation of some foreign works. In ages of fashion, on the contrary, it must naturally happen that the forms of imported art show themselves detached from their stem, since it is the flower, and not the stem, that, in this case, attracts curiosity. Then art becomes handicraft more often than handicraft becomes art. And curiosity, the characteristic of these epochs, demands a misleading and irritating kind of satisfaction, which supplies it with a continuous stream of invention, of invention to order and by formula, of novels and dramas based upon fictitious happenings, of fantastic pictures, of unheard-of-music, of eclectic movements, Curious times want only artists of imagination; loving and believing times want artists imbued with faith and love.

We see that either because of its origin, or of its subject, or of its inspiration, the art of fashion differs from the art of custom. A difference that is, in many respects, analogous, distinguishes the two corresponding kinds of morality. Their origin, in the first place, is quite distinct. The

essentially religious virtues of tradition are the natural
flowering of the wants of the restricted group where they
blossom. Reflected virtues, namely those of a lower class
that seeks to appropriate to itself the moral qualities of an
aristocracy, those of a people which is taking moral or
immoral lessons from another, just as at the Restoration
England copied French morals, these reflected virtues are
an ethical veneer, an arbitrary decoration of the everyday conduct which they overlie, but which is not in touch
with them. In such cases the borrowed virtues are even
unearthed from the past, but from a dead or fashion-
revived past. This phenomenon of moral mimicry, by which
fashion takes on a false air of custom, is not at all rare in
history. But moral *reforms*, where we see, for example,
virtues which had their *raison d'être* among the Hebrew
patriarchs or the Christians of the primitive Church, re-
appearing in the midst of the sixteenth century in Europe,
are, in reality, innovations which have been born in the soul
of an apostle in love with a past which he fails to understand, and which have subsequently spread abroad, thanks
to the general drawing of people's hearts into the ways
of free imitation. In this they absolutely resemble those
literary or artistic *renascences*, another kind of conventional archaism, which have often been seen. The objects
and the motives of the two kinds of morality which I am
comparing are no less clearly distinguished. Customary
duties impose upon the individual certain sacrifices in view
of certain peculiar but permanent wants of his walled-in
and exclusive society, of his family, tribe, city, canton, or
state. Borrowed duties, conventional and so-called national duties, order the individual to sacrifice himself to
more general interests, to interests that are scattered among
a large number of men, but to interests which are often
more transient and less lasting. The man of traditional
times draws the power to accomplish the sacrifice that is
demanded of him from the hereditary solidarity which
makes him one with the series of generations in which he
is a single link, in such a way that, in dying for his family,

for his tribe, or for his city, in order to contribute to the immortality of the great collective person of which he is a part, he thinks that he is devoting himself to himself. Moreover, he usually draws this power from the promises of his inherited and ancestral religion. This double source of energy dries up partly or wholly for the man of an innovating age. In such ages imitation frees itself from heredity, and ties between kindred, between forebears and descendants, are obliterated by the connections between the unrelated individuals who are detached from their families[1] and brought together by the age. In such ages, the clash of different religions or of religion and philosophy tends to engender scepticism. But the men of these periods substitute for these losses in part an entirely new development of the highest kind of moral energy, the sentiment of honour.

I mean honour, not in the sense of family and aristocracy, but in the democratic and individual sense, in the modern sense, since we are unquestionably passing through a period of fashion-imitation, one which is pre-eminently remarkable for its breadth and permanency. This second meaning, dating from the Italian Renascence, according to Buckle, must in reality have been formed wherever the

---

[1] Hence the individualistic character of fashion-morality, analogous to that of fashion-art This means that in the eyes of the artist, as in those of the moralist, individuals begin to count for something in themselves But this does not prevent duty in times of fashion having very general, although very fleeting, interests for its object, just as the works of art of the same times excel in photographing under the lineaments of an individual, widespread, although highly variable, psychological states. I have pointed out above the naturalistic character of fashion-morality and of fashion-art. "In the second half of the sixteenth century," M. Brunetière very truly says, "beneath the religious wars, the great question at stake is to know whether the antique morality, the morality that was founded in theology on the dogma of the fall of man, but in reality upon the experience of the natural perversity of man, is to be ousted from the government of human conduct, and whether *nature* alone will suffice from this time on to maintain the social institution." Here, it will be noted, incidentally, that the inspiration of naturalism and individualism coincides with the inspiration of optimism Is it that pessimism, I mean true pessimism (the pessimism of Christianity and Janseism, for example), not the pure kind, belongs to ages of custom, and optimism to ages of fashion?

spread of *public morality* was rapid through the lowering of certain social barriers. Why is it, we shall be asked, that this desire for personal consideration must grow while the antique bases of morality, the family and religion, are being more and more undermined? Because the same cause which shakes the latter to their foundations is fit to consolidate and extend the former, I mean the progress of communication and of the indefinitely accelerated circulation of ideas in a domain that is being incessantly enlarged far and beyond the walls of clans, classes, creeds, or states. The substitution of fashion-imitation for custom-imitation results in breaking down pride of birth and dogmatic belief, but it also results in arousing, through the progressive assimilation of people's minds, the irresistible power of public opinion. Now, what is honour but a passive, spontaneous, and heroic obedience to public opinion?

We are witnesses to the birth and growth of this new and potent motive, whenever a young conscript passes out from the paternal roof to his regiment. At the end of a short time, he no longer thinks of the father for whom he had had a reverential fear, or of the field which he coveted, or of the young girl whom he was courting with the idea of founding a family; he thinks still less of the catechisings of his curate. All the springs of his laborious honesty and of his relatively pure morals have dried up. But his morality has changed rather than degenerated, and what he has lost in continence or in love of work he has regained in courage and in probity, because in addition to the thought of court-martial he has had to sustain him in his life of barrack-room discipline and at his post of duty on the field of battle the idea of avoiding, even at the price of death, shame or humiliation in the eyes of his comrades. At the same time he is conscious of being useful in the accomplishment of his new duties to a mass of men who have just become his fellows, to the great country which is assimilating him and for which he formerly cared so little, absorbed as he was in his domestic preoccupations.

To this I may add that if his new morality is adapted
to the care of more numerous, less personal, and more extensive interests, his old morality was fitted to watch over
less momentary and more lasting interests. In any case,
the effect of the sacrifices that are required by his new
duties reaches much farther, proportionally, in space than
in time, whereas, formerly, the sacrifices demanded of him
by his duties had a utility that was narrowly hemmed in
by his immediate surroundings, but that was relatively considerably prolonged into the future. All the strictly domestic and patriarchal, local and primitive virtues, female
chastity, for example, are privations that are undergone
for the advantage of a single family, to be sure, but for
the advantage of the whole posterity of that family. Inversely, modern morality, which is very indulgent to the
vices for which our grandchildren will alone have to suffer,
blames severely the faults which may react harmfully upon
our contemporaries, remote though these contemporaries
may be. In this, it seems as if the morality of ages of fashion resembled their politics. Whatever may be the form of
their government, the statesman of to-day differ from those
of other days both in their enlarged horizon of watchful-
ness over a larger number of similar interests subject simultaneously to identical laws, and by their much shorter
range of foresight. Formerly the feudal king of the *Isle-
de-France,* shut up in his narrow domain, looked forward
from the start to the development in future ages of this
fine realm of France and he toiled painfully on in the pursuit of this future ideal. We have seen the kinglet of
petty Prussia sacrifice the present in his calculation of a far
distant, imperial future which his grandchildren, alas! have
seen shine. Nowadays, would any political assembly in
any country whatsoever, beginning with Germany, consent to
sacrifice some actual interest in view of some benefit from
which only the second or third generation to follow would
profit? Far from that, it is to our descendants that we
charge up the bill of our debts and follies. I need not
explain, after all that has been said, how this striking con-

trast, this offsetting by extension of abbreviations in duration, is related to the distinction between the two forms of imitation.

But if it is true that every stream of fashion tends to betake itself to the big and tranquil lake of custom, this contrast can be but temporary. Without doubt, as long as the stream flows, the prescriptions or interdictions of morality will bear less and less upon acts that are useful or prejudicial to our children or grandchildren alone, especially upon certain facts of conjugal fidelity or infidelity, of filial piety or domestic waywardness, of cowardice or patriotic bravery, which were considered in other days cardinal virtues or capital crimes, but whose salutary or disastrous effects are experienced only in the long run. After me, the deluge, society will say. Unfortunately, society might end by perishing from the too frequent reiteration of this phrase. Besides, we have reason for thinking that after a time of progressive but transitory short-sightedness, collective forethought will begin again to apply itself to time after it has vent itself upon space, and that nations will become as widely conscious of their permanent as of their general interests. The moment will arrive when civilisation will, finally, at its culminating point, draw back upon itself, just as it has already done so many times in the course of history, in Egypt, in China, at Rome, at Constantinople. . . . The past speaks for the future Then morality will become again, in many respects, what it has been, distinguished for grandeur and logic. Casuistry will spring up again in a more rational setting. To the duties of honour, an artificial morality which contents an age enslaved to a fickle public opinion, the duties of conscience, as our fathers knew them, will succeed. They will be as imperious, as absolute, as deeply rooted in the human heart, but they will be superior in light and reason. And at the same time, art, turning back from its brilliant vagaries, will drench itself again in the profound sources of faith and love.

There is much to be said in explanation of the historic

phenomenon of renascences, the hybrid phenomenon of
fashion and custom, to which I referred above. It is a
subject which is a little distinct from that of the present
chapter, for in connection with it we do not see a new fashion becoming in its turn a custom, but we see it taking on
the aspect of some ancient custom. This additional relation of the two branches of imitation deserves to be
examined. In science and industry, an entirely new idea
and one that it gives itself out as new, can spread through
fashion; for in its birth it brings with it experimental
proofs of truth and utility. But the case is different in
the fine arts, in religion, in literature, in philosophy itself
up to a certain point, in statecraft, in morals, and, finally,
wherever the choice of solutions is abandoned in large
measure to the discretionary power of the judgment and is
unable to depend upon a rigid demonstration. In this case,
upon what authority, that of facts being pretty nearly lacking, could fashion depend for the triumph of its novelties
over the old strongholds of custom? By what right is
she entitled to array the products of enterprising reason or
imagination against time-proved rules and ideas and institutions? (Therefore, if she wish to succeed, she must assume the mask of the enemy and besiege existing custom
by unearthing some ancient custom long since fallen into
discredit and rejuvenated for the needs of her cause. And
so we see all religious reforms pretending, with more or
less complete sincerity, to return to the forgotten sources
of the religion upon which they were grafted. This was the
pretence of the protestantism of all the sects of the sixteenth
century, the first century to inaugurate the *grande mode* of
modern times. It was also the pretence of the Mussulman
sect of the Ouahabites, which was born in the eighteenth
century and which spread and is still spreading in Asia
and Africa, where it boasts of steeping Islam again in
the primitive Koran (see *Revue scientifique*, November 5,
1887). And this is the pretence of all the sects which
swarm over the old but still fruitful trunks of Hindooism
and Brahmanism and which think that they are restoring

the antique religion of India to its original state. This was also the thought of Buddhism, the Protestantism of the East.

If this is so with religious reforms, it is no less so with reforms in literature or art. When fresh sap begins to circulate in the souls of artists and poets, it is under the form of a renascence of some distant past which it interprets to the outer world. Shall I cite the humanism of the Italian Renascence, the Ciceronianism of Erasmus, the neo-Hellenism or neo-Latinism of the architects and sculptors and painters of the fifteenth and sixteenth centuries, the neo-Gothic flavour of the romanticism of 1830? From the time of Hadrian, the craze for Latin poetry, which had raged among the upper classes at Rome from the time of Augustus, and which had spread step by step to the provinces, began to subside. Why? Because a new fashion put in its appearance, that of the new Greek sophists, whose art had been born again—a true renascence, indeed,—and had aroused admiration and, later on, general imitation. This fascination lasted a long time and produced a factitious and, likewise, archaic reawakening of Greek patriotism.

The same thing is true of legislative reform. The top of fashion, in this connection, was a fashion which, in the sixteenth century, made all the codes of Europe uniform. It consisted of unearthing the Corpus Juris and of introducing under cover of the Roman name all the salutary or pernicious usurpations of lawmakers or kings or emperors. The same thing is even true of political reforms. Sometimes this is obvious. The French parliament, for example, in inaugurating an entirely new and original control of the royal power by judicial authority, invoked the antique customs of the Franks and imagined that they were resurrecting the political constitution that they saw in their dreams. At other times, although it is less obvious, it is none the less true. Even the French Revolution prided itself upon copying Athens and Sparta. Finally, the very boldest of philosophers, men who were the least respectful of precedents, our French Encyclopedists, judged that the support that logic seemed to lend to their plans of social reconstruction was insufficient; and the at times sincere desire to *rediscover* the forgotten attributes of the human race, to reproduce in its primal purity the supposed state of nature, combines in their writing, as well as it can, with their cult of Reason. A great deal of prehistoric archæology is mixed up with their idealogy.

Moreover, renascences, let me repeat, are more apparent than real. Burckhardt shows that the resurrection of antiquity was only one of the innovations of the fifteenth century in Italy, of the Italian Renascence, and that, in its re-birth, Greek and Latin antiquity was strongly Italianised. Besides, this innovation was only a fashion following, like any other, in the tail of certain discoveries, namely, the archæological discoveries resulting from the diggings in the sacred soil of antique Rome or in the libraries of the monasteries. Prior to these numerous finds of statues, inscriptions, manuscripts, and ruins of all kinds, antiquity may well have been taken on faith and admired, but it could not have been imitated.

The Reformation, I may say, was only a German Renascence, just as the Renascence was only an Italian Reformation. The return to life and youth which Italy exacted from the old classical antiquity that she was said to be imitating, Germany demanded from its alleged and still more imaginary imitation of primitive Christianity. (It would be a mistake, between parentheses, to see in the first of these two movements merely the prelude of the second. The Humanists were merely the chance allies of the Lutherans. As a matter of fact, each movement was a complete evolution in itself. The Renascence was not, as has been said, a superficial revolution of people's souls; it was, for a narrow group of souls reared in the aristocracy of art and intellect, *a profound dechristianisation* which, underneath the Reformation, was to spread among us in the eighteenth century.) As the Renascence was connected with discoveries in arts and letters, so the Reformation proceeded, in large part, from the invention of printing. The idea of acquiring by the mere reading of sacred books the highest type of knowledge, a full solution of the most difficult problems, could only have arisen when the sudden and extraordinary diffusion and invasion of books, hitherto unknown, had developed a general epidemic of reading and of the illusion of thinking that books were the source of all truth. It was perhaps because of this, Germany being the birthplace of printing, that Protestantism was German in its origin. Otherwise, this fact would be surprising, for, prior to the Reformation, all great heresies, all attempted rebellions against the Church, started from the South of Europe, a more civilised region than the North.

Fashion and custom have still another relation of which I have not spoken, and which requires to be distinguished both from the revival of an antique custom by a recent fashion and from the consolidation of a fashion into a custom. I refer to the very frequent cases in which a new fashion creeps, in order to introduce itself, under a still living custom which it insensibly changes and appropriates to itself.

For example, it has been noted that long after the importation of bronze among communities that had previously been restricted to the chipping of flints, bronze tools and weapons were made to imitate the forms of entirely outworn tools and weapons of flint. It has also been proved that Greek architecture is explained by the reproduction in stone or marble of the peculiarities of the huts of the primitive populations of Hellas. The most ornate columns of the temples of Miletus or Athens were modelled upon ancient wooden structures. The architectural type of China is explained by the primitive tent. What does this mean but the grafting of new fashions upon the still living trunk of old customs? Does it not imply the necessity of this grafting among societies based on custom, and is it not, above all, an act of art and of morality in order to make innovations live and endure? When the fashion of iron or marble was introduced after the example of foreign

peoples, the only way it could become acclimated was
through adopting the uniform of national usages

An entirely parallel phenomenon is produced when new
maxims or sentiments of morality filter into a social group
whose horizon tends to enlarge and, in order to make themselves acceptable, have to have themselves introduced by the
very prejudices whose place they are taking. Thus in a
clan where only contracts between blood relations have
ever been recognised as valid, contracts are made with
strangers by means of such ceremonies as the intermingling
of drops of blood to counterfeit consanguinity. Thus,
when the feudal disintegration of the Middle Ages began
to give way to monarchical centralisation, the duty of
fidelity to the king, which was soon to be substituted for the
duty of the vassal towards his over-lord, began by affecting
a feudal colour, and seemed to express nothing more than
a more general tie of vassalage, etc.

CHAPTER VIII

REMARKS AND COROLLARIES

AFTER having studied the principal laws of imitation we have still to make their general meaning clear, to complete them by certain observations, and to point out several important consequences which proceed from them.

/The supreme law of imitation seems to be its tendency towards indefinite progression. This immanent and immense kind of ambition [1] is the soul of the universe. It expresses itself, physically, in the conquest of space by light, vitally, in the claim of even the humblest species to cover the entire globe with its kind. It seems to impel every discovery or innovation, however futile, including the most insignificant individual innovations, to scatter itself through the whole of the indefinitely broadened social field. But unless this tendency be backed up by the coming together

---

[1] Let me express the full depth of my thought upon the unknown and unknowable source of universal repetitions. It may be that an immense and all-pervasive ambition is not a sufficient explanation. I confess that at times another occurs to me. I reflect upon the fact that delight in endless and tireless self-repetition is one of the signs of love; that it is the peculiarity of love, both in art and life, to continually say and resay the same thing, to continually picture and repicture the same subject. Then I ask myself whether this universe, which seems to delight in its monotonous repetitions, might not reveal, in its depths, an infinite outpouring of hidden love, greater even than that of ambition. I cannot keep from conjecturing that all things, in spite of intestine struggles, have been made, separately, *con amore,* and that only in this lies, evil and misfortune notwithstanding, the explanation of their beauty And yet, at other times, in reflecting upon death, I am led to justify pessimism. Everything repeats itself, and nothing persists These are the two characteristics of our universe, the second growing out of the first. Why should it be chimerical to conceive of a perfect world, of a world that was both stable and original, where everything lasted, and where nothing repeated itself? But a truce to these dreams!

of inventions which are logically and teleologically auxiliary, or by the help of the prestige which belongs to alleged superiorities, it is checked by the different obstacles
which it has successively to overcome or to turn aside. These
obstacles are the logical and teleological contradictions
which are opposed to it by other inventions, or the barriers
which have been raised up by a thousand causes, by racial
pride and prejudice, for the most part, between different
families and tribes and peoples and, within each people or
tribe, between different classes. Consequently, if a good
idea is introduced in one of these groups, it propagates
itself without any difficulty until it finds itself stopped short
by the group's frontiers. Fortunately, this arrest is only
a slowing up. It is true that, at first, in the case of class
barriers, a happy innovation which has happened to originate and make its way in a lower class, does not, during periods of hereditary aristocracy and of physiological inequality, so to speak, spread further, unless the
advantage of adopting it appear plain to the higher classes;
but, on the other hand, innovations which have been made
or accepted by the latter classes easily reach down, as I
have shown already, to those lower levels which are accustomed to feel their prestige. And it happens that, as a
result of this prolonged descent, the lower strata gradually
mount up, step by step, to swell the highest ranks with their
successive increments. Thus, through assimilating themselves with their models, the copies come to equal them, that
is, they become capable of becoming models in their turn,
while assuming a superiority which is no longer hereditary,
which is no longer centred in the whole person, but which
is individual and vicarious. The march of imitation from
top to bottom still goes on, but the inequality which it
implies has changed in character. Instead of an aristocratic, intrinsically organic inequality, we have a democratic inequality, of an entirely social origin, which we may
call inequality if we wish, but which is really a reciprocity
of invariably impersonal prestiges, alternating from individual to individual and from profession to profession. In

this way, the field of imitation has been constantly growing and freeing itself from heredity.

In the second place, in regard to barriers between families, tribes, or peoples, it is equally true that while the knowledge or institutions or beliefs or industries which belong to any group while it is powerful and triumphant, spread without difficulty to neighbouring groups that have been conquered and brought low; on the other hand, the examples of the weak and vanquished, if we except the case of those whose civilisation is obviously superior, are practically nonexistent for their conquerors. Hence it follows, parenthetically, that war is much more of a civiliser for the conquered than for the conqueror, for the latter does not deign to learn from the former, whereas the former submits himself to the ascendency of victory and borrows from his enemy a number of fruitful ideas to add to his national store. The Egyptians took nothing from the books of the captive Hebrews. They made a great mistake. Whereas the Jews gained much inspiration from the hieroglyphics of their masters. But, as I have said, when a people dominates others through its brilliancy, others, who heretofore had imitated none but their forefathers, imitate it. Now, this extra-national propagation of imitation, to which I have given the name of fashion, is, at bottom, merely the application to the relations between states of the law which governs the relations between classes. Thanks to the invasion of fashion, imitation always descends from the state which is for the time being superior to those which are for the time inferior, just as it descends from the highest to the lowest rungs of the social ladder. Consequently, we shall not be surprised to see the rule of fashion producing effects in the former case similar to those produced by it in the matter. In effect, just as the radiation of the examples of the higher classes results in preparing the way for their enlargement, where imitation is facile and reciprocal, through the absorption of the lower classes by them, so the contagious prestige of preponderating states results in preparing the way for their extension, for the extension of states which were originally families, then tribes, and, later, cities and nations, and which have been constantly enlarged through the assimilation of neighbours whom they have annexed, or through the annexation of neighbours whom they have assimilated.

Another analogy. Just as the play of imitation from top to bottom leads, in its continuation, to so-called democratic equality, that is to say, to the fusion of all classes into one, in which reciprocal imitation is admirably practised through the acceptance of one another's respective superiorities, so a prolonged process of fashion-imitation ends by putting pupil-peoples upon the same level, both in their armaments and in their arts and sciences, with their master-people. It creates a kind of federation between them like that which is called in modern times, for example, the European balance of power. By this is meant the reciprocity of every kind of service or exchange which goes on incessantly between the different great centres which divide up European civilisation. In this way, in international relations, the free and unimpeded domain of imitation has been enlarged with scarcely an interruption.

But, at the same time, Tradition and Custom, the conservative forms of imitation, have been fixing and perpetuating its new acquisitions and consolidating its increments in the heart of every class of people that has been raised up through the example of higher classes or of more civilised neighbours. At the same time, too, every germ of imitation which may have been secreted in the brain of any imitator in the form of a new belief or aspiration, of a new idea or faculty, has been steadily developing in outward signs, in words and acts which, according to the law of the march from within to without, have penetrated into his entire nervous and muscular systems.

Here then we have the laws of the preceding chapters in focus from the same point of view. Through them, the tendency of imitation, set free from generation, towards geometric progression, expresses and fulfils itself more and more. Every act of imitation, therefore, results in

the preparation of conditions that will make possible and
that will facilitate new acts of imitation of an increasingly
free and rational and, at the same time, precise and definite
character. These conditions are the gradual suppression
of caste, class, and nationality barriers and, I may add, the
lessening of distances through more rapid means of locomotion, as well as through greater density of population.
This last condition is realised in the degree that fruitful,
that is to say, widely imitated, agricultural or industrial inventions, and the equally fruitful discovery of new lands
promote the world-wide circulation of the most inventive
and, at the same time, the most imitative races. Let us
suppose that all these conditions are combined and that
they are fulfilled in the highest degree. Then, wherever
a happy initiative might show itself in the whole mass of
humanity, its transmission by imitation would be almost
instantaneous, like the propagation of a wave in a perfectly
elastic medium. We are approaching this strange ideal.
Already, in certain special phases, where the most essential
of the conditions which I have indicated happen to be
combined, social life reveals the reality of the aforesaid
tendency. We see it, for example, in the world of scholars,
who, although they are widely scattered, are in constant
touch with one another through multiple international communications. We see it, too, in the perpetual and universal
contact of merchants. Haeckel said in an address delivered
in 1882 on the success of Darwin's theories: "The prodigious influence which the decisive victory of the evolutionary
idea exercises over all the sciences, an influence which *grows
in geometric progression* year by year, opens out to us the
most consoling perspectives." In fact, the success of Darwin and Spencer has been amazingly swift. As for the
rapidity of commercial imitation as soon as it is given free
scope, it has been a matter for observation in every period,
not merely in our own. Read in Ranke the description of the
progress of Antwerp from 1550 to 1566. During those six-
teen years the commerce of that city with Spain doubled;
with Portugal, Germany, and France it was more than

tripled; with England, it increased twenty-fold! Unfortunately, war put an end to this prosperity. But in such intermittent flights we see the steady force which pushes on to indefinite commercial expansion.

I

It is now proper to bring to light a general observation, a special side of which I have just been indicating in pointing out the passing of unilateral into reciprocal imitation. The mere play of imitation has resulted, then, not only in extending it, but in making it two-sided as well. Now, this effect which imitation produces upon itself, it also produces upon many other connections between people. Ultimately it transforms all unilateral into mutual relations.

We ceased long ago to believe in Rousseau's " social contract." We know that far from having been the first tie between human wills, contract was a bond of slow formation, that it took centuries of subjection to the empire of the coercive *decree,* of the passively obeyed command, to suggest the idea of the reciprocal decree, as it were, of the complex bond by which two wills are linked together in alternate command and obedience. Nevertheless, many people still believe, although the error is quite similar, that exchange was the first step taken by mankind. This was not so at all. Before the idea of exchanging came that of present making or that of thieving, much simpler relations.[1] Perhaps you also believe that at the very outset men talked, discussed, and interchanged ideas with one another like the shepherds of an eclogue? Now, this exchange did not occur in primitive times any more than did that of men's products. Discussion presupposes the concession on both

---

[1] On this subject see Spencer's *Sociology,* Vol III., where he tells how gifts, which are at first voluntary and one-sided (either from the superior to the inferior, or inversely), become, little by little, habitual, obligatory, and reciprocal. But Spencer forgets to tell of the leading part played by imitation in all of this.

sides of the right of mutual enlightenment; but before that
it presupposes the possession of truth, that is to say, of an
individual perception or opinion which attributes to itself
the rightful power of being recognised by all normal minds.
Would the idea of this kind of power be possible without the
preliminary experience of such power as exercised by a
father, priest, or teacher? Is it not *dogma* that has alone
made possible the conception of *truth?* In the same way,
if some reader of idyls were inclined to think that primitive
men, even the gentlest savages, were familiar with courtesy
and mutual consideration, he should be shown the proofs
that urbanity in France and everywhere else, born as it was
of the non-reciprocal homages and compliments paid to
chiefs, over-lords, and kings, is the gradual vulgarising, as
history clearly shows, of this one-sided flattery as it becomes
a mutual thing in its expansion. Alas! We cannot even
believe that war, if by that word we mean the exchange of
blows inflicted by weapons, which are more or less alike,
was the first international relation between human groups
The chase, that is to say, the destruction or expulsion of
some defenceless being, of a peaceful tribe by a brigand
horde, preceded anything worthy of the name of war.[1]

Now, how did the human chase come to make way for
human warfare? How did flattery come to make way for
courtesy, credulity for free enquiry, dogmatism for mutual
instruction? Docility for voluntary agreement and absolutism for self-government? Privilege for equality before the
law, present-making or theft for exchange,[2] slavery for in-

---

[1] I refer to human relations; for in the relations of primitive man to
animals—relations which have no direct bearing upon sociology—the
opposite *seems* to have occurred, since, as we have seen already, man
fought with savage beasts before he had the means to hunt them

[2] In the beginning the administration of the sacrament was gratu-
itous; it was an out-and-out gift (On this subject see Paul Viollet,
Histoire du droit français, p 385). "Little by little, communities came
to respond to these gifts with others, with presents that were spontaneous, and not in the least obligatory, until, finally, these offerings
came to be dues. Fire-insurance companies are societies for mutual aid
They date back to 1786 under this reciprocal form But they were preceded by non-mutual benefit societies, by systematic almsgiving for the

dustrial co-operation? And, finally, primitive marriage, the one-sided appropriation of the wife by the husband, for marriage as we know it, the appropriation of the wife by the husband and of the husband by the wife? I answer: through the slow and inevitable effect of imitation, of imitation under all its forms. It will be easy to quickly prove this. I need do nothing more than indicate the transitory phases that have been traversed in the course of the above transformations.

In the beginning, one man always monopolises the power and the right to teach; no one disputes it to him. Everything that he says must be believed by all, and he alone has the right to deliver oracles. But at last the desire arises among those who have drunk in with the greatest credulity the words of their master, to be infallible like him, to resemble him in that particular as well. Hence those efforts of genius on the part of philosophers which will end one day by bringing about the recognition of every individual's right to spread his own particular faith and to evangelise even his pristine masters. But before this they must limit themselves to more humble pretensions; and imitation of the theologians is so thoroughly the spirit of their dissimulated revolt that they feel happy if, while they submit without discussion to dogma, although to dogma which is for the first time hemmed into a particularly assigned sphere, they succeed in dogmatising in their own little domain by imposing upon scholars and scientists certain capital ideas which are laid down as incontrovertible, the theories of Aristotle or Plato, for example, in as much as they are not contrary to religious faith. On the other hand, at the same period of transition, scientists who also bow down to a certain extent under the metaphysical yoke, know how to dogmatise in their turn. It is a series of dogmatic rebounds which make evident the need of imitation from which this singular stage of thought

benefit of sufferers from fire (see Babeau, *La Ville sous l'ancien régime*, II, 146) The right of divorce began by being one-sided, to the exclusive advantage of the husband, before it became reciprocal, etc.

proceeds. It is nevertheless true that the emancipation of human reason comes from the same source. In fact, there is something contradictory and artificial in the attitude of the mind which already feels its own power, but which, believing in its right to impose its convictions without discussion upon others, nevertheless believes that it is its duty to accept without examination the convictions of others. So much timidity is inconsistent with so much pride. And so the time comes when a bolder and more logical mind conceives the desire of dogmatising without restriction, of asserting and imposing its convictions both above and below. Its example is at once followed, and discussion becomes general. Free thought is nothing else but the mutual conflict and mutual restraint of many such self-asserting, contradictory individual infallibilities.

Originally, one man commands and the others obey. Authority, like instruction, is monopolised by the father or the teacher. The rest of the group has no other function but to obey. But this autocratic authority becomes an object of envy. The ambitious among those that are ruled over conceive the idea of reconciling their subjection with their craving for power. At first they dream of limiting, of circumscribing the authority exerted over them by their rulers, then of diverting it, still in a limited and definite form, to the subjects next in rank. We have here a hierarchy of limited but indisputable commanding powers. The feudal system was the realisation of this idea on the greatest scale. But, as a matter of fact, the military organisation of any period is its most obvious incarnation, and this example shows us that the conception in question, just as the preceding and analogous conception, that of the hierarchy of dogmatic systems, answers to a permanent need in societies, their need of patriotic defence or of educating their children Later on, however, men dare more, they wish to be able to command in certain respects those whom in other respects they obey and *vice versa,* or to be able to command for a time those who have been or who will be obeyed at another time. This reciprocity is obtained by recruiting the men in the public service from all classes, by rotation in office, and by the right of universal suffrage. The mere fact of voting implies on the part of the voter a pledge to submit to whomsoever may be elected and in this way imparts to the decrees of the latter a character of tacit contract. Can the popular sovereignty which is formed in this way be said to be anything else but kingly sovereignty multiplied into millions of examples? Without the example of the latter, as it is notably embodied in Louis XIV, would the former have ever been conceived?

All social changes or advances which have been effected by the substitution of the reciprocal for the unilateral relation, and which I deem consequences of the action of imitation, are attributed by Spencer to the replacement of " militancy " by " industrialism." But the development of industry itself is subject to the law in question. In fact, the first germ of industry is unpaid slave labour or the labour of woman, the born slave of primitive man. The Arab, for example, is waited on, nourished, dressed, and even lodged by his numerous wives, just as the Roman was by his slaves. For this reason polygny is as necessary to him as our numerous tradesmen to us. The relations between producer and consumer begin, then, like those between father and son or between husband and wife, by being abusive. But by dint of working gratis for others, the slave aspires to make someone work gratis for himself, and, thanks to a gradual restriction in the power of his masters in no longer controlling all his acts or all his time, he ends by accumulating savings which first enable him to buy his freedom and then to purchase one or more slaves, his victims in turn. Had he dreamed only of freedom, he would have hastened to enjoy it in isolation, *providing for his own wants himself.* But, as a matter of fact, he copies the wants of his ancient masters; in the satisfaction of these wants, he wishes to be served, like them, by others; and as this condition becomes more and more general, the times comes when all these ancient emancipated slaves, all of whom pretend to have slaves, alternately or mutually serve one another. Hence division of labour

and industrial co-operation.[1] Of course, let it be said once
for all, the desire of imitation would not have succeeded in
effecting either the aforesaid transformations or those I am
about to mention had not certain inventions or discoveries
made them possible. The invention of the water-mill, for
example, in lightening slave labour to a considerable degree,
prepared the way for the slave's emancipation; and, in
general, if a sufficient number of machines had not been successively invented, we might still have slaves in our midst.
Scientific discoveries, notably astronomical ones, have alone
given the opportunity to individual reason to fight advantageously against dogmatic authority. Juristic discoveries
or inventions, the dictation of new legal formulas by writers
or publicists, have alone permitted national sovereignty to
manifold and thereby replace the sovereignty of royalty. But
it is nevertheless true that the desire to imitate the superior,
to be, like him, believed in, obeyed, and waited upon, was an
immense, although latent, force which urged on the transformations I have mentioned; and it needed only the *necessary accident* of these inventions or discoveries to be developed.

[1] The more mutual services of all kinds become, in the course of
industrial and commercial progress, the more arbitrary and capricious
is the character assumed by the wants which are thereby satisfied.
The consumer, who is also a producer, determines more and more how
he is to be served, and when he is to be served. He determines to make
everything cater to his momentary desires, no matter how fleeting and
extravagant they may be This is called, in high-flown language, the
emancipation of the individual. Now, this may be readily explained
through the laws of imitation. In the beginning, capriciousness is the
monopoly of the master, the *pater familias* or king, who has himself
waited upon by his children, his slaves, or his subjects without
reciprocity. It is also the monopoly of the god whom prostrate adorers
serve, without the right of demanding any equivalent from him for the
sacrifices made at his feet Therefore, if reciprocity of services has only
been brought about, in the long run, by a prolonged and free-spread
imitation of the one-sided service by which heads of families, kings,
and the nobility modelled upon them, gods and demi-gods are benefited,
it is natural for consumers, in seeking to ape the rulers of a past time,
in their character of consumers at least, to affect to give to their needs an
air of somewhat royal and divine caprice In this way our growing
democratic independence and self-sufficiency has come in a straight line
from theocratic and monarchical absolutism.

Let us continue. The chase of man is, as I have said, the first international relation. A tribe, a folk, thanks to the discovery of some new weapon or of some new improvement of which it has the secret, exterminates or subjugates all its neighbours. Such undoubtedly were the rapid conquests of the ancient metal-possessing Aryans over the smooth- or rough-stone peoples; such were the American " settlements " of Europeans among the ill-fated Indians, a people without horses or game-supplying guns. Now, how was true war-fare, a two-sided chase, according to the usage of civilised nations, substituted for this one-sided warfare, so to speak? Through the imitative spread among all these peoples of the weapons and tactics which had led to the triumph of one of their number. But they dream of imitating this conqueror still further, they seek to obtain a military monopoly like him, to discover some overpowering weapon which will make them invincible and will again reduce war to a chase. Fortunately, this dream has never been fulfilled except in a slight degree, although the Prussians with their needle-rifles did in fact treat the Austrians at Sadowa as a sportsman does a rabbit. As an intermediate stage between these two terms of evolution, I may mention certain barbarous epochs in which a people which has been completely overthrown and made tributary consoles itself for its defeat by crushing without a motive one of its more feeble neighbours and making it in turn pay tribute. In Gaul, in Cæsar's time, cer-tain peoples were *clients* of others, an international arrange-ment which could be defined as the feudal system applied to inter-state relations.

I have kept to the last an example which, although it is the least important, is the best fitted to illustrate the truth of my ideas. In a democratic society, a society which has always been preceded by aristocratic, monarchical, or theo-cratic rule, we may see the people in the street bow to one another, address one another with mutual politeness, and shake hands with one another. Whence come these usages? I leave to Spencer the task of pointing out in a masterly way, the royal or religious source of all this and of showing how,

the prostration of the whole body became slowly transformed
into a slight inclination of the figure or uncovering of the
head.   Let me add that if removing the hat is but the much
modified survival of the primitive obeisance, it is also the
mutualised form of the latter.   I may say as much of the
homage or flattery of the court whose crude incense, burned
on the altar of the mighty, suffocates us when a puff of it
reaches us over the distance of a century or two in the dedication of some old book.   The compliments which well-bred
people pay each other to-day are far from being so exaggerated, but they have the advantage of being reciprocal.
So, too, are those visits which were formerly, in their character of homage, unilateral.   Politeness is merely reciprocity
of flattery.   Moreover, we know beyond a doubt that the
desire of the petty potentate for ambassadors, of the marquis
for pages, of the courtier for a court, that the general need
of being flattered, waited on, and saluted like a nobleman,
was the secret factor which little by little, in France and
elsewhere, made every man polite.   It began with the court,
then reached the city, then the chateaux, and then all classes
to the very lowest.   The urbanity which characterised the
ancient *régime* from the time of Louis XIV was the intermediate state, analogous to the transitory phases that were
referred to above.   Each of the innumerable ranks into
which the society of that period was broken up forced the
rank below it to pay it gratuitious courtesies, visits and obeisances, which it did not return.[1]   It was a hierarchy of
impertinences, as La Bruyère observes somewhere.   But as

[1] Or, in case the superior did make obeisances, and pays visits and
compliments, it was always the inferior who began the saluting, the visit-
ing, and the complimenting.   At that time there was an obligatory
salutation of class by class—as of rank by rank; to-day, we know only
the salutation of man by man, and it is arranged in such away that
the same man is not always the first to bow.   We find a description in
La Bruyère of the transition of the unilateral to the reciprocal courtesy.   His Ménippe, when people bow to him " *is embarrassed to know
whether or not he should return it,* and, while he is deliberating, you
have already passed him by."   This trait is truly obsolete.   Do we ever
see anyone, in these days, no matter how high his position, hesitating to
return the greeting of the humblest of his fellow citizens?

we near the close of this vanished world, we perceive that courtesies are becoming mutual and that "equality" is approaching. In fact, of all the levelling methods that have been invented in the course of civilisation perhaps none is as powerful and as inconspicuous as that of politeness in manners and customs. What Cicero said of friendship, *amicitia pares aut facit aut invenit*, applies perfectly to urbanity and especially to the life of polite society. The drawing room admits equals only or equalises those whom it admits. Through this latter feature, it constantly tends to diminish, even outside of itself, those social inequalities which within it are immediately effaced. When hierarchical functionaries of very unequal rank meet very frequently in society, their relations show the effects of it even during the interval between their social meetings. Polite manners are even superior to railroads in overcoming distances, not only between civil or military functionaries, but also between classes which eventually draw nearer to one another by virtue of bowing to or shaking hands with one another. In our changing society thousands of people are daily flattered by hearing themselves addressed as *sir* or *madam*. In this, as in so many other respects, in its countenance of the rules of fashion, in its devotion to the philosophic ideas of the eighteenth century, the nobility of the old *régime* helped to undermine its own foundations and "buried itself in its triumph."

II

The preceding considerations upon the transition of the unilateral to the reciprocal lead us quite naturally to treat of a question of greater interest and of one which should have been handled by sociologists, I mean the problem of what is *reversible* and what *irreversible* in *history*.[1] Every-

---

[1] I do not use the words *reversible* and *irreversible* in the same sense which they have in legal phraseology and in the dictionary, but in the construction which is given to them by physicists, especially in thermodynamics, where a mechanism is called *reversible* which can act indifferently in either of two opposite directions.

body feels that in certain respects a society can pass in a precisely opposite direction through certain phases that it has already traversed, but that in other respects it is cut off from any such regression. We have seen above that after having passed from custom to fashion, communities can go back from fashion to custom—to custom that has broadened, out, to be sure, never to that which has been narrowed in;—but can they, after they have substituted reciprocal for unilateral relations, retrograde from the former to the latter? They cannot, and for a reason that I have already implied. "Monopolies," Cournot very justly remarks, "great trading or fighting corporations, the slave trade, negro slavery, and all the colonial institutions which go with it, are things for which the world has no further wish, which have disappeared or which are about to disappear, without our being able to think that they will ever return any more than the slavery or the forum of antiquity or than mediæval feudalism." This is true, but upon what is this conviction based? The reason should be stated, and yet Cournot does not state it. We have learned that this necessary and irreversible transition from monopoly to commercial freedom, from slavery to exchange of services, etc., is a corollary of the laws of imitation. Now, these laws may cease to act, either in part or in whole, and, in this case, a society perishes partially or completely; but the laws cannot be *reversed*.

Again, is it conceivable for a great empire, like the Roman Empire of Marcus Aurelius, to turn about and become first an Italian republic Hellenised by a Scipio, then an uncultivated and fanatical republic governed by a Cato, then a little barbarous village organised by a Numa? Or can it even be conceived that after having passed from a violent to an astute and voluptuous state of criminality, as is always the case, and from crimes to vices, a society ceases to be vicious to again become austere and sanguinary? We could as well conceive of an adult organism retrograding from maturity to youth, from youth to infancy, and ending by returning to the ovum from which it issued, or of a burnt-out star, like the moon, setting itself to retraversing the exhausted series of its ancient geological periods or of its vanished faunas and floras. Dissolution is never, in spite of Spencer's opinion to the contrary, the symmetrical pendant of evolution. Does that mean that the world has really one direction and one goal, or, rather, that all reality, in its constant discontent. with its destiny and in its preference for the unknown or even for annihilation as against its own past, refuses primarily to relive its life, to retrace its path?

I hasten to add that, on one of its important sides, historical reversibility or irreversibility cannot be explained by the laws of imitation alone. Successive inventions and discoveries, which imitation lays hold of in order to spread them abroad, do not follow one another accidentally. A rational tie which we do not need to dwell upon here, but which has been clearly pointed out by Auguste Comte in his conception of the development of the sciences and which has been definitely traced out by Cournot, in his masterly treatise upon *L'Enchaînement des idées fondamentales,* binds them to one another; and we cannot but admit that to a large extent their order, the order, for example, of mathematical discoveries from Pythagoras to us, might have been inverted. Here, irreversibility is based upon the laws of inventive logic, and not upon those of imitation.

Let us stop for a moment to justify, in passing, the distinction that I have just drawn. \The order of successive inventions is distinct from the order of successive imitations, although imitation does mean imitation of invention. The laws, in fact, which govern the first of these two series should not be confused with those, even the logical ones, which govern the second. It is not necessary for *all* imitations of inventions to pass through the terms of the irreversible series which inventions, whether they be imitated or not, must necessarily traverse one by one. We could, if put to it, conceive of a succession of inventions, which were logically antecedent to the final consummate one, unfolding in one and the same master mind; and, as a matter of fact, it is seldom that an inventor does not climb up several obscure rungs in such a ladder before reaching the illustrious step.

The laws of invention belong essentially to individual logic; the laws of imitation belong in part to social logic. Moreover, just as imitation does not fall exclusively within social logic, but depends upon extra-logical influence as well, is it not obvious that invention itself is produced mentally, through conditions which are not alone the apparition of premises in the mind of which it is the logical conclusion, but which are also other associations of ideas, called inspiration, intuition, genius?

Meanwhile, let us not forget that every invention and every discovery consists in the interference in somebody's mind of certain old pieces of information that have generally been handed down by others. What did Darwin's thesis about natural selection amount to? To having proclaimed the fact of competition among living things? No, but in having for the first time combined this idea with the ideas of *variability* and *heredity*.[1] The former idea, as it was proclaimed by Aristotle, remained sterile until it was associated with the two latter ideas. From that as a starting point, we may say that the generic term, of which invention is but a species, is the fruitful interference of repetitions. If this be true, I may perhaps be allowed to set forth, without emphasis, an hypothesis which occurs to me at this point. However numerous may be the different kinds of things which are repeated, if we suppose that the centres of these repetitive radiations, otherwise known as inventions or the biological or physical analogues of inventions, be regularly placed, their interferences may be foreseen; and these interferences or new centres will themselves present as much regularity in their disposition as did the primary centres. In such a universe, everything, however complex it might be, would be regular; nothing would either be or seem accidental. If, on the contrary, we assume that the primitive centres are irregular in position, the position of the secondary centres will also be unordered and their irregularity will equal that of the primary centres. Thus, there will never be in the world

* See Giard's article in the *Revue scientifique,* December 1, 1888.

anything but *the same quantity of irregularity*, so to speak,
only it will appear under the most changing forms. Let me
add that, in spite of all, these changing forms must have a
certain indefinable likeness. The original irregularity is
reflected in its enlarged copies, the derived irregularities.
From this I conclude that, although the idea of Repetition
dominates the whole universe, it does not constitute it. For
the bottom of it, I think, is a certain sum of innate, eternal,
and indestructible diversity without which the world would
be as monotonous as it is vast. Stuart Mill was led by his
reflections to a similar postulate.

Whatever may be said of the conjecture which I have
just hazarded, I am sure that there must be a combination
of the two kinds of laws which I have pointed out to entirely
explain the irreversible character of even the simplest social
transformations. Let us take, for example, the changes in
dress in France during the last three centuries and let us
suppose them to have occurred in an inverse order. The
hypothesis seems acceptable, *a priori;* at least it seems to
involve no greater contradiction than the idea of playing a
melody backwards, beginning with the last note and ending
with the first. Parenthetically, it is a strange thing that in this
way an entirely new melody is produced which, without having anything in common with the original one, is sometimes
satisfactory to one's ear. But imagine the courtiers of Louis
XIV dressed in the black coat and waistcoat, in the trousers
and silk hat of our present fashions. Imagine the trousers
gradually replaced by knickerbockers, the short hair by wigs,
the coats by embroidered, gilded, and many-coloured suits
with side-swords, and our democratic contemporaries decked
out like the followers of the Sun-King! It would be grotesque. There would be such an inconsistency between a
man's exterior and his ideas, between the succession of costumes and that of events, opinions, and customs, that it is
useless to dwell upon the impossibility of the thing. It is
impossible, because the events, the opinions and the customs
of which the clothes should be, up to a certain point, the
expression, are linked together from the time of Louis XIV

by a certain logic whose laws, as well as the laws of imitation, are opposed to the reversing of their melody, so to speak. This is so true that our hypothetical inversion would be infinitely less absurd if it were a question of women's ciothes. We could, at a pinch, without making any other change in modern history, imagine the court ladies of the seventeenth century wearing the dresses and even the hats of the fashionable ladies of the nineteenth century. We could imagine that they were followed by the crinoline and then by the high Greek bodice of Mme. Récamier and Mme. Tallien, and that these metamorphoses led our contemporaries to dress like Mme. de Maintenon or to arrange their hair like Mlle. de Fontange. It would be a little strange, but it would not be out of the question. And yet how is it that the current of women's fashions can be conceived of as turned back, without its being necessary to think of the current of customs and ideas as reversed also, whereas this is not true of men's fashions? This can undoubtedly be explained because of women's infinitely smaller participation in political and intellectual work; because of their dominant interest at all times and places in being physically pleasing, and because of the fundamental immutability of their nature which, in spite of their love of change, rebels against the wear of civilisation.

But let us note the fact that for women, as for men, it is impossible to conceive of a reversion from extreme complexity to primitive simplicity in that succession of inventions relating to weaving which has brought us goods of a more and more varied and intricate character. The laws of logic forbid it. In the same way they forbid us to suppose that the series of weapons which has reached us from the Middle Ages might have been reversed and that we might have passed from the needle-rifle to the flint-gun, to arquebuses, to cross-bows and long-bows, or from Krupp gun to culverin or balista. Besides, the laws of imitation show us the impossibility of admitting that after either men's or women's clothes had been, according to hypothesis, more or less alike in cut and material for all classes and provinces in France under Louis XIV, just as they are in our day, they could gradually become differentiated in different classes and in different parishes as of yore. This is inadmissible,[1] even were we to suppose at the same time that all our telegraphs and railroads had been destroyed after having existed under Louis XIV, and had carried away with them the intense desires for affiliation and assimilation to which they had given birth. For such a violent death on the part of our civilisation would reduce all its imitative functions to inertia, but it would not make them retroactive. A chronicle[2] tells us how Louis XIII was filled with admiration, upon his entrance into Marseilles, for the soldiers of the militia, and was especially pleased to see that "some of them were dressed in savage style, as *Americans,* Indians, Turks, and Moors." It was only under Louis XV, in fact, that a uniform became general. Imagine the effect produced by a return in our day, if one could be made, to such an antique medley of military garments! Such diversity of costume would not be tolerated, that is, it would not seem *natural* or normal, unless it spread abroad as a fashion; and, in this case, the very multiformity would be a kind of uniform, a similitude which consisted of copying the variety of others.

Let us turn our attention to the kind of historical irreversibility which is adequately accounted for by the laws of imitation, just as the laws of reproduction and of vibration are able to explain some, but not all, kinds of irreversibility in nature. A great national language cannot return to the little local dialect from which it has sprung. Not that it cannot be broken up by some political catastrophe into fragments which will become dialects. But, in this case, the differentiation of dialects will be due to the compulsory imprisonment in each province of the linguistic innovations that have sprung up in the place and that formerly would have radiated to the remotest part of the land. Moreover, each dialect that is made in this way will not resemble the primitive dialect in the least, nor will it incline to reproduce

---

[1] What becomes here of the famous law of progressive differentiation considered as a necessity of universal evolution?

[2] See Babeau, *La Ville sous l'ancien régime.*

the latter. It will tend to spread over to its neighbours and to its own good to re-establish unity of language over a vast area. What I say of language applies also to religion. But let us cast a glance over the social life in its entirety.

It has often been remarked that civilisation has the effect of raising the level of the masses from an intellectual and moral, from an æsthetic and economic point of view, rather than of rearing still higher in these different respects the higher peaks of society. But this vague, indefinite formula has been not unjustly the subject of refutation because of failure to point out the cause of the phenomenon in view. This cause we know. Since every invention which has once been launched clear of the mass of those that are already established in the social environment, must spread out and establish itself in turn by winning a place for itself in one class after another until it reaches the very lowest, it follows that the final result to which the indefinite continuation of all these outspreadings from centres which appear at distant points and in high places, must be a general and uniform illumination. It is in this way, by virtue of the law of vibratory radiation, that the sources of heat as they appear one after another tend to produce, according to a famous deduction of physicists, a great universal equilibrium of temperature which is higher than the actual temperature of interstellar space, but lower than that of suns. It is in this way, too, that the dissemination of species according to the law of their geometric progression, or, in other terms, of their prolific radiation, tends to cover the entire earth, which is still very unequally peopled, with a uniform stratum of living beings which will be denser throughout its whole extent than the average density of its present population. Obviously, the terms of our comparisons correspond exactly. The surface of the earth is the domain that is open to the radiation of light, just as space is the domain that is open to that of heat and light and as the human species, inasmuch as it is a living species, is the domain that is open to the spread of inventive genius. After this statement, we can understand how cosmopolitan and democratic assimilation is an inevitable tendency of history for the same reason that the complete and uniform peopling of the globe and the complete and uniform calorification of space are the objects of the vital and of the physical universe. It is so of necessity, for of the two chief forces, invention and imitation, which help us to interpret the whole of history, the former, the source of privileges, monopolies, and aristocratic inequalities, is intermittent, rare, and eruptive only at certain infrequent periods, whereas the latter, which is so democratic and levelling, is continuous and incessant like the stream deposition of the Nile or Euphrates. But we can understand also that it may well happen that at periods when works of genius crowd upon and stimulate one another, in feverish and inventive ages like ours, the progress of civilisation is accompanied by a momentary increase of every kind of inequality, or, if the imaginative fever has centred in one place, of a special kind. In our day, when the creative spirit has turned primarily towards the sciences, the distance between our most distinguished scholars and the most uncultivated dregs of our population is much greater from the point of view of the sum and substance of learning than it was in the Middle Ages or antiquity. In the innovating periods of which I speak the whole question consists of knowing whether the precipitate eruption of inventions has been faster than their current of example. Now, this is a question of fact which statistics alone can solve.

Believing that the transition from an aristocratic to a democratic order is irreversible, Tocqueville refuses to think that any aristocracy can be formed in a democratic environment. But I must be clear on this point.[1] If, in conse-

---

[1] Let us note that through a regular and uninterrupted series of transformations, the ecclesiastical organisation of Christian Europe passed from an evangelical, equality-loving democracy to the aristocracy of the early bishops, then to the modified monarchy of the Bishop of Rome, as it was limited by the Councils, and, finally, to the absolutism of papal infallibility. This is the exact opposite of the evolution accomplished by secular society. But, on the other hand, in this case as in that, the evolution has been from multiformity to uniformity, from disintegration to centralisation.

quence of the cause of which we know, societies hasten·
towards an increasing assimilation and an incessant accumulation of similarities, it does not follow that they are also
progressing towards a greater and greater development of
democracy. For imitative assimilation is only the stuff out
of which societies are made; this stuff is cut out and put into
use by social logic, which tends to the most solid kind of
unification through the specialisation and co-operation of
aptitudes, and through the specialisation and mutual confirmation of minds. It is therefore quite possible and even
probable that a very strong hierarchy may be the destined
goal of any civilisation,[1] although every consummate civilisation which has reached its ultimate fruition is marked by
the diffusion of the same wants and ideas, if not by the same
powers·and wealth, throughout the mass of its citizens.
This much, however, may be granted to Tocqueville—after
an aristocracy which is based upon the hereditary prestige
of birth has been destroyed in a country, it can never come
to life again. We know, in fact, that the social form of Repetition, imitation, tends to free itself more and more from
its vital form, from heredity.

. We are also justified in affirming that national agglomerations will enlarge to a greater and greater degree, and that
they will consequently become less dense and that the contrary will never be realised unless a catastrophe occur. This
is a result (as pointed out by M. Gide in his little work upon
the colonies[2]) of universal assimilation, especially in the
matter of armaments. In fact " it is clear that the day when
we shall all be formed in the same mould, the day when one
man will be worth another, the power of every people will

[1] The Byzantine Empire was the goal of Greco-Roman civilisation;
the Chinese Empire, of Chinese civilisation; the Mogul Empire, of
Hindoo civilisation; the Empire of the Pharaohs, of Egyptian civilisation, etc.

[2] M. Gide expressly refers to the " laws of imitation," for he was one
of the first to accept my point of view, and in his *Principes d'économie
politique* he gives a pretty good place to my theory of value, the application of this general point of view, as I presented it a long time ago, in
several articles in the *Revue philosophique*.

be mathematically proportioned to the number of its population " and, consequently, a struggle between a small state and a big one will be impossible or disastrous for the former. This is an additional argument for the numerous reasons which we have for foreseeing a colossal empire in the future. In every period prior to our own, larger states extended themselves *as far* or *farther* than the then means of communication made practicable. But at present it is plain that the great inventions of our times will make possible and enduring much more extensive agglomerations than those which now exist. This is an historic anomaly, unexampled in the past, and we must believe that it is fated to disappear. The world is more ready at present for a concentration of the whole of Europe, northern Africa, and half of Asia into a single state than it ever was for the Roman or Mahometan conquest, or for the empire of Charles V. Does this mean that we must expect to see a single empire extending over the entire globe? It does not; from the law which I developed above on the alternation of fashion and custom, on the final and inevitable return to a protective tariff of custom after a more or less lengthy period of free trade in examples, it follows that the natural, I do not refer to the factitious, aggrandisement of a state could never pass beyond certain limits. Consequently, we are not justified in conceiving the hope that a single state will rule over the whole earth or that the possibility of war will be suppressed. On the other hand, as the unification or at least the federation of civilised nations becomes more desirable and more longed for, the obstacles in the way of its realisation, patriotic pride and prejudice, national antagonisms, misunderstood or narrowly interpreted collective interests, accumulated historical memories, all these things will not cease to grow. The checking of this growing aspiration by this growing difficulty might be considered the infernal torment to which man is condemned by civilisation. It seems as if the mirage of perpetual and universal peace loomed up before our eyes with more and more brilliancy but at a greater and greater distance.

In a limited and relative sense, however, we may believe that this ideal will be temporarily realised through the future conquests of a people, whose name we do not know, who is destined to play this glorious part. But then, after this Empire has been established, after it has bestowed upon a great part of the world a security comparable to the majesty of a *Roman peace* increased tenfold in depth and extent,[1]

[1] Historians err in feeling, or affecting to feel, an unjustifiable contempt for all great social similarities in language, religion, politics, art, etc., which have been visibly effected by the imitation of some prestigious model, whether or not the prestige be that of a conqueror or merely of a stranger. They are wont to treat with scorn the great agglomerations of peoples, the great social unities, the Roman Empire, for example, which are made possible in this way, and to declare them *factitious.* This does not keep them from highly valuing, over-valuing, in fact, other similarities, other unities, which they consider natural and spontaneous. They are not aware that these are also caused by imitation, by imitation which is, in certain cases, unconscious and unthinking, instead of conscious and deliberate, but which is nevertheless imitation. Superstitious reverence for the unconscious, and ignorance of the leading part played in human affairs by imitation in its many overt or hidden forms, give rise in the best minds to many such contradictions.

Here is an example, which I borrow from the very erudite *Histoire des institutions politiques* of M. Viollet (p. 256). This distinguished historian belongs to the very large number of those who contrast the senility of the Roman Empire with the fruitful and spirited adolescence of the German barbarians. He considers that the great imperial unity is artificial and, by contrast, he is led to consider that every little unity produced by the break-up of the Empire is natural and *spontaneous.* The frightful chaos from the sixth to the tenth century, which was relieved only by the period of Charlemagne, the glorious and conscious imitator of the Cæsars, seems to him to be only a crisis in racial development; its gloom is "an aurora." It all seems admirable to him. first the disintegration, and yet this is evidently a step backward, for I do not know how many centuries, and then, and this seems contradictory to me, the obvious but futile inclination to reconstruct the broken unity, under the form of re-enlarging nationalities. "The Occident," he says, "as it was *happily* and definitely *disintegrated,* having no longer any uncontested tie but that of *a community of religious and philosophic beliefs,* or any similar institutions, but institutions which were born *spontaneously, so to speak, from similar wants,* was about to present the admirable spectacle of a diversity a thousand times richer, more fruitful, and more harmonious than the best-planned homogeneity." Now, let us not forget that, had it not been for the long duration of the Empire, for the age-long propagation of currents of imitation in language, ideas, manners, and institutions, there would have been no *similarity of wants* between so many originally heterogeneous peoples. And, as for community of religious as well as of philosophic beliefs, it may happen that an entirely new social phenomenon, one neither conforming nor contrary to the principles that I have propounded, may appear to our descendants. We may wonder, to be sure, whether universal similarity under all its present or future forms, in regard to dress, to the alphabet, perhaps to language, to sciences, to law, etc., we may wonder whether it is the consummate fruit of civilisation or whether

this was clearly due to those multiple conversions, to those imitative contagions between minds and souls that the unity of the Roman Empire alone made possible. Thus, that which the writer I have quoted so much admired as being contrary to a factitious imperial unity, is, in its origin, imperial. Suppress that, and nothing remains but the unrestricted disintegration which takes us back to a state of savagery.

If we fully comprehended the truth of the observation, that, unless man in society is inventing, a rare occurrence, or unless he is following impulses which are of a purely organic origin, likewise a rarer and rarer occurrence, he is always, in act or thought, imitating, whether he is conscious of it or not, whether he yields to a *so-called imitative* impulse or whether he makes a rational and deliberate choice from among the models which are offered to him to imitate; if we knew this, if this were our starting-point, we would be cautious of admiring, with a childish superstition, the great currents of unconscious and thoughtless imitation in social phenomena, and we would, on the other hand, recognise the superiority of acts of voluntary and rational imitation.

We would also recognise how invincible and irresistible, in virtue of the laws of imitation, is the immense impetus of all things towards uniformity. I do not deny the picturesque side of the "rich diversity" that the chaotic period of the Merovingians and Carlovingians was a factor in producing in the great feudal period. But in modern times has there not been a return to uniformity, and even an enlargement of it; in short, is not our present civilisation by way of being cast in a single, unique mould? Nowadays, have we not to seek the depths of some African desert or Chinese village to avoid seeing the same hats and dresses, the same cigars, the same newspapers?

Thus, in spite of the political disintegration which has persisted, although in a minor degree, a *social level* has been reconstructed. This cannot be imputed to a political unity, as in the case of the Roman Empire, as if it were its sole or principal cause. The Roman conquest favoured and hastened the social assimilation of Europe, and in doing that it rendered a great service to the cause of civilisation. *since civilisation is precisely nothing else than this work of unification, of social complication, of mutual and harmonious imitation.* But, even without the Roman conquest, social unity would have been brought about in Europe—only it would have been accomplished in the same way as that of Asia or Africa was accomplished; that is, less well, and less peacefully. It would have entailed fearful massacres, and, without doubt, the progress of inventions and discoveries would have been less advanced, just as happened in Asia and Africa.

And so I do not join with those who consider that imperial unity

its sole *raison d'être* and its final consequence are not the unfolding of individual differences that will be more valid, more
intense, more radical, and, at the same time, more subtle,
than the differences that were annihilated. It is certain that
after a cosmopolitan inundation has left a thick deposit of
ideas and customs over all humanity, the demolished nationalities will never be reconstructed; men will never return to
their Chinese ancestor-worship nor to their contempt for
foreign usages; they will never prefer to accentuate their
fixed idiosyncrasies rather than to hasten general changes
shared in by all alike. But it is perfectly possible that civilisation may pause some day to draw back and give birth
to new offspring, that the flood of imitation may be banked
in,[1] and that through the very effect of its excessive development, the need of sociability may diminish or, rather, may
become altered and transformed into a sort of general
misanthropy. While this would be quite compatible with

was disastrous because of the very memory that it left behind, a
memory which proved a source of delusion for the Middle Ages.
"This dire idea of universal monarchy lasted for more than a thousand years." Dire in what? Is it not evident that the small degree
of higher order and harmony which persisted in this anarchy of
warring fiefs, the political dust of the imperial block, was due to
the very dream and memory of the Empire, and that without the
pope, the spiritual emperor, or even without the German Cæsar, this
dust might have been incapable of ever regaining life and organisation?

[1] Our inclination to imitate stranger or neighbour does not increase
in proportion to the multiplication of our relations with him. Of
course when there are practically no relations at all, there is no tendency to imitate him, because there is no knowledge of him; but, on
the other hand, when we know him too well to be able to continue
in our envy or admiration of him, we no longer take him for our
model. There is, therefore, a certain *point* between too little and too
much communication, where the highest degree of the need of imitating others may be formed. How shall we determine this point? It
is a difficult matter. We may say that it is the optical point where
we are near enough to have all the illusion of the scenery without
being near enough to be aware of the stage machinery.

It is essential to note the consequence of the preceding fact. It
follows that the multiplied communications between peoples and classes,
through railroads, telegraphs, and telephones, will result in leading
them back to a taste for and a pious observance of their distinctive
idiosyncrasies, and of their particular habits and customs. Is not the
present return to the spirit of nationality due in part, in slight part, to
this cause, in spite of the fact that its chief cause is militarism?

a diminution of commercial intercourse and with the reduction of economic exchange to what was strictly necessary, it would be well fitted to strengthen in each of us the distinctive traits of our individuality. Then the finest flower of our social life, the æsthetic life, would blossom forth, and as it became full-blown all men would come to have a share in it,—a rare and imperfect condition at present. And then the social life, with its complicated apparatus of confining functions and monotonous rehearsals, would finally appear, like the organic life which it follows and complements, in its true colours. It would appear as a long, obscure, and tortuous transition from a state of elementary diversity to one marked by the possession of personal physiognomy. It would appear as a mysterious alembic of numberless spiral curves where one thing is sublimated in another, where out of an infinite number of elements that have been bent and crushed and despoiled of their distinct characteristics is mental and fleeting attributes of personality, its idiosyn- extracted an essential and volatile principle, the funda- crasies, its ways of thinking and feeling, here to-day, vanished to-morrow.

INDEX

A

Accent, spread of, 217.

Adaptation to environment, explanation of living or social types not found in their, 141.

Adoption, fiction of, 53, 250, 315, 352-3, 365.

Agriculture, its rivalry with commerce, 289; its progress dependent upon uniformity of law, 321-2; its failure to progress under feudalism, 335.

Alcoholism, explanation of spread of, 194, 195; spread of, from superior to inferior, 231 N. 1.

Amber, its importation in antiquity, 96, 330

Ammonite, 25 N 1.

Ancestor-worship, 53, 267 *sq*, 275.

Animals, invention among, 3, 4, imitation among, 3, 4 N. 1, 67 N. 1, 198 N 1, 206; domestication of, 17, 42 N 2, 46, 219 N. 2, 235, 236, 274 N. 1, 276-80, 330 N. 1; relation of primitive man to wild, 271-8, 372 N. 1; deification of, 274-8; human speech understood by, 331 N. 2

Animal societies, 4, 59, 60; of La Fontaine's fables, 67

Anthropology, distinction between archæology and, 89 *sq*

Archæology, methods of, 89 *sq*; proof in, of preponderance of imitation over invention, 98; principle of imitation in, 98 *sq*.; the paleontology of society, 103; comparison between Statistics and, *ib.*; branches of, 107; erroneous deduction about primitive man in, 325.

Architecture, transmission of Roman, 9; resemblances between Old and New World, 39 N 1; imitation in, 54; development of Greek and Egyptian, 54 *sq*, analogies in, 56-7; logical conflicts in, 161, 162; repetition of types in, 191; invention of, 235; climate not an adequate explanation of style in, 326; in times of fashion, 335; in the 19th century, 344.

d'Argenson, 218 N. 1.

Aristocracy, initiative character of, 221; influence of theocratic, 223; of cities, 228; the cause of democracy, 231; racial intermixture, characteristic of, 238 N. 1; speech of the, 257; Tocqueville's distinction between democracy and, 303; the relation of militancy to, 305 N. 1; assimilation of usages in the, 335; the future of, 388.

Art, laws of refraction in, 23; differentiation in, 55; analysis of Arabian, Greek, Egyptian, 99; logical conflicts in, 159; interplay of fashion and custom in, 164; the ideal the substance of, 182, conventionality of, 191; evolution of, 207; survivals in, 209; degeneration of, 210, animal drawings, first attempts in, 274 N. 1; transition from fashion to custom in, 298; relation of evolution of, to industry, 303 N. 1; during periods of custom and of fashion, 342, 346-55; religious origin of, 345; its origin in handicraft, 353

Assimilation, of modern civilisations, xxiii., 16, 388-9, of civilisations through imitation, 21, 128; social, point of departure for social advance, 72; produced through cities, 228; due to language, 264; international political, 290, due to mediæval preaching friars, 338.

Astronomy, accumulable discoveries in, 174; modern, reducible to a single formula, 178; discovery of, 235.

Atomism, 178.

164; its relation to reproduction, 253-4; effects of transition from, to fashion and from fashion to custom in language, 255-65; in religion, 265-86; in government, 287-309; in legislation, 310-22; in usages, 322-33, in industry, 333-44; in art and morality, 344-65; paternal prestige the source of, 276; relation of price to, 339-40; empire of, in language, 344. See Custom-Imitation under Imitation.

D

Darmesteter, 266 N. 1.
Darwin, xvii., 12, 17, 37, 67 N. 1, 370, 382
Death, necessity of, 7; a justification of pessimism, 266 N. 1.
Delahante, 119 N. 1, 129 N. 1.
Delbœuf, 7, 76.
Democracy, tyranny of the many during, 84; imitation during, 225; Tocqueville's distinction between aristocracy and, 303, 387; increasing resemblances do not necessitate, 388.
Desire, transmission of, a fundamental social relation, xvi; growth of, to invent, 43, specific character of; 44, 93; for a maximum of belief, 50; a social force, 145; for reason, 149, docility, imitation of, 197; for equality, 303.
Desires, interferences between, 24 sq.; expressed by statistics, 104-7; their relation to invention, 109, 159; tendency of, towards geometric progression, 115, 124; for fraternity, 112, 121 sq, 266; competition of, 115; for truth, 125; for property, 125-6; three phases of, 126 sq., increase of, in civilisation, 148 N. 1; conflict between, 149 sq.; spread of, 210; satisfaction of, by industry, 322; of consumption spread more rapidly than corresponding desires of production, 329 sq.
Diabolical possession, 50-1.
Discovery, of gallium, 12; the successful, of the present determines that of the future, 19; of Cicero's *Republic*, 34; of the

steamboat, 44; of the circulation of the blood, 44, 170; of mineral springs in France, 92 N. 1; of tea, coffee, tobacco, 93; for the pleasure of discovery, 94; of beet sugar, 104; of fire from friction, 235, 270 N. 1. See Invention.
Division of labor, among animals, 60; 61 sq.; original lack of, 327.
Dostoiesky, 207 N. 1, 246 N. 1.
Dubois-Reymond, 125.

E

Eagle, two-headed, spread of, through imitation, 47 N 1.
Ellis, Havelock, v.
Emission theory, 48.
English language, illustration of linguistic refraction in, 22; vowel differentiation in, 143; spread of, 257, 331, grammatical simplification in, 265.
Envy, the effect of obedience, 201; assimilation produced by, 202 N. 1.
Erigeron, spread of the, 17.
Eructation, as an act of courtesy, 42 N. 1.
Espinas, xvii., 3, 4 N. 1, 59 N. 1.

F

Family, the nation developed from the, xxii.; spread of, dialects, 17, 255, 287; relation between imitation and docility and credulity shown in the, 199; the patriarchal, 202-4, 267 N. 1; imitation in the primitive, 250, 269; the, not the unique source of society, 268; religion cradled in the, 280, 287; the, the original social group, 287; origin of and art in the morality 314-15, 345; industry in the, 328; undermining of the, 358. See Adoption.
Fashion, progress of, in European societies, 16; in crimes, 113; interplay of custom and, 164; in dress, 199, 212, 334 N. 2, 385; contemporaneous prestige, the source of, 276; parliamentarism a, 293; sixteenth and eighteenth

398 Index

centuries periods of, 293 N. 2;
the secret ballot a, *ib.*; spread of
municipal law through, 314;
jury system a, 317; trial by torture a, *ib*; birth of political
economy during ages of, 320;
increase of rationality through,
321; tobacco-chewing a, 327;
naval, in America, 334; unchanging, of monastic dress, 334 N. 1,
383-4; in eating, 336 N. 2, 340;
relation of price to, 339; its relation to individualism and naturalism, 341-2; its relation to invention, 343; the assumption by,
of the mask of custom, 361 *sq.*;
Latin poetry a, 362; Roman jurisprudence a, *ib* See Custom
See Fashion-Imitation under
Imitation.

Féré, 76

Feudalism, assimilation of, 62-3;
formation of, 73, 239-43; persistence of titles of, 152 N 1;
a harmonising factor, 186; opposition of communes to, 226; failure of agriculture to progress
under, 335; a stage in the transition from unilateral to reciprocal authority, 374; disappearance
of, 380

Friday, superstition about, 106
N. 1.

Friedlander, 257 N. 1.

G

Garnier, 42 N. 1.
Gaudry, 25 N 1.
Generation. See Reproduction.
Gerontocracy, influence of, in
primitive societies, 268.
Giard, 382 N. 1.
Gide, 388
Glasson, 240, 241.
Gobineau, de, xxii.
Goblet d'Alviella, 47 N. 1, 274
N. 1.
Government, originally an answer
to a demand for security, 174;
distinction between additions
and substitutions in, 180; a polit-
ical idea, 182; etiquette of, 191;
language, an instrument of, 206,
conservatism and liberalism in,
288; compared with religion,
289 N. 1; in times of fashion,

342; relation of art and morality
to, 345. See Ceremonial Gov-
ernment.
Grimm, 22, 260 N 1.
Guibert, Louis, 186 N. 1.
Guyau, 332.

H

Haeckel, 12, 370.
Heredity, inaccurate use of term,
xv.; its relation to imitation,
xxi.-xxii., 25 N. 1, 280, 328, 357,
368; organic progress dependent
upon, 7; analogous to imitation
and vibration, 11; during custom-imitation, 36; first repetition
in, 43; idea of, combined with
that of variability, 382.
Hesitation, opposed to imitation,
165
Historic method, excellence of, 14.
History, interpretation of, 3, 109;
methods of, 8-10, 101; continuity
of, 12; action of imitation the
first principle of, 49; relation of
archæology to, 90, 102; as commonly understood, 92; definition
of, 139; a tissue of tragedy and
comedy, 172; the reversible and
irreversible in, 379 *sq.*
Horse, its disappearance from
American fauna, 46; superseded
as a means of locomotion, 158;
introduced into Egypt, 214; advantage of the, in war, 236;
primitive possessors of the, 277
N. 1.
Houzeau, 331 N. 2.
Hugo, Victor, 98, 226, 352.
Hugonnet, 42 N. 1.
Hypnotism, compared to social
phenomena, 76 *sq*; 199 N. 1,
204, 275 N. 2.

I

Idealism, its relation to materialism, xviii.; in sociology, 2, 3;
177.
Ideas, geometrical progression of,
18, 115; constituting a social
type, 68; imitation of, precedes
imitation of their expression,
207; spread more easily than
usages, 323 N. 1

BIBLIOLIFE

Old Books Deserve a New Life
www.bibliolife.com

Did you know that you can get most of our titles in our trademark **EasyScript**™ print format? **EasyScript**™ provides readers with a larger than average typeface, for a reading experience that's easier on the eyes.

Did you know that we have an ever-growing collection of books in many languages?

Order online:
www.bibliolife.com/store

Or to exclusively browse our **EasyScript**™ collection:
www.bibliogrande.com

At BiblioLife, we aim to make knowledge more accessible by making thousands of titles available to you – quickly and affordably.

Contact us:
BiblioLife
PO Box 21206
Charleston, SC 29413

5203323R1

Made in the USA
Charleston, SC
13 May 2010